Full Upright and Locked Position

Full Upright and Locked Position

Not-So-Comfortable Truths about Air Travel Today

Mark Gerchick

W. W. Norton & Company

New York • London

For information about permission to reproduce selections from this book,
write to Permissions, W. W. Norton & Company, Inc.,
500 Fifth Avenue, New York, NY 10110

For information about special discounts for bulk purchases, please contact W. W. Norton Special Sales
at specialsales@wwnorton.com or 800-233-4830

Manufacturing by RR Donnelley, Harrisonburg
Book design by Chris Welch
Production manager: Devon Zahn

Library of Congress Cataloging-in-Publication Data

Gerchick, Mark.
Full upright and locked position : not-so-comfortable truths about air travel today / Mark Gerchick. — 1st ed.
p. cm.
Includes bibliographical references and index.
ISBN 978-0-393-08110-7 (hardcover)
1. Air travel—Miscellanea. 2. Air travel—Social aspects. I. Title.
HE9776.G47 2013
387.7′42—dc23
2013006528

W. W. Norton & Company, Inc.
500 Fifth Avenue, New York, N.Y. 10110
www.wwnorton.com

W. W. Norton & Company Ltd.
Castle House, 75/76 Wells Street, London W1T 3QT

1 2 3 4 5 6 7 8 9 0

For my mother, the writer

CONTENTS

FOREWORD

Human flight—like electricity and the computer—is one of those amazing gifts of technology we take for granted. Almost half of all adult Americans traveled by US commercial airline in 2012—transiting the skies faster than our species could have imagined even a century ago—and not one passenger's life was lost to a crash. On the other hand, almost half of those 100 million or so fliers found the experience "stressful" and "frustrating" according to polls; the airline industry ranks below even the Internal Revenue Service for "customer satisfaction."

Flying today is a jarring contradiction—amazing and god-awful at the same time. It's incredibly safe, increasingly reliable, and still a relative bargain. But for most, the "magic" of air travel has morphed into an uncomfortable, crowded, and utterly soulless ordeal to be avoided whenever possible. For trips shorter than 250 miles, 46 percent fewer travelers took to the air in 2011 than a decade earlier. Folks gladly pay more to take the fast train, or drive.

In the years since the morning of September 11, 2001, the contradictions of air travel have come to a head. Airlines that survived the decade's financial hellfires evolved into hard-nosed businesses, bent on efficiency and ever more focused on the bottom line. But as the airlines learned to make money, passengers learned to live with stripped-down service, always-full airplanes, and no free lunch—not to mention the stop-and-frisk security for which we can thank the shoe bombers and underwear bombers and liquid-explosives bombers.

Call it a new dynamic equilibrium—albeit one balanced precariously on the unsteady base of volatile fuel prices or some would-be terrorist's impulse to stick a couple of ounces of plastic explosive where the sun don't shine. Optimists among us can foresee improvement for the passengers' lot, but all told, what you see now is more or less what you can expect to get. Welcome to the new normal of air travel.

There are no easy fixes to make it all more pleasant, more comfortable, or more humane, aside from shelling out big bucks to escape to "premium" flying. Commercial air travel is a complicated, interconnected business pushed and pulled by multiple powerful interests, each with its own agenda and its own demands—some justified, some, well, not so much. The list of players begins—or *should* at least begin—with passengers. Yet there are plenty of others: from fiercely competitive airline executives to highly organized labor unions; from thousands of airline shareholders to safety, consumer, and economic regulators; from global aircraft manufacturers to politically powerful airports. And the stage itself keeps tilting in response to uncontrollable forces such as fuel-price spikes, "black swan" events like plagues and terrorism, and the shifting sands of the economy and consumer travel demand.

Even as the skies turn from not-so-friendly to borderline hostile in the new "all-business" aviation world, though, passengers can at least hope to understand what's happening to them along the way. That's the modest idea behind this book: If we understand better what's really going on when we buy our ticket or check our bags or when the cockpit door slams shut—in essence, if we know more about what lies beneath our air-travel experience—we're less the victim.

The aviation landscape that has emerged a decade after September 11 holds plenty of mysterious, often harsh, features. This book explores many of them: the "unbundling" of the very notion of what constitutes a "flight"—a conceptual leap that opened up an irresistible cornucopia of nickel-and-dime revenue for airlines; new questions, and emerging answers, about our health and safety in the air; the annoyances and indignities and minor outrages that together create the dread, yet pervasive, Hassle Factor. In short, this book explores what's going on—at least the things passengers wonder most about—when we're in the air-travel system, and why.

I started thinking about this book in 2008, during some of the darkest days for commercial flying since the attacks on the World Trade Center and the Pentagon, a time when airlines facing a massive spike in the price of jet fuel were hemorrhaging cash and talking about installing onboard pay toilets to make enough money to survive. Financed to the hilt, some of the oldest and biggest teetered on the brink. Labor was (and still is) aggrieved by major cuts imposed by airlines during bankruptcy reorganizations. Passengers, meanwhile, were losing traditional amenities, from magazines to food. Planes were dirty, workers were angry, and passengers were stressed—and not just about the loss of microwaved lasagna or free pillows in coach. Almost any touch of humanity or personal caring seemed gone too. Bad karma all around—and all on the heels of the tragic death of a distraught young mother at the Phoenix airport in the fall of 2007 that seemed to come from nothing so much as just a lack of simple human empathy; a hauntingly sad reflection of the grimly impersonal, by-the-book new world of air travel.

Former American Airlines CEO Bob Crandall once described commercial aviation as a "nasty, rotten business." Even if we can't make the massive enterprise more humane or gentle or generous, though, at least it can be less mysterious and mystifying to ordinary fliers. That alone may make it a little easier to sit back and relax from the "full upright and locked" position.

Exploring a business so uniquely fraught with suspicion, anger, and even hostility between providers and consumers is a particular challenge. When the Department of Transportation recently tried to appoint a four-person "consumer protection committee" to advise it, a key consumer group summarily declared the new body "unlikely" to work because two seats would be filled by representatives of airlines and airports, whose "vested interests" were inherently "adverse to consumer protection."

This book isn't meant, though, to offer a "balanced" view of commercial aviation today—just an honest one. (Nor is it a deep dive into aviation's many technical intricacies; so, experts, pardon me some simplifications to make the read easier.) It's based on my own experience on all sides of the aviation fence—as a federal regulator, an airline and airport advocate, and a close industry observer. It is also based on the wisdom of scores of others who closely watch this giant, influential, and minutely scrutinized industry. They range from veteran pilots to safety experts, economists to entrepreneurs, Wall Street financial analysts to Washington regulators and lawyers, and especially the many extraordinary journalists who cover aviation with acumen and depth.

For my part, I've grown up with aviation. My first serious summer job in high school involved standing out on the hot tarmac at our sleepy suburban New York local airport in my one rumpled poplin suit, counting passengers as they came down the mobile stairs from the daily Allegheny or Mohawk commuter planes. My employer, the county government, assigned me to count business travelers, part of an effort to justify building a new terminal to replace the World War II–era Quonset hut that had long served that function at the Westchester County Airport. Today there stands a facility that handles a million passengers a year.

For a brief stint after college, I was a *Miami Herald* newspaper reporter in Palm Beach, Florida, often working the airport to catch the glitterati and visiting politicos coming off their Gulfstreams and Lears for the winter sun and the polo season. I covered my first and only plane crash there—a twin-engine prop flying tourists to Orlando that ran out of fuel and landed without incident on an open stretch of highway. Not exactly the Miracle on the Hudson, but at least nobody was seriously hurt.

Years later, I led the Federal Aviation Administration's 100-lawyer legal office. ("Led" in the sense of Gandhi's famous phrase: "There go my people. I must hurry to catch up with them. I am their leader.") That meant plenty of time in the air, on rare occasion in a cockpit jump seat. It also meant learning from and arguing with the real players in the business—from top airline execs to weekend recreational pilots to labor leaders and airport mangers, from congressional staff to safety experts and regulators who had forgotten more about how aviation really works than any of us political appointees would ever learn.

Later, working with the US secretary of transportation and his staff to help open international aviation markets (a policy known as "Open Skies"), I started counting my monthly air miles by the tens of thousands—mostly on US commercial airlines but sometimes (thrillingly, I admit) on government jets with UNITED STATES OF AMERICA proudly emblazoned on the fuselage. To celebrate my son's fifth birthday, we slipped him briefly aboard the secretary's sleek Gulfstream IV business jet—code-named "N-1"—for a birthday cupcake and a greeting from the pilot a few minutes before our delegation took off for Asia. He was nowhere near as impressed when, after leaving government, I rejoined the thundering herd of Washington-based aviation lawyers, lobbyists, and consultants.

Heck, I even proposed to my wife on an airplane flying over the Grand Canyon—decades before YouTube made it a cliché. After she said yes, the teary flight attendant sneaked us a bottle of Champagne from First Class.

So I do appreciate the amazing gift of air travel, and I'm glad it's safer, more financially stable, more reliable, and still accessible to tens of millions of Americans—some 85 percent of us have flown at least once, says Southwest Airlines. Yet, that's in the abstract. For all the tired, hungry air travelers wedged into their seat in Row 34 ahead of the screaming kid, waiting for the harried flight attendant to collect their trash and sell them a bag of chips, wondering if their checked suitcase made the connection, or if they'll make it home for dinner, and maybe why they didn't score the upgrade, what really matters is the uncomfortable here and now of commercial flying. This book is for them.

Full Upright and Locked Position

The Disconnect

HOW WE FLY NOW

Not many of today's fliers remember what air travel used to be like at the dawn of the "jet age" a half century ago. Crossing the Atlantic then was really something to tell the neighbors about. Gracious, smiling stewardesses took your coat, stowed your bags and, of course, offered a sip of Champagne. On some flights, there were only two classes of service—First and Deluxe—and only one (albeit unofficial) US "flag" airline, Pan Am. Meals catered by Maxim's of Paris were served on china, fine wine in glass goblets. "Guests" were offered crisp pillows and cozy blankets, often small gifts; they were practically tucked in. And the captain tried to stop by for a personal greeting.

Veteran road warriors wax nostalgic about this distant, lyrical past, some of it true only in the imagination. We forget about the bouncing, bumpy rides, the engine noise in the cabin, the less-than-ergonomic seats, the boredom. Onboard movies—fuzzy projections on pull-down screens—began only in 1961, when TWA showed Lana Turner in *By Love Possessed* on a cross-country Boeing 707. We forget about the hassles, like buying and changing paper tickets only at the local travel agent or ticket office during business hours. And we tend to forget about the price. The cheapest government-approved "tourist class" jet fare from New York to London in 1958 was more than $2,000 in today's dollars.

Even if long-ago air travel wasn't as great as we remember it, it was also nothing like today's experience. Industry veterans talk about how everything changed after Congress deregulated the US airlines in 1978, freeing them to compete on fares and service, but the changes that have swept the industry in the decade since September 11 have been nearly as profound. When it comes to the experience of ordinary air travelers, flying today is almost as different from 1998 as from 1968.

Even ten years ago, nobody paid to check a suitcase, pillows were on every seat, empty seats were common, and airlines were still serving meals and free drinks in coach. But forget the little things. The humans in the back—whom pilots tend to call "the people"—were more than just transitory sources of revenue. And if air travel wasn't always something they looked forward to, at least it wasn't a source of dread. In the decade after 9/11, the mix of economic near-catastrophe, the gnawing threat of airborne terrorism, and leaps in automation and information technology have changed forever the way most of us fly, and the way we think about air travel.

The Decade That Changed Everything

It was almost as though premonitions of millennial doom were aimed at a single industry. Within weeks of the last celebratory firework, the dot-com bust was upon us. The NASDAQ index of technology stocks, which had soared 600 percent in the five years before, suddenly plummeted, half its value lost in the year 2000 alone. The broader stock market—having nearly tripled in five years—abruptly halted its ascent and turned down, taking with it many of the go-go entrepreneurs, road warriors, and multinational firms whom airlines counted on to buy the expensive, wide seats up front.

Demand for the price-be-damned, last-minute airline seats was about to crater, but not before the infamous Summer from Hell in 2000. For air travelers, it was a grueling season of record delays and cancellations and bad weather and packed terminals, compounded by labor strife at United Airlines that virtually defined the term "gridlock." Unhappy pilots denied they were engaged in a collective slowdown, but plenty of flights ready to taxi out to take off suffered mysterious last-minute maintenance delays. With more than one in every four US commercial flights cancelled or delayed, one harried senior federal official put it succinctly: "The tolerable pain threshold was crossed this summer."

The airline industry is famous for its up-and-down financial cycles, and the "up" cycle of expansion—new routes, new airplanes, new investment—was hitting its apex during the late 1990s. From 1995 to 2000, US airline net profits averaged $3.5 billion a year. More people had been flying and fares had risen. Airlines in turn ordered new planes, hired new workers, and expanded their schedules; airports started building new terminals and pushed for new runways. Congestion generated frustrating delays so routinely that the Federal Aviation Administration (FAA) warned that the entire US system—from crowded runways to overstressed air traffic control—could not handle the hundreds of millions of expected fliers.

By early 2001, though, the cycle had reversed. As the dot-com bubble burst, the bottom started to fall out of air-travel demand. Average fares dropped, but even worse for airlines, there was a massive drop in "premium" air travel—the front-of-the-plane business travelers who accounted for a disproportionate share of profits. Revenue from business-type airfares dropped almost 30 percent, even as fuel and labor costs kept rising.

The coup de grace, of course, was September 11, 2001. Overnight, the world of commercial aviation changed profoundly and permanently. Aircrews were scared of passengers, and passengers were just plain scared. Airports became armed camps. It was a world of duct tape and anthrax and shoe bombs and snipers. Fearful business travelers blamed the "hassle factor" and uncertainty about long security lines, but nobody flew unless it was *really* necessary. In the immediate aftermath, business travel demand dropped an estimated 30 percent.

Already facing economic slowdown, belt-tightening corporations seized the opportunity to cut their own travel spending. As the demand for their seats plummeted, airlines rushed to cut payrolls and curtail schedules. Within three months of the attacks, US airlines had laid off some 80,000 workers and grounded 20 percent of the seats they had been flying. Not until three years later would US air travel regain the record levels of August 2001. And for the four years after September 11, there was only red ink—by 2009, net losses added up to a mind-boggling $55 billion. By the middle of the dismal decade, the situation was dire. Passenger travel stayed down, and so did airline revenue. Business fliers refused to pony up four or five times—sometimes as much as ten times—the cost of a coach ticket to ride in First Class on a three-hour flight they didn't even want to take. Selling cheap seats to families, tourists, and backpackers couldn't pay the rent.

Even more ominous, the airlines that had ruled the nation's skies for decades faced a growing threat from such well-financed, low-fare competitors as Southwest, JetBlue, and AirTran, now more stable than their bigger rivals. These low-cost airlines had stayed on the fringes, trying to keep out of the way of the big guys. Not anymore. By mid-decade, they accounted for a quarter of the whole US domestic air-travel market. With more efficient operations, newer planes, and more productive labor forces than their old-line rivals, plus a "no frills" product that let them offer lower fares and still profit, the low-cost "upstarts" kept gaining market share.

The traditional US airlines were in trouble. As their access to credit dried up, assets were hocked, capitalization plummeted, and bankruptcy became all but inevitable. Between 2001 and 2005, all but two of the big airlines succumbed. Bankruptcy reorganization gave the airlines breathing space—to void existing costly labor contracts, stiff vendors, zero-out investors, and cut salaries—and they used it. Nearly a quarter of full-time jobs at the major US airlines—more than 100,000 of them—were eliminated in five years, and average wage rates dropped dramatically.

It wasn't enough. The traditional airline industry urgently needed to redefine itself, to find a sustainable operating model that would run cheaper, faster, and more profitably. Emulating their successful low-cost tormentors, the Old Guard found ways to leverage new technology and build efficiencies, substitute automation for humans, cut "frills," fly smarter to reduce fuel burn, and extract every last dollar passengers would pay. Time-honored assumptions about the very nature of the flying experience were questioned, then rejected. Where was the God-given right to a meal, a checked bag, a free magazine, a refund, a paper ticket, or even a smile?

With an improving economy, the industry began to emerge from its financial ditch. In 2006, US passenger airlines as a whole earned their first profit of the decade—$3 billion. Air travel started to pick up, and profits grew slightly in 2007 amid tentative signs of an economic recovery. The respite was short-lived, however.

The hammer came down again in 2008—in the form of an unprecedented explosion in the price of jet fuel, the indispensable commodity that accounts for 35 to 40 percent of the cost of operating an airline. Until mid-2004, the price per gallon had never risen above $1; by the Fourth of July, 2008, it had jolted to $4.02—and every penny's rise cost US airlines another $175 million annually. Though the price of jet fuel soon receded, the industry's acute vulnerability to fuel prices was etched on the traumatized psyches of fearful airline managers. And there was more pain to come as a recession—and even the prospect of a wholesale collapse of the US financial system—chilled business travel in 2009.

By the end of the punishing decade—with deep-red ink in seven of the ten years—three dozen large and small passenger airlines had been forced to seek bankruptcy protection; another eight or nine stopped flying altogether. Two big airline mergers married United with Continental and Delta with Northwest. In their wake, just four traditional US carriers were left standing—United, Delta, American, and US Airways—along with Southwest, JetBlue, Alaska, and a few other low-fare competitors. The survivors emerged tougher, leaner, and focused squarely on profitability. In the airline boardrooms, outlooks and priorities had evolved too. Forced to grow up fast during the decade that changed everything, the airlines became just another service industry trying to make a profit—albeit one with an amazing product that moved people from point to point with breathtaking speed and safety.

The New Business of Air Travel

Today's air-travel experience reflects the new business ethos. Forget the romance of flight in the Golden Age. Forget the magic and wonder of soaring above the clouds. Forget the "friendly skies." You want elegance and grace? You pay for it.

The death of the baked-on-board chocolate-chip cookie neatly captures the zeitgeist shift: Midwest Airlines ("the best care in the air") baked them on board for a quarter century. Everybody got two of the warm goodies free, the fragrance improving immensely the stuffy cabin air. When Midwest was bought and merged with Frontier in 2010, the new CEO pledged to make the new entity an ultra-low-cost carrier, and the cookie was no more. After a "review," the company spokesman said, "it was determined that the cookie did not align with either the perception or the financial reality of a low-cost carrier." Plus, said the spokesman, "we were the only [similar] airline offering a free perishable snack." And so, "it was determined" the airline would end the tasty, "non-aligning" cookie. Now they will sell you a bag of animal crackers—for a buck in Economy.

The industry's best creative minds set about discovering new streams of revenue, new "products" that offered a modicum of peace and comfort to the journey, but starting with airfares. *Average* inflation-adjusted fares actually are considerably lower than they were thirty years ago, but that's hardly the end of the story. They've risen steadily since 2009, and hardly anybody pays the "average" anyway. With super-sophisticated computers and vast data systems, airlines learned to pinpoint the absolute top dollar each type of passenger could be forced to shell out before he or she smashes the computer screen in frustration and calls Greyhound.

Fares alone weren't enough, though. Air travel is largely a commodity—like a pound of sugar or a gallon of gas. Raise the price (or basic fare) too much and buyers turn elsewhere—to a competitor that starts service on the overpriced route or that offers to save a bundle for fliers willing to take an indirect connecting flight. So how do you make money in the airline business if you can't charge more for your product—a flight?

The Eureka moment came when somebody "discovered" that what airlines were selling wasn't really just a flight at all. Airlines were selling a bundle of separable, flight-related *services*—transportation of luggage, making a reservation, having a seat assigned, snacks and drinks, legroom, even jet fuel—all divisible extras, or "ancillary" (to use a more impressive, if less well-understood, term) services, each priced separately. Fees for these services can easily mean the difference between profit and loss; checked-bag and ticket-change fees alone generated close to $6 billion for US airlines in both 2010 and 2011—more than all of the industry's net profit.

There were also more subtle, even creative, ways to shift burdens to passengers. Innovator JetBlue, for instance, came up with the breathtakingly simple concept of making customers do some of the work. Passengers were asked to pick up their own trash and toss it in a plastic bag passed through the cabin before landing, saving a couple of precious minutes of the "turn time" it takes to ready an arriving plane for its next flight. New checked-bag fees that incentivized passengers to carry and load their own luggage in overhead bins reduced the airlines' cost of unionized baggage handlers. It also created a valuable new product to sell—"early boarding privileges" that ensure you get on board early enough to find overhead space available to load your own luggage into. Brilliant. Passengers also paid indirectly, by bearing the cost of leaner and meaner staffing levels. Staffing airport customer service desks with just enough people to handle normal passenger demand for re-booking cancelled flights or changing seat assignments on a cloudless midweek afternoon can mean utter bedlam when afternoon thunderstorms hit on Labor Day weekend.

Conspiracy theorists might wonder if it wasn't all part of some grand market segmentation strategy conjured up in airline revenue departments: Make the stripped-down mass-travel experience so downright unpleasant that passengers will gladly pay more to buy their way out of the hassles—either actually purchasing a First or Business Class ticket or more likely earning their salvation (and a few extra inches of legroom) through "loyalty" to the airline. As pack-'em-in coach travel got ever grimmer, those lie-flat seats and designer-chef meals and personal attention for the "elite" passengers up front started to look more and more worth the extra dough. And this is America. Anyone can be elite—all it takes is cash.

A cliché that regularly passes for sagacity among self-described aviation experts is that change is the only constant in the airline world. It's a beloved truism that is becoming less true all the time. Some 35 years since the upheaval of airline deregulation, commercial aviation in the United States is today actually reaching toward unaccustomed stability—a modestly profitable, generally competitive, "rationalized" business that can weather the perennial, almost inevitable, external upsets: Three or four traditional airlines, each paired off in a stable global airline grouping, plus a small handful of low-cost carriers that, as they've become more established, are more likely to think like their traditional rivals. There's a new business equilibrium that feels more stable than it has in years.

The Disconnect

This new status quo is welcome to airlines exhausted by the last decade's drama and turbulence, but what does it mean for air travelers? The "product" remains an amazing gift. We can be on the other side of our globe in a single day, hurtling near the speed of sound to land safely in near-zero visibility, all the while engaged in earthly business via "live" TV and Wi-Fi as though we were sitting at home. It's still fairly cheap, too—what else costs less today than it did in the 1980s? And major US airline flying has reached an extraordinary plateau of safety. Think of commercial aviation as the "physical Internet" of the modern global economy. Just ask the late Osama Bin Laden. As the *Washington Post* reported in April 2012, he bragged to a would-be shoe-bomber that another 9/11 "will ruin the aviation industry and in turn the whole [US] economy will come down."

That said, air travelers have lost a lot in the decade since 9/11—and it's more than just some sentimental, semi-mythic vision of the Golden Age of aviation. We're angry about a broken bargain we imagine we have with the airlines. Legally, air carriers owe us only what DOT regulations require, plus whatever *they* say they do. (It's laid out in "contracts of carriage" drafted by airline lawyers that typically run dozens of pages long and are rarely read by anyone except those same airline lawyers.) But for years, passengers struck their own personal, unspoken, bargain with their airline: If I agree to go way up there in that infernal machine, against all my primeval human instincts, you in turn will take care of me, make sure of my welfare, make me comfortable.

Is that expectation so exceptionable? After all, as air travelers we are dependents. In flight, an experience that sets off all sorts of limbic alarms, we relinquish control. We're told when to buckle up, when to get up, when to ask for liquids, even when to pee. We are scolded: Unless we sit down, the plane will not leave. When the captain emerges briefly from the cockpit, we're watched suspiciously to assure we don't rush the flight deck. At least in the back, we largely cease to be individuals. Everyone gets five seconds of conversation with the harried flight attendant: "Drink?" "Coke, please." And as the cart lurches down the aisle, it's "Watch yer knees!"

Even simple dignity and civility can be hard to find in a system now so furiously driven by efficiency and the incessant push for revenues. I imagine my 80-year-old aunt on her way to visit from her London home, pressing the Call button to summon "the stewardess" to please bring a cup of tea. Why does that modest request now seem so impossibly optimistic and out of time?

The gap between our expectations of care and service and the reality of our air-travel experience has become a chasm. We want the cheapest discount fare and, even though we know in our heads it won't come with chilled Champagne and a lie-flat seat, we harbor the long-marketed fantasy. In the last decade, air travel has changed, for good *and* for ill. As passengers, we stand at arm's length with our airline. There are still plenty of regulations, but essentially, flying is a commercial relationship between a buyer (passenger) and seller (airline)—not what lawyers call a fiduciary bond of trust and confidence. Chairman Crandall's "nasty, rotten business" is, really, just a business. And that's the way entrepreneurial airlines want it. When United's CEO warned employees of job cuts after a "disappointing" 2012, he put it this way, as reported by the *Wall Street Journal*'s Corporate Intelligence blog: "In the past, we were just an airline, and not a real business, and we all suffered for it."

That doesn't mean, though, that airlines are "just the same" as every other business. They're not. For one, their product—soaring above the clouds—is unique. We depend entirely on the provider for the quality and safety and value of the service; we have no real way, no expertise, to evaluate or compare it. It's a special business, surrounded by a wonder and fear that seizes the public imagination. When was the last time some aspect of air travel *didn't* make the evening news? When it comes to the commercial airline industry, "just like any other business" just won't—pardon the pun—fly.

Where does that leave air travelers facing the emergent new business of aviation—as self-loading freight, fungible targets of revenue? Can't we reasonably expect a little humanity and even, yes, dignity—maybe even a little bit beyond what the marketplace and the laws of commerce strictly require? Maybe, but we also need to grow up and recognize what has changed. Commercial aviation is a business trying to make a buck, to finally find a model that's economically sustainable. Flying today, concludes a longtime industry analyst, "is what it is." A decade past 9/11, it's often unpleasant, occasionally downright miserable, and there are plenty of uncomfortable truths about it that neither the industry nor regulators like to talk about. But mystery breeds passenger anxiety, discomfort, and even paranoia. We sometimes see demons where there are only capitalists and engineers.

The Hassle Factor

"People love to fly," says a Boeing "passenger satisfaction" official. "They just don't love to fly today." That's putting it mildly. But just what makes air travel so crazy for so many can be hard to pinpoint. It's more than the sum of specific annoyances, more even than the overall impersonality and occasional sheer indignity of the experience. It's something deeply disquieting and sadly exposed in the tragedy of airline passenger Carol Gotbaum of New York.

Gotbaum died at age 45, self-strangled on restraints that held her to a bench at the Phoenix Sky Harbor Airport police facility in September 2007. She was en route to an alcohol rehab facility in Tucson but was not allowed to board her connecting US Airways flight (operated by Mesa Airlines) because, the airline said, she had arrived too late at the gate, some eight minutes before the flight was due to depart.

Distraught, she pleaded with the airline agents: "I am not a terrorist. I am a sick mother. I need help." When Gotbaum began to weep and flail about, gate agents called the cops. Three officers wrestled the 105-pound woman to the ground, handcuffed her, and put her in the airport holding cell chained to a bench, alone and crying hysterically. They only checked on her when the crying stopped. Although the local coroner ruled the death an accident, the city paid the family $250,000 to settle a wrongful death suit. A police investigation found that nobody had acted illegally. But there had been no mercy for a woman obviously in crisis, a human being who really needed to make that plane.

The Gotbaum tragedy is extreme, but it speaks to an unsettling truth about what commercial flying has largely become. For all its technological wonder, air travel is today's mass transit, bound by strict rules, rigid processes, tight schedules, and a desperate pursuit of efficiency and revenue. Perhaps unavoidably, it leaves precious little slack for simple humanity or random acts of kindness or grace. Not just for the relative few already on the edge and trying to cope with the craziness, but also for the millions of ordinary, less fragile travelers who regard flying with a mixture of contempt and dread. Many would rather drive. Even for trips up to 500 miles, air travel dropped 17 percent between 2000 and 2010.

Just stepping through the sliding doors into the rush-hour bedlam of New York's LaGuardia Airport or Heathrow's crowded Terminal 3 makes some people shaky. Airport workers recognize "the stare." Lines of cart-shoving families intersect and snake across one another toward unseen podiums or checkpoints while recorded "threat" warnings drone on, lights glare, and grim-faced security operatives watch impassively. Everybody *else* is moving somewhere with apparent purpose—shades of that nightmare where you are always late, in the wrong line, forgetting to turn in that final paper, oversleeping for the exam.

Now add some small frustration to the background stress: a cancelled flight, a long delay, an officious gate agent or brusque security screener, a fellow passenger who reclines his seat an inch too far or an overfilled overhead bin. Even the most reasonable people can lose it, and many do. Every other day on average, the FAA gets an official report of an incident with an "unruly passenger"—also known as an "air rage" incident. That's more than 3,000 reported since 1995, but those are just the small percentage that lead to criminal prosecution or FAA enforcement action. Flight attendant unions estimate it's more like 4,000 incidents a year,

a dozen a day on average. Based on JetBlue's experience with disrup-
tive passengers in 2011, a *Wall Street Journal* analysis projected that
17,000 passengers were barred from or kicked off US flights annually—
that's almost 50 people each day. Instead of pillows and amenity kits,
today's planes are stocked with passenger "restraint kits" to be used, in
the words of a British manufacturer, "once all efforts at communication
have failed."

Sky-high tension isn't just aloft. At major hub airports, you can sometimes sense a kind of "ground rage." Watch the security screening lines at
busy travel times and you're bound to witness at least a shouting match.
At the international check-in desk, overwrought passengers are so common that some airline staff have a special word for them—"irates." At
Louis Armstrong International Airport in New Orleans in November
2011, a 30-year-old man got so frustrated at a Continental self-check-in
kiosk that he punched out the computer screen. A gate agent in Newark
spent five days in a coma with a broken neck after an altercation at the
gate about a family's boarding passes for a long-delayed flight to Disney
World.

Corralling tired, crying kids for hours in stuffy, crowded boarding
areas is bad enough, but in flight, the inducements to craziness are
magnified by passengers' utter lack of autonomy. If the airport is too
much, you can walk away, hop in a cab, and go get a beer, or maybe a
Valium. Once the plane door closes, though, that choice is gone. We're
infants—literally almost immobilized, belted half-prone for hours in
our reclined seats in a dimly lit tube, window shades pulled down "for
better viewing." We're told when we may visit the bathroom, where we
may not "congregate" (near the cockpit), and when it's time for sleep.
Our senses perhaps dulled slightly by mild hypoxia (a little less oxygen
gets to the bloodstream and, by extension, the brain, at normal high-
altitude cabin pressures), we're regularly watered and, until recently,
fed. Our captain's soothing voice tells us to sit back and relax.

Treated like infants, we're more likely to act like them. Also like

infants, when we don't get what we want—no food, no space in the overhead bin, no more booze, no cell-phone use, no legroom—we sometimes
throw tantrums. Crammed together in our airborne survival tube, we
resent the lack of control, so we complain bitterly about being kept in
the dark when things go wrong. We demand to know precisely why our
flight is delayed, even though we can't possibly do a damn thing about
it—because it gives us at least the *illusion* of control. Regulators recognize the craving: new DOT rules in 2010 require pilots not just to inform
tarmac-delayed passengers what's happening, but to update them *every
half hour*.

Even more than we crave another two inches of precious legroom
or an uncontested armrest, we seek dominion over our tiny personal
environment even in the crowded confines at 35,000 feet. Passengers
get crazy when the guy in front reclines his seat into their knees. It's not
just because we're cramped or bumped, but because they're invading
our domain—that pathetically small realm we "own" on board. In 2011,
a seatback-recline battle got so bad on a fully loaded United Boeing 767
that the plane had to return to the airport, escorted by F-16 fighter jets.
More recently, five sheriffs' deputies were called to the airport when a
passenger on an overnight Alaska Airlines flight flew into a rage after
a nearby passenger declined to turn off her overhead reading light. No
wonder we don't touch our seatmate's "gasper"—that little knob above
your head that lets you, and you alone, manage the airflow to your
minuscule piece of cabin turf. We push our *own* buttons.

Aircraft makers and some airlines get it. The new Boeing 787 "Dreamliner" was designed to add new passenger control buttons. One of them
makes the window darker in five successive levels of opacity—lots more
to control than just a simple plastic window shade. In the same way,
individual seatback movie screens are about much more than just
clearer viewing, or even the actual entertainment programming. Just
as important is the range and number of "choices" and channels. Virgin
America lets passengers order a drink or meal on their own seatback

touchscreens. You could just as easily stand up, walk down the aisle to the back of the plane, and grab a Coke (and it's probably healthier to get the exercise and leg stretch), but ordering by "fingertip control" satisfies more than thirst: it keeps control freaks happy, even sane, in a place where feeling out of control can trigger panic or air rage.

Particularly when alcohol comes into the mix, misbehavior can become extreme. That's what happened on the 11-hour United flight from Buenos Aires to New York in October 1995, when an intoxicated senior investment banker from tony Greenwich, Connecticut, was refused more booze. Seated up front, the banker, age 58, tried to help himself to more, but was rebuffed by the flight attendants. In the words of the FBI affidavit, "A male flight attendant then entered the first class section and saw [the passenger] with his pants and underwear down defecating on a service cart used by the flight crew. [The passenger] then used linen napkins as toilet paper and wiped his hands on various service counters and service implements used by the crew. [He] also tracked feces throughout the aircraft." The banker pleaded guilty to assault, got two years' probation, and paid a $50,000 cleaning bill.

The mystery may be why there aren't more airline folks like Stephen Slater, the veteran JetBlue flight attendant who, confronted by one too many obnoxious passengers in August 2010, famously grabbed a couple of beers from the galley, pulled the emergency-evacuation inflatable chute, and slid to freedom, more or less, on the JFK tarmac—the ultimate "Take this job and shove it."

Air rage lies at the far end of a continuum of stress shared to some degree by most fliers—81 percent of them according to a University of Washington survey taken in the months right after 9/11. Stress has become part of the whole air-travel experience. It's no surprise then that airlines in 2011 ranked *last* out of 47 US industries in the University of Michigan's annual American Customer Satisfaction Index. That year, one airline, Delta, ranked the second-to-worst company for customer satisfaction among the 225 companies in the survey.

So what is it, exactly, that makes for the pervasive hassle of air travel? We can deconstruct the unhappiness into specific pockets of air-travel pain, but beyond the individual irritants and indignities, there's the larger question: Does commercial air travel—even when understood as a kind of mass transit for nearly two million people flying over America every day—really need to be the hassle it's become for so many over the last decade?

"Your Flight Has Been Delayed"

Just that phrase—with all its finality and blame-deflecting passive voice—is enough to make the throat tighten and teeth clench. Delays cost US travelers an estimated 320 million wasted hours in the peak travel year of 2007. That's otherwise productive time worth $12 billion, according to the Congressional Joint Economic Committee in May 2008, not to mention the $19.1 billion those delays cost the airlines, themselves, in operating costs such as overtime pay, extra fuel and maintenance, and lost flying time. During the same busy year, more than a quarter of all flights were delayed. By 2011, that record improved significantly—fewer than one in five flights were delayed—and on-time performance is getting better, largely because airlines are, for now, simply flying less.

Nationwide on-time statistics don't tell the full story, though—especially for the tens of millions of travelers at a handful of America's busiest hub airports, where delays are far worse than average. The three large New York–area airports plus Atlanta, Philadelphia, San Francisco, and Chicago accounted for 80 percent of all delayed flights in 2009, according to a Government Accountability Office (GAO) report in May 2010. Flying into Newark on a summer evening, your chance of arriving on time is closer to 50-50. And when delays do occur, they're New York–sized, too—more than a solid hour on average in 2011.

Even flights reported as "on time"—defined as arriving within 15 minutes of schedule—are commonly delayed well beyond how long they "should" take. Government "on-time" statistics actually measure "on-schedule" performance—whether your flight arrives when the airline *scheduled* it to arrive. So the easiest way to "improve" your airline's on-time performance is just to pad your schedule. And that's what happens. Delta's Flight 715 from New York to Los Angeles was scheduled for six hours in 1996, a *Wall Street Journal* analysis by Scott McCartney found; now it's scheduled to arrive "on time" in seven hours. That 15 percent increase in travel time has nothing to do with Continental Drift. Similarly, my early morning flight from Washington, DC's Reagan National to New York LaGuardia in December 2012 was scheduled for only 61 minutes; the evening rush-hour flight was "on time" if it made the identical journey in the scheduled *89* minutes.

Are airlines playing games to make their widely reported on-time rankings look better, or are they just being more honest with passengers by scheduling realistically? In fact, regulators insist that airlines tell fliers when they can really expect to get where they're going—not just how long the plane *could* fly the route on a "severe clear" low-traffic Sunday morning. On some routes, delays have become so predictable that it would be deceptive *not* to build them into airline schedules. Regulations prohibit scheduling too optimistically—with potential fines for carriers whose flights are so "chronically late" they arrive more than a half hour behind schedule more than half the time. A *USA Today* analysis found that, statistically, flights have in effect slowed down—from 358 miles per hour in 1998 to 342 miles per hour in 2007. Strange that in a world where technology is accelerating the speed of everything, flying from point A to point B typically takes longer in 2011 than it did two decades earlier.

Common wisdom blames delays on congestion—too many planes

trying to land and take off at the same time, while FAA controllers slow everything down to keep them from crashing into one another. It's only partly true. The FAA tries to keep the lid on delays with a process once known as "flow control." An hour outside Washington, DC, where suburban sprawl meets Virginia Hunt Country, is the safety agency's futuristic National Air Traffic Control System Command Center. "It's the FAA's nerve center," said the agency's head in 2008. "NASA has mission control, we have this." The facility oversees the entire national airspace system—a hierarchy of hundreds of airport towers that control planes on the ground and "own the airspace" within five miles of each airport; scores of "TRACONs" (I'll spare you the full name) that handle departing and approaching flights up to about 40 miles from the airport and below 10,000 feet; and the 20-odd "En Route" Control Centers responsible for "handing off" planes flying at altitude across more than five million square miles of US airspace.

Despite its complexity, the object of the exercise is pretty simple—to smooth out the constantly changing stresses on the national aviation system: a line of funnel clouds in Oklahoma, a key runway blocked for maintenance at JFK, an electrical outage that takes down navigational aids for aircraft landing at fog-bound Juneau. The task is to curtail the bottlenecks, current or predicted, that constrict the "flow" of airplanes anywhere from San Diego to Bangor. The mechanics and technologies, though, are complex and time-intensive. Decisions made in flow control on any given day and hour will have a lot to do with whether you make it home in time to kiss the kids before they go to bed.

When the skies near an airport or region get too crowded for comfort (in FAA-speak, when a "sector" of the national airspace begins to get "saturated") the FAA typically issues a "ground delay program." This keeps planes waiting on the ground, not burning fuel in the air, until congestion dissipates along the planned flight route or at the destination. Computers generate an average and a maximum delay time, and every affected flight gets an "expect [sic] departure clearance time" and later, as takeoff time approaches, a "wheels up" time. FAA delay programs have made "circling" airports for hours largely an anachronism. Other tools are used to keep planes in the air safely "separated" by a precise minimum mileage distance, known as "miles-in-trail," that depends on their altitude, aircraft type, location (whether near busy airports or cruising at high altitude, where the norm is five nautical miles) and other factors. Planes can be directed to fly off course along "delay vectors"; ordered to just slow down; or sometimes to simply "hold" over a specific area at a designated altitude until they can be fitted safely into a congested airport landing pattern.

If things are getting really sticky—say, an unanticipated thunderstorm blocks a standard departure and arrival route or there is, again in FAA-speak, "an overabundance of airplanes . . . at the destination airport"—the agency may up the ante, elevating a ground delay program to a full-bore "ground stop." A ground stop means nobody heading to the destination goes anywhere and, what's worse, nobody can definitively say when they will. Adding to the uncertainty is that while ground stops are usually issued for short periods of time, they're extended as long as needed. Ground stops are the times when harried airline gate agents earn more than their pay mollifying choleric Type A's who rage on that the airline "keeps saying different things" about when their flight will leave. The fact is that nobody knows when the flight will leave. How soon will the tornado stop churning along the path to your destination?

How much your flight is delayed often isn't entirely out of your airline's hands, though. Even when the FAA imposes a ground delay, airlines can typically pick and choose which of their flights to the same region go first and which keep sitting at the gate. Air traffic controllers don't normally care which of the airline's Boeing 737s heading to the New York area takes off first. So get this, you Type A's: your airline can decide to move *your* flight to the head or to the back of the line—depending on how much "priority" they give it. They can just trade "wheels-up" times with another flight. Try not to take it personally, though. Delay priority decisions are generally based on economics—like which plane has more passengers connecting to lucrative overseas long-haul markets, which crews are nearing the end of their maximum permitted "on-duty time," and whether your airplane has to be somewhere later tonight to avoid cascading delays tomorrow morning. Does it matter if there are lots of high-paying business travelers or a VIP on board? Airlines don't say.

Contrary to popular belief, the main reason for delay has little to do with "system" problems like heavy traffic volume, congested air space, air traffic control, or bad weather. Together, they accounted for only a quarter of 2011 delays. Nearly a third of the time, delays are the fault of what the FAA calls "circumstances within the airline's control"—things like aircraft maintenance (something on the plane needs fixing), crew staffing (the copilot overslept), late baggage, or fueling. From a broader perspective, though, endemic air travel delay—though reduced recently to one in five or six flights—is just the predictable consequence of a massive, intricately interdependent aviation system straining to operate at the fine edge of its capabilities. Within that window, there's simply precious little margin for the inevitable screwups, acts of God, and "stuff happens" scenarios of the real world. Consider the stresses on a system approaching a billion passengers annually by the mid-2020s:

Tight and Fast

Start with the pure economic incentive to keep hellishly expensive planes in the air when passengers want to fly. The prime revenue directive is to schedule planes tight and turn them fast. The faster you can "turn" a modern jet around—from landing and unloading to loading and taking off again—the more money that shiny new $80 million Boeing 737 generates. (If you're really good at "the turn," like Southwest, you can even squeeze in an extra flight full of paying passengers every day.) Financial analysts obsess about this "aircraft utilization rate"—how many hours a day each plane is flying (from when the door closes to depart to when it opens on arrival) as opposed to just sitting on the ground being maintained, serviced, loaded, or just waiting at the gate. JetBlue's jets flew 11.7 hours a day in 2011, compared to those at American that spent only 9.6 hours each day making money (albeit on longer wide-body routes and different networks). Guess which airline turned a profit.

Stormy Weather

Weather is involved in roughly half of all flight delays, but the really extreme stuff—such as tornadoes and blizzards that shut down airports—accounted for only about 4 percent of delays in 2011. Large jets routinely navigate serious turbulence and heavy snows, not to mention 50-million-volt lightning bolts. What much more commonly triggers delays is the run-of-the mill fog or icy drizzle that hardly merits an umbrella but that limits what pilots and tower controllers can actually see. When that happens, good weather "visual flight rules" won't work to keep airplanes safely separated. The time-honored "see-and-avoid" flying technique requires that the pilot can, in fact, see—typically, for at least three miles in the vicinity of busy airports, with specific minimum clearances between the plane and any clouds. Otherwise, the FAA imposes "instrument flight rules"—and this inevitably slows everything down.

Switching from "visual" to "instrument" rules can easily cut hourly flight operations 15 to 25 percent or more, depending on the airport and its navigation facilities. Planes must stay farther apart to add a safety cushion along busy air traffic lanes, or "airways." That means longer waits between takeoffs as well as staggered landings, all designed to increase spacing between planes—like tapping your car's brakes to lengthen your distance from the driver you're following on a foggy, icy highway. Things move slower on the tarmac, too, as tower controllers need more time to guide huge aircraft along taxiways.

Scheduling Games

When it comes to delays, airlines don't mind being seen as innocent victims—either of acts of nature or some ill-defined government (usually FAA) incompetence. Pilots tell their impatient, tarmac-bound passengers that they're just waiting for air traffic controllers to give them a departure slot. If only those darn controllers would get to work! The truth is, though, the airlines aren't exactly innocents in many delay scenarios: According to the FAA, they *knowingly* schedule more flights at crowded hubs and crowded times than the airport can handle.

The problem is that everybody—especially airlines' best business customers—wants to fly out between eight and nine in the morning and fly back home between five and six in the evening. So airlines naturally try to schedule, advertise, and sell them those conveniently timed flights. But there is a physical limit. Not all of those desired flights can be crammed into those two "preferred" rush hours. The system goes tilt and everybody is delayed. On the other hand, each airline *individually* has every incentive to schedule as many flights as it can cram into the half hour when passengers most want to fly. If they don't, they assume their competitors will. Even if the ultimate result is that everybody's flight ends up waiting on the tarmac, airlines can always blame the predictable delays on the FAA.

Former FAA administrator Randy Babbitt got sufficiently ticked off to call the airlines out. In a tough 2010 speech, he declared that the FAA "will not sit back and be the scapegoat" for delays. "If you have twenty flights scheduled to take off in a single five-minute window, you've just created a bow wave of delays that's likely to last all morning, maybe all day," he said. "It's just not going to work." The airline trade association spokesman offered a "who-me?" response: We're just "schedul[ing] flights to meet the expectations of consumers who want to fly at convenient times"—apparently even if that means nobody's "expectations" are fulfilled.

Except for jawboning, though, there's only so much regulators can do about airline overscheduling. There's no law against it and antitrust laws normally preclude airlines from getting together to agree on saner schedules except in rare situations. At a few perennially delayed hubs—including Chicago, New York, and Washington

National—overscheduling got so bad that regulators had to step in directly with a "temporary" fix—but that was in 1968. Nearly a half century later, that temporary solution is largely still in place: a system of "slots" (hourly takeoff and landing "reservations") that can be bought and sold. The going rate in 2011 to obtain the slots to operate a well-timed daily flight at DC's close-in airport was about $5 million; peak-time slot pairs at London's Heathrow were recently valued at $50 million. LaGuardia slots were a bargain at $4 million per takeoff and landing.

Ripple Effects, Chokepoints, and Murphy's Law

Commercial aviation is the poster child for Murphy's Law. Take the seemingly simple matter of finding an open boarding gate when your plane lands. Without one, you're sitting on the tarmac, maybe just 50 tantalizing yards from escape, but you're not making that meeting, no matter how early your flight touched down. The folks waiting in the terminal to board that incoming airplane to fly elsewhere are cooling their heels too. Especially at busy hubs where each gate may handle more than half a dozen flights every day, airlines assign gate coordinators to do little else than manage that game of Tetris.

Gate availability is just one of the many little airline-caused delay triggers. A late-arriving flight attendant or copilot or a bag-handler's ill-timed coffee break can be at fault. Planes can't leave without the FAA-prescribed complement of one attendant per 50 seats. Or there could be a last-minute "mechanical" or "maintenance discrepancy." Is it just a burnt-out cockpit warning light, or a critical part that requires repair (by an FAA-certified mechanic) before takeoff?

Small glitches beget big delays down the line. They tend to cumulate, each building on the last, cascading across the country throughout the day, with precious little built-in cushion to let flights make up lost time. Blame in part the hub-and-spoke system; most US fliers "connect" to their destinations through only a dozen or so big hub airports like Chicago O'Hare, Atlanta Hartsfield, and Dallas/Fort Worth. (The 30 busiest hubs account for two-thirds of all US flight boardings.) Delays can ripple across the continent when a major hub gets "stuck"—say, a runway ices, air traffic overloads, or some hopeless romantic can't resist ducking past the TSA security checkpoint to kiss his girlfriend good-bye at the gate (an incident that shut down Newark Airport's Terminal C for six hours in 2010).

Some 40 percent of delays stem from the late arrival of your plane from somewhere else, so by the end of the day, short delays have grown into long delays. Flying from the nation's largest hub airports in July 2012, on average, your chance of an on-time departure between seven and eight *a.m.* was nearly 50 percent better than if you flew between seven and eight *p.m.*, according to DOT figures. At ultra-congested airports like Newark International, the difference between early morning departures (about 80 percent on time) and evening flights (about 50 percent on time) was even more dramatic.

Ultrabusy hubs are the fragile backbone of the aviation system when it comes to delays. At Chicago O'Hare, the nation's second busiest airport by departures, flights take off or land at the rate of 100 every hour of the day on average. Add to that the pressure of flight "banking," the airline practice of tightly choreographing schedules to create dense "waves" or "banks" of flights all arriving or departing close to the same time. This reduces the time that travelers have to spend waiting on the ground at connecting airports for their onward flights and also keeps planes making money flying. Tight hub scheduling can leave only 35 to 50 minutes, depending on airline and airport, to move passengers and, hopefully, their luggage, from their arriving domestic flight to the boarding gate for their onward departing domestic flight. It's challenging enough in optimal conditions—now add to the mix an approaching line of severe thunderstorms.

Some mega-hubs are so perennially clogged that DOT has labeled them "chokepoints." Out of 4,000 US public airports, only seven accounted for about 80 percent of all delays in 2011, but the nation's largest aviation market, Greater New York (including Philadelphia and

Teterboro in New Jersey), was the worst chokepoint of all. New York is used to superlatives; its three huge airports handled 3,200 flights every day in 2010, more than 100 million passengers coming and going every year. But consider this: in the first six months of 2011, this one metropolitan area accounted for nearly *half* of *all* US flight delays. Flights bound for Newark Airport *alone* accounted for 40 of the nation's 100 most-delayed flights, according to data compiled for the *Wall Street Journal* in 2011. And here's the kicker: a third of all delays are caused in some way by New York airspace congestion, the *New York Times* reports. In the interconnected architecture of the nation's airspace, New York congestion affects everything downstream. Wonder why your afternoon flight from sunny Dallas to even sunnier Albuquerque is delayed? Blame heavy morning fog over Long Island that slowed your plane's first flight of the day from JFK to DFW.

Bag Wars

For sheer travel anxiety, not much beats standing around the baggage carousel after a long flight while everybody *else* retrieves their stuff from the belt and the remaining bags start to thin out. No wonder travelers cite lost luggage—even if statistically rare—as a serious grievance.

The airline industry doesn't talk about "lost" luggage at all; the preferred term (which also covers pilfered, delayed, and damaged luggage) is "mishandled," presumably on the theory that there's always hope. But whatever it's called, luggage that's not there when you arrive—bleary-eyed and jet-lagged after hours in transit—is no fun. In its "Fly Rights" consumer guide, DOT chirps that "only a tiny percentage of checked bags is permanently lost." But then it adds—rather breezily—that "your bag might be delayed for a day or two." No problem—unless, of course, it's your *only* bag, the one with the baby formula and diapers and the keys to your car.

Airlines were actually losing luggage only half as frequently in 2012 than five years earlier, when there were five to six mishandled bag reports for each 1,000 domestic passengers. How often bags are mishandled seems, predictably, to track pretty closely the ups and downs of air traffic generally. Hefty new bag-check fees have helped reduce the crunch too. The fewer bags checked, the fewer bags lost. As airlines instituted fees for checking bags in 2008 and 2009, the number of checked bags per passenger reportedly dropped 40 to 50 percent; it's no surprise that the rate of mishandled bags also improved 40 percent from 2007 through 2009. Better bag-tracking and bag-handling technology also played a role.

A 3-in-1,000 risk of any passenger losing luggage (really a higher statistical risk for those fliers who actually *checked* a bag) seems low, but it means US airlines are still mishandling more than 5,000 bags every *day*, with nearly two million reports of mishandling in 2011. The good news, though, is that close to 98 percent of lost bags eventually make it back to their owners. According to a 2011 report by SITA, a provider of IT and communications services to the aviation industry, more than 50 percent of those bags worldwide are returned within 42 hours, and the great bulk of the rest get there eventually. There's plenty of financial incentive for US airlines to make that happen; they can be required to pay passengers up to $3,300 for the depreciated value of their lost luggage and its contents. Even if the lost bag is eventually retrieved, estimates are that airlines spend $90 to $100 to deal with a mishandled bag. Retrieving and otherwise dealing with lost luggage cost airlines worldwide nearly $3 billion in 2010—not including unhappy customers and, for US airlines, the lousy public relations from poor DOT consumer rankings.

So airlines spend serious money and effort idiot-proofing the labor-intensive luggage process. TSA estimated in 2008 that six to ten airline or airport workers touch a bag for every TSA officer who does so, according to news reports. Workers at many airports are supposed to hand-scan each bag before loading to make sure it's on the right flight; a warning sounds if it isn't. ("Supposed to" because some baggage handlers reportedly resist scanning; it interferes with the preferred bag-heaving "rhythm.") Scanners also help stop workers from unloading bags meant to remain on a "through" flight. Then there are simpler fixes—like training check-in agents to make sure baggage labels are straight and visible so automatic scanners can read them.

The deeper mystery is this: What in the world really happens when our Samsonite drops into the dark maw behind the airport check-in desk or drop-off? And why does it get screwed up? (Or in FAA-speak, what's the "failure mode"?) Simplified, here's what's supposed to happen to checked luggage making its way through a typical large hub, and why it sometimes doesn't.

Step One: The check-in agent prints out an adhesive bag tag that includes a bar code, a flight number, and a three-letter destination airport code, and it all gets attached to your luggage handle. The bar code will be read later by automated sorting devices using laser scanner arrays.

Failure Mode: A check-in agent uses the wrong city destination code for your bag tag, sending your luggage to San Juan, Puerto Rico (code: SJU) instead of San Jose, California (SJC) or San Jose, Costa Rica (SJO). *Or,* the check-in agent has poor "baggage hygiene." (They really call it that.) They're supposed to stick your roller bag on the belt wheels-up, with at least three feet between bags, which helps avoid jam-ups (a perennial problem with long tubes, skis, and loosely strapped luggage), and oversized bags are supposed to go elsewhere.

If the printed strip with the bag tag attached to your luggage gets shredded, smudged, folded, ripped, spindled or dislodged, your bag can't be automatically sorted and—uh-oh—it's sent to a default pile, where a human eventually has to look at it and retag it. Or the bag has more than one bag tag—it's amazing how many people think it's neat to collect bag tags—which confuses the scanner. Bag-tag bar code readers have only about 80 to 90 percent accuracy, according to *Popular Mechanics,* but bag tags at large airports increasingly incorporate radio-frequency identification chips that improve automatic reader accuracy. Ticketing and tagging errors cause about 16 percent of mishandled luggage world-wide, says SITA.

Step Two: Your bag drops down a conveyor belt behind the check-in podium, where it travels on a belt at 5 to 10 miles per hour (some new systems nearly double that speed) to security screening. Since 9/11, all luggage in the cargo holds of passenger airlines gets screened. Not by humans, but by million-dollar CT-scan machines. The machines image up to hundreds of "slices" of each bag, enabling TSA agents peering at high-resolution screens in a windowless room somewhere else to remotely "see into" about three bags a minute. Newer "in-line" models reportedly screen up to 500 bags every hour. Suspicious contents can be instantly checked against vast libraries of stored image files. (Is that pistol really a novelty hair dryer made in Hong Kong in 1982?) Based on their years of experience, human screeners can "resolve" roughly a third to a half of the bags (it varies) that the CT scans find suspicious, without resorting to a time-consuming manual search of the bag.

Bags that don't look or smell funny (that is to say, explosive) get to move on. Some airports, such as Denver, load them onto 20-mile-per-hour unmanned carts—like miniature roller-coaster cars—called destination-coded vehicles. With the tag on each bag optically scanned, at the correct junction of the conveyor belt another sorting machine diverts the bag and dumps it down another chute, where it lands at the luggage-sorting station or carousel near your flight's boarding gate. (Sometimes, multiple flights will use the same carousel—uh-oh again.)

If your bag *does* set off an alarm—there are lots false positives in the hypersensitive scanning machines—and the screen-watchers can't resolve it, the bag goes down farther to the Baggage Inspection Room—what some airports have affectionately referred to as "the Bomb Room." There, one of a half dozen inspectors wearing blue latex gloves physically opens the suspect bag—they've got hundreds of keys to open luggage locks—trying not to bust the luggage. (The TSA doesn't say how often it happens, but at least at one major US hub, inspectors find "something" every year that requires them to evacuate the room and call the local bomb squad.) If your bag was opened for inspection, you may have found a nice time-stamped note left by the friendly screener. They do try to get your stuff back on the conveyor belt in time for it to be loaded onto your flight; even in the basement inspection room they have flight departure monitors. But don't count on it.

Failure Mode: The object of the baggage process is to move your bags faster than you yourself can move—from check-in desk to departure gate, or from arrival gate to baggage carousel, or from your arriving plane to your connecting flight. When your bags can't get there before you do—say, the underground high-speed conveyor belt (picture Disney World's "Wild Mouse Ride") gets snagged on a fashionable bag strap or outsized zipper pull—you may not see that bag for a while.

Every connecting hub has a minimum "legal" connecting time—often only 35 to 50 minutes. That's how long the airline thinks two things can happen: the first is for you to drag yourself, your bulging carry-ons, and your tired kids off the plane and herd everybody down the hall to another boarding area—inevitably located at the other end of the crowded, quarter-mile-long concourse—where your next flight is leaving; the second is for the airline to retrieve your checked suitcase from the cargo hold of the plane you arrived on and load it onto the plane you're departing on, also maybe halfway across the airport. Not that airlines don't try—notice how baggage carts race around tarmacs at busy hubs to transfer "hot" bags from one plane to another—but bare-minimum connecting times multiply the chance of a baggage screwup.

Step Three: Once your luggage makes it to the bag assembly area below your gate, how hard can it be to get it the last few yards into the cargo hold of your nearby plane? You'd be surprised. Much depends on the ramp agent or "ramper"—occasionally also affectionately known in the trade as the "thrower" or "bag smasher."

Failure Mode: "Touch a bag, read the tag" is the rule, but it's not always followed. Bags can get overlooked, stuck on the wrong cart going to the wrong plane, arrive a minute too late. Not so rarely, they actually fall off moving carts on the way to the plane. Simple "failure to load" accounted for 15 percent of mishandled bags in 2011, according to SITA's report. Let's face it. Bag handling can be boring, repetitive, and tough when it's 12 degrees or 120 degrees on the tarmac, jet engines are screaming, and the pressure is on to load and unload 100-plus bags in minutes to keep the plane on schedule.

Precisely how your suitcase is loaded into the cargo hold depends on the type of aircraft. On large wide-bodies like Boeing's 777, 747, and 787 jets, bags normally go into explosion-resistant 5-by-10-foot cans known as unit load devices, which are then hoisted and slid snugly into the cargo hold below the seating level. Much more fun—if it's not your cherished, hand-tooled leather trunk packed with keepsake crystal—is the way bags are loaded onto workhorse domestic jets like the 737, with its narrow 90-foot-long cargo hold. As described by travel journalist George Hobica of Airfarewatchdog.com, in his interview of a confessed "baggage thrower," it will convince you never, ever, to pack anything fragile.

The ramp agent drives an angled conveyor belt to the door of the cargo hold, where another agent climbs inside. As a bag tossed from the cart onto the belt moves up to the door of the hold, the agent inside heaves it—slides it, bowls it, or throws it—to the end of the hold, where yet another ramp agent is waiting to stack it with the other luggage. This is not a delicate operation. Handlers are expected to be able to fill a 737 cargo hold with 150 bags in less than 30 minutes.

Will They Make Me Check It?

Even when luggage actually makes it there on time and in decent shape—as it most often does—the whole bag-*checking* issue has become a source of air-travel angst. With hefty checked-bag fees and potential delays, "Will they make me check it?" is on every flier's mind. Since

airlines started charging for your first checked bag in 2008, the temptation to cram a week's worth of clothing into a small overnight suitcase
can be overwhelming. Most US airlines have the same luggage size limits: carry-ons can't exceed 45 "linear" inches—basically, 22" × 14" × 9"
(think a good-sized tabletop microwave)—and must weigh less than 40
pounds; Southwest allows a few inches more.

And they are not kidding. Sharp-eyed airline staff are popping up at
check-in counters and boarding gates. Even if you make it to the boarding
gate with that so-called carry-on, you're not home free. Europe's Ryanair
demands an extra "gate bag fee"—equivalent to about $50—assessed at
the door to the airplane if your carry-on is deemed too big. In late 2011,
Spirit Airlines went further, imposing a $100 penalty on folks trying to
sneak aboard *any* carry-on that is too big to fit underneath the seat in
front (and needs to go in the overhead bin) without paying Spirit's "normal" $45 fee for that "service." Sounds extreme, but more traditional
airlines are also working on "how to prevent so many non-complying
bags from reaching the gate" in the ominous words of a United Airlines
spokesman quoted by *New York Times* aviation writer Joe Sharkey.

Getting your overstuffed carry-on past the gate agent is one thing,
but even if the lone agent is too busy to bar the jetway door, you still
have to jam it in the overhead without busting it—or your back. And if
it doesn't fit, you're headed for the dreaded "gate check," where you're
perp-walked, red-faced, back up the aisle against the stream of boarding passengers to the aircraft door; there the ramp worker hands you a
receipt and unceremoniously chucks your bag (naturally, marked "fragile") down a planeside metal tube, hopefully to be loaded aboard.

Lines upon Lines

Air travel can feel like just a series of waiting lines—lines to check in,
lines for screening, lines to board, lines to collect luggage. Lines can
become the travel experience, transforming us into Chaplin-esque

drones shuffling splayfooted through endless queues to be packed, boxed, and shipped.

Air-travel lines are different than most. Normal queues are a response, an orderly alternative to rioting when multiple people are waiting for something they want. Those who sell that "something" want their lines to be as short and quick as possible, so they can sell more of it. Air-travel lines, on the other hand, seem more like a kind of punishment—their purpose, up to a point, to make the journey harder for those who pay less. Call me cynical, but without annoyingly long lines for the bargain-hunting masses, why would other passengers pay extra for "priority boarding"—in essence, a line-jumping pass—or better yet, a business-class ticket that avoids the long line entirely?

Airlines and airports tell passengers to arrive at the terminal up to *three hours* before the scheduled flight departure time. Unless you're trying to fly coach to Mongolia on an expired passport with lots of luggage in August at rush hour, that seems like a crazy long time. Perhaps it helps contain airline labor costs—the second biggest expense category after fuel—by requiring fewer check-in and other airport staff. Sure, tighter staffing can mean longer passenger lines, but you'll make your flight if you arrive early enough to spend extra time waiting in those lines. Think of it this way: airlines are trading their labor costs for your "standing-in-line" costs.

Not that long pre-flight waits necessarily bother the airports or the concessions that rent space from them either. Getting passengers to arrive hours in advance of their flights means more airport "dwell time," which in turn means more time to spend money at airport shopping malls, food courts, and watering holes. And it's not just Gucci and Prada. One of the biggest sources of revenue for all the stores beyond the security checkpoint is simply bottled water—commonly at $2 to $3 for 20 ounces—that can't be brought through the screening line. (According to airport travel columnist Harriet Baskas, bottled water was the top-selling item even in rainy Seattle in 2006.) Telling passengers to arrive

hours in advance also reduces pressure on the whole system—long security screening lines cause fewer missed flights and baggage handlers
have more time to load aircraft—but is it really fair to the infrequent-
flying innocents who actually follow the warnings and show up ridicu-
lously early "just to be sure"?

Crowding and Cramming

Airplanes have never been as crowded as they are today. Well into the
1980s, many flew nearly half empty—literally. Until 1978, the federal
government essentially set airfares (it had broad fare-approval authority) at levels that would ensure that airlines made a predetermined rate
of return. To make those calculations, Civil Aeronautics Board officials
had to make an assumption about how many fare-paying passengers
would typically be aboard any given flight. Through the 1970s, the estimate was that 55 percent of seats on average would be filled.

The reality today is far different. Most reasonably timed flights are
simply chock-full. From the 55 percent target of the 1970s, normal loads
had grown to about two-thirds full by the mid-1990s, then almost three-
quarters full in the 2000s. Today, the big US network carriers—United,
Delta, American, and US Airways—technically average close to 85 percent full. Conveniently-timed flights in major markets are normally even
fuller, though, since the overall average includes half-empty predawn
flights to reposition aircraft for the day ahead, flights during the slow-
est post-holiday winter travel season, and lots of "non-rev" passengers—
commuting or deadheading crew members and airline employees with
travel privileges who fill unpaid seats and so don't get counted in the official load-factor averages. In the real world, to put it simply, don't expect
empty seats.

Crowding means success in the airline business. Airlines spend about
as much to fly a Boeing 737-800 carrying 20 paying passengers as the
same jet crammed with 175 souls—maybe a few more bucks for the extra

soft drinks. So the fuller the airplane, the better financially. For passengers, though, crowding amplifies all the other craziness that's part of mass air travel.

Most obvious is seating comfort—aircraft designers call it "living space"—one of frequent travelers' top two complaints in a 2010 Consumers Union survey of almost 15,000 fliers. Economy seats are all pretty much the same. For instance, they have to withstand a crash that exerts 16 G's (16 times the force of gravity). That's the limit of what the FAA thinks passengers could possibly survive hurtling forward against the seat in front in an "impact-survivable accident"—from 44 feet per second to a dead stop in about a tenth of a second. US airlines' seats are all also about the same width—17 to 18 inches—to fit the common six-across coach configuration on most domestic jets and still keep the single aisle wide enough to let passengers evacuate the plane in 90 seconds in an emergency, as the FAA requires. (In a modest concession to developments in modern American anatomy, Airbus, the leading European aircraft manufacturer, is considering a slightly wider aisle coach seat for its A320 planes, but the other two seats in the row would lose nearly an inch each.)

It's much easier to change the front-to-back space between seat rows, known as "seat pitch," and it's amazing what a difference an extra inch or two can make. Mechanically, it would be a simple matter to lengthen legroom spacing—seats are bolted to rails on the cabin floor and the spacing can be readily adjusted—but there's a serious economic trade-off. Bean counters naturally want to cram the most possible salable seats onto the plane, and the easiest way to do so on large narrow-body workhorses like Boeing 737s and 757s and Airbus 320s is to shrink the seat pitch. Cutting just one inch of legroom for every seat on a 30-row plane generates an entire extra row of six paying seats—and the temptation to do so has proven hard for airlines to resist. One alternative: new seat designs that try to save that inch either by reducing the thickness of the seat cushion or limiting the range of seat recline with an "articulating pan" that moves the seat itself forward as the seatback moves rearward.

Seat pitch reflects each airline's market niche and brand strategy. Ultracheap Spirit Airlines thinks its passengers will endure just about anything for a low fare—including the industry's tightest seat pitch, just 28 inches between seats on its fleet of Airbus 320s. (The norm in coach is more like 31 to 32 inches.) That's about as tight as an adult male can handle without sitting "side-saddle." Plus, Spirit's seats don't recline—presumably for fear of injury to the poor unfortunate in the seat behind; the airline describes its immovable seats, apparently without irony, as "pre-reclined." Nobody enjoys the ride, but Spirit can jam 174 paying seats into 29 coach rows of its A320—some 15 percent more seats overall than other airlines can stuff onto similar jets. United and Delta fill the same type of plane with about 148 seats, and "we-are-the-world" JetBlue, which promises to "bring humanity to air travel," affords all passengers at minimum a relatively luxurious 34 inches of pitch on its A320 planes. But Spirit gets the last laugh: its stock price nearly doubled in value in its first year as a public company and the fast-growing airline remains consistently profitable, with industry-leading, double-digit operating margins into 2012.

Other People

Crowding exacerbates one of air travel's worst horrors: other passengers. When "living space" for each passenger is so scarce, perceived invasions of personal space, even just by reclining your seat, can turn nasty quickly. That's what happened May 29, 2011, on United's late-evening Flight 990 from Washington Dulles to Accra, Ghana. One passenger reclined his seat all the way back, presumably smacking the knees of the person behind. The injured party allegedly slapped the recliner's head. A shoving match ensued, despite the mediating efforts of a flight attendant and a passenger. Rather than head out across 5,000 miles of the

Atlantic with a potentially uncontrollable ruckus in the back, the pilot decided to call it a night. The Boeing 767 with 144 passengers aboard circled for 25 minutes to expend some of the thousands of gallons of fuel that would have made the jet too heavy to land safely and returned to Dulles under F-16 fighter escort. No charges were pressed by authorities. Maybe they sympathized.

Personal-space wars extend well beyond the seatback recline battle to include, as we know, armrest wars, obesity spillover squeezes, and overhead-bin-space fights. The space-deprived middle seat is so anathema, according to a survey run by the Global Strategy Group and sponsored by 3M, that 50 percent of air passengers said they would wait for the next flight in order to get an aisle seat; one in five said they would rather stay *overnight* at an airport hotel for an aisle seat on the first flight out the next morning. According to IndependentTraveler.com, 9 percent of travelers simply refuse to sit in the middle seat on a full flight of more than two hours. Period.

Physical-space invasion is just the beginning when it comes to "other people" issues. Personal hygiene was near the top of the list of passenger annoyances, cited by nearly half of the 1,600 respondents in a 2009 Travelocity poll. Some 30 percent of those surveyed cited coughers and sneezers, and 15 percent objected to sitting next to obese passengers (though 44 percent of these travelers thought airlines should provide a second seat at no cost to obese fliers). Other frequently mentioned "other people" peeves include:

> Fragrant travelers—whether "natural" or due to perfume or cologne.
> The "inappropriately attired"—like the 23-year-old Hooters waitress and student whose denim miniskirt Southwest thought left too little to the imagination to fly in 2007, or the middle-aged gent wearing only women's undergarments and high heels on a US Airways flight from Fort Lauderdale in 2011.
> Make-yourself-at-home fliers—who remove shoes, and sometimes

socks, at the first opportunity; clip nails (alas, not just fingernails); remove nail polish; change soiled diapers, and so on.

> Not-so-cute kids—the nasty little seat kickers who pop up and turn around to drool on you.

> The hygiene-challenged—nose-pickers and serial flatulators included.

Then there are the Mile-High Clubbers who can't seem to resist the allure of sexual intimacy in the three-by-three-foot lavatory or, worse, in the seat across the aisle from you. Purists insist that the "club" is meant to include only those in flagrante while actually *piloting* an aircraft above 5,280 feet. Commercial airline pilots will tell you (perhaps a little ruefully) that this happens about as frequently as fatal US airline crashes do—in other words, almost never. But passenger sex isn't quite so rare. Maybe it's the vibration, the close quarters and dim lighting, or just hours with little to do, but a global annual survey by (who else?) a major European condom manufacturer found in 2005 that 4 percent of surveyed adults in the United States (2 percent globally) claimed to have had some kind of onboard sexual encounter. Professed enthusiasts include even airline gurus like Virgin Atlantic founder Richard Branson, who says his encounter at age 19 with an older woman in a Laker Airways lavatory en route to Los Angeles "was every man's dream, to be honest."

You've got to be pretty amorous. Aside from the obvious physical constraints and the gazillion germs that cover airplane lavatory surfaces, long stays in the loo make cabin crews nervous. On the tenth anniversary of the attacks, Frontier's flight from Denver to Detroit was met by F-16 fighter jets when a couple retreated to the lav for "an extraordinarily long time," according to the airline. So a public service announcement for would-be "clubbers": For $300 to $1,000 or so, there are mom-and-pop air-charter operators who will fly you and your beloved around for an hour in a small propeller plane with a mattress-outfitted cabin about the size of a large SUV. Pilots wear headphones and promise to be very discreet.

And don't forget the technology-addicted. The ones who play movies on their laptop without earphones—whether *Dora the Explorer* or *Debbie Does Dallas*—or, if they use earphones, can't seem to shove their ear buds all the way in (allowing everyone to enjoy the throbbing bass line). Plus the self-important folks who can't power off their iPhones during takeoff and landing like everyone else. Not to mention the drunks, the chatterboxes, and the folks with urinary problems who always insist on the window seat.

Yackety-Yack

The ultimate "other people" in-flight annoyance may be yet to come: the looming threat of the airborne cell phone. You'll be able to learn so much about your seatmate's medical problems or romantic crises or political leanings on those long, full flights! At least 3,000 planes world-wide were already wired for web connectivity in 2012, using onboard satellite technology that could be adapted to let fliers use their own cell phones for in-flight calls. There remain some safety questions in the United States, where federal regulations still bar airborne calls on the view that the devices' electromagnetic transmissions could affect delicate aircraft avionics, but European safety authorities lifted their in-flight cell-phone ban in 2007 (though in-flight calling is still not common in Europe).

The FAA is taking a harder look at the safety of personal electronic gadgets, though it says it's not about to consider cell phone calls. But absent a safety problem—current evidence is, at very most, equivocal on this issue—more widespread mobile phone use (voice and text) seems inevitable. It's already offered on a few Persian Gulf carriers—Emirates Airlines' 90 mobile phone–capable jets handled nearly 20,000 calls per month by 2012—and in-flight phoning is poised to become a competitive differentiator for high-end international fliers. When British Airways announced in-flight texting and web access on its financier-packed all-business flight from London City Airport to New York, it didn't take long for archrival Virgin Atlantic to cross the sound barrier too—allowing in-flight voice calls on its transatlantic services. Virgin says it will only allow six passengers at a time to use the system and that it's only meant for use—get this—"in exceptional situations." We're talking about New York business travelers here, folks. For them, "exceptional" is a 30-point drop in the Dow.

There's a deep split of US opinion about in-flight mobile phone calls—not surprisingly, it falls largely along generational lines. A government survey released in 2008 asked fliers whether to allow cell phone use on planes if it's safe. Nearly 40 percent said "definitely" or "probably" yes; nearly 45 percent said "definitely" or "probably" no, with some 15 percent unsure. Only a quarter of travelers over age 65 liked the idea, though, compared to nearly half of the 18-to-34 crowd. Meanwhile, a major flight attendants' union is opposed, and frequent-flier surveys reflect opposition. The House of Representatives passed and sent a bill to the Senate in 2008 that never became law called the "Halting Airplane Noise to Give Us Peace" Act (aka "HANG-UP"), which would have imposed a permanent federal ban on in-flight wireless phone calls and VoIP (voice over Internet protocol) communications.

Cell-phone-friendly airlines (they do get a cut of call charges) like Emirates profess special efforts to minimize annoyance, such as restrictions on nighttime-flight use. And for now, calls remain expensive—usually charged at international roaming rates—so they tend to be short, on average about two minutes, says Emirates. Still, communication costs invariably decline over time with new technology, and there may well come a day when chirping smart phones join engine whine as normal cabin background noise. Although limited experience with in-flight calling hasn't triggered air rage, turn-off-the-phone battles with the phone-addicted have already turned nasty and Britain's Association of Anger Management has a grim prediction about in-flight voice calls: "It would be a nightmare. We will see air rage statistics increase."

Nickel-and-Diming

Nobody likes to pay for something they used to get for free, but fliers' anger over the tsunami of fees and charges spawned by the airlines' 2008 fuel-induced financial panic is about more than that. It's also about the sheer scope of the new fees, their nagging appearance at every juncture of the journey and the constant drumbeat of marketing of the newly "unbundled" services. Just buying a ticket online requires navigating multiple screens of "options" for lounge access and queue-jumping and "upsells" for more legroom and "are-you-sure-you-don't-want-to-do-the-responsible-thing-and-buy-travel-insurance?"—not to mention the come-ons for hotels, rental cars, and tours. It all drives home the disquieting notion that we're merely transient sources of airline revenue to be mined for whatever we're worth. No wonder that a *Consumer Reports* survey of thousands of air travelers in June 2011 found nickel-and-diming at the top of the passenger grievance pile.

OK, we can live without "free" yummy airplane food or well-used blankets and pillows. These things feel like tangible extras it's reasonable to be charged for, even if they used to be included in our airfare; after all, they cost the airline a little more to provide. On the same view, we might even swallow some modest fee to check luggage—it costs airlines labor and fuel to haul our stuff. But there's a line beyond which we feel seriously ripped-off. Maybe it's the fee just to check in, or to talk on the phone to a human reservations agent, or to stand by for an earlier, half-empty flight, or to stick our briefcase in the overhead, or to book a "free" trip with the frequent-flier miles we've "earned." At some point, the loss of an amenity becomes an insult.

The expertly concocted smoke-and-mirrors rhetoric the industry

deploys to justify the new fee-based business model and defuse consumer (and congressional) "outrage" is nearly as infuriating. Some of
the language is positively Orwellian. New fees are about "giving customers more choice," says Airlines for America, and "making choices
and paying for services you use and value." These "service choices
[*please*, not 'fees'] are not new," writes the trade association's CEO in
a November 2011 *USA Today* op-ed. "Airlines began offering customers the option to pay for service they value" years ago. "If you look at
what consumers want in the US," echoes Delta's CEO in a June 2012
NPR interview, "they want choice." Some might argue that what they
really want is more legroom, a bigger seat, and a free snack at a lower
price. How could anyone object to "choice," "value," "service," and having "options," or be so dense as to confuse these virtues with just forking
over more cash to the airline?

It's not about *adding* new fees, airlines say. They're just "unbundling" the prix fixe journey into a menu of à la carte offerings—merely
deconstructing the journey into goods and services fliers thought were
included in the ticket price. But there's a serious logical disconnect: If
we choose not to take the option of, say, checking a suitcase (since we
"value" avoiding the lost-bag office), shouldn't the basic airfare we pay
go down? If "à la carte" means paying the same check for the complete
dinner, but then adding a *new* extra charge for dessert, why *shouldn't* we
be ticked off? The industry's most straightforward defense of fees came
from the trade association's top lobbyist in July 2011, when she was
called to justify fare hikes to a Senate committee: "The airline industry
is sick, it's anemic," she told the senators. "We have to be able to cover
the cost of flying folks."

No matter how much passengers hate the nickel-and-diming, there's
just too much money at stake for airlines to give it up. On average, fees
for checked bags and hefty charges for "changing" a ticket—altering the
time or date or routing, or sometimes just the traveler's name—added
$22 to the basic domestic ticket price in 2011. Checked-bag fees alone

brought in more cash in the first three months of 2012 than the profits of the ten largest US airlines combined, according to *The Economist*. For the industry, nickel-and-diming made the difference between profit and loss. In 2011, the net profits of US airlines (excluding bankrupt American) totaled $2.3 billion; bag fees earned $3.4 billion. Do the math: these fees are not going away.

No Service, No Smile

Beyond the panoply of specific hassles, for many the most jarring change in air travel over the last decade or so has been the shift from reliance on humans to reliance on technology, from service to self-service. Start with your airline ticket. In 2000, tickets were almost all paper, sent by snail mail or purchased over the counter, and you handed it to a human check-in agent at the airport. Electronic tickets were introduced by United in 1994, but as recently as 2000, only about half of US airline tickets (a much smaller portion in other parts of the world) were electronic. By mid-2008, paper tickets—which cost about ten times what e-tickets cost to handle—were virtually eliminated. You could still get one if you paid extra—about 1 percent of passengers on staid British Airways did just that—but why bother? With e-tickets, there was no muss, no fuss, no worry about lost tickets, no tedious "re-issuance" of paper. Just book online, download to your smart phone, print your own bag tags, and go right to the gate.

That's fine if you are young and tech savvy (and the Wi-Fi's working). Now ask your 80-year-old aunt to do it. Good luck.

The unceasing drive for cost-lowering efficiency means that air travelers increasingly remain untouched by human hands—not counting those of TSA screeners. Human interaction is becoming a costly anachronism. Combine wages, pension benefits, and taxes, and the average all-in cost of a full-time worker for major US airlines came to a hefty $83,000 in 2011, according to researchers at MIT. Technology makes the self-service journey possible. "Paperless" boarding eliminates the wasted five seconds it takes to hand your pass to the gate agent at the jetway door, for the agent to scan it and say, "Thank you and have a good flight." Why bother when you can have the electronic boarding pass texted to your mobile phone and you just silently flash the bar code at the automatic gate scanner's red eye?

By 2020, the International Air Transport Association (IATA) says the industry group's "Fast Travel" initiative will let passengers handle their own airport check-in, bag-tagging, rebooking, boarding, and even lost-luggage claims. The goal, according to an October 2012 IATA strategy paper: "reducing the number of passenger/agent touches"—in other words, a "seamless curb to airside experience" with the least possible human involvement. It's all liberating, time-saving, efficient, and modern—but it also means one less smile or human glance along the way.

The Margin

Very early every morning, a document stamped FOR OFFICIAL USE ONLY is delivered to the spacious tenth-floor office of the head of the Federal Aviation Administration, which overlooks the National Mall in Washington. Prepared overnight by the FAA's emergency operations staff, the "Administrator's Daily Alert Bulletin" catalogs everything that went wrong in the skies over the United States the previous day: a bomb threat in Boston, a tug hauling a small jet that crossed a taxiway in Raleigh without clearance, an electrical outage at an Indianapolis air traffic control facility, an "operational error" when a pilot or controller mistake brought airplanes a little too close together near Los Angeles. But the top line of the document always reads COMMERCIAL FATAL ACCIDENTS. For years, thankfully, the next line has been the same: NONE REPORTED for US airlines.

Facts aside, an estimated 30 million Americans say they're "anxious" fliers—and those are just the ones who admit it. Look around the cabin next time your plane throttles up and starts its takeoff roll. Fingers grasp armrests, breathing slows, and everything gets very, very quiet. Flying is not something we're designed to do; it's a jarringly unnatural experience. The mind rebels: something as heavy as this airplane shouldn't be able to fly; there's nothing below me for miles; no way to get out of here if I try; if only one thing breaks . . . the atavistic fear of falling, all amplified by the visceral awareness, as the airplane bumps and thunders down the runway, that our survival is now beyond our control.

The fear is natural but not realistic. Flying is safe in any rational sense, maybe safer than ever. More than three *billion* people flew on US airlines from 2007 through 2011—that's 10 times the entire population of the United States—and only 50 died, all in a single regional airline turbo-prop crash. Statistically, the risk is almost inconsequential. How inconsequential? What people really want to know is their risk of dying (by accident) on a random flight. MIT statistician Arnold Barnett calculated that risk in the United States in June 2009 as roughly one in 23 million. You would have to fly every single day for the next 63,000 years before you would be likely to die in a jet airliner crash, Barnett estimates. You're more likely to freeze to death or drown in your own bathtub, about 10 to 40 times more likely to face injury or death in an automobile, by one estimate. Choose any American kid at random; he or she is more likely to be elected president of the United States than to die on any given jet flight, and 10 times more likely to win an Olympic gold medal.

Crashes aren't even as deadly as they used to be. Nobody walks away from a 500-mile-per-hour vertical dive into the ground, but that's only a small portion of even serious accidents. According to an NTSB review of airliner accidents from 1983 to 2000, of "survivable" crashes, 95.7 percent of the occupants survived, thanks to tougher airplanes, better-trained crews, and tighter regulations. US Airways' Chesley Sullenberger's fatality-free, engines-out landing on the Hudson River is only the most famous "miracle" of recent years.

Fatal crashes in the United States are becoming near-random events, years apart—a safety record so reassuring statistically that it poses its own safety problem: complacency. How do you improve on near-zero fatalities? Airlines and regulators talk about "continuous safety improvement," but the real worry is how to stay atop the safety plateau, maintain the margin, find the unknown unknowns.

The low-hanging safety fruit—rickety airplanes, unreliable

instruments, flying blind into weather—was picked years ago. The task now is more subtle—ferreting out incipient dangers and potential weaknesses: finding a weak junction of wire and clamp, forecasting invisible "clear-air turbulence," separating huge hunks of speeding aluminum trying to land on foggy parallel runways at rush hour, keeping alert on a 12-hour journey. In the "new normal" after 9/11, it can also mean detecting a few ounces of plastic explosive hidden in somebody's skivvies.

My former boss, a respected aviator who led the Federal Aviation Administration, had a safety goal he called "nine nines." By this he meant an aviation system where things worked safely 99.9999999 percent of the time, where the odds of a fatal air crash were essentially one in a billion. We're not there yet, but we're not all that tremendously far away, either—maybe now closer to seven nines. Maintaining that margin gets tougher, though, with every new stress on a system already near capacity, where the tolerance for error is shrinking. As remarkable as the safety record is, people in the airline business, and its regulators, don't talk much in public about air safety in a serious way. So passengers tend to get two alternative unrealities: bland, patronizing reassurances that all is well or, left without any reality check, "we're-all-gonna-die" hysteria.

The happy-talk approach fits aviation's ingrained tradition of macho understatement. Commercial pilots learn early in their careers about TMI (too much information) when dealing with passengers. Hair-raising approaches to mountain-ringed airports are merely "challenging." Gut-wrenching turbulence is "a little chop." A "loss of aircraft separation" can mean a fiery midair collision, and smashing into a mountainside is "controlled flight into terrain." Who doesn't snicker a little when the pre-takeoff safety spiel tells us to use seat cushions for flotation "in the event of a water landing"? A water landing? Here's what Worldcue Airline Monitor, which rates airline safety risk for multinational companies, calls some of the world's most god-awful scary air carriers in the far corners of the globe: "non-preferred."

Reassuring happy talk, when it comes to air safety, isn't new. It's been the industry default mode since the early, much riskier, era of commercial flight. (Even as late as 1965, the start of the jet age, the US airline accident rate was more than 10 times the 2011 rate, according to government safety data.) In those days, airlines carefully avoided even mentioning the "S-word." Delta Airlines' predecessor airline famously changed its earliest marketing slogan for the five-hour flight from Dallas, Texas, to Jackson, Mississippi. "Speed, Comfort, and Safety" in 1929 soon became "Speed, Comfort, and Convenience." Touting safety only reminded people that—by logical implication—where there is safety there's also risk.

Some 85 years later, airlines and regulators still squirm when talking about air safety—except for pious bromides like "Safety is our number-one goal" or "a sacred trust," or "the first priority." In polite company, aviation people talk about aircraft "reliability" instead of safety. A plane that plummets to earth in a spectacular fireball after its engines explode is less than "reliable." Airbus even took heat for fearmongering when advertising for its new long-haul A340 jet used a photograph highlighting the plane's four engines flying over stormy seas, with the phrase "4 engines 4 long-haul." The problem was that Boeing's competing long-haul jets have only two.

In truth, airlines and safety regulators haven't really trusted the flying public to handle what shouldn't be a dirty secret: air safety is not absolute. The notion that air travelers need reassurance, not nuance, when it comes to safety is embedded in the aviation mind-set—even when that soothing "all is well" message is questionable, as in the crash of ValuJet Flight 592 in May 1996, discussed in chapter 9. Despite deeply troubling safety questions surrounding the incident, federal safety officials' immediate response was unqualified: "When we say an airline is safe to fly," the head of the FAA told a Senate hearing three days after the ValuJet crash, "it is safe to fly." A month later, after an intensive review, the FAA grounded the airline.

In fairness, that historic, reflexive approach may well be changing, at least if regulators' muscular response to serious safety incidents involving the new Boeing 787 in early 2013 is any indication. First publicly launching a wide-ranging investigation of the newly certified plane, then imposing the ultimate remedy of grounding the entire fleet several days later when a second battery failure triggered cockpit smoke alarms and forced an emergency landing, DOT and FAA weren't exactly in a "rush to reassure." On the other hand, until the second frightening incident forced the emergency landing, the secretary of transportation did seem almost compelled by institutional protocol to issue a ritual full-throated assurance that he'd have "absolutely no reservations" about hopping aboard the plane.

That said, even a more open approach to discussing aviation safety issues—one less patronizing to fliers and less protective of industry public affairs sensitivities—isn't likely to make the very rare aviation disaster a less titillating focus of public interest or seemingly unquenchable media attention. MIT professor Barnett, who studied *New York Times* front-page stories in 1988 and 1989, long before 9/11 heightened the air-travel fear factor, found near-obsessive levels of news focus on air mishaps. In those years, he found, America's "newspaper of record" published 1.7 homicide stories for every thousand murders, 2.3 stories about AIDS for every thousand deaths from the disease, and just .02 cancer stories for every thousand cancer deaths. For every thousand air-crash deaths, though, the *Times* published 138.2 plane-crash stories. Air-crash deaths drew nearly 100 times more ink than even murders.

Confronted with "disasters" and "catastrophes," we exaggerate our sense of personal vulnerability, no matter how truly remote the danger. At Reagan National airport, a thoroughly routine "missed approach"— where the plane on final approach aborts its landing and "goes around" for another landing to avoid some potential hazard—becomes a terrifying scrape with death; for one passenger, her "life flashed before her." Some 59 percent of Americans told a Gallup survey just after 9/11 they were either "very" or "somewhat" worried that they or a family member "will become a victim of terrorism."

The reality is that aviation safety is all about relative risk, and keeping that risk at an acceptably low level. In the commercial airline business, with lots of lives at stake, the tolerance for risk is—and should be—very, very low. But the notion that "one accident is one accident too many" is just an aero-political aspiration. The real-world goal, again, is just to keep the "margin"—an adequacy of extra protection, precaution, and redundancy that keeps risk tolerably low even when somebody makes a mistake or something fails. Getting beyond the dual unrealities of absolute safety and unwarranted fear, air travelers can take a mature look at what's really worth worrying about, and what's not.

Don't Worry

1. THE AIRPLANE'S NOT GOING TO BREAK

The great majority of fatal accidents have nothing to do with an aircraft malfunctioning, and the few that do almost never involve "just one thing." In nearly every disaster, there's a weird confluence of multiple failures, each very unusual, all happening at almost the same wrong time. Modern airliners are among the world's most intricate machines. Each has thousands of components—a Boeing 747 jet engine alone has some 25,000 parts—but surprisingly few are actually critical to the safety of the flight. For each type of aircraft, FAA rules painstakingly list which pieces of equipment are *not* essential to safety. A Boeing 777 can take off with broken cabin passenger address loudspeakers, for example, but not if two *adjacent* speakers are broken. For complicated machines like the Boeing 777, that "master minimum equipment list" runs more than 250 pages.

Nearly all the "safety-critical" systems have backups if they go bad. Even the total failure of an engine almost never causes a crash. The FAA won't certify a plane to fly commercially unless it can take off safely after losing an engine at the worst moment during the takeoff roll, as it's speeding down the runway at the point of no safe return. And once aloft, most jet airliners today can fly more than an hour, often much longer, with an engine completely shut down—an event so rare (about one per million flights worldwide) that most pilots today never experience it, except in flight simulators.

2. TURBULENCE DOESN'T CRASH AIRLINERS

Fear of turbulence is pervasive, if only because every flier encounters it. Pilots can often see and avoid turbulence generated by convective weather patterns—essentially, thunderstorms—whose downdrafts and updrafts can toss planes around as much as hundreds of feet (though rarely as far as it feels). Another kind of turbulence comes from weird air currents that spool off the wingtips of airplanes during takeoff or landing. These eddies and vortices can create powerful, unstable wakes for planes following even miles behind. Known as "wake turbulence," the phenomenon is one reason why FAA rules dictate specific minimum distances between airplanes depending on size and weight. But what most troubles nervous passengers is "clear-air" turbulence—the invisible, sudden, buffeting that typically comes without warning. Often it's the result of passing through or near the edge of jet streams, rivers of fast-moving air where large temperature gradients between nearby air masses can create horizontal and vertical wind shear. Sometimes, clear-air turbulence happens when fast-moving air slams into mountains or other high terrain that generate "mountain waves" of roiled air, as Rocky Mountain fliers can attest.

The FAA categorizes normal levels of turbulence—or "chop" (FAA definition: "somewhat rhythmic bumpiness")—as "light," "moderate," and "severe." Rare severe turbulence, the kind of gut-wrenching roller coaster that comes from wind shear or flying into another jet's wake, can be really scary even for veteran road warriors. (It can also be seriously dangerous for unseated and unbelted cabin occupants, including flight attendants, who suffer nearly a dozen serious injuries a year from turbulence, on average.) Being tossed around by random unseen forces triggers two atavistic fears—loss of control *and* fear of falling. But even mild or modest routine turbulence unnerves inexperienced passengers; watching the massive aluminum wings while they seem to flap up and down makes some people crazy.

The fact is, though, that naturally occurring turbulence almost never brings down modern airliners. Why "almost"? Because the last officially determined turbulence-caused commercial airliner crash occurred three decades ago when an 85-passenger Fokker jet flew into a tornado while at low altitude near Rotterdam, Netherlands. Lesson: don't fly into tornados . . . or mature thunderstorms, either.

And no, turbulence won't pull the wings off. The FAA will not certify a new plane as fit to fly unless it can provably handle nearly impossible stresses. (Consider that modern jetliners absorb direct lightning strikes on average every year, without a fatal US crash in a half century.) A test aircraft must pass a torture test in the design hangar. Cables attached to the ceiling are fitted around the wingtips of the test jet and yanked upward by powerful pulley motors until the entire wing bends upward—about 25 feet in the case of the Boeing 787—without any buckling or structural failure. That's about 150 percent of the most extreme forces the aircraft is ever likely to encounter in the air. Think about that next time your coffee jostles on a bumpy flight.

3. SAFETY'S NOT JUST REACTIVE

Critics worry that the statistically remarkable safety record of major US airlines has made the industry complacent—fat, dumb, and happy. The fear is that a cost-focused industry and its sympathetic regulators wait until something breaks to fix it instead of anticipating or searching for hidden weaknesses—a "tombstone mentality."

It's not a baseless concern. Why should it take an accident, followed by the ritual media hype and congressional excoriation, to accelerate government safety action that could otherwise remain mired in process and red tape for years? The FAA is trying to change the paradigm, emphasizing the identification of safety weaknesses before they become disasters, to prevent accidents before they happen. "Proactive," or precautionary, safety also lets government safety experts focus on established priorities without being whipsawed by the latest mediagenic "outrage"—say, a controller snoozing in an otherwise-manned tower—which may in fact be less urgent.

Still, the tombstone mentality is somewhat a matter of perspective and perception. When something does break, the public expects, first, that somebody (safety regulators and industry) will make sure that this same "something" never breaks again. After a plane crash, media focuses its attention, politicians demand action, a few chosen heads roll, and safety experts at the National Transportation Safety Board (NTSB)—an agency independent of the FAA or DOT—investigate and recommend improvements. At a minimum, pilots and crews are warned what to look out for and how to correct it. Training and flight procedures change.

As time goes on, after millions of flights, dangerous mysteries become fewer and fewer. Invisible wind shear and wake vortices spinning off wingtips and the icing dangers of supercooled freezing rain, even miscommunication between pilots in the cockpit and with controllers, all once befuddled pilots and downed planes. Today they're well understood and far better avoided. In little more than a decade, entire categories of once-commonplace safety threats are nearly extinct. Midair collisions, for instance, were a constant, terrifying prospect—until an improved onboard "collision avoidance" system was widely adopted starting in the 1990s. The gadget, a kind of onboard radar, not only warns pilots that another plane is too close, or soon will be, but it also tells the pilot just how to get out of the way—a mechanical voice loudly demands "CLIMB; CLIMB NOW" or "DESCEND. DESCEND." That safety aid is now considered so accurate and reliable that pilots *must* follow its mechanical "resolution advisory" orders even if human traffic controllers issue the pilot conflicting instructions.

In the same realm lies the once-mysterious phenomenon known as controlled flight into terrain (CFIT)—when a perfectly competent crew flies a perfectly good airplane into the ground or a mountainside or the ocean. Once a cause of crashes nearly twice every year on average in the mid-1970s, CFIT accidents in US airspace virtually evaporated with the advent of improved "ground-proximity" warnings that loudly alert pilots where there's a little too much "proximity" to terra firma. Fly too close to a dark mountainside in a nighttime rainstorm and the system, using a radio altimeter, sternly commands the pilot in no uncertain terms: "TERRAIN: PULL UP!"

4. SAFETY "WATCHDOGS" AREN'T PUPPIES

It's not exactly "No more Mr. Nice Guy," but government safety regulators have, over the last several years, grown tougher about keeping airlines and manufacturers on their toes. Putting aside perennial industry complaints about a "rampage" of safety rule enforcement, there has been a discernible change of tone since 2009. Regulators' slightly cooler, more distanced approach is reflected in a new FAA lexicon. Airlines are no longer the government's "customers" and "partners"; now they're demoted to the more neutral "stakeholders." Today, the "customers" are the flying public—at least rhetorically. The FAA's "vision and values statement" used to read "We are responsive to our customers and are accountable to the taxpayer and the flying public." As of April, 2010, it's "We are accountable to the American public and our stakeholders." Catch the drift?

Until 1996, the FAA's job, by law, was both to "promote" civil aviation and to regulate its safety, a dual mission that was cast in sharp relief after September 11 left the airlines reeling. The notion that the feds were "too cozy" with the industry is perhaps too simplistic; still, the priority was on rescuing the critical, comatose industry, not fining it. The former head of the FAA's thousands of safety inspectors, the chief of its Flight Standards Division, L. Nick Lacey, explained it this way to ABC News in May 2010: "The previous administration, after 9/11, pretty much called the watchdogs off in terms of enforcement actions or things that would cost the industry any money at all. Either said or unsaid, that was the operating tone in the field. Now under this administration, they seem to be more actively looking and willing to bring about civil penalties."

In fact, as the industry stabilized financially and regulators felt more empowered, attitudes and approaches changed. FAA enforcement penalties against airlines almost doubled in the first full fiscal year of the Obama administration—to $14.7 million in 2009 from $7.6 million in 2008, according to the ABC News analysis. Or consider the FAA's summary grounding of the brand new Boeing 787 in January 2013. The first such sweeping regulatory action in three decades, the "emergency airworthiness directive" came as a real shock to many in the industry used to more benign "partnering" with friendly regulators, especially given the thousands of jobs and tens of billions of revenue dollars riding on the success of the new American superplane. The former head of Continental Airlines (also a former Boeing exec) promptly decried the federal safety order as "heavy-handed, draconian," and "the product of a cover-your-ass administration," the *Seattle Times* reported.

Not so cozy anymore.

Practically every major US airline—and lots of smaller ones—has been fined in the last few years for failing to obey FAA safety orders, and the penalties are getting large enough to catch their full attention. They include a $5.4 million fine issued to US Airways in 2009 for not properly inspecting possible cracking of an Airbus A320's landing-gear part and $3.8 million the same day to United for flying a Boeing 737 more than 200 times before workers discovered the cause of low fuel pressure—two *shop towels* stuffed into openings in the engine's oil-sump area instead of the prescribed protective caps. More fines don't mean flying is less safe, though, maybe just the opposite: safety inspectors and regulators are arguably running a tighter ship.

The record fine of $24.2 million went to American Airlines in 2010 for maintenance lapses on its older McDonnell Douglas MD-80 jets. In 2006, the FAA ordered all airlines flying that type of aircraft to inspect electrical wiring bundles deep within the wheel wells, concerned that chafed or frayed wiring could cause a catastrophic fuel-tank explosion. (Technically, the issue was whether clips holding the wiring bundles were spaced too far apart and how the bundles were themselves tied.) Some 18 months later, FAA inspectors visiting American's Tulsa maintenance base and Dallas hub found planes whose wiring was still not properly fixed. When FAA inspectors refused to extend the inspection deadline again, in order to comply with FAA's inspection order American was forced to ground its entire MD-80 fleet of nearly 300 planes. Thousands of flights were cancelled, stranding more than 100,000 passengers over several days. The FAA told American's bankruptcy court in July 2012 that the airline could face even bigger fines for past maintenance violations—potentially as much as $162 million.

Even Southwest Airlines, with its vaunted safety record—no passenger fatalities in its 40 years—has had problems obeying FAA safety orders. In 2008, it was fined $10.2 million (later lowered to $7.5 million) after it flew 46 planes for more than 59,000 flights without conducting FAA-required inspections for fuselage cracks. Four of the planes were found actually to have had inch-long cracks that required repairs. Some of the inspections had been ordered *three years* before they finally were made. Even the $54 billion Boeing Company likely took notice in July 2012 when the FAA proposed a $13.57 million fine for failing to meet a deadline to submit for the FAA's approval certain servicing instructions to enable airlines to reduce the risk of fuel-tank explosions.

Pretty tough, but the FAA has the legal authority to get tougher still—fining airlines up to $27,500 for each safety "violation." Theoretically, that could mean $27,500 for *each* flight of *each* plane that doesn't comply with an FAA safety rule, known as an "airworthiness directive." So if an airline misses an FAA deadline to perform an ordered safety inspection on just one small part on only a handful of airplanes with busy flight schedules, the fine can still run to millions of dollars.

The FAA has other tools of persuasion too, maybe more effective than fines. With a few keystrokes, the agency's media office can e-mail virtually every aviation reporter and editor and news producer in the country (and others around the world) an official news release about an airline safety penalty. That kind of publicity is an airline public relations staff's worst nightmare. And don't try to negotiate to soften the language. "The FAA does not negotiate the contents of a news release or whether it will issue one," agency policy states. At the extreme, the FAA can yank a bad actor's "certificate" to fly, the airline's very right to operate.

As the industry focuses ever more sharply on the bottom line, regulators seem to be sending a warning against cutting corners: even small lapses can mean sizeable fines. American Eagle was fined $330,000 in 2010 for flying a regional jet a dozen times with passenger seats that wouldn't raise to their "full upright and locked position" for takeoff and landing. Frontier was fined $380,000 the same year for failing to replace outdated seatback safety placards that illustrated a prior cabin-seating configuration. Are the watchdogs stirring?

OK, Worry

So what *is* worth worrying about? As the system gets more crowded and less error-tolerant, and the drive for efficiency and sustained profitability commands center stage, there are still weak links that need attention before somebody gets killed.

1. NAPTIME IN THE COCKPIT . . . AND THE TOWER

Human error causes most fatal airline accidents. When it comes to safety, you don't want the human sitting on the left side of the cockpit to be fatigued. Up to a point, planes *can* fly themselves—flight management computers do a great job flying jets when cruising at altitude. Beyond that point, those moments when a pilot's split-second response is critical, fatigue can mean the difference between a bumpy ride and a catastrophe.

Speeding down the runway for takeoff, pilots can have only one, maybe two, seconds to react to a key warning light or alarm and make the decision whether it is safer to raise the nose and lift off or to hit the brakes and abort. React too slowly and there's no option. The plane *has to* fly or you run out of runway if you try to stop. It's similar landing in heavy crosswinds on an icy runway, or making the right call about when to pull back or push down the yoke (the control column that orders the plane's altitude and direction) in a sudden blast of wind shear six miles above the remotest regions of the South Atlantic when the autopilot shuts down. These are what some pilots call the "full alert" moments— times that call for skilled, trained, split-second decisions not slowed or dulled by exhaustion.

By their own admission, though, pilots *do* fly fatigued. A National Sleep Foundation poll of commercial pilots in March 2012 (more than two-thirds flying for airlines) found that one-fifth of the 202 pilot respondents admitted to having made a serious safety error due to sleepiness. The same year, a British pilots' union survey of 500 members found 43 percent admitted falling asleep at the controls at some time in their careers. In 2011, half of Norway's airline pilots told a public-broadcasting survey that they dozed off behind the yoke at one time or another; 2 percent admitted doing so "often," sometimes without alerting their copilot. In a 1999 NASA survey of more than 1,400 pilots at 26 regional airlines, 80 percent admitted to "nodding off" in the cockpit at some time in their careers. Body-clock confusion isn't limited to international long-haul pilots crossing a dozen time zones in a day; domestic pilots can face even more frequent circadian rhythm disruptions and heavier daily workloads. So if you're wondering, the FAA allows pilots to take the popular sedative Ambien (generic name Zolpidem)—as long as it's more than 24 hours before flying and no more often than twice a week.

Asking airline pilots if they're overworked may be a less-than-scientific way to assess the true extent of cockpit sleeping, but pilot fatigue has been, for more than two decades, high on the list of "most wanted" air-safety improvements published by the independent safety experts at the NTSB. Still, it's not a *sexy* safety issue. There's no new gadget that will correct the problem, and everyone knows that an effective solution—such as hiring more pilots—would cost airlines big money, maybe trigger new labor-relations issues with the pilots' unions, and encounter fierce resistance from cost-focused managers. The gridlock means that, despite tinkering over the years, rules about how long pilots can fly, and how often and long they must rest, haven't changed much since Ronald Reagan was leaving the White House. Until 2010, the last time the FAA even tried to update the rules comprehensively was in 1995; airlines and their supporters clogged the FAA mailroom with more than 2,000 written "comments" mostly opposing the changes.

Regulators turned to another approach that might avoid industry blowback, a cost-free way to fight cockpit fatigue: simply let pilots take naps in the cockpit on long flights. Sleep scientists at NASA were for it, and so were pilots. Experts largely agreed it would be better for pilots to nap in a controlled way on long flights than risk dozing at a critical moment or when the second pilot is out of the cockpit. But the FAA ultimately balked at changing its longstanding prohibition on cockpit sleeping.

There were real concerns that the remaining "awake pilot" could become sleepy or incapacitated, or that a groggy "resting" pilot wouldn't function effectively in an emergency immediately on being awakened. But among the political folks in the regulatory agencies, there was also a less scientific worry—they call it "optics" in Washington-speak—about "controlled rest in the cockpit." No matter what you called it, sleeping up front violated the *Tonight Show* Rule: if it's grist for late-night comedians, it doesn't happen. And sleeping pilots would make passengers nervous—almost as much as they would delight those comics and editorial cartoonists. Little has changed when it comes to the sensitive politics of the issue. When safety experts at the NTSB proposed in 2011 to let air traffic controllers nap briefly during late-night shifts when other controllers were present, the secretary of transportation was adamant: "We're not going to pay controllers to nap."

Pilot fatigue remained a nagging back-burner issue until a wintry February night in 2009 when Capt. Marvin Renslow, according to NTSB investigators, made a series of faulty piloting decisions that doomed his Colgan Air commuter flight and its 49 passengers in an ice storm near Buffalo, New York. Crash investigators cited fatigue as a factor; Renslow's relatively inexperienced copilot, 24-year-old Rebecca Shaw, was hardly well rested. To get to her Newark, New Jersey, flight in time, she had hitchhiked by air all night cross-country from her Seattle home before sacking out on a couch in an airport crew lounge. Her long-haul commute to her $16,254 job wasn't that unusual. A July 2011 National Research Council report found that more than 20 percent of pilots live more than 750 miles from their jobs. Of 137 Newark-based Colgan pilots, 93 commuted to work by air, sometimes for hours.

The gory details of the Colgan crash—fatigue, pilot error, hiring and training issues—reignited the battle over pilot rest rules, and the FAA in late 2010 came up with what it hoped was a modest proposal—albeit complex at 145 pages—that airlines would accept. As finalized, it would mean that pilots would get ten hours of rest instead of eight hours between flying shifts, with an opportunity for eight hours of uninterrupted sleep, and they could be scheduled to be at the controls no more than eight or nine hours a day, depending on when they started work. Their total workday, including time on the ground and commuting by air to their job, could last no more than nine to 14 hours a day, down from the grueling 16-hour workdays that the previous rules could allow.

The industry went through the roof. Some 8,000 public comments poured into DOT; most opposed the proposed new rule. American, for example, claimed the rule would require it to hire 2,325 more pilots and spend a half billion dollars more every year. The airlines' trade association estimated that an initial draft rule proposal issued in late 2010 would cost carriers $19.6 *billion* over 10 years to comply—15 times more than what the FAA projected. Weathering the withering criticism, though, regulators issued a revised final rule—the first significant change in flight and duty time in almost 30 years—a few days before Christmas in 2011. Still, it won't take effect until 2014, and aspects of the rule could be tied up in court for years.

Air traffic controllers nod off too, especially during overnight "mid-shifts" when flights are sparse and they're alone in the tower, surrounded only by softly glowing instruments and quietly buzzing fans. (The controllers' union, the National Air Traffic Controllers Association, or NATCA, prefers the term "restorative break" to "nod off.") Major hubs like O'Hare, Dulles, Boston, and the New York airports have at least two controllers on duty all night, but dozens of other busy airports with few overnight flights may have just one controller. One of them used to be Washington's Reagan National Airport, just three miles and less than a minute's flight time from the White House. That changed on March 23, 2011, when the sole controller, pulling his fourth consecutive graveyard shift, took a half hour's nap while on duty. Two inbound flights heard only silence when they tried to radio the tower. Both landed safely on their own while in contact with regional traffic controllers, a common procedure at smaller, "uncontrolled" airports, but the "nobody home at Reagan" scenario caused a media firestorm.

It wasn't the first time. In 2006, a Comair commuter jet had crashed while trying to take off from the wrong runway in Lexington, Kentucky, while the lone tower controller—working on two hours of sleep—was distracted. So when the National Airport incident hit the *Washington Post* front page the next morning ("Tower at Reagan National Goes Silent as Planes Attempt to Land"), all hell broke loose. By day's end, congressional inquiries were brewing, the secretary of transportation— the executive department that includes the FAA—had launched an investigation and ordered a second controller to man the tower, and the head of the FAA had suspended the hapless napper. By late afternoon, a "nationwide review" of the air traffic control system was under way, and an "interim plan" was in the works. New reports of napping controllers slowed only after the FAA announced a plan that still barred sleeping but let late-night controllers take a "break" as long as they "conduct[ed] themselves professionally" and were "available for recall." And used an alarm clock?

2. COMMUTER AIRLINE SAFETY—A DIFFERENT LEVEL?

It may be extreme, but some serious people with serious safety concerns —including one former DOT Inspector General—have gone out of their way to avoid commuter airlines. I don't and, since these airlines account for more than half of all commercial flights in the United States every day, I probably couldn't. The fact remains, though, that, all told, com- muter carriers just don't have the same safety record as the major air- lines that typically contract with them to fly their passengers.

"Regional airlines," a term often used interchangeably with "com- muter airlines," such as Delta Connection or US Airways Express or United Express look like the major airlines they serve, but most are really subcontractors, completely separate businesses flying under the big airline brands. Forget the names and logos painted on their planes; these carriers—including SkyWest, Mesa, Colgan, ExpressJet, Republic, and Pinnacle—are on their own, with their own pilots and training and maintenance. The big airlines call them "partners," but that's just marketing lingo. Most (though not all) sell seats on their commuter-sized planes (generally under 100 seats) to the major airlines for a negotiated per-flight fee.

Over the last decade, nearly all of the US commercial airline fatalities involved regional airline crashes, and, as the *Wall Street Journal* reported in 2009, commuter airlines from 2003 until then had ten times the serious accident rate per flight than the major airlines. The real risk to any individual flier is still tiny, but it is higher. This isn't news to regulators. After a series of commuter-airline crashes in the mid-1990s, the FAA announced grand plans for "one level of safety"—translation: trying to make commuter flying as safe as the major airlines. "Safety summits" were held and speeches given, but some concrete proposals met powerful resistance, including from flight schools and aviation colleges that turn out new pilots as quickly as possible for entry-level industry jobs.

Nearly 20 years later, "one level of safety" for all airlines, big and small, remains largely an aspiration. Commuter captains still must meet the same minimum FAA experience standards as their large-airline brethren to earn an air transport license, but those are minimums. In the real world, there can be a chasm in training and experience. A full-fledged "air transport pilot" needs a minimum 1,500 hours of flying time—equivalent to flying five to six hours every workday for an entire year—but virtually every captain at the big airlines has thousands more hours of actual flying experience than the minimum required.

The gulf has been even wider when it comes to regional airline first officers. Until new Congressionally mandated FAA pilot training rules required all airline pilots and copilots to earn full "air transport" ratings, copilots needed only a "commercial" license, the same as crop-dusters and beach ad banner-towers. For that you must be 18 years old, have a private pilot's license, and have flown for 250 hours (essentially several months). Though regional airlines typically insist on more experience

than that, some are scrambling for pilots to meet the tougher requirements expected to take effect in 2013.

3. FLYING IN THE DEVELOPING WORLD IS NOT THE SAME

One of my college professors in the 1970s, an eminent and ancient his-
torian, lived by the rule that he would only travel to places where he
could get the *New York Times* (he meant in hard copy) no more than one
day late. Some might say the same about commercial aviation. Safety
records where you can get the printed *Times* are, by and large, far better
than in places you can't—that is, mainly, in the developing world.

Exact statistics change from year to year, but generally speaking the
risk that you will die on any randomly chosen scheduled flight in North
America, Western Europe, and the most developed Asian countries is
considerably less than one in *ten million*. Worldwide, the average risk is
around one in *two* million, and roughly the same for recently industri-
alized nations such as South Korea, Mexico, and Brazil. In the world's
least-developed regions, though, the risk of dying on a scheduled flight is
only about one in 800,000, as MIT's Arnold Barnett calculated in a 2010
article. For the whole decade 2002–2011, the fatal accident rate per ten
million flights (passenger and cargo) was 27 times worse in Africa (43.9)
than in North America (1.6), according to the European Aviation Safety
Agency. Africa's accident rate improved in 2011, says IATA—to 9 times
worse than the global average.

Why the big safety gap? A major reason is lax, sometimes even nonexistent, air traffic control. Crossing thousands of air miles from the
Sahara to southern Africa, planes fly across vast swaths of what's known
politely as "uncontrolled airspace." Even surrounded by treacherous,
mountainous terrain, some sizeable Latin American airports lack precision navigation and landing systems to guide planes landing at night or
in low visibility. As recently as 2008, Russia had the world's worst rate of
"hull loss" accidents (in which the airplane is destroyed), due partly to

aging and unreliable Soviet-built airplanes, a proliferation of hundreds of newly privatized start-up airlines, and spotty airline maintenance. In some countries, there's no government aviation safety regulatory authority at all; instead, the national airline essentially regulates itself.

That doesn't mean you can't fly outside the United States without Valium. There are decent airlines in every region; often they include carriers aligned with the global airline "alliances"—like Star, oneworld, and SkyTeam—which have a strong economic incentive to guard the safety reputation of the members of their commercial groupings. Size counts too. Over the last decade, the world's 25 largest airlines carried half the world's 11.5 billion air travelers and had only six fatal accidents, resulting in 873 deaths. The remaining thousand commercial airlines accounted for all the other fatalities—87 percent of the total of 6,566 deaths worldwide, according to a *Financial Times* analysis of data compiled by the Ascend consultancy in 2011.

Still, knowing which foreign airlines to avoid isn't always easy. For years, US safety officials didn't really know and certainly didn't want to say. It was a delicate diplomatic question, after all. Most foreign airlines are "flag carriers" (their nation's flag is painted on the plane's tail) and icons of national pride, however sketchy their safety records. The issue came to a head, though, after the sadly unnecessary 1990 crash of Avianca Flight 52 from Bogotá, Colombia, when the Boeing 707 simply ran out of fuel over Long Island while circling to land at JFK in bad weather. The Spanish-speaking crew didn't get across to English-speaking air traffic controllers just how desperately low on fuel the jet really was; it requested "priority" to land but failed to explicitly declare a "fuel emergency."

In the wake of the crash, the FAA quietly began checking how other countries were regulating their airlines that flew to the United States. The results, initially kept confidential, were not exactly reassuring. Particularly sensitive were problems with Russia's CIS and former Soviet states whose civil aviation systems were then caught in the midst of political upheaval. But when it emerged that the US embassy in Moscow had barred its own US diplomats from flying within Russia (sometimes requiring them to resort to train travel), aviation regulators in Washington had little choice but to see that all US travelers had the same cautionary information.

Beginning in September 1994, they did. Rather than blacklist specific foreign flag airlines, though, the FAA checked on whether their home countries were properly regulating them. This avoided directly slamming particular carriers (after all, their countries could reciprocate). It did, though, catch a few airlines—such as Israel's El Al until late 2012—with estimable international safety records but whose nation's regulatory oversight was deemed insufficient (for example, because of a lack of written regulations or laws or numbers of inspectors or air traffic routings). Airlines from those countries could continue existing flights but could not expand their US air service or start flying to the United States if they weren't already doing so. The FAA list changes periodically but typically includes about two dozen countries—mostly in Africa, Central America, and Central Europe—that don't cut it.

The European Union's approach seems more direct. Brussels simply blacklists "unsafe airlines" from flying to the EU. But the EU's list of nearly 300 banned airlines is populated largely by small local or regional carriers from countries like Afghanistan, Angola, Benin, Congo, Equatorial Guinea, Gabon, Kazakhstan, the Kyrgyz Republic, Mozambique, Sierra Leone, Sudan, Swaziland, and Zambia—airlines that have little or no intention of flying to European capitals anyway. In 1999, the UN's ICAO agency established a "universal" program to internationalize aviation safety auditing of the world's airlines, wherever they flew.

4. WHEN AIRLINES DON'T OBEY

When a yard-long tear in the top of the fuselage of a Southwest 737-300 flying over Yuma, Arizona, in 2011 forced an emergency landing, the FAA quickly ordered every airline flying that "classic" version of the venerable 737—dozens in US fleets—to complete detailed metallurgical inspection of the heavily flown planes within five days—too bad about the havoc played on schedules and stranded passengers. The FAA order was broader and more urgent than most, but hardly unique. Almost every weekday, on average, regulators issue airworthiness directives (ADs) telling US airlines to check for or correct unsafe conditions. Often the fix is relatively simple—for instance, replacing a $240 metal pin on a landing-gear assembly for one type of 777. In rare cases, though, an AD can ground scores of planes for urgent and costly inspections that must occur before their next flight.

The FAA's air safety directives—about 250 are issued every year—are not optional. They have the force of law. They indicate that there is a known safety problem that must be corrected or checked within a specified time in order to make or keep a plane safe to fly. That doesn't mean, though, that airlines always do precisely what they're told to do when they're supposed to do it. Often the failure is inadvertent—a sloppy repair that doesn't completely comply or genuine confusion about exactly what the FAA wants (certain complex technical directives can run hundreds of pages long). Sometimes, it's a failure of record keeping—the check or repair is made but not properly documented. But in the real world, there's also pressure to keep planes moving on time and to keep costs down. What if postponing the FAA-required inspection for a few days would avoid the cost and schedule grief of yanking a large jet out of the flight rotation just before it's due to be down for its next four-to-six-month regular maintenance anyway?

How serious is the risk that airlines won't do what safety inspectors and regulators tell them to? The FAA inspectors may be "tough as nails," as a former agency head told a 2008 annual "forecast conference," but in reality, much, if not most, safety regulation is based on trust. It practically has to be. Even with some 4,500 FAA safety inspectors and technical specialists combined, the government can't closely oversee everything that happens daily in an aviation system as vast as America's.

We're talking about well over 25,000 airline flights every single day, plus 5,000 aircraft repair stations and 600,000 US pilots. "FAA is unlikely to ever have enough safety inspectors to oversee every aspect of aviation," DOT's Inspector General acknowledged in 2012. Fortunately, US airlines normally comply with safety edicts, and so earn that trust. A large-scale FAA audit in 2008 of 5,600 government safety directives found 98 percent compliance by airlines. In most industries, that's a great result. In aviation, though, anything short of 100 percent isn't.

5. JET GERIATRICS

Older aircraft are a bit like older people—they keep going, but it takes more and more to keep them healthy. And by the end of the difficult decade after 9/11, US airlines were flying some of the oldest jets in the developed world. According to websites that track aircraft fleet ages, like Airsafe.com and Airfleets.net, some MD-80 and -90 jets flown by American and Delta averaged 20 years old; so did a third of Southwest's fleet of Boeing 737s. US Airways' Boeing 767s averaged 22 years old. While big US airline fleets today overall average some 12 to 16 years old (several low-cost carrier fleets are half that age), as of 2008, *half* of the world's 4,400 aging aircraft (those at least 21 years old) were flying in the United States, according to an analysis reported by ABC News that year.

Buying pricey new airplanes was simply not a priority during the difficult years soon after September 11. Those shiny new wide-bodies taking off from Seattle's Boeing Field were headed for Dubai and Beijing, not Dallas or Chicago. For years, the official line was that new planes were better for fuel efficiency, but that no plane, properly maintained, is too old to fly safely. In one sense that may be true. Chronological age matters less when it comes to an aging airframe than the number of flights the airplane has made, specifically how many "cycles" of pressurization and depressurization stress it has undergone. Every time a plane is pressurized, forced air pushes on the airtight fuselage from inside out. (Think of blowing up the same balloon repeatedly.) A 14-hour New York–Tokyo flight pressurizes the aircraft only once—much less than the stress on the structure of a short-haul narrow-body jet that flies that same day to four or five cities. The long-range jumbo jet may be fine for two or three decades, but even a much newer 737 on a workhorse schedule can have problems in half the time. The Southwest 737 that ripped open in Yuma was a middle-aged 15 years old.

Even if industry lore holds that planes need never get "too old," there's still a caveat: They need ever-more-careful inspection and TLC the older they do get. After thousands of takeoffs and landings, tiny fatigue cracks in the metal can develop and spread, then link with other tiny cracks to undermine the aircraft structure—especially around fastener holes where rivets hold together the overlapping aluminum plates of the fuselage. This type of metal fatigue was blamed when an 18-foot slab of fuselage ripped off a 19-year-old Aloha Airlines 737 "island-hopper" at 24,000 feet between Hilo and Honolulu in 1988, blowing a flight attendant out of the aircraft after explosive decompression. The plane had recorded nearly 90,000 pressurization cycles—more than a dozen flights every day for its not-so-long lifetime.

The concern is as old as pressurized flight—likely behind the rash of fatal crashes that doomed the very first commercial jet, the De Havilland Comet, in the 1950s. (That aircraft was designed with rectangular windows subject to particularly high pressurization stress at their corners.) It wasn't until November 2010, though, that safety regulators finally offered a "comprehensive solution" to metal fatigue for older planes—special structural inspections, including ultrasonic testing for flaws hiding deep within the metal—though it won't take full effect for some airplane models until 2016.

Meanwhile, who's making sure the cabin roof won't shear off our 30-year-old DC-9? Until 2000, major US airlines maintained and repaired their own planes—at massive maintenance bases staffed with thousands of American workers licensed by the FAA—and maintenance

isn't cheap, accounting for at least 10 percent of the cost of running a
major airline. Today, at least two-thirds of the "heaviest" aircraft maintenance is contracted out to about 4,800 independent, FAA-licensed
"repair stations," including about 700 located abroad. It's far cheaper
than doing it in-house, where heavy aircraft maintenance by union
mechanics reportedly costs about $100 an hour, including overhead
and other expenses. According to an October 2009 NPR report quot-
ing industry analysts, that's twice as much as at independent nonunion
shops in the United States, and about three times more than in some
foreign repair locations.

There's plenty of debate about the quality of this outsourced airplane maintenance and also about how well the FAA monitors it—an
issue that grows in safety importance as planes age. As aircraft technology gets ever more sophisticated, so does the task of maintaining
it. A typical passenger jet today has more than four million parts,
Boeing estimates, and the newest A380 jumbo jet contains more than
300 *miles* of wiring alone. Traditional maintenance work—fixing loose
airframe rivets, tightening fasteners, and checking hydraulic lines—is
just the start. Every five years or so, each airliner is virtually disas-
sembled, then checked inch by inch—a month-long maintenance visit
known as a "D check." Walls, floors, ceiling panels, lavatories, and galleys are removed to look for cracks and corrosion. Landing gears and
hydraulics are largely replaced. Engines are separately inspected and
tested. Fluids are sent for laboratory analysis. Even fuel-tank interiors
are checked.

Only 100 or so of the FAA's several thousand safety inspectors are
assigned to oversee the 700 foreign repair stations that perform this
work, and industry critics worry that outsourcing today's complex
maintenance is exceeding the FAA's limited ability to oversee it, at home
and abroad. The DOT's Inspector General, for instance, found it "imperative" in 2012 that the FAA "provide more vigorous oversight of this
[repair] industry," both foreign and domestic, and the FAA has assured

concerned members of Congress that it will tighten up monitoring. Still, with thousands of aircraft-maintenance jobs in the United States on the line, you've got to wonder if some of the brouhaha isn't really as much about economics as safety. The president of the Teamsters, which represents about 20,000 airline mechanics, says outsourcing maintenance abroad is "a betrayal of passengers' trust." On the other hand, the pilots who fly the planes haven't made it a priority issue. Meanwhile, apparently the only maintenance-related US commercial airline crash in the last decade involved an Air Midwest turboprop flight from Charlotte, North Carolina, in 2003 that lost control on takeoff. NTSB investigators faulted in part lousy maintenance work—performed in Huntington, West Virginia.

6. SOMETHING'S GOTTA GIVE

Nobody dresses up to fly anymore; air travel has become routine, commonplace, accessible—so much that it's stressing the system. We're cramming more planes into more congested airspace, flying them longer and farther, turning them faster, and overtaxing busy runways and airports and air traffic control systems that have expanded little in the last 20 years at least. The last new big US airport opened in Denver almost two decades ago, planes still navigate with World War II–era radar-based technology, and the pressure on controllers to move the airborne aluminum only accelerates. The gnawing worry is just that something's gonna give. What keeps aviation-safety folks up at night?

Separation Anxiety

More flying means more workload for air traffic controllers—and a greater chance of error. In the year between October 2009 and October 2010, FAA "operational errors" jumped more than 50 percent. The most serious type of errors—the kind that really *could* end in midair disasters—climbed nearly 50 percent in just two years. The error frequency has since leveled off but remains almost double the error level of 2007. While there's debate about whether the jump was due at least partly to more accurate *reporting* of errors, the disquieting bottom line is that planes are coming closer together than they're supposed to nearly a half dozen times every day, on average.

Most often, that doesn't mean really dangerously close. Even nearly five miles apart can constitute what the FAA calls a "proximity event" that transgresses the agency's complex and conservative separation standards when a small plane is landing behind a much larger jet. Even 50 nautical miles' separation can be the bare minimum between jets cruising over the ocean beyond radar range. But the most serious mistakes are growing too. The most "severe" or "category A" incidents— those that pose an imminent threat of collision and require evasive action—more than doubled from mid-2008 to mid-2011 and now occur almost weekly on average.

These errors, too, have leveled off, but there's another lurking issue behind the numbers: Lots of today's air traffic controllers are relatively green, hired in the last few years to fill the spots of experienced controllers who, as twentysomethings, were recruited en masse to replace the nearly 13,000 PATCO air traffic controllers fired by President Reagan for staging a walkout in 1981. In recent years, those 1980s new hires have been hitting the mandatory retirement age of 56 (it's a tough job) in droves. That means "trainees" (and what the FAA calls "developmentals") manned about 26 percent of the radar scopes nationwide in 2010, albeit under experienced supervision. The number rises to near 40 percent of the controller workforce at some of the busiest facilities, such as Denver and the Southern California terminal radar control area, or even the tower at ultrabusy LaGuardia.

Runway Screwups

Forget about midair disasters. The deadliest aviation accident in history occurred on the tarmac—in the Canary Islands in March 1977— when two fully loaded jumbo jets collided almost head-on approaching takeoff speed on a foggy runway, killing 583 people. That was a quarter century ago, but at busy, crowded airports with multiple taxiways, high-speed turnoffs, and low visibility, pilots still get confused, tower radio communications still get garbled, and planes still make dangerous wrong turns at night. Busy controllers hustling to get planes in the air can have little time to play tarmac traffic cops.

New airport guidance technology and sustained FAA focus seem to have kept the worst problems (the "bare-miss" category especially) in check when it comes to commercial airliners. The most dangerous kinds of incursions dropped from 53 in 2001 to only 7 in 2011, even though total runway incursions held constant at around 1,000 every year. Together with runway *excursions*—where the plane undershoots or overruns the tarmac—runway screwups still make NTSB's "most wanted" list of safety improvements. And they have since the list's inception in 1990.

Horizontal Man-Made Mini-Tornadoes

The airspace around airports can hold only so many planes safely at any one time. Congestion ups the risk they could smack together, but it also amplifies another serious, if less obvious, risk to safe flight: "wake vortex." Jet aircraft trail behind them potentially deadly wakes of air turbulence that swirl off their wingtips. In some atmospheric conditions, you can even see these whorls coming off landing jets in super-humid air or low clouds near airports. As airline pilot and writer Patrick Smith vividly recounted in his *Salon* "Ask the Pilot" column, these normally invisible horizontal mini-tornadoes can drive to the ground a plane that's following behind the wake of another. It's especially dangerous when the following plane is flying near stall speed at low altitude, on takeoff or near landing. Pilots say the effect of flying into a vortex can be like "hitting a wall." Just two months after the 9/11 attacks, 260 passengers and five on the ground died when American Flight 587 leaving JFK apparently hit the powerful wake of a loaded Japan Airlines 747 taking off moments before; the pilot overcorrected and the rudder failed as the plane's tail (vertical stabilizer) tore off.

Tower controllers take care to warn pilots cleared to land behind a larger jet: "Caution, wake turbulence." But how far planes need to stay separated to avoid wake turbulence depends on the type and size of the aircraft involved, and their speed. Large, heavy wide-body jets generate more turbulence, so most single-aisle jets must stay four to six nautical miles behind them on landing, for example. The superjumbo A380 creates such a wake that small jets were originally required to stay back 10 nautical miles, though that distance has since been reduced to eight nautical miles. All of the required extra spacing between jets at busy hubs in order to avoid wake turbulence further clogs the system. As aircraft grow larger, it takes more time to safely "fit" them on the same flight paths in the same airspace.

Superplanes

Over the last decade, the size and complexity of jet airliners has grown swiftly. Driven by the economic imperatives of efficiency and the need to make the most of limited access to congested airports, planes like the A380 are meant to carry up to 850 passengers. Boeing's 747-800, the latest version of its venerable jumbo jet and the world's longest commercial jet at 250 feet, holds about 500 passengers. There's even talk of an expanded A380-1000 that would carry a *thousand* travelers. For efficiency, it's got to be a lot cheaper to fly one A380 than two Boeing 777 flights: one fuel-guzzling takeoff and one landing, one cockpit crew; one boarding gate, one takeoff and one landing "slot" at congested airports.

But for all their remarkable capabilities, indeed because of them, the new generation of superplanes amplifies the challenge of maintaining the safety margin. Look no further, again, than the Dreamliner. The new jet is so chock-full of innovative, complex technologies that it not only promises greater passenger comfort, 20 percent more fuel efficiency, and economic access to new long-haul markets, but it also challenges the capability of government safety officials to stay on top of its design and development (much of it outsourced abroad) in certifying the plane's "airworthiness." In the long and involved certification process required

of all new aircraft, manufacturers must show that their new designs comply with hundreds of detailed regulations—except when those design
features are so "novel or unusual" (as in the case of much of the 787) that
there *are* no existing safety standards. That's when the FAA essentially
has to make up new rules—commonly known as "special conditions"—
for specific new planes, as it did in approving the 787's novel method of
using lithium-ion batteries in 2007. When problems arise with "novel
and unusual" aircraft technology, even if it's been tested in flight for hundreds of thousands of hours and more than a year in commercial service
carrying over a million passengers, regulators not surprisingly want to
be "1,000 percent sure."

Far less esoteric are the safety challenges posed by the mere size of
some new aircraft, like the Airbus 380 and the new, extended-length
Boeing 747-8. Merely moving these monsters safely on standard airport
taxiways demands lots of attention from the control tower. The wingspan
of the A380 is just 12 yards shy of the length of an entire football field, its
tail rises eight stories, and its maximum takeoff weight exceeds one million pounds. When the wing of one operated by Air France clipped the
tail of a Delta commuter jet at JFK in 2011, the A380's occupants barely
noticed; meanwhile, the Delta plane spun around more than 90 degrees.
Takeoffs and landings become more complex events too—because of the
huge wakes and blasts of jet-wash these planes generate. An airport's
entire landing sequence may have to shift to put safe distance between
the new airborne behemoths and traditional jets.

Their sheer size also raises some old-fashioned, low-tech safety
questions. Such as how passengers are supposed to escape from one
that's burning after skidding off an icy runway, or ditching into the
Hudson River. Fear not, the FAA has a rule. Before the agency approves
a new large aircraft to fly in the United States, the manufacturer has to
prove by "real-life" tests that the plane, fully loaded, can be evacuated
in 90 seconds—with half the available exits blocked, in complete dark-
ness. No simulations allowed. Inspectors are watching. Airbus actually

managed to get all 853 mock passengers and 20 crew off a test version of its A380 cabin in just 78 seconds. Like all such simulations, though, it was a far cry from a "real" evacuation—no wind, no blood, no freezing rain or ice, no smoke, no infants, no panic, and only one broken leg resulted.

Aside from their massive girth, today's superplanes can fly nonstop almost halfway around the globe—crossing oceans or polar wastes or empty deserts or unpopulated rain forests three, four, or even five hours from a safe place to land if something really bad happens. Aircraft that can fly 9,000 statute miles (think nonstop back and forth *twice* across the United States)—including the Boeing 787, the Boeing 777-200LR, the Boeing 747-8 and the Airbus A340, A350, and A380—are expressions of their underlying economics. Ultralong nonstop flights—including with two-engine aircraft—are cheaper to operate, pose less stress on pressurized aircraft, and are more convenient for passengers than multiple separate connecting flights.

FAA rules used to prohibit long-haul flights on two-engine jets for safety reasons—in case one engine failed. Until the mid-1980s, planes had to stay within an hour of a landing spot, precluding twin-engine nonstop crossings of even the relatively puny Atlantic Ocean. A quarter century later, 12-hour flights have become commonplace. More than 5,000 flights traverse the North Pole every year, and daily 19-hour journeys from New York to Singapore merit not the slightest fanfare. What changed? Safety regulators grew comfortable with the ultrareliability of jet turbine engines—confident enough to let the "diversion time" (the time needed for the plane to get to a safe landing strip if an engine fails) grow. The first cautious step was to let planes fly up to 90 minutes, instead of 60 minutes, away from a suitable airport (this allowed TWA to fly a two-engine Boeing 767 from St. Louis to Frankfurt in 1985), then up to three hours in 1988—enough to make most of the globe accessible to two-engine jets.

Today, FAA-approved twin-engine jets like the 777 can fly nonstop virtually anywhere in the world except the South Pole (on most routings), a small piece of the South Pacific, and the North Pole in winter weather—as long as they're specially maintained and inspected. Regulations for these "extended range twin engine operations" (ETOPS) flights stipulate, for example, that the same maintenance technician may not perform the same tasks on both left and right engines, to avoid the chance of someone making the same error on both. And even today's minimal range restrictions are disappearing. At the end of 2011, the FAA allowed certain Boeing 777 models to fly as far as five and a half hours distant from a suitable landing spot—even if it's a remote landing strip on a mid-Pacific coral atoll like Wake Island, Midway, or Kwajalein, or, at the far, far end of Alaska, tiny Shemya Island. Air New Zealand expects the more direct routings to save 100 minutes of flying time from Auckland to New York across the vast reaches of the South Pacific.

Safe ultra-long-haul flying requires an incredible level of engine reliability and so far it's worked. In March 2003, a United 777 with 255 passengers had to shut down an engine with low oil pressure en route from Auckland to Los Angeles, about as far from anywhere as geographically possible. As designed, the plane flew on for 192 minutes against strong headwinds to land perfectly in Kona, Hawaii, on the one remaining engine. Comforting, but some pilots still refer to the ETOPS program as "Engines Turn or Passengers Swim."

7. THE BIRDS

Something more prosaic to worry about: birds. The first recorded bird strike on an aircraft was in September 1905 when Orville Wright's early biplane hit what was thought to be a red-winged blackbird; the first fatal strike occurred in 1912 when a gull jammed control cables on a pioneering flight in the ocean off Long Beach, California. Birds have been a serious safety issue ever since—most famously when birds sucked into jet engines triggered the 2009 Miracle on the Hudson when US Airways Flight 1549 glided down to a safe "water landing" on the Hudson River off the Upper West Side of Manhattan.

What happens when a bird flies into a jet aircraft engine isn't pretty, but it is quick. The animal hits the blades hard—on the order of 200 miles per hour (plus the speed of the jet engine fan blades turning) if the plane is landing or climbing. A small bird hitting even a relatively slow-moving jet creates an impact not unlike dropping a bowling ball onto a fan blade from 10 feet in the air, according to a Pratt & Whitney paper presented at a 2009 conference on the subject. One estimate is that when a large bird like a Canada goose is involved (some have been reported to fly nearly to 10,000 feet), the energy generated by the impact approaches that of a 200-pound weight dropped from 50 feet high. The Miracle on the Hudson plane hit a whole flock of these creatures, shutting down both engines. The good news for planes, but not birds: more than 85 percent of bird strikes do no significant damage. The bird either bounces or gets emulsified into what's known scientifically as "snarge."

As serious bird strikes doubled in the last decade at 13 major US airports, they've moved up the list of aviation safety priorities. Nearly 10,000 "wildlife strikes" were reported in 2010, double the average in earlier years, though fewer than 600 of them were considered "damaging" strikes by the FAA. By 2012, the FAA was getting three dozen bird-strike reports every day on average, and birds hit the planes of both the vice president and the secretary of state the same day in April. Meanwhile, DOT's Inspector General warned that the FAA needs to work harder to oversee airport efforts to eliminate the bird hazard.

Roughly half of bird strikes occur on takeoff and another third on landing; about 15 percent are at higher altitudes away from airports. There's even an official name for the problem in the acronym-crazed aviation world: BASH—for "Bird Aircraft Strike Hazard." Airports try to get rid of the critters (scare them, shoot them, send in the border collies and falcons), but the problem is getting worse—especially in places like New York's JFK, set amidst acres of coastal wetlands and the Jamaica Bay wildlife refuge, and Sacramento, sited on the Pacific Flyway bird migration route. And quieter planes with fewer engines are less frightening to airborne wildlife.

S--t Happens

When something as awful as an air crash occurs, we search for someone, or at least *something*, to blame or to fix. Angry postmortems and earnest investigations hunt the culprit or cause. The sad fact is that as commercial aviation has become so safe, fatal accidents are almost flukes—random events each of little predictive significance, a confluence of rarities at just the wrong moment. Engineers rebel at the notion, but sometimes they're mainly a matter of very bad luck.

Consider the spectacular July 25, 2000, crash in Paris that ultimately ended the life of the Concorde, the one and only supersonic passenger aircraft. Though first flight-tested in 1969, the sleek jet in many ways remained for decades the world's most technologically sophisticated commercial aircraft. The aircraft that took off from Charles de Gaulle Airport was airworthy (though experts have questioned the particular plane's weight and balance and tires), the crew highly qualified, the weather good. The immediate cause of the disaster was determined to be just a tiny piece of debris—a thin strip of titanium metal, 17 inches long, that lay at the end of the runway, having come off a jet that had departed four minutes earlier. The metal strip ruptured the Concorde's tire. The tire debris in turn hit the plane's undercarriage at 300 miles per hour, ultimately exploding a fuel tank and dooming the plane. Call it fate or misfortune; sometimes even with the best technology, stuff happens—stuff nobody can prevent.

Damned Statistics—The "Safest"

In the end, every passenger naturally wants to know the safest way to fly—the safest airline between the safest airports sitting in the safest seat on the safest kind of airplane. There's no easy answer about comparative safety. The industry line is that everything is safe and it doesn't matter where you sit or what plane you're on. That's not just blowing smoke; there's a real data problem. There just haven't been enough major accidents, at least in the First World over the last decade, to draw broad conclusions.

Lots of airlines have had a crash or two, but these events are increasingly near-random anomalies where the wrong combination of circumstances happens at just the wrong time and it's really nobody's fault—like a bird strike or lightning bolt. That isolated accident is a meaningless measure of the airline's overall safety record, even less a predictor of what's going to happen on tomorrow's flight. And if one airline crashed once in the last 25 years, and another crashed twice in the last 35 years, which is really "safer," especially if one operates ten times more flights every day?

Nearly every large scheduled US passenger airline that's been around for at least ten years has had fatalities—exceptions include Hawaiian, JetBlue, and Southwest—but none in more than a decade, according to AirSafe.com. United and American have each had half a dozen fatal crashes over their half century of corporate existence. In comparison, by 2012, Air Zimbabwe and Air Jamaica had not had a single fatal crash in 30 years. Are they "safer?" When you get finished sifting the statistics, taken all together, the big US network airlines have roughly equivalent accident rates—on par with such venerable foreign airlines as British Airways, SAS, Lufthansa, and ANA.

The same rarity of accidents makes it hard to judge the "safest" airplanes. Until its first and only crash in 2000, the Concorde had been the world's statistically safest airplane for more than two decades—no accidents, no incidents, top-notch maintenance and crew. The moment its tire ruptured on a piece of runway debris, though, it became statistically among the most dangerous planes in the world, because it had flown fewer than 100,000 total flights in its life span, skewing its safe-flight percentage.

There are lots of ways to parse the numbers to try to find which types of aircraft are "safest"—fatalities per flight, crashes per year, accidents per number of takeoffs, incidents per years of operation—but statistics are statistics. By one measure (fatal crashes per million flights) compiled by AirSafe.com, as of 2010, the least accident-prone of common large commercial jets was the Boeing 777, then the Airbus A320, followed by a tight grouping of the newer-model Boeing 737s, then the Boeing 757, the Boeing MD-80 and -90, and the Boeing 767. By another, equally defensible, measure of fatal accident rates—this one published by Boeing—the popular newer-model Boeing 737s just barely edge out the Airbus 320 and its cousins. Imagine that.

Even harder to rank is the safety of airports, given differences in terrain, climate, and congestion. Frequent fliers all have their "least favorites" or, as pilots prefer to say, "most challenging." (The most challenging can actually have strong safety records; experts liken it to lower auto accident rates on difficult, winding roads than on smooth, wide straightaways.) Among the sportier airports:

> Washington's Reagan National. To avoid overflying sensitive buildings like the White House and Capitol, and for noise abatement, pilots on the busy River Visual approach make a sharp turn to line up with the runway, fully leveling out only about 300 feet above the Potomac just before touchdown. Plus, straying off course can earn you a face-to-face with a fully armed fighter jet in seconds.
> New York's LaGuardia's short runways are bounded by Flushing Bay; superbusy airspace means near-constant congestion.
> At San Diego's Lindbergh Field, lots of private planes compete with

airlines, the normal approach drops down steeply, and a 100-foot-tall parking garage sits off the end of the main runway.

> At Orange County's John Wayne International, tough local noise restrictions demand that pilots cut power quickly after a steep climb-out on takeoff.

> In Juneau, Alaska, strong northerly winds whipping down the Gastineau Channel through mountainous terrain can create power-ful unanticipated turbulence for landing or takeoff.

Some foreign airports are reportedly even more interesting. In the Caribbean, the prize goes to St. Barts, a tiny island playground of the "one-percenters." The Gustaf III Airport's 2,100 foot airstrip ends at—actually almost right *on*—a gorgeous white-sand beach, where topless beachgoers have been known to distract pilots. But the all-time favorite scary airport for decades of frequent fliers was Hong Kong's former Kai Tak, a key hub for international jumbo jets until it was replaced by Hong Kong International in 1998. Veterans remember the Runway 13 landing approach over Kowloon that came so close to surrounding tenements that passengers could see not only the flickering light of residents' TVs, but, some swore, even the shows they were watching.

The only "what's safest?" issue that has anything like a satisfying answer may be where it's safest to sit in the plane, at least according to an analysis done by *Popular Mechanics* in 2007. Reviewing every plane crash in the United States since 1971, the magazine found that the farther back in the plane you sit, the better your chances of surviving a crash—about 40 percent better near the tail than sitting in the first few front rows. Of 20 crashes the magazine studied, the back-of-the-bus passengers fared better in 11, and *much* better in seven, while front-end passengers did better in only five crashes. Meanwhile, a British study in 2008 found proximity to an emergency exit to be key to safety. Your chances of escape in a fire are better than 50-50 sitting within five rows of the exit, but you're likely not going to make it sitting six or more rows away.

Best bet for truly anxious fliers: Seat 34D (or thereabouts) in the back of an A320 near the rear exit, and land at Denver—its three-mile-long Runway 16/34 is the nation's longest for public use. Or just sit back with a cold one and contemplate the odds—they're *way* in your favor.

The Pointy End

E ven in the no-drama mundanity of today's air travel, there's still a larger-than-life aura about the middle-aged white guy in the pseudomilitary hat up there in what pilots call the "pointy end" of the plane—if only because we entrust the pilot with our lives.

Weaving the slightly hairy final approach to Washington National or Quito or Juneau, bouncing through the low-visibility "goo" on a stormy night with gusting crosswinds, we may contemplate mortality, but not for long. Chatting away, watching the movie, pecking at laptops in the dimly lit cabin, we have faith. The pilot's twang—"buckle up until we get through this little bit of choppy air"—reassures. Nothing to worry about here. We're not going to die tonight. Sit back and relax.

A favorite pilot joke: "The only difference between God and an airline pilot is that God thinks he's a pilot." In no other profession does the law, tradition, and the unique physical isolation of the airborne craft give more responsibility and power to a nonmilitary official. A "pilot in command," the FAA's term for the person, ideally the captain, who bears ultimate responsibility for the safety of the flight, no matter what. When the aircraft door closes, the captain's word is law.

We want our airline pilots to fit this mold. Like Sully Sullenberger— not just a fine pilot who deftly floated that US Airways jet safely onto the Hudson River with no engines, but a guy adulated as a miracle worker. We want pilots who look and talk like pilots are *supposed* to—the way

Warren Burger looked exactly like a Supreme Court Chief Justice. Tall and fit, military bearing, a little gray at the temples. And we love that soothing "aw-shucks-we're-out-of-gas" pilot drawl—echoes of the legendary Chuck Yeager and the hollows of West Virginia, as Tom Wolfe observed in *The Right Stuff*.

Never mind that that airline pilots aren't really heroic adventurers, that they worry more about paychecks and pensions and work schedules than dead-stick landings and the magic of flight. On average, airline captains today are overwhelmingly white, straight, and male, just over age 50, often with years in the military. (Rough estimates are that only 1 percent of US airline pilots are African American and 5 percent are women.) They tend to be conservative in their personal habits, play golf, drive boats and other mechanized toys, and love their families. They're fastidious and well ordered—neatly groomed even when casual. Pilots tuck in their Polo shirts. Nearly all have a bachelor's degree, and many have a master's or higher degree. They're healthy in body and, presumably, in mind. "We've been tested, poked, and peed in a cup our whole lives," says a longtime pilot for American.

The pilot icon is powerful and traditional, reinforced by the fact that pilots think and act and talk and do their jobs much the way they did 50 years ago. But in the decade since September 11, there have also been real changes in what happens up in the pointy end of the plane, and how pilots relate to their passengers, their machines, and their jobs.

The Disembodied Voice Behind the Steel Door

Most obvious of these changes is the Inviolable Cockpit (or, in correct terminology, the "flight deck")—isolated physically and psychologically behind the bulletproof door. The ruins of the World Trade Center were still smoldering when airlines took steps to beef up security: first, by fortifying the cockpit. The imperative was obvious: protect the "front office" from potential threats "back there." Cockpit doors that once gave way to a hard, swift kick were replaced by reinforced steel (costing an estimated \$30,000 to \$50,000 apiece, installed) designed to withstand not just bullets and small explosives but a 300-joule hit—the impact of an NFL lineman running at the speed of an Olympic sprinter. Add to that serious locking systems and new security protocols for entering the pilots' *sanctum sanctorum*. The goal was to keep terrorists away from the controls, but the effect was also to explode the old pilot-passenger paradigm.

By law and ancient tradition, the airline pilot's first responsibility—as with any captain at sea—is the care and welfare of his passengers or, as airline pilots sometimes call their flocks, "the people." By September 12, 2001, the same "people" had become potential threats. So much for visits up front to meet the captain and friendly, serene pilots strolling through the cabin; now it was all about protecting the cockpit.

Nothing more epitomized the abrupt attitudinal shift in this relationship than the voluntary arming of pilots. By 2003, trained airline pilots could volunteer to become "federal flight deck officers," sworn law-enforcement officials entitled to carry firearms into the cockpit—and many did. The Department of Homeland Security won't say, but estimates are that well over 10 percent of commercial airline pilots are qualified to tuck a pistol into their flight bags, and training classes in New Mexico are consistently full. The largest pilots' union estimates that armed pilots are on about 15 percent of domestic flights. The goal of the program, according to the law that created it, is "to provide a final, deadly-force deterrent to an attempted hostile breach of the flight deck." The pilots' new job description: "defender of the flight deck"—the last line of defense in a potential death struggle for control. Not exactly the avuncular chaps who once pinned junior pilots' wings on little Johnny.

Nobody gets in or out of the cockpit easily. When pilots need what FAA delicately refers to as "a physiological needs break," it's a minor production. Calls on the intercom to the flight attendants, peering through the peephole, guarding the cockpit door with a drink cart, everybody

on alert—you wonder how the poor guy can relieve himself. Just fetch-
ing the pilot a bottle of water entails a security ritual—a predetermined
"secret word" or word exchange that crew and pilot agree to during a
preflight crew briefing, sometimes a secret knock or a numeric-pad code
entry. So pilots thnk twice about leaving the cockpit. Better to call for
an F-16 fighter escort if there's a disruption in back.

In truth, not all pilots mind the lack of passenger contact. Sure, they
understand they're in a customer-driven business and instinctively feel
protective of their charges in back. "I see an 80-year-old lady," says a
Delta pilot, "and that's my mom traveling." But that's not what they love
about flying, and it's not quite personal. More like: "If I, the pilot, get
there safely and securely, so will the hundreds of folks sitting a few yards
behind me. If I'm OK, they're OK."

Observe the way pilots communicate, a fine balance of honesty and
patronizing obfuscation. There's the script to rely on, but if there's an
"anomaly" (pilot-talk for anything from a balky radio switch to a hair-
raising near disaster)—a medical diversion, an engine problem, major
turbulence—pilots keep it short and nonspecific, with a unique brand
of understatement. There's never a "storm" or "lightning" or "wind
shear" or "icing." Instead, it's "rain showers," "bumpiness," or a "slight
chop," or seeking "a more comfortable altitude." A flaps malfunction is
a "flight control issue"; a failed landing gear is a "hydraulics issue." An
emergency landing is an "unplanned arrival." Pilots try to be honest, but
minimalist. "Big technical descriptions terrify people," says one pilot.
"Passengers don't understand the redundancy built in" to modern jets—
in other words that there's a backup if something important breaks.

The new cockpit isolation changed the dynamic with passengers,
but the "front office" has always been a refuge of order and sequence
for pilots, where routine and repetition and ritual are recognized and
the power and control of flight are centered and unmistakable. The first
thing its occupants do when arriving for duty on board is start "building their nest," setting up the cockpit "just so." Seats and headrests are

rearranged, hats and personal items stowed. One pilot touches the cabin door frame in the same place every time he climbs aboard. Another arranges the flight plan and other papers on the console between the seats by securing them with a rubber band that is *always* in just the same spot. Still another captain, a germ freak, carefully cleans each cockpit button and toggle switch with alcohol swabs.

Actually, the pointy end is not entirely private. For much if not most of the flight, Big Brother is watching, or at least listening. By federal rule, airline cockpits are under mechanical surveillance. Automated voice recorders capture for posterity everything said, every sound in the cabin, during the last two hours of the flight. The point is to assist accident investigators trying to determine what went wrong if a large plane goes down, but the "black boxes" (really not black at all but high-visibility bright orange) capture every off-color joke, every slur at airline management, every heartfelt personal revelation to your buddy who's been occupying the same SUV-sized space with you for the last eight hours. And that means posterity. To be recoverable after a crash, they're built to survive 3,400 times the force of gravity, water pressure at 20,000 feet for 30 days; and 30 minutes of heat up to 2,000 degrees Fahrenheit, not that much less than the surface of the Space Shuttle on reentry.

Until recently, airliner cockpit voice recorders held only a half hour of sound, so pilots who said something off-key had plenty of time to just keep quiet as they landed and taxied to the arrival gate, confident any embarrassing statements would be recorded over and so disappear forever. Crash investigators at the National Transportation Safety Board wanted to know more, though, and the new two-hour recording time required as of 2012 equals nearly the entire length of the average domestic flight.

Audio recordings worried workplace privacy advocates, but what really disturbs airline pilots more is another NTSB "most wanted" recommendation—for *video* surveillance of the airborne nest. Crash investigators would dearly love to see in living color, as well as hear, what was happening in the cockpit of a downed airliner—for example, whether pilots were sleeping or one became suicidal, or who had what controls.

Pilots say they understand the desire to find out "what happened" shortly before a crash, but expanding cockpit surveillance makes them livid. By law, cockpit voice tapes are to be used only for crash investigations; they must remain strictly confidential—only written transcripts are normally made publicly available as part of an investigation; pilots agreed to audio recorders in the first place, in the early 1960s, only on that condition. (On the other hand, air traffic control tapes of cockpit-to-ground communications are public and accessible.) To their consternation, though, some of these disturbing—and, for grieving families, intensely private—"last words" tapes have since found their way to the Internet.

Videotape ups the ante in a YouTube world. Count on clips of crashing cockpits rocketing instantly around the web. More prosaically, who wants to be videotaped up-close and personal in their workplace for hours on end? Some veteran pilots say it would make them "walk off the job" and exercised unions lobbied hard against cockpit video. So far it's worked. The FAA has proposed standards for the safe installation of video in airline cockpits, but it hasn't ordered airlines to actually install it.

Siri on Steroids?

If more isolated pilots have grown a little more distant from and patronizing toward passengers, their relationship with their airplanes has only become more deferential since the 1990s, as aircraft automation and technical sophistication has accelerated. No, planes don't somehow "fly themselves" automatically, but for most of the flight big jets aren't really being flown by humans, either. Pilots are relying on something called a flight management computer. Their "inner Sullenberger" is an assemblage of integrated computer-driven systems that does so many things so reliably that flight engineers, once the traditional third officers in jet cockpits, became largely superfluous by the mid-1980s. What computer automation really does best, though, are routine tasks—like holding a constant speed and course and altitude—so pilots can anticipate and respond to the hard stuff while scanning for errant private planes and assessing the darkening thunderclouds up ahead.

Before the flight, the onboard computer is loaded with information about the route of flight, the weight of the plane, the fuel load, current and predicted winds and temperatures, and planned altitudes. In flight, the computer reports to the flight crew via a small computer screen (a "control display unit") that sits between the two pilots. At the heart of the computer system is the autopilot—"George," as pilots often call it. As in, "George is changing our heading 2 degrees" or "George is acting up today" or "What does George want?" George flies the plane better than humans 99.9 percent of the time in normal conditions—so well, in fact, that pilots are strongly encouraged to "engage" him/it as soon as possible after takeoff. You'd think human pilots might resent these automated doppelgängers, but they don't. Many are hard-core techies, after all.

Pilots are mainly there to monitor what's happening during normal cruise—essentially all of the flight that occurs after the plane takes off and starts to climb until it sets up for final approach 50 miles or so out. (Another old pilots' joke: "In the cockpit of the future there will be only one pilot and one dog—the pilot to feed the dog and the dog to bite the pilot's hand if he tries to touch anything.") The autopilot (along with autothrottle) flies the preloaded flight plan, adjusts the throttles and pitch of the plane to control speed and altitude, and smooths out changes in heading and speed. The flight management computer monitors the plane's precise position, checking it against GPS, signals from radio navigation beacons, and distance-measuring equipment on the ground. The altitude stays precisely steady—avoiding the need to constantly fiddle with controls to correct for thermal dips and gusts—and it stays headed on the preassigned route of flight. The passengers' ride is smoother and it's a helluva lot easier on long-haul pilots than flying the plane "by hand"—actually manipulating the controls to make frequent slight corrections—for hours on end, as pilots had to do before George arrived. Other "electronic crew members" implement human direction. With the autopilot engaged, pilots can turn the plane 8 degrees to a new heading by twisting a dial or knob and, if necessary, punching in "heading mode" on a cockpit console, which in turn electronically directs the plane's physical control surfaces (ailerons and rudder) to move the precise distance to effect the desired turn.

The goal is to make flying essentially mistake-proof or, more realistically, as Boeing puts it, "error-tolerant." Over the last decade, both Boeing and Airbus have made leaps in creating ever-more-intricate cockpit automation that is not always applauded by pilots or, for that matter, by safety experts. They fret that all the whizz-bang automation may distract from, or even undermine, the basic "stick and rudder" skills pilots need to get out of a jam or, more precisely, to handle "anomalies." In an online aviation newsletter, one Airbus pilot calls the advanced Airbus 330 "a video game, not an airplane," while a Boeing pilot blogger describes the ultrasophisticated 787 cockpit as "17 computers in a Kevlar frame" that "seems like it was designed by Apple."

How much cockpit automation is too much is a hot topic for airline pilots and aerospace manufacturers alike. It has been since the first autopilot—a gyroscopic, biplane-mounted contraption—wowed the crowd at a 1914 aeronautic exhibition in Paris when it let the daredevil pilot-inventor Lawrence Sperry not only lift his arms from the biplane's steering stick but actually walk out onto the wing as the plane kept flying straight and level. (Two years later, the same young pilot crashed into Long Island's Great South Bay while demonstrating the technological wizardry to an engaging New York socialite; reportedly some body part bumped the gyro device and both fliers were rescued, naked, by duck hunters. It was a very early example of overreliance on cockpit technology.)

Now flight computers and autopilots can—and do—land heavy jets and bring them to a complete stop on the runway. The "auto-land" function is not often used, but it can still be the best way to get an equipped aircraft on the runway in pea-soup fog—near what pilots call "zero/zero" ceiling and visibility. Using a very precise radar altimeter to show just how many feet the plane is poised above the runway, it determines just when to "flare" the plane—raise the nose at the last moment before touchdown (figure 10 yards or so above the pavement) to slow the descent and avoid a "hard" landing—then automatically brakes it to a stop.

The next logical step—announced at the Paris Air Show in June 2011—is essentially a "panic button" for pilots about to crash. The device—the designer calls it a "digital parachute"—would let computers take full control of an aircraft in jeopardy and return it to safe flight. It's handy to have in worst-case situations where pilots have become disoriented and stall at higher altitudes. Ultimately, such a gadget might even be able to land an aircraft at the nearest appropriate runway, even with an incapacitated pilot.

Does all the new whizz-bang automation make pilots superfluous, mere automation managers? Not until passengers feel comfortable flying on pilotless drones. Human pilots still normally do the challenging tasks like takeoffs and landings. Auto-land can get a plane on the ground, for example, but won't work well in wind shear or heavy crosswinds; human "hand-flying" is more sensitive and may provide quicker, smoother corrections to last-second wind bursts. And besides, pilots like to land their own planes—not just for safety in tough conditions, but also out of pride. Landings are one of the few phases of flight that passengers actually feel and can appreciate. "Passengers always grade you on the finish," says an American 767 pilot.

Humans are also better, by and large, when it comes to handling the "anomalies." Like when the automation stops working, the hydraulics fail, an engine stops turning, or the middle-aged man in 23D is having a heart attack. An international 777 pilot with more than 30 years' experience puts it drily this way: "Today's aircraft technology has made flying so much more reliable and the [flight management] systems do work all the time—except once in a while they don't."

The broader issue—call it the "2001 question" from Stanley Kubrick's movie of that name—is raised in an FAA report: "For any given situation, who will have final control authority?" The pilot or the flight management computer? Aircraft manufacturers and their automation designers have somewhat different philosophies. Airbus has tended to favor the machine—its automation is designed essentially to prevent the plane from getting outside its safe "flight envelope" no matter what the pilot does. Meanwhile, Boeing tends to give the pilot the final word—and its adherents can be adamant. A Boeing-flying Delta captain puts it this way: "When shit hits the fan, a pilot should be able to disengage all the magic and fly the airplane with basics. . . . All you can do is hope the software engineers haven't screwed you with some magical sub-mode that, [sitting] in an office with a nice warm cup of coffee, makes sense at the time." For every fan of Airbus's "make-it-impossible-to-crash" approach, there's a proponent of Boeing's support for new cockpit technology only where "there is no adverse effect to the human-machine interface."

The debate is not just a matter of philosophical nuance. Consider what happened in 2010 when one of the first commercially flown A380 superjumbos, among the world's most sophisticated new airliners, blew an engine over Singapore. The three highly skilled senior Qantas captains on board were deluged with 54 computer-generated error messages on their cockpit screens, and it took all three nearly a half hour just to unravel all the warnings. Only then could the pilot in command land the massive plane by hand, with 469 passengers on board.

Demigods and Whiners

Pilots whom passengers see as demigods, airline management sees as high-maintenance, high-cost whiners. And pilots tend to reciprocate that high regard. The last decade's financial stresses only exacerbated labor-management tensions. That couldn't help but affect the tenor of the flying experience, subtly but pervasively, for travelers. When everybody from pilots to flight attendants to baggage handlers are angry at their employer, passengers sense it.

As airlines declared bankruptcy, one by one, during the last dismal decade, they used the legal leverage that Chapter 11 provides to dump labor contracts, cancel debts, and renegotiate pay levels downward. By the end of the decade, pilots' salaries at the big airlines were down as much as 40 percent and so-called work-rules changes meant more work for that lower pay. By 2012, the once-glamorous, high-paying job of commercial airline pilot ranked 104th on a list of the 200 best and worst US jobs prepared by CareerCast.com, based on income, employment outlook, environment, physical demands, and stress. Airline pilots were ranked a notch above hairstylists and a little below autobody repairers.

More lasting than the pilot salary squeeze was the decade's impact on junior pilots' prospects for career advancement. As strapped airlines cut capacity, stored unused planes in the desert (the lack of humidity minimizes corrosion), and curtailed new routes, fewer pilots were needed. Thousands were furloughed, others downgraded ignominiously from captain to first officer, or from large aircraft to smaller ones. Then the FAA decided in December 2007, after decades of debate, to extend the mandatory pilot retirement age from 60 to 65. Copilots who had been patiently waiting their turn to move from the right-hand seat to the captain's chair on the left, some for up to 20 years, now had to wait longer for the old guys to leave.

By 2011, the most *junior* captain at American had 19 years' flying experience, according to the *Dallas News*, and very, very few major airline captains were under 40. American has seven pilots *over* 60 for every one under 40, with the average captain and first officer aged 54 and 49 respectively. It's all a far cry from the 1980s, when it was not uncommon to see major airline captains in their mid-thirties, with only five to eight years of seniority.

At the average large passenger airline in 2011, pilots and copilots combined averaged close to $180,000 in total salary, pensions, and benefits added together, according to government data compiled by the Air Line Pilots Association. (Express cargo pilots at UPS and FedEx made about 50 percent more than the average passenger pilot.) Typically, airline captains made almost a third more than their generally younger and less-experienced first officers, and the most senior international passenger airline captains pulled in a quarter million or so a year, benefits, bonuses, and overtime included.

Of course, beyond the monetary compensation—not to mention that few captains work more than four days a week to satisfy monthly minimums of 70 to 80 hours at the controls—there's also plenty of psychic reward. Listen to Paul Morrell, a former Northwest pilot, now deceased, reflecting on one of his last flights: "As an airline captain . . . I fly above things; I take in the awesome beauty and raw natural power of God's nature and universe. I can turn down the lights in the cockpit on a dark night and count the stars, see satellites, watch the planets, the constellations, and even the *aurora borealis* on winter nights at the higher latitudes. I've flown over the Rockies, the Badlands, the Grand Canyon . . . and I can describe them all as if they were my best friend." Even for the old-timers, the senior captains, it's still about the jolt they get from flying. For those who got in at the right time, it's not exactly a hardship profession, even if some say it's not what it used to be.

Still, as hard as it is to weep for the handful of former $300,000 senior captains who became $200,000 senior captains, consider the other end of the pilot spectrum—the tough world of pilots at the regional or commuter airlines, the carriers that handle half of US flights and typically contract with the big airlines to deliver more than 160 million passengers a year to big airline hubs. Airline pilots get their start at these commuter airlines, and they're hardly getting rich; many are barely getting by.

As major airlines filed for bankruptcy protection over the last decade, one of their first acts was to cut what they paid these carriers, their regional "partners." Next down the food chain, the regional airlines, now hurting, cut what they paid their already-strapped pilots. As reported by pilotcareer.info for 2011, regional airline *captains*—average age 41, with ten years' experience—make only about $70,000, far less than their major airline counterparts. Entry-level regional *copilots* earn as little as $20,000 a year—just half again more than the minimum wage, annualized.

That said, pilots have to start somewhere, and it's not an easy path. They "fly hard," in the words of an American Airlines pilot who apprenticed in the Air Force instead of the commuter airlines, sacrificing pay and conditions to accumulate enough hours for a shot at the majors. Their working days consist not of one takeoff, a six-hour cross-country cruise, and a single landing, but rather a series of short-haul flights in high-traffic-density airspace, multiple takeoffs and landings at crowded airports, and pressure to turn the plane around fast for the next haul of passengers to connect with a major airline's hub. Not to mention surviving on Big Macs and crashing on couches in crew lounges. How could it not affect safety?

How Pilots Think

There's still a strange duality to the airline pilot's mind—poets soaring through the skies and, at the same moment, emotionless engineers and managers. Isolate the problem, ignore the distractions, focus on solutions, even when all hell is breaking loose. Pilots rarely admit to fear, but acknowledge flying moments when they are "fully alert." Their final words recorded on black boxes recovered after a disaster often reflect a determination up to the last moment to fix the machine, more powerful than fear or even resignation to imminent death. As Sullenberger's Airbus jet is screaming toward the Hudson River at

170 miles per hour, a few hundred feet up, with every warning horn in the cockpit blaring, he calmly asks his copilot 17 seconds before the potentially fatal impact: "Got any ideas?" To which the equally calm answer is "Actually not."

The calm seems born of a preternatural self-confidence—their earth-bound spouses and teenage kids sometimes say "God complexes"—that reassures subordinates and passengers alike. Veteran airline pilots make decisions definitively and swiftly, even if not always correctly, and they rarely look back. "Follow me over the hill, boys" works better than collegial debate in a crisis. And how could they not have confidence—given the awesome power and responsibility that goes with flying big airplanes full of hundreds of souls?

A fully fueled 747 waiting at the gate and loaded with 400 passengers isn't going anywhere unless the pilot agrees it is ready to fly. It doesn't matter if company dispatchers are tearing their hair out trying to keep on schedule or if the departure gate needs to be cleared to unload the next jet waiting on the tarmac. Recently, an Atlanta-based pilot "refused" an MD-88 when one of its two coffeemakers, located in different galleys, shorted out, raising concern about an electrical-circuit problem on the plane. American Airlines pilots were accused of using a raft of "frivolous" maintenance discrepancy write-ups to cause schedule havoc in a September 2012 labor fight. Then there's the widely recounted tale of the major carrier pilot who, during an intense labor-management standoff in 2000, reportedly refused to fly a nearly full, fueled-up Boeing 777 to Frankfurt, Germany, because the toilet-paper holder in a coach lavatory was broken.

The captain can also refuse to fly if he's concerned about a sketchy passenger. Pilots are notified of, and often meet, those of their passengers who are armed. (Including federal air marshals, prisoner escorts, VIP "protective" agents and police, there can be quite a few.) And if the captain insists on more fuel aboard his flight, it has to be loaded—even if airline bean counters object. In an emergency, the pilot in command even has the legal right—indeed, the duty—to refuse a direct instruction from air traffic control if he genuinely believes it will endanger his flight. (Pilot response to controller in that case: "Unable.")

Pilots cherish this power and authority—enough to shoulder the huge responsibility that comes along with it. A senior Delta captain, puts it this way: "For me it's about being totally in control when I'm flying an airplane. I'm solo. Every decision is ultimately mine, for good or bad. Autonomy. Independence. If a doctor makes a mistake, he buries one person. I have five seconds to decide [about a whole planeload]." As pilots, "we're in an organization, but we're at the top of it," he adds. "When it comes down to it, all we have [from others] is input."

In that sense and in other important ways, for all that piloting has changed, it remains much the same as it was at the dawn of the jet age. There's still the reassuring adherence to routine, repetition, and ritual, the incessant checks and double-checks, the rhythm of the cockpit interaction, the circadian confusion, the bad food, the constant struggle against boredom to stay sharp. In the end, though, even whiny passengers, terror threats, and endless labor battles can't wash away the power and romance and the joy of flight.

What Pilots Do

Plumbing the pilot mind is one thing, but what do those people *do* up there for hours behind the reinforced locked door?

Start with the takeoff. Takeoffs are a kick for pilots. Even the most seasoned captains who've made thousands of them still talk about the "rush" they get from 75,000 pounds of thrust per engine at their command (on the original Boeing 777), hurtling down the runway, and lifting off. Pilots and first officers (aka copilots) are required to brief each other on all the what-ifs before every takeoff. If an engine fails, what heading do we fly to return to the airport, what runway do we use, who will fly the plane, and who will communicate with the tower?

Once the takeoff roll starts, the pilot will abort if something's not right, typically as long as the plane's speed is below 100 knots (some airline standard operating procedures prescribe 80 knots). Faster than that, it gets dicier. Then pilots generally "reject" the takeoff only for four things—an engine failure, an engine fire, a wind-shear warning, or if the pilot for some reason doubts the plane will fly. And taking off safely isn't just a matter of going as fast as you can and then pulling back on the yoke. There's a specific threshold of runway speed the plane needs to reach. Take off too early and you risk a stall—and crash. Take off too late and you risk running off the end of the runway—and crash.

There's a well-learned ritual to avoid these unpleasant outcomes. The pilot flying the plane (whether it's the captain or the first officer) handles the controls while the other pilot (now called the "pilot monitoring," formerly the "pilot not flying") keeps his eyes locked on the airspeed and engine-performance gauges in front of him. As the plane accelerates down the runway, the nonflying pilot "calls out" the plane's increasing speed (always in knots, not miles, per hour)—"ninety knots . . . one hundred . . . one-ten"—until the speed hits "V-1," the predetermined critical "decision speed." In the last seconds before reaching V-1, the captain (and commonly *only* the captain, even if the copilot is flying the plane) makes the key decision to either take off or "reject" the takeoff. If everything's normal, the plane accelerates down the runway until the nonflying pilot gives the signal to lift off: "Rotate." The nose rises off the runway into the air and the plane gathers speed going airborne and reaching velocity V-2—the speed fast enough for safe flight, even if one engine decides to stop working.

Takeoffs and landings can be intense, honest-to-God piloting tasks that the flight crew enjoys. But these busy times can be fairly few and far-between, punctuating long hours of relative boredom while the plane is cruising straight and level at high altitude on autopilot. In those hours, an experienced American Airlines 767 pilot estimates, the job demands only about 10 percent of the flight crew's active attention.

Cruisin'—"Staying Ahead of the Plane"

When pilots aren't manipulating the controls, their primary work is, as some put it, to "stay ahead of the plane." Monitoring what's happening around them, how the plane is flying, and what's likely to happen next, whether other aircraft are nearby, what the weather's doing, how much fuel is left, where they could land in an emergency—anticipating the what-ifs. The pseudoscience term is "maintaining situational awareness." Lose it and the plane, with all its technology, is flying *you*, rather than the other way around. Pilots sometimes refer to "not having the big picture"; some air traffic controllers used to call it not "getting the flick," as in not seeing the whole movie.

"Staying ahead" starts long before takeoff, even before passengers board. There's the traditional walk around the aircraft at the gate— typically the copilot's visual inspection of landing gear, tires, undercarriage, checking for fuel or hydraulic leaks, looking at the fan blades in the jet engines for nicks or anomalies. Then there's the time-honored challenge and response of the preflight checklist. Before aircraft "pushback" from the gate, every item is visually checked, every key button or switch or circuit breaker pushed or toggled or verified, every gauge read. Dozens of preflight items must be checked on a jet airliner. The flight crew has done it a thousand times and could easily recite it in their sleep, but they need to do it carefully and take it seriously every single flight.

Once in flight, the checking continues—confirming that the plane is really where the onboard navigation system says it is and that the aircraft is performing "nominally," or within acceptable limits. They're checking that the preflight weather briefings they printed out at the flight operations office an hour before takeoff are still valid, by monitoring high-frequency radio reports from other planes up ahead on the same flight tracks and altitudes.

They're also keeping a close eye on how much fuel is left and how fast it's being expended, a particular concern since spiking fuel costs pushed airlines to carry as little "extra" as needed for safety so as to cut excess weight. Headwinds that slam against Europe-bound planes at 140 knots (160 miles) per hour, or turn five-hour flights from Los Angeles to New York into seven-hour journeys going the other way against the jet stream, can drain the required fuel reserves with remarkable speed. When Australia's Qantas Airlines in 2011 moved its nonstop Sydney flight from San Francisco to Dallas, nearly 1,200 miles farther from Australia, passengers were occasionally treated to unplanned visits to refueling spots like Noumea in New Caledonia in the far South Pacific. So pilots en route keep an eye on weather, not only at the scheduled destination, but also at remote landing strips that might be needed in an emergency—when a monsoon over Midway or a snowstorm in Shemya in the Aleutians might matter.

Passing Time

Isolated from passengers and other crew for ever-longer stretches of automated cruising, the front office can get pretty boring. Transoceanic pilots don't even have to check in regularly with air traffic controllers by high-frequency radio anymore; an automated communications device called ACARS (aircraft communications addressing and reporting system) can automatically report to ground controllers how the flight is going, along with its position. Pilots battle that boredom much as they have for decades—by talking, eating, griping, and sometimes dozing, though not necessarily in that order.

What can they possibly find to talk about for hours on end?

Hangar Flying

The term is from an earlier age, when pilots hung around the airplane hangar chewing the fat when the weather was too lousy to fly. Tall tales of amazing feats of piloting—landing in howling crosswinds, debating off-the-wall air traffic controllers who, in one pilot's words "sometimes want you to defy the laws of physics," harrowing scrapes with strange-acting folks who just might have been scoping things out for bad guys. Protocol requires hangar fliers to pretend to believe one another's stories—however embellished. Don't they get bored telling the same stories over and over? "Hell no," says a Delta pilot. "It's a different audience" every trip. Sometimes they even learn a technique they later use to avoid a fatal mistake.

Women

There's an unmistakable macho—some say downright sexist—cast to the cockpit, an old nautical term pilots vastly prefer to the more politically correct "flight deck." The captains and more senior pilots who set the tone are often ex-military. (Veterans accounted for 90 percent of airline hires in 1992, though only 28 percent of new hires in 2008, according to Aviation Information Resources.) "When you're with women, you talk about flying," they like to say, "and when you're flying, you talk about women." It can get a little nasty. A Southwest Airlines pilot in June 2011 took off on a rant against "ugly" flight attendants that was eventually heard by thousands. Forgetting his open microphone, the man complained loudly about a "continuous stream of gays and grannies" at his Houston base, home to the airline's "ugliest." The pilot was suspended, then reinstated after "diversity training." More typical is a somewhat softer edge. After all, airline pilots are exposed to literally every creed and ethnicity every day they fly.

On the other hand, as mentioned, only some 5 percent of the Air Line Pilots Association's 53,000 union members are women, and there are estimated to be only about 450 female airline *captains* worldwide (about one in nine women airline pilots overall)—not all that surprising given the 20-year career track to make captain at major US airlines and women's relative lack of seniority in the profession. Some male pilots prefer it that way. A Delta pilot, for example, professes to having "no problem" flying with a woman pilot—unless the woman is in the left-hand seat as pilot-in-command. "That," he confessed, "could be a little weird."

Dumb and Greedy Airline Execs

Bitching about airline management has long been a favorite way to pass the hours in the cockpit. It's almost mandatory. Nearly every major airline pilot *knows* he can run an airline better than the folks in charge. Griping about airline bosses—how little they do for how much they make, "how great it used to be" at the airline—is more than a constant source of cockpit chatter; it's practically the lingua franca of pilots worldwide.

The Scheduling Game

When and where pilots fly, what days they have off, where they fly to, is determined monthly at most airlines through an elaborate, seniority-based "bid" system that everybody tries to game. Beating the system means everything from stringing together the most consecutive days off to avoiding working the most weekends to scoring a weekend layover in Paris or Bali, not to mention being home for the family graduation or anniversary or Little League championship. The game can border on the obsessive. Two Northwest pilots overflew their Minneapolis destination by nearly 150 miles in 2009 when they were apparently so busy playing with new scheduling software on their laptops that they forgot where they were flying. Their explanation for 78 minutes of radio silence was entirely believable to those in the business.

Distractions—Food, Sex, and the Written Word

Sometimes sick of talk, pilots read. FAA rules limit cockpit reading to "publications . . . related to the proper conduct of the flight," at least during what the FAA calls the "critical phases of flight"—taxi, takeoff, landing, and generally flight below 10,000 feet—but some pilots give that a liberal interpretation once the plane is cruising at altitude. Besides, the back page of *USA Today* includes a map of national weather; what could be more relevant to flying? If you happen to also glance at the sports scores inside the paper hours out over the ocean, who's to know?

The FAA's "sterile cockpit" rule prohibits "nonessential" activity such as eating or chatting or reading during those critical phases, but once the plane is safely en route, it's an open secret that pilots read almost anything—at least as long as it doesn't absorb their attention. Beyond flight manuals and FAA notices, that can include car and airplane magazines, crosswords, maybe even a little light porn. (Female pilots have filed sexual harassment lawsuits alleging they found trashy stuff left behind by preceding crews). But heavy reading is frowned upon. Studying law books to prepare for the bar exam is considered too distracting.

Newer electronic distractions—like personal laptops and smart phones—present a temptation, too. They can't come out during the "sterile" parts of the flight, and some airlines ban them altogether. On the other hand, the FAA in late 2011 allowed American Airlines pilots to substitute iPads for pounds of bulky paper navigation charts and flight manuals they're otherwise required to carry; these "electronic flight bags" are likely to proliferate. For less "official" electronics, though, real-world practice seems to vary, at least on long flights. Does it *ever* happen that DVDs show up in cockpits on long overnight flights over the ocean when boredom can be overwhelming? Well, there *are* electric power outlets in the cockpits, and laptops fit nicely propped up on the cockpit glare shield; pilots concede it's not unheard-of. "The copilot is looking to the captain," says an Atlanta-based pilot who flies long-haul. "What if the captain asks if there's anything good on Netflix?" The FAA was concerned enough to issue a carefully worded notice to the airlines in April 2010 to emphasize that distracting personal electronic devices in the cockpit can "constitute a safety risk."

Another distraction that captures the imagination, though undeservedly, is cockpit sex. It's a fantasy—even if that doesn't mean it never, ever happens. In August 2011, for instance, a photo surfaced of an accommodating Cathay Pacific flight attendant apparently "pleasuring" a pilot in the cockpit—though there was no evidence it was actually in flight. The sedate *New York Times* reported the individuals were "in decidedly compromising positions." Allegedly stolen from the pilot's laptop, the photo quickly went viral, forcing the eminent Hong Kong airline to halt a multimillion-dollar international advertising campaign featuring the slogan "Meet the Team Who Go the Extra Mile to Make You Feel Special." That incident aside, forget the male fantasies of unattached young hotties cavorting in the cockpit. Multiple rounds of US airline employment cuts have raised flight attendants' median age from 30 in 1980 to 44 in 2007; in 2012, American's averaged about 51 years old.

A more mundane cockpit time-killer is eating. What pilots consume depends partly on what their unions negotiate with each airline, partly on what cash-strapped flight attendants haven't wolfed down first. Some enjoy First Class fare; others make do with "crew meals"—a kind of hybrid that still involves some aspects of "real" food.

Eating in the cockpit still has its rituals. In the days of unreliable refrigeration and iffy catering, pilots and copilots were not allowed to eat the same meal (seniority got first choice), and sometimes had to stagger their mealtimes. The reasoning: if the first eater survives for a couple of hours, odds are that the other pilot won't keel over from eating the dish. That's still the case in some international destinations for certain food. Flying out of a Southeast Asian hub on a big US airline, only one pilot gets the seafood. Still, food poisoning is rare. An FAA study of pilot "incapacitation" in the cockpit released in 2004 found that only two out of 39 incidents during a five-year period were potentially due to food poisoning. Domestic pilots living on airport fast food were probably poisoned just as often.

Struggling Against Sleep

Even with all the talking and eating and griping and reading, during that fourth or fifth engine-droning hour across the Pacific at night, a quick nap can be almost physiologically irresistible—particularly when your internal clock says it's three a.m., the autopilot is engaged, and only the soft, warm glow of the instruments lights the nearly silent cockpit. That's when one pilot tells the other he intends to "meditate" for a while ... with his eyes closed. Or that he plans to take a "flight management respite" or "study the back of [his] eyeballs" or lie back and "examine the circuit breakers" whose switches lie just above his head on the ceiling instrument panel. Occasional cockpit napping—albeit in violation of FAA rules—is no secret in the trade.

By contrast, on ultra-long-haul flights, the FAA *wants* pilots to sleep—just not while they're at the controls. Regulations require "augmented" crews (normally, an extra pilot) for very long flights, even an entire second crew (a total of four pilots) for those 16-hour trans-Pacific jaunts, and there need to be "adequate sleeping facilities" for relief pilots. A reserved First Class seat will do, but that costs the airline serious lost revenue, so large intercontinental jets are designed with hideaway sleeping nooks for crew that passengers never see. Depending on the airline, crews on extended-range Boeing 777s, for instance, rest in bunks in "upstairs" space above the coach cabin. (There's a special escape hatch down to the main cabin; look for the "dummy" overhead luggage compartment above a coach seat in the far back.) Up a narrow stairway near the tail of new-model Boeing 747s, over the rear lavatories, there's a place for eight flight-attendant bunks, each six and a half feet long by 30 inches wide, almost a twin bed.

For the longest of the long-range jets, sleeping accommodations for pilots can be pretty comfy, depending on the aircraft and how the airline configures it. The 787 features a "loft" space for cabin crew above the main cabin, reached by a small ladder; there's also a pilot-only double bunk just behind the cockpit. Meanwhile pilots on some of Airbus's new 9,000-mile-range jets enjoy their own enclosed bedrooms, complete with proper-sized bed, comfortable seat and reading light, in-flight entertainment, and a pilots-only lavatory. On the A380 and the A340, the world's longest-range commercial airliners, look just behind the cockpit.

Just in case, though, long-range planes like the Boeing 777 and 747-400 have fail-safe mechanisms to keep pilots awake and alert. A "crew alertness monitor" pops up a visual caution message—"pilot response"—on the cockpit computer screen if the aircraft's controls or switches or radios aren't touched for a preset period of time, say 15 to 20 minutes. A few minutes later, if there's still no activity, a cautionary beeper sounds. If there's *still* no response after 30 minutes or so, all hell breaks loose; a loud and continuous "wailer" alarm goes off—an especially rude awakening.

When the Cockpit Goes Wrong

It's rare, but even pilots, these icons of calm and stability, sometimes behave badly, miscommunicate, or just screw up.

Pilot intoxication—by drugs or booze—is an obvious, if rare, concern. Denzel Washington's cinematic antics in the movie *Flight* aside, the last major crash in the United States known to involve alcohol occurred in 1977, when a Japan Airlines DC-8 cargo jet crashed on takeoff at Anchorage, according to a report by Alan Levin in *USA Today*. The rule for pilots is simple: at least eight hours "from bottle to throttle." (Some airlines require 12 hours.) And blood alcohol levels in the United States must be below .04 percent—half the legal limit in most states for driving a car. Airlines can have their own tougher *zero*-tolerance rules; some suspend pilots with just .02 blood alcohol. (Half a glass of beer is roughly at the limit in the UK.) Violators face severe punishment. Beyond firing and disgrace, there are criminal sanctions—15 years in federal prison is the penalty for operating a common carrier under the influence.

Still, it happens. Of 11,000 vocational pilots tested at random each year, a dozen or so fail, which translates to a one-in-a-thousand chance of having a pilot with a problem, even if not obviously impaired. That said, nobody in aviation hesitates to turn in a pilot smelling of booze, be they security screeners, fellow employees, or passengers, though there have been some close calls abroad. Like the Aeroflot flight to New York in December 2008, where Moscow passengers refused to take their seats aboard the Boeing 767 after the pilot slurred and garbled his "welcome-aboard" greeting. The airline blamed the mutiny on the passengers' "mass psychosis" but nonetheless found a new crew, according to press reports. (According to the London *Telegraph,* a *Moscow Times* correspondent on the plane reported that a carrier representative reassured concerned passengers that "it's not such a big deal if the pilot is drunk. ... Really all he has to do is press a button and the plane flies itself.")

Alcohol is one thing, but when pilots lose it psychologically, it shakes our faith in their deserved reputation for preternatural cool. After all, many have endured high-stress flying, handling a fighter jet in tight formations, landing on aircraft carriers at night in rolling seas, some even certified in the military to transport nuclear weapons. So pilot freakouts like the March 2012 incident involving a 49-year-old JetBlue captain who had to be locked out of the cockpit and restrained are incredibly rare. During the New York–Las Vegas flight, he told his first officer, "We're not going to Las Vegas," followed ominously by "We need to take a leap of faith." On the other hand, airline pilots don't typically get rigorous psychological evaluations once they're hired.

The chilling story of Egyptair Flight 990 still haunts the profession. On Halloween Night 1999, the Boeing 767 crashed into the ocean 60 miles south of Nantucket Island, en route from New York to Cairo. The NTSB found nothing wrong with the aircraft. Instead, it concluded that the first officer had committed an act of mass suicide-homicide. In the drily analytic language of the official post-crash findings, the plane's "impact with the Atlantic Ocean" was "a result of the [copilot's] flight control inputs." The reason for his action was officially not determined, but the cockpit audiotapes revealed that, when he was alone in the cockpit, the first officer disconnected the autopilot, shut down the engines, and put the plane into a dive. Then he calmly repeated—11 times—*"Tawakalt ala Allah."* Translation: "I rely on God."

Possible suicidal impulses aside, a more subtle kind of cockpit dysfunction has long been seen as a serious, sometimes fatal, safety issue. The psychobabble term—"cockpit resource management"—covers a lot of ground, but it's all about how pilots interact with each other and with the complexities of the airplane, how they communicate and make piloting decisions, prioritize problems, and delegate tasks in a crisis; how flight problems get solved or not. The 1978 crash of United Flight 173 brought the issue into stark focus. On approach to Portland from Denver, the crew of the DC-8 became preoccupied by an instrument-panel light that had failed to illuminate to confirm that the landing gear was down and locked. They were so engrossed in diagnosing the landing-gear problem that the plane was left to circle the airport for an hour. It simply ran out of fuel and hit fir trees and electric power lines short of the runway.

The spectacular crash of Air Florida Flight 90 into the Potomac River on takeoff in a Washington, DC, snowstorm in January 1982 is still the textbook example of failed cockpit teamwork, though. As the plane accelerated down the runway to take off, ice-clogged exterior sensors generated cockpit readings that overstated the plane's actual engine thrust. Throughout the Boeing 737's takeoff roll, the copilot tried to warn that the instrument readings showing adequate engine takeoff power were exaggerated, but he ultimately deferred to the flying pilot's misplaced faith in their accuracy. Here's the cockpit voice recorder transcript from AVweb.com:

15:59:51   CA (Captain): It's spooled. Real cold, real cold.

15:59:58   F/O (First Officer): God, look at that thing. That don't seem right, does it? Uh, that's not right.

16:00:09   CA: Yes it is, there's eighty [knots of speed].

16:00:10   F/O: Naw, I don't think that's right. Ah, maybe it is.

16:00:21   CA: Hundred and twenty [knots].

16:00:23   F/O: I don't know.

16:00:31   CA: V-One [the takeoff "decision" point]. Easy, V-Two [the rotation point]

16:00:39   [Sound of stick shaker—a device that noisily vibrates the control yoke to warn of an imminent stall—starts and continues until impact]

16:00:41   Tower: Palm 90 contact departure control.

16:00:45   CA: Forward, forward, easy. We only want five hundred [feet of altitude].

16:00:48   CA: Come on forward . . . forward, just barely climb.

16:00:59   CA: Stalling, we're falling!

16:01:00   F/O: Larry, we're going down, Larry. . . .

16:01:01   CA: I know it.

16:01:01   [Sound of impact]

The Air Florida captain wasn't really hearing his copilot's reservations about the takeoff speed, but a deeper issue troubled safety experts: the copilot, assessing the problem correctly, couldn't bring himself to overcome the ingrained deference to his superior and just grab the controls. The airline paradigm, after all, is military and hierarchical—that's why they're called "captains" and wear more stripes on their sleeves. And in military flying, where most senior airline pilots still come from, the chain of command is sacrosanct. Today there's much greater focus and training on how pilots work together and communicate in the cockpit. In the past, says an experienced Delta captain, "the first officer would watch [his captain] fly into a mountain before he would say something. Today he'll speak up quickly when he sees a deviation." But "that doesn't mean we take a vote" on how to fly, he quickly adds.

Communication lapses inside the cockpit can amplify subtle failures to communicate with ground controllers and accumulate to trigger disaster. Look no further than history's deadliest airline accident, when two fully loaded jumbo jets collided on a fog-shrouded runway in the Canary Islands in March 1977. A KLM flight taking off from one end of the runway hit the top of the Pan Am plane taxiing in the opposite direction. The senior KLM captain mistakenly assumed the Pan Am plane had already left the single runway and that his Boeing 747 had clearance to take off, even though members of his own flight crew were in doubt and initially questioned the captain's misunderstanding. Amid a cascade of other communication errors, the copilot, age 32, seemingly hesitated to repeatedly challenge his superior. The final words on the cockpit voice recorder came from the Pan Am captain staring into the onrushing lights of the KLM jumbo jet: "Goddamn, that son-of-a-bitch is coming straight at us!" Six seconds later came the KLM captain's reputed last words, a phrase not uncommonly heard on post-crash voice recorders: "Oh, shit." Pilots are now required to "read back" to controllers what they've been told to do, to confirm that they hear and understand the instructions. A simple acknowledgment won't do when dozens of planes are sharing the same radio frequencies near busy hubs at rush hour. Just answering "Roger" is mostly for Hollywood.

Sometimes in international flying, the communication problem is as basic as simple language comprehension. Take the 1993 crash of a US-made China Northern Airlines MD-80 in a fog at Urumqi in northwest China. About 10 seconds before impact, the Chinese pilots heard an audio alarm from the plane's ground proximity warning system indicating that the plane's landing approach was dangerously steep. The cockpit voice recorder picked up the pilot's last words in Chinese: "What does 'pull up' mean?" In 2008, English became the official (not just traditional) worldwide language of aviation—required of international pilots and controllers everywhere.

Fares, Fees, and Other Games

There's nothing "win-win" about airfares. For all the marketing hype, it's a zero-sum game. Either you pay more or the airline makes less. Call it market forces, but for the last 35 years there's been a simmering battle for revenue between bargain-hunting passengers and profit-seeking airlines. Flying is still a bargain, relatively speaking, but at the end of the decade after 9/11, the momentum in the tug of war showed signs of shifting. By fits and starts, the airlines were beginning to gain the upper hand.

After years of cheap and stable prices—average domestic fares actually *dropped* nearly 16 percent between 1995 and 2011, adjusted for inflation—the cost of flying has recently been climbing. According to government figures, fares rose 8.3 percent between 2009 and 2010, and another 8.3 percent between 2010 and 2011, unadjusted. In 2012, fares climbed another 4.2 percent. Hidden in the averages were double-digit percentage hikes for increasingly scarce seats on some popular routes, and international fares, spurred by fuel costs, were rising even faster. For the next 20 years, FAA predicts, fares will continue to rise. Based on rosy assumptions that vigorous competition and lower operating costs will keep fares down, though, the agency anticipates that these increases will slightly trail inflation. Still, fares are only part of what we pay for a flight—don't forget to add those annoying fees and surcharges.

Rising fares don't mean that flying is overpriced, though, in any relative terms. Flying round-trip from New York to London almost a half century ago, in June 1969, cost $400 in Economy and $750 in First Class on Pan American (no Business Class then)—the equivalent of $2,500 and $4,400 in today's dollars, even factoring in inflation. That's more than double today's economy fare (inflation-adjusted) and almost exactly what it costs today to travel between the two cities in Business Class—now with lie-flat bedlike seats that improve on old-style First Class. And as airlines like to remind us, in the entire decade from 2000 to 2010—albeit mostly before recent years' fare hikes—the price of the average domestic ticket *fell* a few dollars—from $339 to $336—while inflation climbed 27 percent.

Recently rising fares don't mean that airlines are getting rich, either. Lots of the new fortune has been going to oil companies. The 11 largest US airlines, members of the trade asociation Airlines for America, earned 12.6 percent more in 2011 than they did the year before, but they had to pay out 15.5 percent more in total operating expenses. That's no way to make a financial killing. And for all that the airlines profited when fuel prices dipped in 2010 and 2011, they lost three times that much earlier in the decade. Of 53 principal US industries ranked by *Fortune* in 2009, airlines were dead last in profitability, about the same place they'd held for years. Even in the recent "good years," airline profit margins have been nothing to write home about—just 2.2 percent in 2010 and a meager 0.3 percent in 2011, not much different for 2012, for the big US passenger carriers together. Excluding extraordinary losses by bankrupt American makes industry profit margins look better, but not that much better, still in the 2-to-3-percent range for 2011, marginally higher in 2012.

Still, US airlines haven't been losing money like they used to. Even kiss-your-sister profits easily beat than the fiscal disaster of the mid-2000s when all but one major airline went bankrupt, some repeatedly, and the industry dropped a cool $62 billion over the decade. Today's airlines expect to actually make money.

What triggered the turnaround, as much as anything, was finan-cial fear—almost desperation—over wildly soaring fuel prices, the air-lines' biggest single operating expense. Carriers left no stone unturned to cut everything else. Not just removing one olive from every First Class salad—American Airlines famously saved $40,000 that way in the 1980s—but hacking away at their labor forces; deferring replacing, sometimes even deferring cleaning, old airplanes; and cutting salaries. But they couldn't cut the price of jet fuel, which accounted for one-third of all their costs. As long as fuel expenses were out of control, so was the whole business. By the summer of 2008, rumors swirled on Wall Street that one, maybe two, of the largest US airlines could no longer get the financing needed to survive and might have to dissolve outright.

There was little left for the airlines to do but try to control the other side of their financial ledgers: revenues. Financial stability, even sur-vival, depended on more cash coming in. In concept, boosting reve-nues was simple: extract more money from passengers in fares, fees, and other new charges. What largely saved the major airlines, what let them finally secure the control over fares they had long sought, seems almost perverse. It was the industry's financial disaster that followed September 11. Scores of fare-cutting low-priced competitors were washed away in the tidal wave of red ink. Meanwhile, regulators sud-denly worried about the fate of the entire aviation sector grew more comfortable with mergers among the desperate survivors—even if the combinations left fewer, bigger airlines with more market power, and the risk of higher fares. When the dust cleared, only a handful of large-scale competitors remained—all traumatized by fuel prices, recession, and demand-depressing disasters—and all equally desperate to raise money and fares.

Bargain hunters could search Expedia to their hearts' content, but real "deals" on flights grew ever fewer. Even the Southwests and JetBlues—the perennial spoilers of airlines' attempts to raise industry fare levels—were feeling the fuel price pinch and grew more willing to go along with fare hikes. Most important, airlines in the United States—less so for still-distressed carriers in Europe and elsewhere—rediscovered the forgotten law of supply and demand. Rather than try to out-expand their rivals and battle to control city-to-city routes, they focused on extracting the most they could get for the product they put on the shelf. Expansion could wait.

As airlines learned to flex their muscles, fares rose and revenue grew. Fuel prices remained a dangerous threat, but increasingly less a truly existential one. When the price of Jet A (the kind of jet-fuel mixture used in the United States) soared again in 2010 and 2012, the airline industry didn't crater under massive losses as it had during the fuel spike of 2008. To the contrary, except for bankrupt American, major US airlines turned operating profits, or came close. A tougher, more focused airline industry had become a business that had learned to cope. Airlines were nothing close to money machines—they hardly covered the cost of invested capital, even over the short term—but Wall Street analysts stopped biting their nails every 90 days wondering who might not survive the next quarterly financial report.

That doesn't make fare-paying fliers happier, but for many, the unhappiness is about more than the upward glide-path of fares, or even the new irritant of pervasive fees. It's the whole context of the air-travel experience in which those irritants fit. Weird fares and novel "extras" feel like just another way of being jerked around, nickel-and-dimed, perceived as "marks" for airline schemes to lighten our wallets or give us less for more. As means of extracting passenger cash become ever more sophisticated, we *feel* taken, somehow victimized and manipulated, no matter how little or how much fare we really pay to fly.

The Black Art of Finding Your "Dammit" Price

Airline pricing rule number one: nobody is supposed to get a "deal." The goal is to make you pay your top dollar for your airline seat—the price that just hits, but doesn't exceed, your point of resistance. Call it the "dammit" price—as in, if the fare goes up just another few bucks, we're cramming the kids in the backseat, dammit, and *driving* the ten hours to Grandma's. Everyone's got a dammit price—the airfare we will pay unhappily, but still pay—and the airline's job is to find it. If you feel you actually got a good deal and would have paid an even higher fare if necessary, somebody in the airline's revenue management department probably screwed up.

Airlines have gotten really good at finding our dammit price. About two years ago, I'm ashamed to say, I did something hardly any experienced air traveler ever does—I actually paid full advertised retail fare for a domestic First Class ticket. The plane—a midweek hub-to-hub flight—was completely full. Of the 34 front-cabin passengers, I was one of only four who had actually coughed up the full $1,120 one-way fare for the transcontinental flight. (A helpful flight attendant confirmed it.) The rest of them, presumably more "loyal" to the airline than I, had been able to upgrade or were flying on corporate discounts negotiated by their high-volume businesses. To be honest, for the $721 full-coach walk-up fare, I could have taken the one remaining coach seat *way* in the back next to the lavatory, wedged for six hours in the middle between a mom with her "lap infant" and a guy who could have played pro linebacker, but I was tired, hungry, and had to work on the laptop to prepare for an important meeting. So I paid the extra $399 to sit up front. If it were $500 more, I would have just sucked it up and sat in back, but the airline had found precisely my breaking point. Almost creepy.

Getting the price right for every seat on every flight—hitting just enough "dammit" points to fill every seat on the plane at the highest *possible* fare—is an incredibly complex job. It all starts, though, with a simple notion that was once unthinkable and, until deregulation, practically illegal: an airline can charge different fares for identical seats on the same flight. At first it seemed counterintuitive to charge different prices for the same product depending on what sort of passenger was buying it—lower for the plan-ahead tourist or retiree with time to burn ("service-flexible" folks in airline jargon), higher for the $900-an-hour Wall Street lawyer who absolutely, positively has to catch the eight a.m. flight to Washington and could hardly care less what the price is. As it turns out, those willing to pay the "nobody-in-his-right-mind" full coach fare (or close to it for tickets bought only shortly before the flight) make up 8 to 10 percent of passengers, industry veterans estimate—airlines jealously guard the exact number—but they contribute one-third to half of all airline fare revenues. Naturally, these customers are the airlines' objects of deepest desire. (Another rough rule of thumb: about one-third of passengers contribute about two-thirds of the total revenue for a typical domestic flight, though that varies greatly by market and other factors.)

To make sure there's always a seat for them, airlines hang astronomical price tags on some of those last-minute seats. The challenge is predicting how many "price-is-no-object" fliers will show up at the check-in desk 30 minutes before final boarding frantically waving their corporate gold cards. Save too few seats and those high rollers are stranded at the gate watching the guys with the backpacks and backward-facing baseball caps fill the plane. Save too many, though, by keeping the fare too high, and you face an even worse fate: a seat that flies empty.

Here's why an empty seat is such a disaster: During June 2010 and again in June 2011, major US airlines filled an average of about 86.0 percent of their seats. They would have made a profit those months, not suffered a loss, if they had filled *one more seat* on each domestic flight (a typical 160-seat plane)—boosting the average load to 86.8 percent. Just that one more seat made the difference between the flight's profit and loss, according to an Oliver Wyman consulting report for investment firm Raymond James. There is nothing more valueless than an empty airborne seat; airlines call them "spoilage," just like rotten fruit.

Predicting precisely what fares will fill the plane while squeezing every last dollar for every seat has been the goal since the 1980s, but it took computing power a hundred times greater than available only a decade ago to hone the process known as "revenue management" to a fine art—sometimes known in the industry as "the black art." It was worth the investment. Sophisticated fare management can grow airline revenues up to 7 percent, says a global airline consultant—more than most airlines' entire profit margins. Oversimplified, here's how the alchemy works:

Some 330 days before your flight, most airlines allocate all the seats on your plane into different so-called "fare buckets," a dozen or so buckets in Economy Class alone. Each bucket reflects the class of service (First, Business, Economy), price, ticket restrictions (whether the ticket is refundable, upgradeable, changeable), and advance-purchase requirements. The cheapest Economy bucket holds the tickets that require the most hassle to use—you have to buy them three weeks in advance, you get no refunds if you miss the flight (yes, even if Granny dies), you leave at six a.m. on Sunday, make a connection or two, and land at the least convenient airport, all while risking a change fee larger than the price of your ticket.

For the airline, that extra hassle serves an important purpose: it keeps folks who are willing to pay a little more for a little more convenience from buying those lowest-bucket tickets. The airline wants these cheapest tickets to go *only* to the most penny-pinching travelers—tourists who can't afford $499 to get to Disney World, but who can and will jump through any hoop, buy months in advance, and stay over the weekend, to fly there for $99. These least expensive tickets make little, if any, profit for the airline, but it's better than flying an empty seat and earning nothing for it. There's also a good chance these infrequent fliers will pay extra fees for checked bags and snack packs. Plus, these cheap fares let the airline advertise ultralow "starting at" fares. ("Take the kids to the Magic Kingdom—"starting at" $99! Restrictions apply.)

Everyone would like to nab the superlow $99 tourist fare, but it's the last thing the airline wants to sell the business traveler, the sales exec who will readily (if not too happily) pay $149, maybe even $399, to get to the can't-miss business meeting in downtown Orlando. To make the suit pay more, the airline erects "fences" around the cheap $99 fare buckets. Business travelers are welcome to buy these cheap tickets—as long as they, too, pay weeks in advance, forgo refunds if their schedules change, and, as used to be more common, commit to spending Saturday night in Orlando instead of at home watching the kids play soccer. What weary road warrior wants to scale those fences?

Once early buying leisure purchasers drain the $99 "bucket," it's closed (though it could later reopen, as noted below). For the next purchaser, the only seats left are in the next-highest fare bucket, with a price tag of $149. As weeks and months go by, buckets of cheaper tickets close, and the only seats left for sale are in the still-open higher-fare buckets. Just a day or two before takeoff, if the process worked right, only a handful of open seats are left on the plane, and they all carry a hefty price premium. These are the seats that are effectively being held for same-day walk-up business travelers who, the computers predict, will show up and pay whatever it takes. Their extra cash buys no more legroom or comfort; it just compensates the airline for "saving" that $399 seat until the last minute instead of selling it last month for $99 or last week for $249—in other words, for taking the risk that seat might never be sold and fly empty, worthless to the airline.

What's amazing is how little is really left to guesswork by the airline. Predicting the precise number of expected last-minute purchasers is a science based on vast stores of historical sales information for similar flights. Crunched by high-speed computers using MIT-developed algorithms, that data is updated 24/7 as every new ticket is sold. The result is extremely—annoyingly—accurate in predicting just how much passengers are likely to be willing to shell out for each seat on each of thousands of flights.

It wasn't always so sophisticated. Revenue management started as simple overbooking. Airlines sold more seats than the plane held because they knew there would be no-shows—even though predicting how *many* likely no-shows was more art than science before the mid-to-late-1980s. Nearly all airlines still "oversell" their domestic flights—5 to 10 percent is common—but some inexpensive "impulse" flights (think $60 midweek jaunts from L.A. to Vegas) reputedly can be oversold by as much as 45 percent. Much depends on the airport, flight time, day of the week, and cost—there are supposedly fewer no-shows among polite Midwesterners than hard-charging Manhattanites—but overbooking predictions have proven amazingly accurate. US airlines leave only about 12 of every 10,000 ticketed passengers at the gate, and more than 90 percent of *those* folks volunteer to give up their seats in return for compensation. (If the airline has to "involuntarily" bump, the passenger is entitled to a sizable payment from the airline, depending on how long she is delayed and the cost of the ticket.) That still means nearly 200 ticketed and bumped passengers on average will have a very bad travel day, but that's out of more than 1.6 *million* daily fliers in the United States.

Simple overbooking worked well enough when every seat carried the same price tag and the goal was just to fill as many seats as possible. Today's more ambitious goal—to earn the most from each and every seat on the plane—depends on supercomputers overseen by cadres of well-educated twentysomethings hidden away in cavernous rooms deep in airline headquarters—"revenue management analysts," often hired out of business school and paid in the high five figures to manage seat "inventory" on thousands of flights. In row upon row of six-by-eight cubicles, they stare at double-wide computer displays that show for each flight the dozen-plus fare buckets and monitor how each flight is selling nearly "in real time." The essence of what the inventory analyst handling next Thursday's early morning flight from Tulsa to Denver sees on her screen boils down to a series of alphanumeric symbols (they differ somewhat by airline), something like this:

F2, Y9, B7, M4, Q3, T0

Translation: There are still at least 25 unsold seats on the 160-seat Boeing 737, spread among six fare buckets. Two of them are pricey First Class seats ("F2"). The airline will try to sell them rather than give them away as upgrades to "elite" frequent fliers, so it may well hold them for sale in the "F" fare bucket until the very day of the flight, hoping someone will pay top dollar.

The rest of the open seats are all physically identical, in Economy, but carry wildly different price tags. There are at least nine seats that remain in the most expensive, "full-fare" "Y" bucket and they cost five times the identical coach seats in the super-discount "T" bucket—which plan-ahead vacationers willing to forgo refunds eagerly emptied weeks ago. Why not put some of those slow-selling "Y" seats in a less-expensive bucket to make sure they sell? The airline is betting that *some* business travelers will have to get to Denver at the last minute, price be damned, and will pay the "full Y" fare. Fare buckets for B, M, and Q fares hold tickets whose restrictions vary inversely with their price.

As noted, history tells the analyst how the flight "should" be selling. The computer knows just how the same or similar flight sold out yesterday, a month ago, a year ago, even years in the past, but that's just the start. It also knows how many days before the flight each fare bucket emptied, the price, class of service, whether it was sold online or through an agent, whether the purchaser was a frequent flier, and how many seats then remained. Meanwhile, the airline computers are keeping up with new purchases in real time—updating and recalibrating whenever anyone anywhere buys or cancels a ticket or makes a reservation, fine-tuning predictions for the same flight tomorrow or next week or next month. Staring at her screen, the analyst knows just how many seats at each fare level *should* be left to sell two weeks before takeoff; how many discount, advance-purchase coach seats *should* "normally" be left on an early morning flight between Tulsa and Denver on a Thursday in the third week of July; and just how many no-shows and frequent-flier award ticket passengers to expect.

If *actual* real-world sales ("booked loads" in analysts' lexicon) aren't up to what the computer predicts they should be—based on the history of that flight or similarly timed ones for that day, week, or season—the analyst can make adjustments. To juice up sales, for instance, she might move four of the eight pricey "Y" fare seats into the cheaper "M" fare bucket, or even reopen long-closed buckets of deeper-discount tickets. Real-world events can change the equation too, boosting or dampening demand. Shoe-bomb threats and reports of airborne pandemics are bad for business—and may force analysts to open more discount buckets to fill planes. Conversely, human analysts, but not the airline inventory computer system, know that on certain Saturdays in the fall, the demand for seats to South Bend Indiana (by Notre Dame football fans) will suddenly surge. And airline revenue managers are rumored to stand ready at the end of the NFL season to rush to close the low-fare buckets for flights between the two Super Bowl cities as soon as the whistle ends the conference playoff games that decide who's playing in it.

Buy Now!

It's not just the bucket magic that makes fares maddening. Walk across the hall from the revenue managers to the airline pricing department, where more geeks in more cubicles stare at more computers to decide basic fare levels—the price tags that get slapped on each fare bucket. Should the cheapest discount fare on your flight be $99, $199, or $599? They (and their computers) make lots of these decisions every day. Worldwide, estimates are there more than 100 million airfares and fare combinations at any given time, and hundreds of thousands of daily fare changes.

Two facts especially drive the airfare roller coaster. The first is that every airline knows almost instantly, to the penny, what every competing airline is charging for every kind of ticket on every route, and what those fares will be in the next few hours. An airline-owned electronic clearinghouse known as ATPCo (Airline Tariff Publishing Company) publishes everybody's up-to-the-minute fares to all the other airlines and online fare systems four times every weekday and once every weekend day for domestic flights, almost every hour for international fares. That means fares may stay on the market for as little as three hours for domestic tickets and just one hour for international ones.

The second key fact is that no airline can bear to have its fares "out of line" with the competition for long; travelers buy tickets—and choose airlines—based, first and foremost, on what's cheapest. Fliers may *say* they'll pay more for better service, but they vote with their wallets, airlines lament. Charge just $1 less than your competition on the same route and your airline "ranks" higher on the online travel agency fare display that's scoured by thousands of consumers hunting for the very lowest advertised fare. And a few dollars cheaper can make a difference. Two of the industry's highest-margin players—bare-bones Spirit and Ryanair—offer little but low, low base fares, and that may be enough. There's an old industry saying: "If you could save people five bucks, you could strap them to the wing." (Don't laugh—an enterprising Italian firm has designed a kind of half-standing airline seat separated only 23 inches from the seat ahead, eight crucial inches less than normal, and a European airline actually suggested "standing room" travel for short flights.)

Combine these two facts of fare setting and you get a never-ending game of speed chess. Take a seat at the computer screen. The flashing hieroglyphs warn that, overnight, your competitor cut its fares on one of your key routes, but only for advance-purchase tickets usually sold to leisure travelers. Should you match that cut to keep bargain-hunting passengers on your planes, or just ignore it, or maybe even "up the ante" by slashing your own fares even further, or broaden the fare sale to include the more expensive fares normally purchased by same-day business travelers? Heck, you could even "double down" and launch your own fare sale on other competing routes. Or let's say your rival *raises* its fares. You may want to go along with the increase in hopes other airlines will follow suit and make the fare increase "stick." But if others balk—traditionally Southwest or other low-cost airlines—everyone has to abandon the fare hike to stay competitive. Back to square one.

There's a lot to consider and not much time to decide. Delay matching a competitor's fare sale and he gets valuable extra time to offer the lowest fare in the market and steal your passengers. Timing is also key to raising fares. Hiking ticket prices on a Thursday night lets an airline hedge its bets, testing to see if competitors will follow. If they don't, the airline can back down without losing much business since hardly anyone buys tickets over the weekend when the fare hike will mainly take effect. If other airlines don't match your fare hike, you can quietly rescind it Sunday evening before fliers boot up their office desktops on Monday morning. For front-line pricing analysts, the fare game can be a rush—a demanding daily diet of strategy, transmission-and-response, moves and countermoves.

Sometimes it gets to be *too* much. Despite the impressive technology and arcane mathematics, maybe a dozen times a year there are fare mistakes that generate amazing short-lived fare bargains. These "fat-finger fares" are typically the result of human error. Somebody makes a typo in a fare transmission. A coder misplaces a decimal point, generating a €5 transatlantic fare. A programmer enters "40" instead of "41" in a key coding field, suddenly slashing Los Angeles–Fiji fares to $51, or San Jose–Paris tickets to $28. (No wonder that airlines tend to avoid using the letters *o* and *i* in their fare codes—they're too easily confused with the numbers "0" and "1.") A manager forgets to add a fuel surcharge and hundreds of domestic flights suddenly cost $130 less. Or, as occurred in July 2012, United Airlines gives away First Class round-trip US–Hong Kong seats in exchange for $43 and *four* frequent-flier miles, instead of the usual $11,000.

Airlines sometimes honor an "amazing" mistake deal if it was purchased in good faith—but usually only if it's not *too* amazing. Some use a kind of "too-good-to-be-true" test. Not that they're so worried about a few ultracheap tickets, but rather because of the potential massive revenue impact when the mistake hits Facebook and several other websites dedicated—believe it or not—to finding "mistake" fares, for a subscription fee.

Pity, though, the poor air traveler trying to score a bargain, or at least a well-priced ticket, under less unusual circumstances. Having finally found one, he hits "Select" or "Add to Cart" and by the time he hits "Purchase" ten minutes later, his fare bucket is empty or fare levels have risen, his low fare replaced by a higher one. It could all get more frustrating if, as predicted, the whole fare-setting system goes 24/7—an unending process where fares change continuously, anytime, any day, not just at defined clearinghouse deadlines. Surfing the web for cheap fares for Thanksgiving? Better have fast fingers.

Parsing the Fare Code

The mysteries don't end when you do "Buy Now." Your ticket (or e-ticket receipt) is laden with hidden meaning—especially the strange alphanumeric code, the half dozen characters near your name. This is what tells the airline's entire staff just how much you are "worth" to the carrier in revenue. Not surprisingly, it has a lot to do with the way you're treated and the service you get. Think of that code as a tattoo that follows you throughout your journey, advertising to everyone—from gate agent to flight attendant to rebooking agent (if the flight gets cancelled) to the folks in the lost-bag office—just where you stand in the airline's pecking order. Whether you paid big money to sit up front, or merely snagged a mileage upgrade, whether you're likely a once-a-year bargain flier, or a "regular" full-fare business traveler. Don't you think they sneak a peek at your fare code when there's a complaint or special request for a bulkhead or exit-row seat, or when a flight is cancelled and you need to be "reaccommodated" swiftly on another flight?

In First Class, your "status" may show up on the passenger manifest, a printout that lists passengers' names. The airline's ground staff hands it to the cabin crew just before the door closes for departure, and it's typically taped up in the galley on longer flights. On some carriers, the list shows where everybody rates in airline priority—which precious few passengers actually paid the full fare (it says "FULL" next to their names) as well as the "eliteness" level of front-end fliers, paying or not. British Airways has gone one better—senior flight attendants in its customer "Know Me" program now get an iPad that instantly identifies the "high-value" passengers on board. In First Class, your priority on the manifest determines who gets to choose their dinner entrée first and, maybe, whether the nice flight attendant will cadge a few extra scotch whiskey miniatures for you to take with you. Full-fare fliers definitely get the steak, but expect the lasagna if you're a non-elite award upgrade.

Booking codes aren't exactly secret (they differ from airline to airline and change a little from year to year) but neither are they designed to be understood by mere mortals. Most of the letters and numbers indicate ticket restrictions—is it refundable, changeable, how long in advance you had to buy it, how long you must be willing to stay over at the destination to qualify for the fare, if it's good for "high season" or only on weekends or slower travel days. A domestic fare basis code that reads QL7NR, for example, is a moderately discounted coach fare (Q) good only on certain days of the week (L) with a seven-day advance booking requirement (7), and the ticket is not refundable (NR) if you don't use it.

The first letter of your code is most important, as it shows your fare class. Take a deep breath and try to follow: First Class should be "F," but it isn't always. "*Full Fare* First" is, but discount First is "A," and some all-business flights are "P." Actually, the most impressive codes start with "R," a designation once reserved for supersonic fliers on the now-retired Concorde, currently used for the ultradeluxe First Class "suites" on some international superjumbos.

Business Class might logically be "B," but it isn't. For some reason its often "C" (sometimes "J"). Full-fare business is relatively uncommon. It's for the senior executives who need to comply with their company's "no-first-class" expense rules, but are happy to pay top dollar for a Business Class seat that might get upgraded to First Class. Actual business fliers can usually get much cheaper discounted Business Class fares (often "Z").

The real opacity is behind the curtain in Economy Class, with its myriad levels of relative misery. The top end is the venerable "Y" fare—the fully refundable, always upgradeable fare normally purchased almost exclusively by the truly desperate, by wealthy foreign tourists with clueless travel agents, or by those trying to game an easier upgrade. Fewer than 10 percent of fliers buy "full Y." (The less-known "Y-UP" fare buys a First Class seat for close to the "full coach" price, but the "Y" in the fare code sometimes fools corporate travel bean counters who won't pay for First Class into thinking you're in Economy.) Below Y are nearly a dozen Economy Class fare codes—like "B" or "M" (airlines differ)—that carry ever more restrictions, but still cost enough to qualify as "standard" fares that can be upgraded. Much less expensive and much more restrictive are "Q" and "V" and "W" fares (some carriers use "L" and "K")—no change or cancellation without a hefty penalty, and a long advance purchase requirement. Lower still are the "You-want-to-pay-*what*?" fare classes like "S," "T," and sometimes "K"—ultracheap tickets (occasionally, forgotten remnants of past fare sales), sometimes called "junk fares," that can carry almost punitive restrictions. No refunds, no changes, no upgrades, no frequent-flier miles, no online assigned seat. Just "use it or lose it." And good news for taxpayers: the federal government uses its buying clout annually to negotiate super-cheap fares for federal official travel—feds pay at most $105 to fly from downtown Washington to New York's LaGuardia, for instance, while same-day retail costs the general public more than $400.

/ / /

All the complexity, the bucket magic, and the gaming can drive ordinary fliers a little batty looking for the best deal, and not without reason. According to MIT mathematician Carl de Marcken, finding the cheapest airfare between two cities is, in fact, an unsolvable mystery. A software genius who went on to start a major aviation software firm, de Marcken calculated in a 2003 academic paper that there could be 25,401,415 possible fare combinations for a passenger flying round-trip between Boston and San Francisco on American Airlines over a three-day period. Even using the world's most powerful computers, the scientist found, it is theoretically impossible to answer the simple question: "What is the lowest fare between city A and city B?"

Can you blame the hapless flier for his frustration? Even if average fares are a screaming bargain, we expect them to reflect, at least vaguely, some objective measure of value—like the distance of the flight, or what we paid last year, or what it costs to take the train. How can it be cheaper to fly from New York to Boston via London, England, than to fly direct between the two East Coast cities? It's a scenario that Stanford mathematician Keith Devlin says actually occurred.

The Resistance

Griping about airfares is nothing new. Twenty years ago, the iconic head of American Airlines, Robert Crandall, found "the whole fare system [had] become chaotic, inflexible, illogical, and unfair." By the opening of the new millennium, that view was ever more widely shared. A prisoners' revolt was brewing. The trigger for many, especially business travelers, were the hated "fare fences." These mendacious obstacles seemed erected for the sole purpose of depriving road warriors of the cheap fares that were intended exclusively for what airlines unlovingly call "the VFR market"—for "visiting friends and relatives." In the bizarre world of revenue management, fences were there to make sure that, to get the good fare, you had to suffer.

Plenty of business fliers saw fare fences as naked coercion, with no independent rationale or cost justification. After all, what more does it cost the airline to return the business traveler home on Saturday afternoon rather than on Sunday morning, or, for that matter, to refund an unused ticket for a seat that another passenger will almost certainly purchase to board an otherwise booked-solid flight? What's the "real-world" reason for fares to double or triple if the ticket is bought 13 days, rather than 15 days, in advance, and what immutable law of commerce decrees "nonrefundability"? Just because an airline *declares* a ticket nonrefundable, it doesn't make that edict sensible or fair or reasonable.

True, revenue-management fences are hardly unique to airlines. Restaurants offer an "Early Bird Special," but only if you're willing to eat it at five p.m. Your $89 motel room in Washington, DC, suddenly jumps to $299 the week the cherry blossoms pop. But those price discriminations somehow seemed more predictable and understandable, their rationale more obviously grounded in the "real world." Then there was air travelers' uncomfortable sense of constantly being managed and manipulated for maximum profit. Road warriors were ready to shoot themselves rather than face another "Saturday-night stay" weekend at the airport motel. For angry air travelers, fare fences were another reminder that the money-grubbing airline just wasn't going to give them a break.

To the amazement (and horror) of much of the industry, some of the airlines' best business customers started to balk. As dot-com boom became dot-com bust, they began to say no to Business Class, no to fare fences, no to "full" fares five times the cost of an advance purchase discount ticket. Even before the 9/11 attacks, the first quarter of 2001 witnessed a startling decline in the percentage of First Class and full-fare Economy tickets sold. The month before the 9/11 attack, fare yields had already plummeted 12.5 percent from year-before levels and revenue from the kinds of fares normally purchased by business travelers was down nearly a third. Forced by recession to downgrade, the road warriors' new normal became "Premium Economy"—still a coach service, but a step up from steerage. As businesses flew less and flew cheaper, airline revenues tumbled.

The Big Mistake

If the recession of 2001 helped trigger the passenger rebellion, the Internet changed the whole passenger-carrier dynamic. It didn't entirely level the field in the hunt for commercial advantage, but it gave passengers a potent weapon against the power of the airlines' sophisticated revenue-management systems. Any would-be flier with a smart phone could go online to readily identify and compare travel options and make spending choices strategically. Southwest Airlines founder Herb Kelleher summarized it this way, as recounted in an article by noted aviation writer and journalist James Fallows: "Once it became painfully obvious, thanks to the Web, that there were $1000 seats and $150 seats in the same market, on the same planes, at the same time, business travelers wouldn't accept it anymore. The high-fare, last-minute, walk-up business customers—that person is gone forever." Even more succinctly, for folks in the airline revenue departments, the Internet was bad news.

The Internet's effect on ticket distribution costs was dramatic. The airlines' cost of selling an average ticket plummeted from $45.93 in 1999 using a traditional travel agent—and paying them the traditional 10 percent ticket commission—to only $25.12 for selling the same ticket online, using an Internet travel agent like Expedia, according to a GAO study. Selling a ticket on an airline's own website was even cheaper—$11.75 by the end of 2002—when nearly a third of all tickets were being booked online. With half the US population using the Internet by then, the industry took the final step and eliminated traditional per-ticket sales commissions entirely. For airlines tired of legions of commission-hungry travel agents, it seemed like a cost-saving coup—but it soon became a classic case of "be careful what you wish for."

The Internet created user-friendly shopping malls for air travel—online travel sites like Expedia and Travelocity in 1996 and the airline-owned Orbitz in 2001 that collected and compared available fares from most airlines, making comparison shopping easy. Everyone was his own travel agent. "Screen-scraper" sites made it easier still, collecting the cheapest of the cheap from across the digital universe. Consumers learned not only how to comparison-shop for fares, but now they could evaluate money-saving tradeoffs, too. How much extra was it really worth to fly Thursday if you could fly Saturday at half the price? Click the mouse. Is there a better deal if you take the earlier flight or a connecting flight or drive to another airport where competition from Southwest keeps fares down? Click the mouse. Where only 1 percent of Americans used the Internet in 1991, nearly 50 percent did just a decade later, as online ticketing got easier and faster. A few keystrokes told fliers—*and* their company budget expense hawks—how they could save by sucking up a little travel inconvenience.

This was not good for an industry banking on "managing" customer ticket choices to maximize revenue. Consider the Chicago road warrior with an unpredictable schedule of sales calls, the kind of flier dear to the airlines' heart. He's habituated to buying high-priced same-day tickets on his hub airline, hoards his frequent-flier miles, and occasionally gets a freebie upgrade from his full-fare coach ticket. As long as his ticket says "Y"—signifying Economy Class—his company doesn't ask questions. The Internet changes the picture, though. Now his company expense monitors can easily see just how much the company is spending—and how much it could *save*—on the latest sales trip to L.A. If our warrior switches planes in Denver, his $837 walk-up "Y" fare drops to $500; if he could only plan ahead a couple of weeks, the flight would cost only $279. And if he drives to Milwaukee to catch a low-cost airline, it's only $189. Suddenly, the warrior isn't getting the upgrade, the airline's not getting the $837, and videoconferencing sounds like a great idea.

Scores of websites devoted themselves to outstrategizing the airlines, and "experts" touted the "secrets" of getting deals (hint: fly on less-busy days, use more competitive airports, book early, and be nice to the gate agent). Airfare guru Rick Seaney of FareCompare.com, founded in 2004, even pinpointed the exact best *hour* to buy your ticket: Tuesday at three p.m. Eastern Daylight Time. (His theory: carriers tend to launch sales Monday night, the week's busiest night for online bookings; competitors' first practicable chance to match those sales is Tuesday morning's uploading of fares to the industry's electronic clearinghouse; and those lower fares take a few hours to filter through the system to online booking sites.) And how far in advance to buy? An Airlines Reporting Corporation study of more than a hundred million domestic ticket transactions, released in 2012, found the cheapest fares available six weeks before the flight—they were 5.8 percent cheaper than average.

Googling "how to get cheap flights" generates more than 150 *million* hits—an array of chat rooms, websites, and online "communities" dedicated to beating the airlines at their own game—when to buy, where to sit, what fare buckets are still open, what seat inventory is available, the chance of an upgrade. The Internet also helped with "creative" ways to leap or evade fare fences such as the old Saturday-night-stay requirement. A favorite tactic in the 1990s was so-called "back-to-back" ticketing: Buy two separate, highly discounted round-trip tickets (one starting from your home and one starting from your destination), both with Saturday-night stays, and simply discard the return portion of each ticket. The combined cost of the two restricted tickets was often far less than a full-fare ticket that did not require the weekend stay. (Competitive pressure has since killed the Saturday-night-stay penalty in all but a few markets.) "Hidden-city ticketing" is still a popular beat-the-system tactic that airlines condemn. An example: airlines may charge much more for a nonstop flight from New York to Chicago, a high-demand business route, than for a flight from New York to Denver that connects *through* Chicago, where passengers change planes. How hard is it for a smart New Yorker with a meeting in Chicago to simply buy the cheaper ticket all the way to Denver and hop off the plane at O'Hare?

Outraged airlines cried foul, threatening to sue or confiscate the frequent-flier miles of "wrongdoers." American claimed the misdeeds "could be construed [as] common law fraud" and others insisted the stratagems were illegal or, at a minimum, violated the "contract" between airline and customer. Fliers must "agree to" this "contract of carriage"—typically dozens of pages of legalese drafted by the airline's lawyers—before they can buy a ticket online.

A simpler and less risky form of customer resistance was just to switch to different airlines, especially low-cost carriers, with fewer hocus-pocus fares and convoluted ticket restrictions. It wasn't that the low-cost competitors managed their seat inventories less carefully than traditional carriers; they just did it in a more intuitive, consumer-friendly, and less obviously manipulative way. Southwest, for instance, markets just three categories of fares—refundable, nonrefundable, and "wanna get away" discount fares (it actually uses multiple fare buckets, but customers see just the three fare labels) and erects no round-trip or "stay-over" fences or added bag fees. From 2000 to 2010, these low-cost airlines more than doubled their national market share. Today they carry one-third of all US passengers, control about 30 percent of the domestic travel market (up from 10 percent in 1999), and serve about 460 out of the 500 largest routes. And you can find plenty of nice brief-cases on Southwest, JetBlue, and their low-cost cohorts.

The Empire Strikes Back

The industry's annus horribilis in 2008 brought the low-energy conflict to a boil, as frightening fuel prices and a historic recession amplified the intense financial pressure on the industry. Airlines needed more than just new ideas for putting fliers in more expensive seats; they needed a whole new business model that didn't depend solely on basic airfares.

Their response, as we've seen, was nothing less audacious than a whole-sale redefinition of what you got for the price of your ticket. In this new universe, paying just the basic fare normally gets you to your destina-tion, but not without some extra inconvenience, discomfort, or stress. To avoid that, you had to pay extra.

Sure, it was a sharp break from decades-old flier expectations, but this shrewd redefinition—once passengers bought it—may well have saved the airline industry as we know it. The two most important fees are for checked bags and for "changing" a ticket—changing the time or date or routing, or even just the passenger's name (mercifully, truly minor misspellings are generally, but not always, allowed). The two cat-egories of charges added nearly $6 billion to US airline revenues in 2010, twice what they had just two years earlier. The next year, ancillary fees worldwide climbed to $22.6 billion. Carriers like Spirit were collecting on average more than $100 in add-ons from each round-trip passenger; fees constituted a full third of all its revenue.

Fees quickly became a deadly serious business, starting with what air-line consultant IdeaWorks calls "the Holy Grail of revenue treasure"—checked-bag fees. American led the pack in 2008, charging a mere $15 to check the passenger's first bag. (Other airlines had previously charged for checking additional bags beyond the first one.) In retrospect, that was a screaming bargain. At the extreme, United collected a cool $400 to check a single "overweight" suitcase (defined as more than 70 pounds) on a long overseas flight in 2012 and American charged $450 for flying that bag to Asia. But even at $25 for the first checked bag each way, tak-ing the family—and four bags—to visit Grandma means paying nearly as much for bags as for one of the tickets.

How could there not be a big profit in bag fees? It's hard to calcu-late precisely what it costs our airline to haul an individual bag, but bear with an oversimplified back-of-the-envelope stab at it. Boeing estimates (in its "767 Fun Facts") that a loaded 767-400ER flying from New York to London burns about 45 gallons per passenger. Since the "standard" passenger weighs 190 pounds (five pounds more with winter clothing), a 71-pound suitcase—about 40 percent of that passenger's weight—should burn about 18 gallons to haul across the Atlantic. At $3 per gallon of fuel, that's $54. Even if we double that to account for the cost of extra labor and handling our extra-heavy suitcase, the airline is out something close to $100 to fly that bag to London. But it's charging twice that amount—$200 is the going rate in 2013 on such bags for the big carriers—for a markup of nearly 100 percent! (Even assuming these cost numbers are off a bit—airlines don't advertise internal cost figures, and fees change—you get the drift.)

Bag-fee profitability looks much the same on shorter, more typical, domestic flights, where big carriers mostly charged $25 to check your first standard bag in 2012 ($35 for the second one). A *Wall Street Journal* analysis in late 2008, albeit when fuel prices had dropped to around $2 a gallon, found that an airline's "all-in" cost to fly that suitcase on an average three-hour domestic flight was only about $15, mostly for labor. Even accounting for today's 50 percent higher fuel prices, hauling bags is plainly one heck of a good business for the industry.

Airlines accordingly take "enforcement" of bag-checking seriously. It even triggered a mini-riot in the Canary Islands in February 2011, when Ryanair bag police stationed at the aircraft door tried to extract an extra $47.50 "oversized gate bag fee" from a Belgian student boarding Flight 8175 home from vacation. The ensuing show of mass passenger resistance led Spanish police to bar 100 of the 168 "disruptive" passengers from flying. No more winking at the check-in agent as you try to carry on your mini-refrigerator.

Besides bag fees (and the slightly hoarier fuel "surcharge" we'll get to in a moment), the next most lucrative—and annoying—charge is the so-called change fee. There's nothing new about the concept of discounting fares for purchasers willing to take the risk they won't make the flight, but the sheer extent of today's fees for rebooking or changing a reservation, and the rapid escalation in the size of the penalties in recent

years—change fees now net airlines six times what they did in 1999—
have made these the ultimate "gotchas" for air travelers with uncertain
schedules. Beyond the mystery of how a few keystrokes by the reservations agent to change your ticket merits a payment of $150 (domestic),
or $250 (international), the penalties have become large enough that
many unused short-haul tickets are rendered practically worthless once
the change fee is offset. On the other hand, there's a logic behind these
fees. If you cancel your flight, the airline legitimately doesn't want to
be stuck holding an empty seat that loses all value when the plane takes
off, or for passengers holding seats to "shop around" for a cheaper fare
while simultaneously keeping the airline from "finally" selling the seat.
Fair enough, but how many empty, unsold seats have you seen lately?

Airlines will gladly sell you a way around the change fee, of course—
it's called a "fully refundable" ticket, and it can cost three to five times
the price of a discount coach ticket. If you risk it and don't pay the extra,
say some carriers, don't go whining for a refund if you can't make the
flight. Vietnam veteran Jerry Meekins, age 76, tried that, initially to no
avail, in April 2012, when doctors told him his esophageal cancer was
too far advanced for him to use his $197 Spirit Airways ticket to visit his
daughter. The airline's initial response was—not to put too fine a point
on it—cold: "We don't do refunds," declared the airline's spokesman. A
week or so later, under threat of mass boycotts by outraged veterans and
others, the airline relented.

The industry's embrace of fees is understandable. In several ways,
money from fees is better than money from raising airfares. Fees don't
affect competition as much as base airfares; they're largely insulated
from competition. When airlines compete for passengers, it's mainly
over basic fares—passengers compare fare "sales" on Expedia or Orbitz or in the morning paper. Fare wars drive prices down, at least until
a victor emerges to raise them again. But fees are different. Very few
airlines compete vigorously on how much to charge to check a suitcase
or change a reservation; with rare exceptions, traditional airlines all

charge about the same. As Spirit's CEO happily observed in a 2012 interview with FlightGlobal.com: "There [are] no bag fee war[s]." Plus, fees for checked bags, early boarding, seat selection, telephone reservations, and food, for instance, aren't subject to the 7.5 percent federal excise tax on basic airfares. If bag fees were taxed, says GAO, it would generate near a quarter-billion dollars in tax receipts.

The new fee-for-all regime did more than unplug a rich new stream of cash for the airlines, though. In the ongoing tug-of-war with bargain-hunting passengers, nonnegotiable fees were almost an antidote to the passenger-empowering Internet. In effect, the new regime helped muddy the fare waters that the Internet had made dangerously transparent for consumers. Fliers could knock themselves out comparison-shopping on Orbitz, but until recently, hefty fees and surcharges—up to a third of the base fare on some tickets—were largely unseen by purchasers until late in the transaction process, and the panoply of extras and add-ons made it tougher to compare the full cost of their journeys, apples-to-apples.

Say you searched online for a flight from JFK to Paris at the start of 2012. American charged $870 in Economy, almost double the fare advertised by Air France. Who wouldn't jump at the cheaper Air France ticket? But go to the "checkout" screen and look closer—the fare Air France showed on the first screen didn't include a mandatory $400 fuel surcharge! Add back in the $400, and the "real" price for the Air France flight was (you guessed it) $870, just like American's. Since then, a new regulation requires airline advertising to show shoppers the full cost of the flight, including mandatory surcharges. Then there are all those other extras and fees to consider. In the end, who knows which airline will really get you to Paris cheaper? And that's the point.

Perhaps the toughest hurdle to establishing the new fee-based business model was getting fliers to accept it. The airlines' world-class spin-meisters went to work, producing some focus-grouped classics. United's explanation for eliminating meals in Economy Class in August 2008,

even on long transatlantic flights? "We need to tailor products and services to what customers value and provide them more choice" as well
as "test new options." Like hunger. Or the airline trade association's
explanation for checked-bag fees: "Airlines [were] offering customers
the option to pay for services they value"—little extras like not having
to cram a vacation week's worth of sneakers, sun dresses, baby toys, and
snorkeling gear into an overnight bag.

In this line of thinking, new fees weren't really quite new fees at all—
just payment for new *services*. OK, maybe not exactly *new* services, but
services airlines *could* have charged for separately before if they had
just thought of it or wanted to. Then there was the appeal to our baser
selves: Why should *you* pay for that slob in the next seat to check his bag
when *you* managed to cram your own overstuffed roll-aboard into the
overhead bin? Finally, there was the simple beg: airlines have lost piles
of money, so they "needed" the extra fee revenue.

At first, the new fee approach sparked remarkably little consumer
blowback—partly because the new fees started small, and partly because
they were introduced gradually as the waters of public outrage were
tested. When British Airways initiated its first fuel surcharge in May
2004, it was just $4 a flight. Competitors condemned it then as "goug-
ing" and "counterproductive" but failed to rile consumers—maybe
because fliers faced the same soaring gasoline prices while filling their
cars and empathized with the embattled carrier's need for a small and
"temporary" add-on.

But seven years after this first modest fuel surcharge, British Airways was slapping a whopping $420 extra charge on longer transat-
lantic round-trips; US airlines followed suit. By then, even the concept
of "surcharge" had undergone Orwellian revision. No longer was it an
amount added to the usual charge to defray the *extra* burden of a sudden
uptick in airline fuel costs; "surcharges" were paying for virtually *all* the
fuel burned on a flight. There was little "sur-" about them. An October
2008, analysis of Boeing data in London's *Daily Telegraph* showed that

surcharges paid for 95 percent of all the fuel on a British Airways New York–London 777 flight. The total surcharge to be collected from passengers was just over £19,000; the total fueling cost for the flight—just over £20,000.

In fact, the surcharge might pay for even *more* than the cost of fuel as fuel prices dropped. Defying gravity, fuel surcharges almost never come down as fast as the market price of oil they're supposed to offset. To the contrary: between April 2011 and May 2012, airline fuel surcharges rose twice as fast as oil prices themselves, according to a study by Carlson Wagonlit, a corporate travel manager, reported in the *Los Angeles Times*. DOT warned airlines in 2012 that fuel surcharges "must accurately reflect the actual costs of the service covered," but airfare analyst Bob Harrell put the issue succinctly in the March 2012 *Business Travel News*: "As far as I've been able to tell, fuel surcharges have nothing to do with fuel."

Were the fee floodgates opened when consumers largely acquiesced to big-dollar fuel fees? If these triggered no rebellion, why not implement other fees that also, truth be told, went beyond just "covering costs"? Personal favorites: the fee to cut to the front of the boarding line (airlines elegantly call it "preferential" boarding for those with "preferred status"); the $15 I had to pay to get assigned a "Choice Seat" next to my wife in Row 17 in the middle of Economy (I didn't actually have a "choice"); a new fee under consideration for early *exit* from your flight. (How would that work—ask flight attendants to form a "flying wedge" around "preferred" exiters?) Another goodie is the surcharge—up to $30—to fly on "peak days." The "peak" in 2010 included three-quarters of the summer; the day after the Super Bowl was a super-double-peak day, when the surcharge more than doubled.

Is there any limit to how far airline fees can go? Maybe only the limits of corporate imagination. IdeaWorks, a kind of think tank for the ancillary-revenue world, even offered a weekend "ancillary revenue training camp" in 2012 for airlines and vendors—at a mountaintop lodge along Virginia's scenic Skyline Drive (early-bird airline price: $2,200). They promise to teach you the "seven steps to . . . ancillary revenue bliss at your airline." Carriers have already been extraordinarily imaginative:

› Charging up to $25 to talk to a human reservations agent to book your flight.
› Charging extra to buy your ticket online. (The fee-free alternative to Spirit's "passenger usage fee": *drive to the airport*.) And if you don't print out your boarding pass at home, there's a $5 "passenger convenience fee" for the agent to press the printer button.
› Charging for "preferred" seats. Airlines figured out how to sell the extra space that FAA requires for evacuation at exit rows, but only "elites" get to see all the open seats on some online seat maps; non-elite fliers see only less desirable ones (middle seats next to the lavatory)—an incentive to be "loyal" or pay extra for a "preferred" seat.
› Charging passengers to put their carry-on bags in the overhead bin—up to $100 per bag on Spirit if you get caught at the boarding gate without paying the standard $45 carry-on charge earlier, a fee that netted the carrier $50 million in 2011.
› Charging serious money to book "free" mileage-award tickets—up to $90 on one major carrier. And more to change those "free" tickets or "redeposit" your miles. And even more if you request your "award" more than a week or two before the flight. For some award tickets on foreign airlines, add fuel surcharges of hundreds of dollars.

The only real limit to fees is when regulators say no or customers balk.

Don't count on either happening anytime soon. When it comes to fees, regulators see their job mainly as making sure airlines clearly disclose them to consumers, especially in advertising. Starting in 2012, when airlines advertise fares, they have to include in them those fees that all customers have to pay, such as fuel surcharges, but not fees for optional extras like checked bags or seat assignments which passengers can avoid, at least theoretically. The few times regulators invoked their broad legal authority against unfair or deceptive practices to question fees, it wasn't because they found the fees themselves substantively unfair but because, however bizarre, they weren't adequately *disclosed* by the airlines that conjured them. In 2009, for instance, DOT challenged Spirit Airways' disclosure of its $2.50 "natural occurrence interruption fee"—a charge to pay for the airline's cost of accommodating travelers disrupted by bad weather (the "natural occurrence")—and its $8.50 "international service recovery fee" to recoup the airline's extra operating costs of flying to foreign countries. Spirit dropped those two add-ons, but kept its "passenger usage fee"—a charge up to $16.99 just for the privilege of buying a ticket anywhere except at the airport.

DOT knows full well the cries of "re-regulation!" it would hear from the industry if it tried to adjudge the substantive fairness of particular consumer fees. When asked about fees for aisle or window seats that kept families from sitting together, for instance, the secretary of transportation told a Senate hearing in 2012 that he was not above "doing a little jawboning" of airline CEOs, but, bottom line: "We can't tell airlines what fees they can charge."

Even if US regulators get more aggressive about fees, with so much money at stake, don't expect the airlines to back down. When DOT in July 2011 had the audacity to ask the industry merely to detail publicly how *much* it was raking in from 16 new categories of ancillary fees (not just for checked bags and ticket changes, but also for things like blankets, entertainment, Wi-Fi, and snacks), the airline trade association blasted the proposal as "excessive," "unjustified," "not legitimate," and "inhibit[ing] the industry's ability to generate jobs." Not to mention that federal debt hawks were casting a longing eye on taxing some of those airline fee revenues—and it's much easier to tax what you can see. Heated rhetoric aside, airlines—after all, private, deregulated businesses—can fairly question a requirement for such ultra-detailed financial reporting; neither is it clear what consumers stand to gain by knowing precisely how much each airline rakes in from selling lounge passes or snack packs.

Regulators are one thing, but what about consumers? What if passengers rebel, or start to refuse crazy fees? Airlines are trying to make sure that doesn't happen, at least when it comes to their most lucrative frequent business fliers. This group gets a pass, or at least a break, on most fees. Bag fees in particular operate as a kind of regressive tax: only about one-fourth of air travelers—the least favored—actually paid them in 2011. Not First Class or Business Class fliers. Not international travelers with a first bag. Not most frequent fliers, who know better than to check bags and can likely get a waiver as "elite" fliers when they do. Not holders of credit cards that are co-branded with airlines—they get a free bag too. It's disproportionately the poor souls who travel twice a year, back deep in Economy, without a clue, who pay those bag fees.

In one sense, though, checked-bag fees affect all fliers, not only those who get stuck paying them. They're an incentive for folks to try to cram every nonliving thing into their overstuffed carry-on luggage to avoid the fee, and this generates other costs. Carry-on bags that required TSA screening reportedly increased some 50 percent since checked-bag fees started in 2008, according to a *Huffington Post* report of TSA statistics— some 59 million more bags in 2010 than in 2009. That means more taxpayer money for TSA staff, and longer security screening lines—not to mention the growing hassle of merely boarding the airplane, already a mad scramble for overhead-bin space that relegates slow-moving innocents to the dreaded "gate check." Checked-bag fees rake in the dough for airlines but impose costs on every traveler one way or the other.

There's a point at which fliers start to feel seriously ripped off. Could airlines end up killing the golden revenue goose? Empowered by social media, consumers slowed the fee craze in the banking and communications industries where, just as with the aviation industry, competition makes it hard to raise "base fares" and profits have waned. Consumers grudgingly swallowed an array of bank fees for services long assumed to be free, but when Bank of America tried charging $5 a month for the privilege of withdrawing one's own money from one's own account with one's own debit card in late 2011, it was a step too far. An estimated 610,000 depositors switched their accounts—enough to capture the market's attention and push the global financial behemoth to back down.

Could that happen in the airline industry? It did before, in 2001, when lots of business fliers "just said no" to premium fares that were way out of whack with discount coach prices. The reality, though, is that most fliers have far fewer competing options for their air travel than for their banking. And those options kept getting more limited as the industry's hunt for elusive profits engendered a new approach to growth in the aftermath of the horrible year of 2008.

The Airlines' Coup de Grace

The new fee-for-all business model blunted consumers' best weapon in the fare wars—the Internet. But there was another, even more potent, weapon at the airlines' disposal that would redress the bargaining power they had lost to consumers. It was a lever they had largely ignored until the existential threat of the 2008 fuel spike forced them to use it. The airlines rediscovered the law of supply and demand.

The idea that the price of almost anything desirable (even a coach seat on an airplane) goes up when there is less of it available is Econ 101, but it was a notion that airlines and their cowboy entrepreneurs had resisted for decades. Staunching growth, cutting flights or seats, went deeply against the industry's hypercompetitive grain. When times got tough for airlines, they normally did just the opposite: they *added* flights, bought new planes, tried to "dominate" existing routes, and started new routes—all to grab their competitors' market share or to keep competitors from grabbing theirs. The drive was to fly every-where—"ubiquity." United even launched a costly public-relations stunt to celebrate becoming the first to fly mainline (not regional subsidiary) flights to all 50 states in October 1984—a one-year free First Class pass for anyone who could hit all 50 states in 50 days. "Grow to profitability" was the zeitgeist; contraction meant defeat.

More sober heads in the industry had long and quietly understood that if everybody grew fast, all at the same time, there would soon be too many airline seats chasing too few passengers—leaving half-empty planes, razor-thin margins, and no leverage to raise fares much above breakeven levels. But nobody would be first to retreat—some leaner, meaner competitor might swoop in—and there was no real-world cata-lyst to reverse the time-honored grow-to-succeed worldview. Then the price of fuel hit an astounding $4 a gallon.

By the middle of 2008, respected Wall Street analysts were warn-ing not just of ugly balance sheets or even multiple bankruptcies, but that one, maybe two, major US airlines might have to dissolve outright. The industry suddenly hit the brakes. By the end of the dreadful year, almost all new routes were frozen and the number of airline seats flown dropped to levels not seen for five years. As North American carriers parked 800 planes, curtailed schedules, and flew smaller planes with fewer seats, it was as if one of the nation's largest airlines had simply vanished. Even indefatigable Southwest, an airline that had grown roughly 6 percent annually for decades, retrenched. By the middle of 2012, the number of domestic flights had dropped almost 14 percent from five years before.

But it wasn't just fear that rewired the industry's growth fixation. The other essential ingredient was *confidence*. Each major airline was convinced that the *other* major airline survivors would also restrain their own growth. All weakened in that grim environment, none had the stomach or the resources to exploit the others' retrenchment. Fac-ing the same soaring prices for fuel and the same souring economic environment, nobody worried about losing customers to some fast-expanding start-up, much less to another member of the industry's Old Guard.

That confidence was bolstered by the fact there were only a handful of US competitors left standing to worry about. By 2011, there remained only four of the ten large-scale national airlines that were flying when the industry was deregulated 33 years earlier. The decade's industry consolidation had tempered the competitive urgency. Each of the major players knew its place. At all but a few of the country's dozen largest air-travel hubs, just a single big airline controlled most of the traffic. (At these "fortress hubs," consumers typically faced the highest average airfares.) So when it came to cutting capacity to leverage the power of supply and demand, the survivors could play "follow the leader," comfortable the rest would in turn stop or slow their own growth. As *Airline Weekly* succinctly observed, "the practice of pushing up prices by squeezing supply . . . only works when everyone's playing the game."

Wall Street had long pushed for airlines to "rationalize" their capacity, but now the effects were striking, and quick. "Load factors"—the percentage of seats filled on planes—soared to unheard-of levels, more than 80 percent on average, more than 90 percent on busy routes. (Before industry deregulation, government economists used 55 percent load factors as a presumed norm.) At those levels, practically speaking, almost every city-to-city flight at a decent hour was pretty much totally full. (For technical reasons, when average load factors across an airline approach 90 percent, there's likely to be a body in every seat on flights at reasonably convenient times.) Planes had never been so crowded.

Basic economics kicked in. With fewer seats available and no let-up in the demand for them, airfares stabilized, then rose. Average fares climbed some 20 percent from their low in mid-2009 to mid-2012, even adjusted for inflation. As the economy slowly crawled out of deep recession, airlines found themselves on the right side of the supply-demand balance for the first time in recent memory. Consumers could comparison-shop the Internet to their hearts' content, but it didn't matter. By tightening the lid on capacity, the industry had found a way to stabilize airfares on an upward path. There was still plenty of worry that volatile fuel prices would erode airline financials or undermine consumer willingness to pay higher, fee-supplemented fares, but by the start of 2013, airlines seemed to have largely regained the upper hand. And absent some new catastrophe or massive fuel spike or economic swoon, it began to look like they would keep it.

The Tax Man

Strapped fliers looking for villains can't fairly blame the rising cost of air travel solely on nasty, greedy airlines, though. About 15 to 18 percent of every ticket (estimates vary) goes not to the airlines but to nearly a dozen federal and local government agencies—figure $50 to $70 out of the average domestic ticket. Airlines don't pay most of these taxes—they're passed on to passengers—but high taxes make it more expensive for consumers to buy the product that airlines sell. The effective tax rate on flying has hardly changed over the last decade, according to MIT's Airline Ticket Tax Project, but it's still a lot of money. The industry argues vigorously that flying is taxed more heavily even than "sin" goods like tobacco and liquor.

Still, consider what's in that portion of your domestic airfare the airlines don't get. The biggest piece—a hefty 7.5 percent federal "ticket tax" on your basic fare—goes to a "trust fund." The money, more than $10 billion a year in the last decade, is to be used only for aviation purposes, mostly to pay for the FAA and to modernize the air traffic system, not to pay off the national debt or build bridges or buy weapons systems. The idea is that fliers, rather than every member of the general public, ought to pay for the aviation system they use. The other big federal tax—a "segment fee" of $3–$4 you pay every time you take off and land—also finances the FAA.

The other major government add-ons go to two places—the Department of Homeland Security and the airports you use. DHS's "September 11 fee" goes for screening. You currently pay $2.50 for each of those luggage rummages and pat-downs—no extra charge for the highly personal version, and no tipping allowed. Airlines have managed to beat back increases in these screening fees for the much-beloved TSA, but they're likely to rise eventually as the airlines' own checked-bag fees incentivize travelers to cram more and more carry-ons through TSA inspection lines. Your airport, too, gets to assess a local "passenger facility charge" of up to $4.50 for each leg of your round-trip (up to $18 if you have two flights connecting in each direction) to pay for runways, terminals, and capital projects—did you think the airport ambience was free? For flying internationally, add an international arrival and departure tax (near $20 each way), Customs and Immigration inspection fees (together, $12.50), and a fee for agricultural inspection ($5). It's all built into the price of your ticket.

Practically all foreign countries impose their own various taxes on air travel—often only loosely related to any bona fide aviation service; some seem based primarily on the anachronistic assumption that anybody who can afford to climb aboard steerage in a jumbo jet must have deep pockets. The UK's "air passenger duty," for example, adds well over $100 to the price of an Economy ticket from the United States to London—double that tax for premium class. Germany's Air Transport Tax (or "ecological air travel levy") raises about $60 per long-haul passenger, and then there's France's "Solidarity Tax" (they call it an "air-ticket solidarity contribution")—$5 for economy, $50 for premium fliers across the Atlantic—which is supposed to fund health care and treatment for pandemics in developing countries.

Airlines argue that they're just being deputized as federal revenue agents to collect taxes that often have little to do with aviation just because they're big, easy, unloved targets, and that added taxes threaten to stifle air travel and eventually suppress demand. In fairness, they've got a point. Heavy taxes raise the cost of flying, and that does eventually dampen demand. An extra $65 per passenger isn't trivial for a working family of four trying to get to see the Grand Canyon. On the other hand, the tax angst isn't all about losing passengers. In 2011, a congressional showdown over reauthorizing the FAA temporarily left the government without power to collect aviation taxes. During the tax holiday from July 23 to August 7, did airlines refund the taxes to passengers? Did they lower fares by the same amount as the uncollected tax to encourage more people to fly? Nope. Nearly all of the large airlines simply kept their fares the exact same as before the tax freeze, then pocketed the difference, a windfall worth millions of dollars.

Sickening

Lieutenant Patrick V. Murphy, age 22, was leading his 101st Airborne infantry platoon near Vietnam's A Shau Valley in 1968 when a Soviet-made RPG antitank rocket blew his leg off. He was the only one in a series of four leaders of his platoon to make it out alive—first choppered to a field hospital, then, after two dozen surgeries and two years of rehab, back home to Maryland. The decorated combat veteran earned a master's degree in business administration, married a pretty Army nurse, and took a job with an obscure federal agency, the Civil Aeronautics Board.

Fast-forward 27 years. Now a senior US Department of Transportation official in charge of negotiating international aviation agreements, Murphy returned to Vietnam, this time to make a deal with Hanoi to open commercial flights between the two former enemies. Once again, Murphy almost didn't make it back—no longer because of enemy fire, but because of some nasty bug he picked up on the Boeing 747 that flew him across the Pacific.

Waking from a nap on the 11-hour flight, the half-asleep vet made a near-fatal mistake: he didn't bother to pull on his shoes before walking in his socks to the lavatory, where he likely came in contact with some horrible bacteria that was lurking on the floor. By the time he landed at Noi Bai Airport, Murphy was woozy and feverish. Systemic septicemia, a life-threatening, fast moving bacterial infection in the bloodstream, had set in. Thanks to a fast-thinking embassy doctor and a quick evacuation to a Bangkok hospital, Murphy survived; years later, he and I became business partners in a Washington consulting firm.

Murphy's dual bouts with mortality in Vietnam may be unique, but getting sick from air travel surely isn't. Flying can literally be sickening. Beyond the fares and fees and food and discomfort, beyond the myriad hassles, the nastiest part of flying may be unseen—the unpleasant stuff in the cabin air and the seatback pockets, and on the little knob that locks the lavatory door. You don't have to be hypochondriac to get a little grossed out.

To be clear, air travel can be unhealthy, but it's exceedingly unlikely to kill you. The risk of contracting something *really* bad—such as tuberculosis, severe acute respiratory syndrome (SARS) or, like Murphy, septicemia—is tiny. But your odds of catching *something*—the makings of a bad head cold, a gastrointestinal virus—appear to be far greater aloft than on the ground. In a 2004 Canadian study published in the *Journal of Environmental Health Research,* one-fifth of all 1,100 passengers surveyed after a series of flights lasting two and a half hours reported having caught a cold. The air travelers were *at least* five times (maybe as much as 113 times) as likely to catch cold than non-fliers, though other factors, such as travel stress and exposure to germs before or after flying, could have played a role. Still, how healthy can it be to be sealed for hours in a densely packed, superdry pressurized metal tube with a couple hundred other random folks?

Health isn't something the airline industry likes to talk about. When *USA Today* tried to survey US airlines in 2007 on how each handled inflight medical emergencies, the airline trade association flatly refused to cooperate. Understandably. Health scares keep people off airplanes. In the decade since September 11, fear grew that global air travel had become a major vector for potential pandemics like avian flu (H5N1) and the deadly form of pneumonia known as SARS. Although SARS killed about 900 people worldwide during a 2003 outbreak, the panic surrounding it nearly cratered Asian tourism for months, punishing the airline and tourism industries of China, Taiwan, Hong Kong, Singapore, and other Asian countries.

Fear is one thing, but how bad really is the health risk of flying? The truth seems to lie somewhere between germ-phobic hysteria and the sunny bromides of some in the industry. There clearly are risks, the medical experts say—after all, a speeding high-altitude jet isn't the most "natural" environment for humans—but there's plenty of debate about the extent of those risks, and even about what really happens to our bodies and our health after we climb aboard.

Cheek by Jowl

There's no way around one fact of airborne life: very close quarters, sometimes for hours on end. And our exposure to the airborne environment is intensifying as flights grow longer, capable of half-circling the Earth nonstop, and ever more consistently packed solid. Some airlines have even eliminated one of the lavatories in order to add more paying seats. So a coast-to-coast jet like the Boeing 757 with 160-odd passengers in the Economy cabin may be reduced to only two lavatories—creating an 80-to-1 lavatory-passenger ratio, far tighter than the more traditional 50-to-1 ratio generally offered. (Federal rules don't dictate bathroom ratios.) And aircraft interior designers are developing even tighter lavatories—assuming that's anatomically possible—to let airlines squeeze up to six more seats on new versions of the popular Boeing 737.

It all means more up-close-and-personal time with our hundreds of plane mates and so a greater risk of catching something. The likelihood of contracting onboard tuberculosis, for example, a disease that sickens about 9 million people across the globe each year, seems to depend largely on three things: how long you are on the plane, how close you are to an actively infected passenger, and cabin ventilation. According to the World Health Organization, the greater risk is on flights longer than eight hours where you're sitting within two rows of the sick person. That's not to say the risk is great—a 2004 analysis by the University of Texas Health Center put the probability of catching TB from another passenger with active TB symptoms during an 8.7-hour flight at about one in a thousand, similar to infection rates in other confined spaces.

Tuberculosis aside, some more exotic and deadly diseases like SARS and swine flu that spread through airborne droplets (think coughs and sneezes) have been tied directly to air travel. Most famous was Air China Flight 112 from Hong Kong to Beijing in March 2003. On the three-hour flight were 120 passengers, including a 73-year-old Chinese gentleman who was coughing lightly throughout it. Within eight days, 20 fellow passengers and two crew members were stricken with SARS, and five subsequently died. What freaked people out was that victims included passengers seated as far as seven rows ahead and five rows behind the sick man, though it isn't clear whether the spread came from breathing common air or from other means (such as touching a contaminated surface).

Remain Seated

Beyond communicating disease, when we're packed in on board, we're largely immobile. There's no real room or opportunity to "move about the cabin"—and that's a health concern too. Pilots recommend we stay belted "just like we do up here" in case of "unexpected turbulence" (not to mention the expected variety). Getting out of our seats is not encouraged. Moving up and down the aisles interferes with flight attendants trying to serve drinks or sell headsets or collect trash. And it can still make people nervous: *Is he going to rush the cockpit?*

The whole pull-down-the-shades, watch-the-screen, light-deprived cabin environment seems designed to keep us soporific, slouched securely in our seats, tapping on our laptops or iPads, staring at the cycle of movies and sitcom reruns, dozing in the torpor of the low-oxygen cabin. The problem is that "just sitting there" can pose a significant health risk; long-haul immobility can even kill.

This nearly happened to a fiftyish senior economic official in my office at the Department of Transportation, whose job took him all over the world to international aviation conferences. When he didn't show up at a morning staff meeting in Washington, we learned he had been hospitalized, having collapsed in the aisle after landing in Frankfurt on the way home from Singapore. After 13 hours dozing and reading and eating in his economy seat, he had stood up to grab his bag from the overhead bin and promptly hit the deck. Medics at Frankfurt's massive international hub had seen it all before—a classic case of deep vein thrombosis (DVT), also known as "Economy Class syndrome." Virtual immobility during long flights—probably exacerbated by low cabin pressurization and dehydration—causes blood to pool and become "thick" or "sticky" in the veins of the calf. If the resulting blood clot breaks off and moves to the heart or lungs, sudden death can occur.

Our economist was lucky to get quick, skilled treatment, but the risk he faced is growing as flights get longer and passengers get older and less fit. The prestigious British medical publication *The Lancet* estimated in 2001 that, based on a randomized trial, as many as 10 percent of long-haul fliers over age 50 may suffer thrombosis in the calf, albeit temporary and without symptoms. A study in 1986 of 61 sudden natural deaths among long-distance passengers arriving at London's Heathrow Airport over a three-year period found 18 percent were due to pulmonary embolism. The risk appears to grow with the length of the flight; a 2009 study in the *Annals of Internal Medicine,* reported in *USA Today,* found the risk of blood clots on airplanes grew 26 percent for every additional two hours of flight time beyond four hours. No surprise that Hawaii, a long flight from almost anywhere, is a hot spot of Economy-class syndrome.

Just 20 years ago, 12 hours was seen as a kind of outside limit on nonstop flights. Today, some two-dozen international commercial flights every day run over 15 hours. Even on typical domestic flights—which averaged some 17 percent longer in 2011 than in 2003—we're also packed in longer. The average flight distance is longer in part because Southwest, JetBlue, and other carriers that don't rely on connecting hubs now fly longer nonstops, including cross-country. But even where flight *distances* are the same, flight *durations*—and thus our stretches of onboard immobility—are lengthier, as we've seen.

What We Breathe

For years, nothing has freaked out health-anxious fliers—or triggered quite so many popular misconceptions—as the air we breathe on board. How much of the worry is justified remains hotly debated; facts tend to be selected carefully to support opposing views.

Fact: A fully loaded jet has one of the smallest volumes of air per person of just about any enclosed public place. It is a simple matter of space and economics. Planes are tight places to start with, the more densely-packed the better from the standpoint of both revenue-seeking airlines and bargain-seeking fliers.

Fact: How much air we get on board matters. Good ventilation seems to reduce the risk of infection. In 1977, an Alaska Airlines Boeing 737 with 54 people aboard was stuck on the ground in Kodiak, Alaska, for close to four hours without an operating ventilation system; within three days, 72 percent of the passengers showed symptoms of influenza, spread by a single sick passenger. With ventilation turned off, onboard carbon dioxide levels are predicted to rise quickly above "comfort levels" established by ASHRAE, the official standard-setting body. So air travelers may actually face their greatest exposure to airborne germs not while flying but, rather, when the plane pulls up to the gate, the chime sounds, and everybody scrambles, huffing and puffing, to get up and grab their carry-ons and wait for the door to open. That's also when cabin ventilation switches from air filtered by jet engine–powered systems to other sources of air, including the plane's auxiliary power unit or the airport's ground-based, diesel-powered turbines that may lack equally sophisticated germ filters.

Fact: Cabin air may be "just as good," in a sense, as the air in modern office buildings—today's jets exchange their air completely much more frequently than office buildings do. But each individual flier typically gets only about half the amount of "outside" airflow (roughly 7 to 10 cubic feet every minute) as the national standard-setting experts recommend for indoor environments like offices. More important: airplane cabins cram together lots more breathing humans per square foot than do offices. As in a busy elevator, these "other people" contribute their exhalations and gases and coughs and sweat and dead skin—and their viruses and bacteria—to the airborne mix. Everybody shares.

In other words, germ freaks should probably worry more about proximity to sniffling seat mates than about airflow. As an NYU medical expert observed, air purification can't protect passengers against the common cold. "All the passenger next to you has to do is sneeze, and you're done," he told the *New York Times* in March 2011.

It *is* better in First Class—but only because there are fewer passengers sharing the up-front real estate and the air that comes with it. (*Very* roughly speaking, Economy passengers each have about half the personal space of each Business Class passenger, even less compared to each First Class passenger.) Premium passengers don't get the "good air" first. It doesn't emanate from the cockpit, waft its way in relative purity through First Class, then plow back through Economy. In reality, cabin air moves downward from the ceiling along the entire length of most jet airliners and ultimately leaves the cabin through floor ducts or grilles beneath the windows.

Fact: Cabin air is not all "fresh"—only about half comes in from outside the plane through the jet engines. Moving through the engine compressors, the air gets very hot, then is cooled down by heat exchangers and fed into the plane's main air-conditioning "packs." This outside fresh air mixes with cabin air that's been recirculated and fed through high-efficiency "particulate arrestor" filters, which are supposed to clean away impurities. Airlines boast these HEPA filters are the same kind used in hospital emergency rooms, and they do remove microscopic particles larger than 0.3 microns—less than one two-hundredth the width of an average human hair. That's fine enough to catch pet dander and vapors and bacteria like strep and TB as well as viruses suspended in larger droplets, as in a sneeze.

Fact: Airlines really don't limit "good air" to cut fuel costs. Nor, by all accounts, do they reduce cabin ventilation rates to save money. Early versions of the Boeing 747 did let pilots reduce ventilation for purposes of "economy"—but that was when half-full planes were not uncommon; new Boeing models reportedly don't have that option, though pilots can turn off air packs for safety reasons, such as a malfunction. Some Airbus planes do have a "Lo" or "Econ" setting that can reduce airflow about 20 percent on relatively empty flights, but it's reportedly rarely used. Recirculating some of the cabin air does save fuel—jet engines need to pump less outside air to the cabin—but the savings are modest. And while breathing recirculated air certainly sounds bad, it's not really like inhaling your neighbor's breath. Research indicates that, with high-performance filtering and the ceiling-to-floor airflow, re-circulated air is no more likely to transmit disease than outside air is. Happily, and for fairly obvious reasons, lavatory air is exhausted directly overboard, not recirculated back into the passenger cabin.

That doesn't mean it's Irish Spring in the cabin, though. Not since 1990 has tobacco smoke billowed from the rear of each section of the cabin, permeating much of the atmosphere (smoking was banned on short flights in 1988), but there remain plenty of other contaminants unique to commercial airplanes:

> Toxic fumes can enter the cabin from engine-oil leaks or oil-seal problems, or via hydraulic or de-icing fluids. Boeing paid a flight attendant an undisclosed sum in late 2011 to settle claims regarding toxic fumes in the cabin of a 2007 flight from Memphis to Dallas.

> Ozone, the key component gas in smog, irritates the nose and eyes; as little as one in ten million parts of air, the most FAA regulations allow in cabins at certain altitudes, can cause airway irritation and reduce lung function. Airlines fly where ozone concentrations are high—between troposphere and stratosphere, particularly near the Poles.

> Pesticides can enter cabins via "disinsection" of aircraft. Some foreign health authorities require arriving planes to be sprayed—sometimes with a neurotoxin called permethrin. The goal is to keep stowaway mosquitoes and rodents from importing tropical diseases like malaria, dengue fever, or Lassa fever from remote areas. The EPA is investigating whether the chemicals affect infant and fetal brain development; a 2012 National Research Council review found pesticides in the cabin to be a "moderate concern."

> Allergens are inescapable as carriers, for a hefty fee, let small pets fly in under-seat containers in the passenger cabin, suspending dander, skin flakes, and tiny saliva particles in the cabin air. A Swiss report in 2010 found common cat allergens on 100 percent of aircraft seats tested, according to MSNBC. DOT has rejected demands, though, for "peanut-free" areas or a ban on peanuts (that would have eliminated Southwest Airlines' entire meal service).

> Cosmic radiation from massive solar explosions, normally absorbed or shielded by the Earth's atmosphere, can be 100 times more intense at jet cruising altitudes and near polar latitudes where that protective atmosphere is thinner. Most experts say not to worry, at least not unless you're a pregnant crewmember who regularly flies long-haul, but FAA has a handy online tool for concerned fliers to predict their likely radiation dose from planned flights.

Not exactly pleasant, but compare today's cabin air environment to the so-called Golden Age of elegant air travel in the 1930s. Here's how legendary aviation writer Ernest Gann described it then:

> We sweat in the cockpit, though much of the time we fly with the side windows open. The airplanes smell of hot oil and simmering aluminum, disinfectant, feces, leather, and puke . . . the steward-esses, short-tempered and reeking of vomit, come forward as often as they can for what is a breath of comparatively fresh air.

Kind of makes you appreciate today's somewhat stuffy cabins.

What We Touch

What we touch on board is at least as nasty as what we breathe. Germs are everywhere on cabin surfaces. Think about the humble little lock on the airplane lavatory—that metal knob you pull across the slot to secure the bathroom door on pretty much any jet. On a typical plane, hundreds of hands will grip that knob every day—before and after their owners have completed their lavatory business. Hand-washing in tiny airplane sinks—holding down one of the already-germy faucet handles to wash the other hand—won't eliminate the germ load.

Or those sticky tray tables. In 2007, a University of Arizona researcher found that 60 percent of those tested on three major airlines were positive for the super-resistant, often-fatal methicillin-resistant Staphylococcus aureus (MRSA) bacteria. A germ that kills 20,000 Americans annually, MRSA tends to get into the body through open skin and cuts. Surfaces on the New York subway were more sanitary, according to the study. Then there are the seatbacks and overhead luggage bins that hundreds of travelers with sniffles or worse grip to steady themselves every day while passing down the airplane aisle. As reported in the *New York Times* in March 2011, the common cold and flu virus can survive for up to 72 hours on plastic surfaces, according to microbiologists; presumably that includes tray tables.

But the germiest areas in the entire cabin could well be the seatback pockets—the time-honored repositories of chewing gum, lunch leftovers, used tissues, and other unpleasantries. As the *Wall Street Journal*'s Scot McCartney recounts in gruesome detail in his aptly named "Middle Seat" column riff on airborne nastiness, the *middle* seatback pocket in particular—where parents tend to deposit soiled diapers and God knows what else—is a place where road warriors know never, *ever* to thrust a hand. And note to true germaphobes: those little air nozzles above your seat—called gaspers (really)—are twisted by scores, maybe even hundreds, of dirty little fingers before yours. Who knows how often *they* get a thorough scrubbing?

What may be the industry's greatest recent contribution to passenger health is the likely unintended consequence of a cost-cutting move—eliminating free pillows and blankets in coach. These objects came in direct contact with passengers' faces and skin, sometimes after, say, a dozen or so other passengers had the chance to thoroughly enjoy them, allowing successive users to touch, even inhale, the contents—sweat, saliva, the soles of the shoes of someone who used that pillow to raise his legs. These "amenities" were cleaned (or discarded)—eventually. But unless they appeared "visibly soiled" to the overnight cleaning crew, it could be awhile. Not that the airlines hadn't noticed the hygiene issue. When US Airways, for instance, started selling clean pillows and blankets to coach passengers in late 2008 (other carriers followed suit through 2011), the airline's spokesman was quick to tout their superiority to the previous "free" version of the amenities. "It's a better product because you know what you're getting," he told Bloomberg News. "No one will be worried about where their pillow or blanket has been." Comforting.

The cabin itself gets cleaned, of course, but there, too, it's a matter of degree. There's the "tidying up" after every flight—essentially dumping the used newspapers and lunch remains, and, when time permits, straightening the seat belts. Then nightly, after a thousand or so humans have made the metal tube their airborne home, cleaning crews—Southwest calls theirs "aircraft appearance technicians," but many airlines use outside contractors—wipe down lavatories, tray tables, and other surfaces, search seatback pockets, and vacuum the carpets. Airlines vary, but a serious "deep clean" of the cabin may wait a month or more. This "major effort clean" is an overnight affair—carpets and seat coverings shampooed, interior walls and fixtures washed, galleys disinfected, air vents cleaned, and toilets scrubbed.

Deep-cleaning a Boeing 777 can take a dozen workers up to eight hours; a jumbo A380 can take more than twice the effort. Then every five years or so, the aircraft undergoes a complete months-long maintenance overhaul usually known as a "D check" or "heavy maintenance visit." The whole aircraft interior is substantially dismantled, carpet is replaced, seat covers stripped off, and interior furnishings refurbished. The result is amazing: according to one pilot-blogger on Airliners.net, this super-cleaning reportedly removes up to 300 *pounds* of dirt from a large jet.

Cabin hygiene has improved over the last decade as the industry has climbed from the financial depths; it could hardly have gotten much worse. Airlines in bankruptcy can be less than fastidious. For example, according to a *Chicago Tribune* report in January 2009, what are now monthly or more-frequent deep cleans at United had earlier become semiannual affairs; occasionally they were deferred for as long as eighteen months. Things had gotten so bad in the industry that simple, basic cleanliness became a competitive selling point. Lufthansa's online ads touted the "cleanest" airplanes. United invited reporters to observe their most finicky aircraft-cleaning managers at work. Emirates proudly accepted an award in 2008 (sponsored by a cleaning-product supplier) as the World's Most Hygienic Airline. Apparently its "mini deep clean" included injecting "biocide fog" into the cabin ventilation system. Plus, there's a specialist "de-infestation" team that "makes sure there are no cockroaches on the aircraft," according to a Dubai business news service.

Put it this way: airline cabins *are* cleaner now than they were in 2008, but just how much remains uncertain. Nor is it fair to blame all the germy-ness of air travel on actual flying. Long before you step aboard, thousands of index fingers have punched the same "Print" button on the kiosk screen you're using to check in with your e-ticket. Most everyone goes shoeless (required), some sockless (not recommended), through security checkpoints, traipsing fungi and worse across the same patch of floor as thousands of others. And God knows what gets dumped in the gray TSA bins from which we fish out our change, key chains, and toiletries on passing through security. When do you think they disinfect those bins?

What Passes Our Lips

Watch any two-year-old and you know: humans take in more nasty stuff through the mouth than through the lungs or skin. In just a few decades, airline cuisine in the back of the plane has evolved—or, rather, devolved—from unremarkable to laughable to nearly nonexistent. Even where there *is* food, though—for international flights or buy-on-board offerings on some domestic flights—from the standpoint of health, you might still consider going hungry, at least if you believe federal food inspectors.

For the most part, airline food is prepared by a small handful of airline caterers (all but a few carriers long ago dropped more expensive in-house "flight kitchens") who've drawn fire from the federal Food and Drug Administration for occasionally less-than-appetizing practices. Here's how FDA inspectors described what they found at the Denver facility of the world's largest airline caterer, LSG SkyChefs, in a December 2009 warning letter to the company:

"Live and dead roach-like insects too numerous to count" and "live and dead roaches" in the silverware and hot kitchen areas; numerous roaches and flies in other food-preparation areas, "employees handling food with bare hands or with unwashed gloved hands," and "holes in wall surfaces, creating areas for insect and vermin harborage." Not to mention "brown leaking fluid draining from at least two garbage bins, apparently creating standing pools of the brown fluid." Kitchen-floor samples found Listeria, a dangerous bacterium that can cause food poisoning. And LSG was not alone. The FDA also found problems at facilities of two other big US airline caterers, Gate Gourmet and Flying Food Group—ranging from high coliform counts and "unclean hands" of employees, to improperly chilled fish, beef, and chicken. FDA reports for 46 of the 91 caterer kitchens showed suspected violations or objectionable practices at 27 of them, according to a *USA Today* report in June 2010. For their part, the big catering companies say they have quickly, aggressively, and "proactively" addressed FDA's concerns; in the words of one, their "goal is to be 100 percent compliant with all safety regulations."

Caterer preparation areas aside, there are plenty of other ways for airline food to go bad. Lapses in refrigeration are one risk. The shrimp served on the evening flight to China may sit for hours in various venues—caterer holding rooms, trucks hauling them to the airport, the elevator truck to the plane, then the catering carts that slide into the aircraft galleys—before they grace the First Class tray tables. Those carts are themselves supposed to be refrigerated, but how often do their doors stay open during meal services? And did you know that even well-regarded airlines like Air New Zealand and Qantas reuse the plastic cutlery on international flights, washing and repacking it in those little wrappers—up to ten times in some cases?

With "free" food all but eliminated in domestic Economy, the tap water on board is a bigger worry. Let's be clear, there's *no* reported history of any widespread health problem associated with contaminated onboard water but for more than a few airline crew members, the rule is simple: Don't drink it. Don't even brush your teeth with it. Some flight attendants won't even wash their hands with it or drink coffee or tea made with it. (No, Virginia, they don't make the coffee with bottled water.) Nobody paid all that much attention to the water on planes until 2002, when Zach, a 13-year-old kid from Alamo, California, put the results of his school science project online. He had tested the tap water on family flights to Australia and New Zealand and his water-testing kit revealed "really gross" (his description) masses of bacteria. Noticing Zach's online report, enterprising *Wall Street Journal* reporters conducted their own water sampling on 14 flights in 2002. Here's what they reported finding in the water they tested, from a story in November that year: "A long list of microscopic life you don't want to drink, from Salmonella and staphylococcus to tiny insect eggs. Worse, contamination was the rule, not the exception: Almost all of the bacteria levels were tens, sometimes, hundreds, of times above U.S. Government limits."

Among the ingredients: *Pasteurella pneumotropica,* a rodent-borne bacteria; *Pseudomonas,* a resistant cause of skin and respiratory infections; and, *Citrobacter,* a fecal bacteria that can cause diarrhea. The EPA says safe drinking water should contain no more than 500 colony-forming units (CFU) of bacteria per milliliter. The *Wall Street Journal's* experts found more than *four million* units in a single sample, roughly the same concentration as in a tainted raw hamburger.

The EPA's own tests in 2004 appeared to confirm the problem, though the airline industry trade association questioned the testing methods used. Inspectors found that about 15 percent of all water samples on 327 randomly selected commercial flights tested positive for coliform bacteria—an indication of the possible presence of disease-causing organisms. Water on two of the EPA-tested planes had *E. coli,* a leading cause of food poisoning that's found in the intestines, suggesting the lavatory tap water might even be contaminated with feces. It was not exactly the kind of publicity the airlines were looking for. Rather than prolong it, the industry quickly agreed to a "voluntary" EPA onboard water–testing program with more frequent sampling and disinfection that will take full effect in 2013.

One reason the water on airplanes can be dicey is that, in most cases, water tanks are filled where they land—that includes Lagos, Mumbai, and Oaxaca, not just Seattle and St. Louis. What else can they do? Flying tons of homegrown US Grade-A water around the world would be hugely expensive in fuel. A long-range Boeing 777 holds well over a ton of water, more than 300 gallons. And once impure water, foreign or domestic, gets into the airplane's massive tanks, bacteria and other tiny organisms can remain there, even after they're emptied and the plane is assigned to other routes. Even if the water itself is pure, how well does the local airport ground handler who pumps it into the plane sanitize its own water cabinets, trucks, carts, and hoses?

Airlines want the "bad-water" issue to go away and, in fact, airplane water quality seems to be improving significantly. Still, sampling conducted from 2005 to 2008 by the EPA and reported in 2009 continued to show limited instances of coliform. So the EPA's understated advice to "concerned passengers" in 2005 still makes sense for the cautious: Worried fliers "may want to request canned or bottled beverages and refrain from drinking tea or coffee unless made with bottled water." No kidding.

"Physiological Needs"

The technological leap from biplane to jumbo jet didn't overlook that one hygiene essential, the airplane toilet. In the early days of flying, the head was about as rudimentary as it gets—a bucket emptied overboard. The loo in the early versions of the legendary DC-3, the commercial aviation workhorse before and shortly after World War II, consisted of a plastic-lined bucket with a wooden seat above it, fondly known as the "honey bucket."

"Blue water" toilets followed. Still found on some older jets, an electrical circulating pump sloshes chemical solution through rings around the stainless-steel bowl, emptying into a central tank that is drained into tanker trucks at the destination. These commodes used a lot of costly-to-carry water and often got stopped up with diapers, pantyhose, and other items too big for the plumbing lines.

The airplane toilet "revolution" really arrived with the vacuum-powered toilet first installed by Boeing in the early 1980s. Flushing in flight opens a valve in the sewer line for about 15 seconds; this causes the air-pressure difference at altitude to suck out the contents into a sealed tank located in the aircraft belly. These beauties not only need far less water (roughly a half gallon); they *rocket* the waste away into onboard tanks—at up to 68 miles per hour on Airbus jets. Still, there's a downside. When you flush, the vacuum's force can spray whatever's in the toilet into a fine aerosol that remains suspended in the bathroom air. Some of it ends up coating the lavatory floor and walls, potentially adding to the coating of fecal bacteria on the faucets and door handles. Advice to germophobes: put down the lid and don't breathe until you get out of there—without touching that grimy little knob on the door, of course.

The most enduring myth about airplane toilets, though, is the "blue-water bomb." Stories of lavatory ice crashing to the ground are so pervasive that the FAA's Chicago district office once had to issue an official "blue ice" disclaimer, updated in November 2010, to calm residents around O'Hare. ("One possible explanation" for the reports, the FAA said helpfully, was that flocks of Canada geese eat fruit and, "if the fruit is blue, it will come out blue when the bird passes it.") Just to set the record straight, though: Toilet waste is not dumped outside airplanes in flight. That valve is located on the *outside* of most aircraft so that ground crews can service and drain it; it cannot be opened in the air. But don't get too comfortable. Standing in the flight path, it's still possible (but very unlikely) to get hit with a little ice—galley and lavatory sinks vent outside the aircraft.

High Altitude in Death Valley

Humans need a lot of oxygen to survive, but there's not nearly enough available in the outside air at cruising altitudes. At 35,000 feet above sea level, most people pass out from oxygen starvation in less than a minute. Modern aircraft compensate by pressurizing the air to concentrate the available oxygen. That makes it feel, oxygen-wise, as if you're at a much lower altitude—say, an 8,000-foot Rocky Mountain pass where the atmospheric oxygen concentration is 75 percent of what it is at sea level. Even at that "virtual" altitude, though, cabin pressurization does weird things to the body. Air trapped inside you—in the middle ear, the sinuses, and the abdomen—naturally expands. Normally, the pressure equalizes as air flows through your ears' Eustachian tubes and sinuses, unless you have a cold or sinus infection or other obstruction. In that case, it hurts like hell—also the main reason that babies are forever screaming their heads off on landing or takeoff.

The pressure of air in your lungs is what forces oxygen into your blood, across the lungs' alveoli. At higher altitudes, less oxygen gets to the bloodstream. On longer flights, this can cause a kind of low-grade oxygen deprivation—or mild hypoxia—that leads to headaches, fatigue, even fainting, the single most common health event aboard airplanes. So why not just make the "virtual" altitude lower than 8,000 feet, pressurize the plane more so we feel like we're back at sea level? Mainly because it would be too tough on the airplane. More pressure inside the cabin stresses the airplane fuselage—pushing outward against the aluminum skin and structure of the plane—resulting in more maintenance costs and potentially shorter life span for the aircraft.

For jet designers in the 1950s, the 8,000-foot "cabin altitude" was essentially a compromise between passenger comfort and fuselage durability. Early postwar studies actually recommended that jet-cabin altitudes be set at a more comfortable level of 5,000 to 6,000 feet. Besides, when regulators chose 8,000 feet in 1957, they likely had in mind fit young military pilots, not aging Baby Boomers. For the latter, a big draw for Boeing's new 787 is that it lowers passengers' "virtual" altitude down to about 6,000 feet; Airbus claims its A380 is closer to 5,000 feet. That said, 21 million residents of metropolitan Mexico City don't think twice about living 7,400 feet above sea level, nor do denizens of Flagstaff, Arizona, and Santa Fe, New Mexico (both at about 7,000 feet elevation).

Outside Death Valley, though, few people live in the extreme dryness of an airplane cabin, with roughly 10 percent relative humidity (think Death Valley in the summer at midday). The lack of humidity derives from the extreme cold of the air that ultimately enters the cabin from outside the plane at cruising altitude. At temperatures around *minus* 65 degrees Fahrenheit, that outside air holds precious little water—less than 1 percent absolute humidity. The only reason humidity inside the cabin is even tolerable—on the order of 10 times higher than outside the plane—is the passengers themselves. To put it delicately, the main source of onboard humidity is—sorry again—the breath and perspiration and other bodily effluents of passengers. The more crowded the plane and the more recirculated air, the moister it gets.

Ultra-dryness for long periods means more than just dry skin and chapped lips; it's also a likely culprit in colds and other infections that so often follow us off the plane. Humidity levels may have as much to do with whether you're about to suffer a raging head cold or gastrointestinal problem as germs in cabin air or viruses on sticky tray tables. Our key defense mechanism against colds is the "mucociliary clearance system," a thin layer of mucus kept in motion by the cilia—tiny, beating hairlike tissues in the nose—that trap invading germs and move them from the nose and throat to the stomach acids that destroy them. Dry cabin air can thicken the mucus to the point where the cilia cannot move it, inviting more nasty stuff in to cause upper-respiratory infections.

None of this has escaped the notice of airplane manufacturers. Higher cabin humidity, just like higher pressurization and lower virtual altitude, has become a selling point for new planes like the Boeing 787 "Dreamliner." Boeing promises to keep relative humidity in the 787 cabin at close to 16 percent. Meanwhile, Lufthansa is providing its First Class A380 cabins a relatively sultry 20 to 25 percent humidity level, and cockpits in fancy corporate jets sometimes get special humidifiers. Still, the high water mark, so to speak, is the "spa showers" that Emirates Airlines reserves for its ultra–First Class A380 passengers—even though the $10,000 one-way New York–Dubai fare entitles you to only five minutes of blissful drenching.

For the rest of us mere mortals, there's perennial talk of equipping planes with humidifiers but debate continues about their safety, effectiveness, and the cost of hauling around enough humidifier water to make a noticeable difference on long flights. Drier is better for delicate airplane systems—including avionics and sophisticated computers. British Airways tried adding humidity to early model jumbo jets in the 1980s, but mineral deposits in the water gummed up water passageways and spray bars so badly that the air-conditioning system reportedly started shooting out small white pellets. Then there's the problem of corrosive condensation on the cold outer skin of the plane, like on the outside of a cold glass on a warm, humid day. Insulation blankets that fit between the outer shell of a 737-300 and the airplane's cabin walls have been found soaked with up to 80 pounds of unwanted water. Humidifying cabin air remains a serious challenge.

Four Chimes

On some airlines, four chimes ringing in quick succession in the cabin is the signal that there's a medical emergency onboard; passengers are likely to hear them more often as the flying population ages. Health problems—preexisting and those triggered on board—cause more than a dozen serious in-flight medical emergencies on US planes every day. Airlines understandably hate to talk about them, and the government doesn't require them to. An analysis done for *USA Today* by MedAire, a firm that provides 24/7 emergency medical advice to some 60 airlines around the world, sheds some light. It found that the rate of in-flight emergencies nearly doubled in six years—up from 19 per million passengers in 2000 to 35 per million in 2006, and that fliers over age 50 accounted for 59 percent of emergencies and 83 percent of in-flight deaths in 2006. In 2010, MedAire alone fielded more than 19,000 airborne medical emergency calls.

Some 2 to 13 percent (studies vary widely) of such emergencies are serious enough to require the plane to divert from its scheduled destination—figure at least twice a day on average. Probably the most common onboard problem, in one study more than half of all incidents, involves vasovagal syncope—better known as fainting. Losing consciousness briefly is usually harmless; the passenger is overtired, overstressed, undernourished, or overheated and just needs to recline and drink water. But here's the tricky part for unlucky onboard diagnosticians: in rare cases, fainting can mean a massive heart attack or brain hemorrhage that, if left untreated for long, will leave the victim a vegetable, or dead. After fainting and gastrointestinal problems, cardiac events are relatively rare, but they account for a quarter to nearly half of those medical emergencies that result in flight diversions, and are the cause of most onboard deaths.

Far down the list of full-diversion-triggering emergencies, maybe 3 to 4 percent, are psychological events like panic attacks, even though they must be among the most common in-flight medical problems. After all, roughly one-third of US fliers has some degree of anxiety about flying, surveys say, though only about one in 16 Americans has a phobia that keeps them off airplanes entirely, according to the National Institute of Mental Health. Add to that the stresses inherent in today's crowded, claustrophobic, and increasingly lengthy flying experience and for some, anxiety can turn to panic. Veteran flight attendants can be experts at treating potentially explosive phobias with little more than some calming words, a reassuring hand, a glass of water, and maybe a few corny jokes—probably one reason only 1 to 2 percent of in-flight freak-outs require flight diversions, according to an FAA study of mid-1990s flights.

What's unique about medical emergencies at 35,000 feet is obvious: the availability of timely, qualified medical help is a crapshoot. Flights over the US mainland can almost always find a place to land within an hour or so, but for planes flying over the mid-Pacific or the Poles, it's another story. FAA rules for extended-range flights permit advanced commercial jets to range up to three hours from an emergency landing strip; a relative few are specially certified to stray as far as five and a half hours away. Even if it takes only an hour to get on the ground, though, that's still a very long time if you're having a stroke or major coronary. And don't count on sophisticated emergency medical assistance on remote Pacific atolls or tiny Aleutian islands with emergency airstrips.

When it comes to assistance in an urgent medical situation on board, what's on the plane is what you get. That's one reason that registered nurses were among the first official non-pilot airline personnel, the original "air stewardesses" introduced by Boeing Air Transport in May 1930. (For $125 a month, these young women also carried bags and checked for oil and gas leaks.) Even today, flight attendants are the first line of assistance.

Surprisingly often there's also a doctor, nurse, or emergency medical technician on board. Northwest Airlines estimated there was one on 96 percent of its flights, as *USA Today* reported in 2008. As for medical equipment, US airlines carry a first-aid kit meant for flight attendants. For use by volunteer doctors, there's also a 15-pound suitcase stuffed with medical devices for resuscitation and injections, and medications for heart attacks and allergic reactions, as well as a tank or two of oxygen and an automated external heart defibrillator. If there are no medical professional volunteers to help, it's up to the flight attendants, who are trained in first aid.

Though heart attacks have long been the major cause of in-flight death, onboard automatic defibrillators are relatively new. UK-based Virgin Atlantic led the way in 1990, an American Airlines flight attendant made the first US in-flight save with one in 1998, and another 81 lives were saved in the decade that followed. Still, emergency defibrillation works only about a quarter of the time at best, and then only on certain kinds of sudden heart conditions.

Just in case the onboard medical volunteer treating your heart attack happens to be a psychiatrist instead of a cardiologist, most airlines also contract with a ground-based 24/7 medical advisory service for emergency diagnostic and treatment help. They're limited in what they can do, though. Diagnosing someone remotely by radio necessarily omits the most basic first step—actual examination of the patient. Communications can get scrambled, too. Since nobody gets into the secured cockpit after September 11, medical information must still be relayed in most cases by cabin intercom from the back of the cabin to the pilots, who then pass it on to the ground-based doctors—remember playing the "telephone" game? The director of MedAire described to the *New York Times* the process of ground-based diagnosis and treatment as a matter of "experience and gestalt."

Ultimately, the captain makes the call whether to divert to the nearest airport; health experts—on board and on the ground—can only advise. There's a lot at stake in the decision, and it's rarely easy. Balanced against an often ambiguous medical risk—is it indigestion or a massive heart attack?—is more than just the hefty cost of landing at an unintended airport: on long hauls, estimate more than $100,000, counting fuel, overtime, new crew, and passenger accommodations, depending on the location. There's also the disruption of hundreds of other passengers' travel plans, as well as potential safety issues if an emergency landing involves an unusually "heavy" aircraft with unexpended fuel or an unfamiliar approach in bad weather to a little-used airstrip. Think of it this way: the last place you want to be in a medical emergency is in an aluminum tube 40,000 feet above the Arctic on a stormy night.

Death Onboard

Precise statistics are hard to come by, but a passenger probably dies on a US commercial airliner every few days on average, about half the time because of a heart attack. The risk of dying on board from illness has become considerably greater than dying in an aircraft accident. Airlines don't have to report onboard medical emergencies to the FAA unless they involve injury or death of a pet, in which case a detailed monthly report is required.

Human death on board is frequent enough, though, that airlines have protocols for how to handle it. Mostly, crews try to isolate the body as much as possible, often moving it to an empty row or to the more spacious First Class cabin and covering it with blankets. (First Class passengers waking from a nap to find themselves seated next to a corpse might be justified in questioning the wisdom of buying their $6,000 tickets.) On a full flight, this can mean just laying it down, covered, on the galley floor, as far as possible from other passengers. Some long-haul carriers routinely carry body bags.

There aren't a lot of good options, especially on a typically full airplane. Storing the body in a lavatory is not advised. When rigor mortis sets in, it can be a mess trying to remove the remains from the cramped space. So Airbus came up with a solution on its ultra-long-range aircraft, the A340-500, which Singapore Airlines flies daily up to 19 hours between Singapore and Newark over some of the most remote points on Earth, skirting the North Pole on the shortest routing. To minimize the discomfort of other passengers flying for nearly an entire night and day with a corpse in full view, the ingenious aircraft designers in Toulouse came up with a new design feature for the jetliner: a discreet pull-out cupboard adjacent to one of the exit doors. Long enough to store a body, with straps to prevent movement in turbulence, the mortuary drawer (aka the "corpse cupboard") respectfully holds the deceased without disturbing the survivors.

No-Brainer

Only four times since the Civil War had New York City seen more than a trace of snow in October—until October 29, 2011, when a freak nor'easter dropped a few inches in Central Park, then churned north to dump more than a foot on central Connecticut and Massachusetts. Falling heavy and wet, the snow brought down still-leafy trees and tree limbs, cutting power to roughly three million.

It also shut down critical bad-weather instrument-landing systems at New York's major airports, forcing more than 150 flights to divert. Among them was the nearly full JetBlue Flight 504 from Fort Lauderdale. Like other diverted planes, Flight 504's pilot asked to land in Boston, an ample facility where the weather was better. But Boston was having its own problems. It was already crowded with two dozen planes diverted from New York, including a massive Lufthansa Airbus 380 that had no place to park except at the end of a runway, closing it to other landings. Another Boston runway was blocked by a military jet trying to unload soldiers wounded in Libya, which required extra room on the tarmac for ten ambulances, according to an Associated Press report by Joan Lowy. There was simply no room in Boston for hapless Flight 504.

Hartford's Bradley International Airport, less than 100 miles north of New York, was the logical alternative. Ringed by old tobacco barns and bucolic New England hills, Bradley is a relatively small facility with limited international services and only 23 gates. That afternoon it lay directly in the snowstorm's northward path.

By one thirty p.m., when Flight 504 with 129 passengers and six crew members landed at Hartford and pulled off onto a taxiway, some 23 other diverted flights were already sitting there or on the way. That included an American Boeing 767 inbound from Paris after about eight hours in the air. In the space of two hours, the airport's gates were filled and, as the weather worsened, new arrivals crowded the tarmac. The airport struggled to deplane more than a thousand stranded passengers amid intermittent power outages that hobbled refueling, de-icing, and deplaning. Meanwhile, Flight 504 sat on the tarmac for seven and a half hours, after its three-hour flight.

Things turned nasty on the JetBlue A320. "We ran out of water," said Andrew Carter, a Florida sports reporter who phoned his editors from the plane, according to various reports. "The bathrooms are all clogged up and disgusting," he reported. "When you flushed, nothing would happen." The power on board was also going off "every 45 minutes or so for five minutes or so, and that would freak people out. . . ." There was no food. Babies, without formula or fresh diapers, wailed. Passengers were cursing, yelling, and threatening to call the police. (One who did call 911 was told there had already been a dozen calls from the plane.) The pilot beseeched the airline, then airport officials, for help: "Is there any way you can get a tug and a tow-bar out to us and get us towed somewhere to a gate or something? I don't care, take us anywhere," he pleaded, his words posted on LiveATC.net.

The 30 to 40 cubic feet of personal space per passenger on a loaded Airbus 320 is a small fraction the size of a standard prison cell. Even inmates get exercise time. When local firefighters finally arrived to remove a paraplegic in distress, other passengers began screaming: "Get us off this plane!" Around nine p.m., nearly 11 hours after an on-time takeoff from sunny Florida, firefighters helped passengers down the slippery aluminum stairs in heavy snow—heading to a terminal crammed with a thousand others forced to spend the night on cots hastily assembled by the National Guard.

It wasn't the first time hundreds of passengers were stranded for hours on crowded, smelly, snowbound tubes—not hardly. For years, an average of two to three flights every day had been sitting on the ground for more than three hours. In the big picture, those extreme delays were rare—less than 0.1 percent of all flights—but it still meant that nearly a thousand domestic flights waited for more than three hours in 2009, stranding more than 100,000 unfortunate passengers. Just slightly shorter incarcerations—from two to three hours on the tarmac—hit hundreds of flights every week. And punishingly long delays on the runway were nothing new; the issue had been a focus of consumer angst for more than a decade, ever since four thousand passengers famously were trapped in foul cabins for up to nine hours in a Detroit blizzard that, as we'll see, slammed Northwest's main hub on January 3, 1999.

Tarmac strandings seemed qualitatively different from the everyday hassles of air travel. Incarcerating scores of humans packed tightly on stationary cylinders for six, seven, eight hours moved beyond the routinely stressful to the realm of the inhumane. It crystallized a disturbing sense that airlines, desperate for the almighty buck, just didn't give a damn. Fliers could understand that an industry struggling in punishing economic times couldn't focus on customers as individuals, but still they were *human*.

Somebody had to do something to fix it. But unless the airlines "fixed it" themselves—and they hadn't, despite more than a decade of complaints—there was really only one realistic alternative: federal regulation. When it comes to commercial aviation, federal regulators are the last, often the only, cops on the beat, not just for safety issues but also for protecting consumers from "unfair or deceptive" industry practices. States and cities have almost no legal authority over interstate airline service. Federal commerce, safety, and labor laws "preempt" state laws in almost all commercial aviation matters. Customers normally can't even sue airlines for lousy service (except for some limited small claims court actions). Since the deregulation of the industry in 1978, market forces are supposed to control how airlines behave. But when that doesn't work, calling the cops means calling the feds—specifically the Department of Transportation—to enforce rules on the books or, as with tarmac delays, to make a new rule.

DOT takes this responsibility seriously, though in truth sometimes more as an aspiration. "It's DOT that protects the public," says the Department's General Counsel. Still, the folks at DOT have rarely been confused with Dirty Harry when it comes to enforcing aviation consumer rules. Not because their hearts weren't in it, or because of any lack of public outcry, but rather because consumer enforcers for years haven't had the bodies, the money, the clout, or, in some cases, the legal authority to get tough.

That's all of little comfort to the masses of air travelers unhappy with their airlines. More than 10,000 of them every year file complaints with DOT's Office of Aviation Enforcement and Proceedings—the equivalent of nearly a half dozen complaints every hour of every workday. Folks lost their bags, lost their vacation, lost their refund, lost their sanity. Topping the list are flight problems, delays, lost bags, and "customer service"—a catchall that covers everything from rude flight attendants to lousy in-flight movies.

Those who make the effort to complain to DOT, though, are just the tip of the iceberg. Consumer enforcers estimate that for every airline complaint they receive, passengers send another 50 complaints to the airlines directly. If that's true, that means an amazing *half million* air travelers are sufficiently ticked off every year to take the time to make a formal complaint about their air-travel experience.

Here's what DOT really does with *almost all* of the 10,000 traveler complaints it gets:

> It counts them.

> It pigeonholes each into a category—overbooking (called "oversales"), "mishandled" (sometimes just plain lost) luggage, flight delays and cancellations, ticketing and refunds, fares, customer service, and other "unfair and deceptive practices."

> It forwards each to the complained-about airline, reminding it to respond in some "substantive" way to the complainer within 60 days. (TSA "customer service" complaints are sent to the Department of Homeland Security.)

> It publishes a neat statistical monthly summary of all the complaints it receives, ranking each airline by complaint totals.

Basically, that's it. In the great majority of cases, there's no DOT investigation and rarely any other follow-up or action to actually "fix" the problem complained of. DOT just passes your beef along to the airline that allegedly caused it, requiring it to send you "a substantive response." What DOT's consumer "protectors" do, mostly, is keep really good records.

It's not that enforcers are trying to bark louder than their fairly gentle bite. When irate passengers telephone DOT's "consumer protection hotline," the first thing they hear is this recorded disclaimer: "If you have an airline service issue, we recommend that you first contact the airline. . . . Most service issues . . . do not violate any federal rules. The airline is in the best position to address and resolve those concerns." In other words, you're on your own. And have a nice day.

To be fair, every week or so on average, DOT actually does some proactive—OK, punitive—enforcing. It investigates a consumer violation and assesses a fine, though not that often against a major US airline. Most penalties involve advertising airfares without including costs like taxes or surcharges, or failing to make clear that the flight you thought was on a big airline is actually flown by its regional "partner" carrier. Even when DOT does levy a fine, it has an unofficial "forgiveness" policy.

Airline violators who don't fight the fine and settle by signing a docu-ment ("consent decree") agreeing to it typically get the "half-off" dis-count. That also lets them (a) refuse to admit they did anything wrong and (b) promise never to do it again. If they don't, in fact, do it again for a year, or if they promise to spend more money on complying with the rules, DOT typically "forgives" the *second* half of their fine.

Getting penalized for consumer rule violations annoys airlines to no end, but it hardly makes them tremble in fear of DOT consumer enforc-ers. The DOT hammer threatens not even to dent the financials of these multimillion-dollar corporations. In 2009, for instance, DOT levied about 30 consumer penalties for a total of some $2.6 million, but only half of them fell on big US airlines and most of *those* fines were $50,000 or less in up-front cash. True, that was roughly twice the size of the pen-alties assessed in either of the two preceding years, but still a pittance for an airline industry that takes in nearly $175 *billion* each year.

Most consumer protection fines don't even address traditional con-sumer issues like deceptive advertising and overbooking. According to an August 2008 DOT presentation to foreign regulators, more than half the DOT penalties from 2000 to mid-2008 involved civil rights viola-tions, including discrimination against disabled passengers. And get this: in the ten years up to 2006, only $2.1 million of the $14.9 million in assessed penalties was actually paid, an Inspector General investi-gation found. Even if all fines were paid in full, though, consider that by 2012, the average consumer penalty assessed against all air service providers and sellers was less than $75,000—about a half dozen First Class round-trip seats to Europe.

When Congress lifted the hand of regulation from the industry in 1978, it gave DOT what looked like broad legal authority to make sure the traveling public didn't get screwed in the competitive free-for-all that might ensue. Rather than explore the outer boundaries of that power to fight "unfair" and "deceptive" practices, though, the feds have tended to focus on issues like omissions in fare advertising "fine print," inadequate disclosure of information about code-sharing, and, at the behest of Congress, air travel access for disabled fliers—all areas where, in fairness, DOT legal authority is most explicit and established. Of course even if DOT *had* chosen to push its envelope, legal authority is one thing; the practical ability to actually make vast private enterprises behave is quite another. That takes money, bureaucratic clout, a credibly sized staff, and high-level political will. And there wasn't a whole lot of that for DOT's consumer protectors, at least until late in the decade after 9/11.

By law, every e-ticket includes DOT's toll-free telephone complaint "hotline." But who's at the other end of the line to handle all those complaints and enforce the rest of DOT's consumer requirements? By 2000, just 17 government employees—including both administrative and legal staff—were there to "protect" America's 100 million or so annual consumers of air travel. Even at a high point of consumer-office staffing in 2004, only some 41 individuals, about half of them lawyers, were assigned to the task—and each lawyer juggled an average of 17 cases or projects, according to a 2006 Inspector General report.

Today, DOT's aviation consumer protection office, part of the DOT General Counsel's office, has a staff of about 45 (half lawyers, half investigators and analysts, including support staff). That's barely larger than the 41 people who performed much the same functions in 1985, the year the responsibility shifted from the old Civil Aeronautics Board to DOT. Consumer enforcers have been added in the last few years—reportedly half a dozen more lawyers today than in 2008—and more money has been allocated, but it's all still barely a footnote to the FAA's annual billion-dollar-plus budget for aviation safety enforcers, inspectors, and regulators.

Aside from warm bodies, monitoring the way America's dozen large airlines (those with more than a million annual passengers) treat consumers takes serious money. Yet, the entire enforcement travel budget for the office as late as 2005 was a mere $3,500—maybe enough to send a couple of agency lawyers to a single out-of-town meeting with a miscreant airline. And even the pinched resources available are spread thin. DOT is legally required to undertake a comprehensive investigation of specific kinds of consumer complaints—the 600-plus each year involving disabled travelers and civil rights—and that leaves even less for all the other thousands of complaints. With this level of "resources"— Washington-speak for bodies, money, and clout—how could aviation consumer protection be anything more than reactive and, even then, only to the worst instances of consumer-unfriendly behavior?

It's not just a matter of government-wide belt-tightening; there's also a deeper, long-standing ambivalence about just how much consumer protecting the feds should do. That policy call shifts with Administrations *and* with sensational, action-forcing events like mass tarmac strandings, but the debate is as old as deregulation, when Congress sent a dual message to DOT aviation regulators: let airlines compete more like "normal" businesses, but make sure the public is treated OK in the process.

Since 2009, the aviation consumer-protection pendulum has been swinging back to greater activism. In 2011, to the consternation of some in the industry, the Obama DOT set a new record for consent order fines—47 penalties totaling nearly $3.3 million (though fewer than half were assessed against US airlines)—then broke that record the following year, issuing 49 such fines for a total of $3.6 million. From 2009 through 2012, DOT's 203 consumer penalties, totaling $16.5 million, nearly doubled the number and amount of fines assessed during the four preceding years of the Bush administration, when 105 penalties totaled $8.8 million.

The get-tougher approach reflects more than just a political shift in attitude or a more favorable policy view of consumer regulation. There was also a sense, perhaps driven in part by disgust at "outrages" like tarmac strandings, that ordinary passengers, increasingly outmatched in their dealings with a tougher, smarter, more concentrated airline industry, just needed more help. And there was also a growing confidence that the industry, now no longer on economic life support, could and should step up better to its consumer responsibilities. Bottom line: regulators are today enforcing the rules more stringently and more frequently, DOT consumer protection is getting somewhat more money and attention, and new rules, mainly focused on keeping air travelers "informed," are being issued. A leading aviation law firm describes the recent shift, with only a touch of hyperbole, as "without question . . . the largest expansion of airline consumer protection rules in decades."

It's taken years, though, for that pendulum to swing, and despite industry indignation over supposed "re-regulation," the real-world effect of this new regulatory activism on the airlines, in dollars and cents, has been pretty modest. So where does the state of consumer protection leave today's unhappy customers—the 10,000–plus air travelers who complain to DOT every year, or the estimated half million who complain to the airlines, or the millions of other folks who just don't bother? Can they count on aviation consumer regulators to tame the excesses or come to their rescue when things go awry? A common observation among DOT consumer enforcers: "Let's get real about expectations."

The No-Brainer

If enforcing consumer rules already on the books seems like an uphill battle, a lightning rod for industry anger, and a long slog for aggrieved passengers, it pales in comparison to the years-long task of making *new* rules to protect consumers. Even proposals that barely affect the way airlines operate day-to-day trigger sometimes-fierce industry opposition, even eliciting accusations, as a popular industry journal framed an op-ed, that regulators had launched a "war against the airline industry."

Even no-brainers can take forever—like a DOT consumer rule to require airlines to release passengers cooped up waiting on the tarmac for more than three hours. The saga of that seemingly simple commonsense regulation shows starkly how tough it can be in the unreal world of Washington to regulate a more humane air-travel experience, and how long it can take for the "cops" to arrive. When it all started with planeloads trapped in the Detroit blizzard of January 1999, no one could have imagined that regulatory help would take more than a decade to come—until two days before New Year's Day 2010—consume vast resources, and trigger an arduous battle that some industry advocates are *still* fighting.

The massive blizzard that hit the Midwest on January 3, 1999, blanketed Northwest Airlines' global air hub in Detroit in more than a foot of drifting snow and 20-degree temperatures. Even as the storm hit, though, Northwest kept landing its planes, even though there was no place to park them. All of the airport's gates were occupied by planes that had been unable to fly out in the storm. In the end, nearly three dozen fully loaded flights sat motionless on the tarmac—one for eight and a half hours. The planes' passengers, without food or water, gagged on the stench wafting from overflowing lavatories. As distraught families emerged with harrowing tales, the consensus to "do something"— pass a law, issue a regulation—seemed crystal clear.

News media pounced on the Detroit story and stayed with it for days. Sobbing moms and starving babies snowbound for hours made for compelling coverage. Meanwhile, Congress was just returning to Washington from the Christmas holiday, ready for action. And almost before the snow stopped falling, class-action lawyers were gearing up to file a massive false-imprisonment and negligence lawsuit. (Two years later, shortly before trial, Northwest settled it for $7.1 million—reportedly some $2,000 for each of the unlucky 600 passengers stuck for more than eight hours.) On the tenth floor of DOT headquarters in Washington— from the richly paneled office of the secretary of transportation down the hall to the General Counsel, his top lawyer and political consigliere— tarmac delays suddenly rose to the top of everybody's crowded inbox.

DOT was, and is, a sprawling bureaucracy of 60,000 workers, cobbled

together in 1967 by President Lyndon Johnson. Its Highway Administration funnels federal billions to build and maintain highways. Its
Federal Transit Administration does the same for subways and buses.
The National Highway Traffic Safety Administration tests automobile
safety and issues safety ratings. The Federal Aviation Administration
oversees the safety of airlines, pilots, and airports. The Federal Railway
Administration supervises railroad safety.

Even though aviation is just one of DOT's "modes" of transport, it
gets far more than its fair share of high-level political attention, mainly
because it gets far more of the *public's* attention. When the discovery
of a single snoozing air traffic controller at a Washington, DC, airport
in 2011 can fuel national outrage, major aviation screw-ups like the
Detroit strandings often top the secretary of transportation's daily
agenda. Those mediagenic enough to make the network news, or at least
the major cable channels, can draw an earful from White House staff.
Within three days, widespread news coverage of the Detroit debacle had
everybody in the "do-something" mode.

Many in Washington assumed that DOT would put out a new tarmac-
delay rule, using its legal authority to stop "unfair and deceptive practices." Holding innocent travelers for hours aboard smelly, crowded
aircraft certainly seemed "unfair." But enforcers prefer specific "thou-
shalt-not" proscriptions that nobody can quibble with and detail precisely what airlines must do with customers trapped in tarmac hell.
Consumer protection rules like these are far, far slower and harder to
implement than FAA safety rules to correct a specific defect or unsafe
condition on a particular type of aircraft. In an emergency, FAA has special authority to make safety regulations effective literally overnight,
even ground entire fleets of jet aircraft if it suspects a defective or dangerous condition. New consumer-protection rules, in contrast, can take
forever. Even the no-brainers.

Making new consumer regulations is a process measured in years. In
a 2001 review, GAO estimated that many significant aviation rules took

three to four years, start to finish; consumer rules with "teeth"—ones that cost the industry serious money to comply with—can take far longer. The ban on smoking aboard aircraft—the granddaddy of airline consumer regulation—took *27 years* to effect completely, starting from the Civil Aeronautics Board's initial step in 1973 to require separate "smoking" and "no-smoking" sections until a complete across-the-board ban took effect in 2000.

Why does it take so long to fix even an obvious problem like tarmac delays with a new rule? Three words: process, consensus, and outrage.

Process

Regulations are like laws, except they're not passed by elected legislatures. To help ensure they're sensible and legitimate and reasonable, everybody—literally, every single member of the public—is entitled to make known his or her views on most proposed federal rules. Conversely, regulators must be able to prove they "duly considered" every last one of those views or comments. The notion is as old as the New Deal, and if regulators don't take all views into account, courts can strike down their regulations. What this means, in practice, is that controversial rule proposals can trigger thousands of comments, even orchestrated campaigns of comments in support or opposition, and months and months of agency "review" of all those submissions.

That's just the beginning of the process requirements for a new rule. Another requirement—and a favorite legal land mine for regulatory opponents—is the so-called cost-benefit test; regulators have to prove that the quantifiable benefits of a proposed rule outweigh the likely cost to the industry of complying with it. For the tarmac-delay rule, that meant proving that the "quantifiable benefit" of liberating trapped passengers from long-delayed planes was greater than the cost to airlines of getting them off the stranded plane. This analysis can all get pretty squishy. How exactly do you quantify the "benefit" of not having to spend the night stranded on the tarmac? Priceless? K Street economists for hire will happily produce "regulatory evaluations" to prove that most any regulation is or is not "cost-beneficial." For the final tarmac rule, DOT's consultant produced a 90-page report that—ta-da!—showed that the rule's benefits would exceed its costs by $69.1 million over 20 years. Here's a surprise: where DOT estimated the rule would cost airlines and fliers $100 million over 20 years, industry-friendly economic consultants predicted nearly 40 *times* that cost.

Battling economists aside, there are plenty of other legal hurdles designed to make regulations hard and K Street lawyers prosperous. (Full disclosure: I used to be one of them.) New rules can't unduly affect "small entities" or Indian tribal interests. They can't impose new costs on states ("unfunded mandates") or interfere with international trade. Even seemingly simple information-gathering—for instance, requiring airlines to report how many tarmac delays lasted more than three hours—can require special White House approval because of a Carter-era law known as the Paperwork Reduction Act. Think of the regulatory process as a game of Chutes and Ladders—fail to cross a *t* or dot an *i* and you're sliding back down to the start of the game.

Consensus

Beyond process, though, there's an equally essential and unwritten prerequisite for timely regulation: securing consensus—or close to it—among "stakeholders." Almost everybody with something to gain or lose by reason of a rule—every important stakeholder—must agree, or at least acquiesce in, the proposal. If not, that stakeholder has to be "rolled"—a politically risky and rarely desirable move. The more opposition from stakeholders, the more time and hassle it takes to put an essential, if unwritten, rule into effect; the more consensus, the better the chance that something useful will happen. Of course, developing consensus can involve delicate compromises and trade-offs that water down a rule, but if a key player throws itself against the regulatory machine, as happened with the tarmac-delay rule, it can delay the process for years until another "outrage" again stirs the pot of public indignation.

In theory, stakeholders include every member of the public who has an interest or concern. In reality, the stakeholders who can change the fate of regulation are the affected businesses who are prepared to invest money and time to enlist K Street and Capitol Hill operatives, to generate political heat to make sure that any rule that emerges goes their way, or at least doesn't do them much harm. Stranded fliers may have been the victims of tarmac delays, but they weren't really seen as stakeholders. The *key* stakeholders were the airlines.

Major airlines are always powerful stakeholders at DOT, and why not? In a real sense, what's good for the airline industry is in fact good for large swaths of the American economy. US passenger airlines alone directly employ nearly 400,000 US workers, and rank among the top industrial sectors in contributions to the GDP. They contract with thousands of American businesses—from Fortune 100 megafirms like Boeing and jet engine–maker General Electric down to the mom-and-pop airport cleaning outfits that vacuum the airplane cabin carpets overnight. Communities large and small depend on them for access to markets and for tourism. San Jose, California, for instance, recently estimated that a single new daily flight to Tokyo would generate $90 million in business and economic growth annually for the region.

Politics aside, DOT *wants* airlines to be financially healthy. Stable airlines are more likely safe, reliable airlines. So the Department listens hard to the carriers—even to hyperbole about the "crushing" burden of complying with even the simplest consumer rules. Given their historic unprofitability and heavy tax burden, sometimes it's not all hyperbole.

To make *sure* DOT and other agencies are listening, though, the US airline industry collectively spends millions of dollars every year on lobbying, hiring some of the best public relations and lobby shops K Street has to offer. On dicier issues like security or hygiene or consumer rights, individual airlines that would rather lie low can let their powerful trade association—Airlines for America (formerly the "Air Transport Association of America," a name suited to its New Deal origins)—do the talking. After all, what airline wants to be known individually for leading the charge against better-rested pilots or "free" airplane baby seats or free oxygen for disabled travelers or, for that matter, ending tarmac strandings? The association spent more than $8 million on lobbying in just the first two years of the Obama administration and in 2011 paid its CEO $3.6 million, the highest for any similar transportation association according to the *Washington Post*. Airlines pay plenty to belong to A4A, but it's worth it.

Airlines aren't the only powerful DOT stakeholders, though. Major airports are critical engines of local economies and huge employers in their own right. More than a million people work directly at the country's commercial airports, almost as many as at Wal-Mart, the nation's largest private-sector employer. Atlanta's Hartsfield, the country's busiest airport, has more than 58,000 "on-airport" workers, making it Georgia's largest single employment center, with an estimated direct economic effect of more than $32 billion on the metro area's economy. Typically owned by municipal governments, big airports have deep political clout. So too does aviation labor, another major stakeholder. Leading national unions in the highly organized industry include elements of the powerful Teamsters and Machinists. Separate unions represent pilots, flight attendants, machinists, maintenance workers, and baggage handlers. And aerospace manufacturers like Boeing, with nearly 175,000 employees alone, are among America's export champions. Who's going to mess with *their* many fierce protectors up and down Pennsylvania Avenue?

Ordinary air travelers are stakeholders too—arguably the most important ones when it comes to achieving consensus on consumer-protection rules. Who's being trapped on those snowy tarmacs anyway? Everybody in the airline industry purports to speak for the interests of air travelers, and regulators by law have that responsibility, but inside the Beltway, consumers are too often just heavily outgunned.

Outrage

Powerful commercial forces can help block regulations, but they mainly just capitalize on the inertia already built into the system by the demand for process and consensus. Just as it's far easier to kill a bill in Congress than to pass one, delay is the default option for most proposed regulation. It's easier and costs less politically to kick the can, appoint a study commission, and order up a GAO report than to propose even a mildly controversial regulation. Unless, that is, there's some kind of galvanizing event that captures the attention of the public, the news media, and Congress. Would there be serious talk of an assault-weapons ban without Newtown?

Outrage at the treatment of thousands of snowbound fliers made action against tarmac delays seem inevitable, even imminent, after the Detroit debacle in the winter of 1999. That it took more than a decade reflects how problematic it can be for travelers to rely on the government to fix what's wrong with air travel, to overcome the built-in inertia and, sometimes, the sophisticated industry opposition.

Inside the Beltway

Geographic fortuity added to the prospect for quick action against tarmac delays in 1999: Northwest's Detroit hub lies within the congressional district represented for more than 50 years by "Big John" Dingell, then the powerful chairman of the House Energy and Commerce Committee and a man famous for demanding and conducting tough investigations. (John D. Dingell Drive bisects the airport itself.) Within a week of the strandings, congressional investigators were dispatched, and four days of televised hearings were scheduled for mid-March. Meanwhile, the House Transportation and Infrastructure Committee rushed to craft a "passenger bill of rights" and the Clinton administration—Vice President Gore himself—proposed corrective legislation.

The overflowing congressional hearings in March 1999 seemed designed for a hanging of Northwest; instead they proved how resilient the airline industry could be. Room 2167 of the Rayburn House Office

Building is one of those imposing, high-ceilinged, deep-carpeted hearing rooms on the House side of the Capitol, equipped for C-SPAN and live TV with lots of space below and in front of the wall-to-wall dais for witness and press tables. It's big enough to hold the largest committee in Congress, the 59-member "T & I" Committee, as it's known, which oversees vast reservoirs of transportation "pork"—federal money for highways and bridges and airports. By the time of the hearings, the huge room was filled, with a line waiting in the crowded hallway to get in. Big John himself was the first witness. Loaded for bear, he set the tone by charging the airlines with a "public-be-damned" attitude.

Every good congressional hearing needs a villain, a foil for congressional inquisition, and Northwest, the hub carrier at the Detroit debacle, was designated to play that role. Setting the stage for mediagenic outrage, the committee first called "victims" stranded on the tarmac to testify about their horrific experiences. Afterward, by the ritualistic choreography of Capitol Hill hearings, the designated villain or target—in this case, Northwest—appears to take its spanking. Except something surprising happened when Northwest showed up for the hearing's continuation the following week: It didn't follow the script. Instead, the carrier dispatched its senior VP and General Counsel, a polished and charismatic Harvard-trained advocate wise in the ways of the Hill. Northwest also got help from another witness, the Honorable Andrew Card. Identified modestly as a "Fellow" at the Chamber of Commerce, Card had served earlier as White House chief of staff to President George H. W. Bush and, before then, as the previous administration's secretary of transportation. What a coincidence. The distinguished former cabinet secretary, "representing the interests of the business community," made a lousy target for congressional diatribes.

Even tougher to attack were the "regular guy" Northwest employees positioned in the audience. Greg and Larry, for example, were two airline workers who had spent long hours with little or no sleep trying to clear snow during the Detroit blizzard. At an opportune moment in the presentation, the Northwest witness "casually" acknowledged the heroic pair to members of the committee. Then came a veteran Northwest pilot witness who had personally gone out of his way to help snowed-in passengers get home from the airport. As it emerged, the captain had actually escaped the worst of the Detroit tarmac strandings, having ridden in on a plane that managed to unload within one hour of landing to deal with a passenger medical emergency. That aside, in crisp uniform with four stripes on the sleeves, he looked every bit the senior airline captain.

The issue at the heart of the hearing *seemed* pretty simple: shouldn't there be a law requiring airlines to let their passengers off a tarmac-bound plane after a specified time? Not so simple, said the airlines. In fact, it was really a question of vast complexity, fraught with implications for regulatory policy, the free market, and even aviation safety. Former secretary Card pronounced passenger-rights legislation to be "unnecessary intervention in the marketplace" that "might stifle innovation," and warned darkly that it could "raise safety issues."

Then the airline trade association's distinguished General Counsel spoke up to announce that the airline industry was taking its own "voluntary" actions that would preempt and render superfluous any government rule. Precisely what were those? Counsel professed himself "very pleased to announce" that the airlines were "reaffirming their commitment to customer service" with a brand-new—wait for it!—Airline Customer Service "Commitment." What this commitment really appeared to boil down to was a qualified promise that passengers would get flight delay and cancellation information that was "timely and accurate," at least "to the extent . . . reasonably available." They would also be told the lowest fare available if they asked. And passengers with confirmed reservations, a valid ticket, and who had "adhered to the airline's policies" could "expect" not to be bumped from their flights.

Although nothing specific was promised about tarmac delays, this rather thin "commitment," rolled out as hardly less than a consumer

Magna Carta, at least gave an industry playing defense something to talk about. And lo and behold, it worked well enough to forestall immediate action. Airlines were apparently so impressed with the outcome that, three months later, with even greater fanfare, they scheduled a formal press conference to unveil a "plan" that included no fewer than *twelve* promises. They would assign an employee (sorry, a "special representative") to handle passenger complaints. They would make "every reasonable effort" to provide food, water, restroom, and medical services during very long tarmac delays (without specifying how long a delay was *too* long), and they would *try* to return lost checked bags in 24 hours. And how about this? They would even "disclose" to fliers the airline's rules on cancellation, frequent flier programs, and accommodating disabled passengers.

Building on the beneficence, Continental issued a press release announcing its own version of the plan, entitled "Customer First." The airline applauded "the joint effort of the airline industry, the U.S. Congress, and the U.S. Department of Transportation to address the key service elements that most affect our customers." If that weren't caring enough, the airline added: "We want our customers to let us know how we're doing by calling our Customer Care Department at 1-800-WECARE2." The "Customer Care Department"? Who could impose job-killing regulation on such caring folks?

Hokey, perhaps, but in the end nobody legislated and nobody regulated tarmac delays for years to come. Instead, 22 months after the Detroit debacle, and just five days before the hotly contested presidential election of 2000, the DOT issued a one-page "fact sheet to help consumers" avoid flight delays. Among the handful of handy "tips": fly early in the day, fly nonstop, and avoid "certain airports [that] are more congested than others." Nothing said about multi-hour strandings, much less a regulation to limit them. Instead, DOT advised "defensive planning" by passengers, since "airline delays and cancellations are not unusual." The government's solution for consumers was to advise "defensive planning"?

Whether a tougher DOT would or could have done more is hard to know. The entire tarmac-delay issue went into deep freeze a year later when the September 11 terrorist attacks and recession made congestion delays the least of anybody's worries. In the four years that followed, the priority was to save a critical industry. Tarmac delays and passenger rights, generally, dropped back down the agenda.

By 2007, though, air traffic had bounced back, airlines were again making money, and the economy was picking up. And with it all returned the crowding and delays. All it took for tarmac strandings to reemerge was a little bad weather, bad judgment, and bad luck. All of that came together on Valentine's Day 2007 at New York's crowded JFK Airport when an ice storm failed to change to a rainstorm as forecast. Even as the weather worsened, JetBlue kept boarding planes and pushing them back from boarding gates; meanwhile, other planes continued to land. What ensued was a cruel game of "musical gates" that left nine jets stranded on taxiways for up to ten hours with nowhere to go. Cue up the by-now-forgotten tales of screaming babies and overflowing toilets—and right in the media capital of the world! Better yet, the bad guy was the hippest, coolest airline around, a stylish newcomer that clad its pilots in blue, served organic potato chips, and vowed to humanize air travel.

Whereas Northwest initially retreated to a defensive crouch after its Detroit mess eight years earlier, JetBlue quickly did the opposite, issuing abject apologies to anyone who would listen. Within 48 hours, the airline's CEO told every media outlet he could—from late-night Letterman to early-morning financial cable news—that he was "mortified" and that "words cannot express how truly sorry we are." One-upping the airline trade association's "Customer Commitment"—the tack that helped forestall regulation eight years earlier—JetBlue issued a "Customers' Bill of Rights." The "bill" itself still focused on better informing passengers and compensating them for delays, but the airline also announced something new, even groundbreaking: pilots were instructed to return to the gate after five hours unless takeoff was imminent. Five hours is a

very long time, but still it was a specific time period, the first that any of
the traditional network airlines (except once-burned Northwest) would
clearly embrace.

Nearly eclipsed by the JetBlue media frenzy was another stranding—
remote from any Manhattan media hub—that had occurred just six
weeks earlier. Bad weather forced American Flight 1348, headed to Dallas, to divert to Austin, where it sat on the tarmac for nearly nine hours.
Airlines didn't know it at the time, but among the outraged strandees
was one who would become the carriers' arch-nemesis in the tarmac
regulation fight. Kate Hanni, an Internet-savvy real estate agent from
California, had been traveling on the stranded flight with her husband
and two kids to an Alabama resort.

Well-heeled, well-spoken, and ill-used by the airlines, this mom
soon became a minor celebrity, and the airlines' worst nightmare. She
launched a website, FlyersRights.org. She organized a "strand-in" pro-
test on the National Mall in Washington, using a mock-up of a jet cabin.
She even came up with a theme song—an adaptation of the Animals'
1965 hit called "We Gotta Get Out of This Plane." She enlisted her California congressman in an anti-stranding crusade, haunted Washington,
and did lots of TV trying to build a grassroots push to "fix" extended
delays. Maybe she couldn't tell an aileron from an elevator, but Hanni
had a clear goal: a "Bill of Rights" for air travelers that included a three-
hour deadline for airlines to get their stranded passengers back to the
gate. Ms. Smith Goes to Washington.

Between JetBlue and Hanni and a nasty resurgence of flight delays
(still averaging five every day in 2007), the George W. Bush DOT faced
new calls for a tarmac rule that had teeth. Yet the Department, led by
a former Arizona transportation director best known for privatizing
highways and encouraging motorcycle helmets, was, to put it gently, in
no rush to regulate. In time-honored Washington fashion, DOT called
for more study of the stranding problem by its nonpartisan Inspector
General. It didn't take long for the Inspector General to return with a

clear recommendation: Airlines should specify a time limit—a number of hours—after which they will deplane passengers. It was essentially what Congress and regulators had pressed for eight years earlier.

Testifying before an impatient Senate panel two days later, on September 27, 2007, the acting head of the FAA could only respond that a "senior staff working group" was "well along in its consideration of various alternatives" and professed that "something must be done to minimize" strandings. Still, airlines betting the outgoing Bush DOT would keep "slow-walking" the issue were proven right when the agency kicked the can again. Instead of proposing a rule, DOT announced that it was *thinking* about proposing a rule—but professed it first needed to hear from the public. What did DOT not know about the problem nearly a full decade since the Detroit blizzard? The first two questions that DOT posed to the public in its notice hardly suggested that a tough rule would emerge: "What costs would (a rule) impose on [airlines]? Would it have any negative consequences?"

DOT also used another timeworn Washington tactic to buy more time: create a "commission" to undertake even further study. (In fairness, the Inspector General's 2007 report had suggested as much, though this suggestion was far down the list of its more action-focused recommendations.) The rather grandly named "National Task Force to Develop Draft Model Contingency Plans," populated by three dozen semi-senior airline officials, airport executives, and trade association lobbyists, plus Hanni and one or two other consumerists, was chaired by the lawyer in charge of DOT's aviation consumer office. Although the group toiled throughout 2008, it quickly became apparent that nothing like an agreed time limit for getting stranded passengers off planes—not even a "voluntary" rule—would emerge. The ultimate report, issued just a week after the election of Barack Obama, carefully emphasized that it was merely "advisory in nature" and that tarmac deplaning timing issues were extraordinarily complex. A week later, a frustrated *New York Times* editorialized that the DOT task force, "stacked with airline and airport executives ... treated the definition of a lengthy delay as if it were some conundrum of astrophysics." The *Times* predicted: "Surely the incoming administration will be less captive to industry on this issue."

The time for regulatory foot-dragging had just about elapsed. On Capitol Hill, senators Barbara Boxer and Olympia Snowe impatiently asked the DOT secretary flat-out to set a maximum of three hours for deplaning passengers caught in tarmac delays, since "voluntary" airline plans would be "completely ineffective." Just six weeks before the Obama inauguration, in one of its last major regulatory acts, the Bush DOT on December 8, 2008, finally proposed a tarmac-delay rule— without any specific time limit on deplaning stranded passengers. For nine years since Detroit, the airlines had succeeded in holding the line against what their trade association called a "hard and fast" rule.

The new administration had different ideas. Less hesitant to regulate and facing an upswing in air traffic and delays, the new DOT didn't take long. In January 2009, senators Boxer and Snowe reintroduced a "Passengers' Bill of Rights" that would force airlines to unload passengers after three hours, and Kate Hanni's California congressman, Mike Thompson, introduced a companion bill in the House of Representatives. Senate Democrats also tried unsuccessfully to tack the three-hour rule to a long-stalled bill to fund the FAA. Meanwhile, a *USA Today* analysis in August 2009 found that extreme tarmac delays were not all that rare: nearly 200,000 domestic passengers had suffered them in the previous two and a half years. The tarmac-delay issue was, as they say in Washington, "gaining traction"—just as the Obama DOT's new political appointees were measuring their drapes and looking to become "change agents."

For the airlines, it was long past time to change the playbook. Policy arguments against "micromanagement" or "government intrusion" that resonated with Republican think tanks were largely ineffective. More persuasive was the fact that multi-hour tarmac strandings just kept happening. One of the worst occurred on August 8, 2009, when 47 passengers were held overnight in Rochester, Minnesota (population 106,000), for six hours—not just aboard a "normal"-sized jet, but aboard a *very* cramped, 50-seat, one-toilet commuter plane. En route from Houston to Minneapolis, thunderstorms forced Continental Express 2816 to land at midnight at the small airport, and there it sat for the entire night, just 50 yards from the terminal. An angry DOT issued its first ever "stranding" penalties—$175,000, part to the airlines involved, part to the ground-handling servicer—and a warning from the new secretary of transportation, a former congressman known for the "common touch" with constituents. Secretary Ray LaHood wrote on his blog: "Reasonable people are outraged."

With the regulatory winds shifting ominously, in September 2009, the head of the airline trade association and his top lawyer quietly paid a "courtesy call" on DOT's newly confirmed General Counsel. According to a memo of the meeting, the executives suggested that the industry just "might be prepared to agree to a firm time limit on tarmac delays." DOT's new top lawyer, Robert Rivkin, told them to send it in writing. By all indications, no such letter arrived.

Even with regulatory action seemingly imminent, the drawn-out Washington process seemed unable to conclude without a little more posturing on all sides. Robert Crandall, the former CEO of American Airlines and an iconic figure in the aviation industry, broke ranks to support a tarmac-delay rule. "Every responsible airline executive ... thinks these things are an outrage," Crandall intoned. Meanwhile, Hanni sued Delta Airlines and a consulting firm for $11 million, claiming they had hacked into her computer. And Continental Airlines' CEO, Jeff Smisek, labeled DOT's anticipated tarmac-delay rule "very stupid" and "inane."

With dialogue deteriorating and vitriol rising, DOT mercifully put an end—more or less—to the debate. On December 30, 2009, nearly 11 years after the Detroit snowstorm strandings, it issued the long-awaited tarmac-delay regulation. With some exceptions for safety and security, the final rule did what consumers and Congress had asked for in 1999.

It required airlines to get stranded passengers off planes after a specific period of time: three hours.

Tarmac strandings essentially ended. In the rule's first year, starting in May 2010, only 20 domestic flights sat on the runway for more than three hours compared to nearly 700 in the same period the previous year. And despite the dire warnings, the rule triggered no financial calamity for the airlines. DOT responded aggressively when airline-friendly consultants issued an alarming report, based on only one month of experience with the new rule, that it would cost the industry $200 million a year and impel airlines fearing heavy fines to cancel flights prematurely. In an unusual official statement, DOT quickly branded the study "misleading and premature." (On the other hand, the critics were at least partly vindicated when a GAO report more than a year later agreed that the rule would indeed increase the likelihood of cancellations beyond expectations, though also reducing hardship for stranded passengers.)

Neither did regulators run wild in the streets penalizing airlines for exceeding the three-hour limit as opponents had claimed to fear. During the entire first year of the tarmac rule, in fact, only one airline was fined, albeit heavily. In November 2011, DOT penalized regional carrier American Eagle $900,000 for stranding 608 passengers on 15 different flights. Though the fine was a record, it was actually far less per stranded traveler—about $1,500 on average—than the $27,500 per passenger the airlines feared DOT might assess.

On Your Own

For all the political and legal tussling, all the hearings and heated rhetoric, all the reports and studies and commissions and working groups and regulatory twists and turns that preceded it, the tarmac-delay rule was at most a modest consumer victory. After all, extreme (three-hour) tarmac delays, for all their drama and media attention, are among the rarest of air-travel woes, affecting even in their very worst months fewer than one in a thousand flights. And far from a panacea, the new rule couldn't stop the stranding of JetBlue's Flight 504 in Hartford in October 2011—an incidental reminder that in today's tightly scripted, interdependent aviation system, screwups can snowball no matter what the rules.

The tarmac-delay saga bespeaks a broader lesson for air travelers about what they can expect government to do to make air travel less difficult. Surely, the tarmac rule should have been far easier to accomplish. After all, it had all the right ingredients: logic, public outrage, media attention, sympathetic victims, attractive champions, angry and engaged political leaders, and an overconfident industry that didn't know when to fold 'em. If *this* issue of extended tarmac incarceration took a decade's bloody battle to fix, what kind of heroism would be needed to deal with much more ordinary hassles of air travel?

The skirmish over the tarmac rule is only part of an ongoing struggle between consumer regulators and industry—a conflict that seems to have grown more antagonistic, even angry, over the last several years. Airlines decry "the crushing and increasing burden of new government rules," and warn darkly of government "regulatory tentacles," Washington pundits opine in industry journals that DOT has become a "rule-making machine" that is "working against [the airlines] at every step."

Especially irksome to some in the industry is regulators' push since 2010 for more "transparency" in the information that consumers get from airlines, particularly about airfares. In a world of fast-changing prices, obscure fees and surcharges, and "buy now" sales pitches, helping fliers better comparison-shop effectively bolsters consumers' bargaining power. Though fare advertising rules don't dictate core airline business functions, the annoyingly detailed proscriptions on how airlines can advertise—what taxes and fees must be included in quoted fares, where and when checked-bag and other ancillary fees must be disclosed—have triggered a firestorm of industry opposition. That included a federal lawsuit and legislation proposed by Rep. Tom

Graves (R-GA) and co-sponsored by Rep. Ron Paul (R-TX) and others that advanced the theory that DOT was trying to "hide the government's taxes and fees" as part of a "hidden agenda," in one carrier's words, to raise taxes.

A new rule giving consumers 24 hours to cancel or change purchased tickets so frosted ultra-low-cost Spirit that the airline imposed a $2 surcharge on all flights, blaming DOT for the "unintended consequences fee." And there aren't many rules the industry *doesn't* find intolerably intrusive—even true no-brainers like requiring airlines that lose your bags to refund your checked-bag fees. The perennial antagonism about regulation speaks to the broader relationship between the feds and the airline industry—a relationship that is alternately, sometimes simultaneously, collaborative and combative, dependent and resistant. Parents of adolescents will understand.

US airlines grew and prospered under the protective cloak of government—early on, when close oversight by safety regulators reassured nervous fliers that it was OK to go aloft in that contraption, later when economic regulators essentially set fares to ensure a healthy profit margin, more recently when $5 billion in federal grants (and up to $10 billion available in loan guarantees) bailed out the industry after 9/11. And billions of dollars go every year to improve airline efficiency (and profitability) with better air traffic control, better airports, more access to foreign markets, and keeping airline customers feeling safe and secure. For years, the FAA even had an explicit "dual" legal mandate—both to regulate and to promote aviation. Nor is the industry shy about asking for help. In April 2012, Delta's CEO, Richard Anderson, urged a "national *airline* policy" to support the airline industry, not just a national *aviation* policy.

At the same moment, the industry, to paraphrase Greta Garbo, just wants to be left alone. "We ought to be able to run like any other business," says the head of Airlines for America. United's CEO, Jeff Smisek (after Continental and United merged), was even more direct in a 2010

J.P.Morgan aviation conference: "The day I rely on government to help this industry you should make sure that I get fired. Look, my goal in Washington is just to prevent them from doing more harm. And candidly what I'd like them to do is just leave us alone for a while. Because every time they try to make things better they just make things worse."

However strange or strained the relationship between the airlines and government when it comes to regulation, the implication for ordinary air travelers is relatively simple. The bloody, drawn-out saga behind the tarmac-delay rule reminds us that any notion that Washington can or will fix all the excesses and discomforts of today's air-travel experience is wishful thinking. The DOT concedes as much, succinctly, in its Consumer Guide to Air Travel. The online advisory offers travelers a kind of subtle warning: "In this new commercial environment, consumers have had to take a more active role. . . ." Put more simply, if you have a problem with air travel, don't expect the feds to come charging in.

And good luck.

Escape

Step into your personal First Class suite aboard a Singapore Airlines A380 and you're in another world. You sense it when the drop-dead gorgeous flight attendant gracefully hands you a perfectly chilled flute of vintage Dom Pérignon and shows you to your three-foot-wide leather armchair. Your private mini-apartment is almost seven feet away from your nearest neighbor.

Plug your laptop into your mahogany "business center" desk or, better yet, grab the high-tech headphones and click on your high-resolution 23-inch LCD monitor to catch one of three dozen new movies, or countless television shows. When you're ready for your six-course dinner, you can't go wrong with the Lobster Thermidor or the Rack of Lamb, cooked to order with fresh vegetables, all served on Givenchy china. (There's not just one celebrity chef but a half dozen on the airline's "International Culinary Panel." But heck, United touts a whole *"Congress of Chefs."*) And wash it down with a Grand Cru Burgundy.

Care for a nightcap? Enjoy a snifter of fine XO cognac (or, on Emirates, a sip of designer water from your own personal minibar). And when you're ready for sleep, don your PJs and a nattily dressed attendant—one of three for the 12 First Class passengers on the 471-seat plane—will make up your stand-alone bed, complete with crisp linens, full pillows, and an Egyptian cotton duvet. For once, the airline marketing hype—"enter an island of calm in a sea of tranquility"—doesn't seem like such a stretch. Now you know what flying can really be.

Oh, and the cost? The round-trip from Los Angeles to Tokyo (12 hours out, 10 hours back) will set you back a cool $12,000, taxes included.

Well I can dream, can't I?

"We All Hate the Airlines"

Back to reality. As we've seen, for the non-elite, non-corporate, and non-wealthy fliers—what snarky flight crews sometimes refer to as "self-loading freight"—the airlines' decade from hell only made things worse. Nasty, impersonal, and crowded. Here's the way an irate blogger put it:

> We all hate the airlines. We hate the experience on the plane and in the airport. The airlines never see themselves as our advocates, friends, servers; no, they are our prison wardens and enemies. . . .

A bit much, but we get the picture.

Every Economy Class flier has his or her own tale of woe. After a decade of cost-cuts and capacity squeezes and driving for revenue, the back of the bus is just not a happy place. Plenty of airline execs and Wall Street investors would say it's about time; it's not *supposed* to be.

Witness the remarkable success of Ryanair and Spirit, airlines that seem to share much the same service philosophy: Give fliers the lowest possible fares, collect the most revenue you can from them in "extras" and fees, get them safely to their destinations (or at least to reasonably close exurbs), and otherwise forget about them. Spirit Airways CEO Ben Baldanza put it this way in an inadvertently released e-mail to a subordinate regarding a disgruntled couple from Orlando who sought compensation after a delayed flight caused them to miss a concert: "We owe him nothing as far as I'm concerned," he wrote. "Let him tell the world how bad we are. He's never flown us before anyway and will be back when we save him a penny." (And be careful of that "reply-all" function.)

Life in the back of the flying bus pretty well bottomed out toward the end of 2008 as fuel prices peaked, the economy started to tank, and—in a sign of the times—a major airline tried to charge $2 for a bottle of water. A few years later, America's air travelers were still not happy campers—far from it. The University of Michigan's extensive annual customer satisfaction survey in 2011 ranked the US airline industry the lowest of all 47 industries surveyed and below every federal government department surveyed except Homeland Security and Treasury (home of the IRS). US airlines improved in 2012—to 45th out of 47 industries.

In other words, forget about the magic of flight. Forget "sit back and relax." Just get us out of here! From shelling out a few more bucks for a few more inches of legroom to realizing the "dream" of International First to acquiring your very own personal jumbo jet, that same imperative has helped generate the cash that stabilized the entire aviation industry.

The Poor Man's "Escape"—Buying Perks by the Pound (Or Inch)

Coach misery generated cash. Folks who couldn't or wouldn't pay three, five, even ten times their discount coach fare for the quantum leap in comfort to Business Class might yet spring a few bucks more for a little less stress, a few formerly-free "frills," a marginally more tolerable coach experience. Buying a few perks was the first baby step up from the depths of standard Economy—still a long way from Business and light-years from International First Class, but at least something to smooth a few of the rough edges.

Sell legroom almost by the inch. Those exit-row seats where the FAA insists on some extra room to facilitate emergency evacuation? Rename them "choice" or "preferred" or "select" seats, and sell 'em! Imagine that gate agents used to *give* these gems away for a smile! Or pay $40 to cut to the front of the check-in, security, and boarding lines. That way you can be sure to grab the limited space in the overhead compartments for *your* overstuffed roll-on before those aggressive bastards fill them with *their* oversized carry-ons.

Rebundle those little shards of escape and minor perks into a new fourth class of "better-economy" travel where there's a "free" checked bag, a few extra legroom inches, maybe even almost-assured overhead space and an assigned seat. Now, that's living! Heck, for another $200 at some hubs, one major airline offers "personal 1-on-1 Five Star" service—the same cramped seat, but "curbside meet & greet," lounge access, "discreet" check-in, a faster security line, an escort to the gate, and "pro-active flight monitoring." And just a few bucks more buys you "protection" (Associated Press's word, not the airline's) against falling victim to that same major airline's checked-bag and reservation-change fees if you have to reschedule your flight. This helpful offering, a marketing official explained, "will eliminate the [passenger's] fear about what-ifs," though "less-discriminating" risk-takers can still go unprotected.

Business Class: The Absence of Pain

Business Class on domestic flights (US airlines market it as "First Class" on planes with only two classes) is a huge step up from the brutally utilitarian, six-across, just-get-me-there coach cabin, but it's hardly Nirvana. Marketing hype about "unmatched" luxury, elegance, and tranquility aside, Business Class is really designed to make flying a non-event, which is what frequent business travelers really want. As online business travel editor Joe Brancatelli puts it, "You go into [domestic] First Class because it's less horrible than coach." Your stress level doesn't elevate. Your heart rate remains constant. You can work, even focus, even "bill time" for clients. There's no joy, but also no drama. And you're not much the worse for wear when you arrive. Kind of boring, really, and that's the goal. A product for which business travelers are willing to pay $789 instead of the $151 it would cost them in coach for the two-hour flight from Atlanta to Chicago—or $3,200 instead of $500 in coach to fly round-trip from New York to Los Angeles on a two-week advance purchase.

For the vast majority of "normal" air travelers, though, domestic Business Class seems pretty darn swell. You can cross your legs and type on your laptop. There are free drinks (in glasses, no less), sometimes food, depending on flight duration, and decently comfortable seats. Your suit jacket sits on a hanger (not crumpled into a tightly crushed ball at the back of the overhead). And it's all calmer and quieter. Today's domestic Business Class isn't all that different from what most air travelers experienced at the beginning of the jet age. In 1964, Economy Class seat pitch averaged 36 inches on US airlines, according to the *Harvard Business Review,* nearly the same as Business Class today and, of course, meals were served.

International Business Class is another matter entirely, and it should be. Flying squeezed in 29E to Chicago for a couple of hours isn't fun, but hey, no big deal. Even flying across the Atlantic in coach can be a tolerable, if unpleasant, transit that leaves you at least minimally functional after a day's recuperation. But 16 hours from Chicago to Hong Kong or from Sydney to Dallas, now within the nonstop range of the most modern wide-body jets? Discomfort seems to increase exponentially with time spent aloft. By nine or ten hours in coach, you're ready to relinquish your firstborn for a big lie-flat seat, a semblance of "real" food, and some peace and quiet. For non-elite, ordinary fliers, International Business is definitely something to write home about.

Consider the quintessential long-haul business flight, New York to London, evening departure, morning arrival, about seven and a half hours. On global business airlines like British Airways and American, roughly 20 percent of the passengers reportedly fly Business Class (another 5 percent may actually buy First Class)—an extraordinarily high ratio, with lots of execs and financial types. After a long day on Wall Street, and sitting through the early rush on the Van Wyck Expressway (a misnomer if there ever was one for the infamously jammed highway in Queens) you arrive, frazzled, at the crowded Kennedy terminal. Regular folks face a bedlam of anxious, confused, excited travelers heading to all corners of the globe, staring blankly, if desperately, at the chaos around them. For you in Business, though, there's a separate and far shorter line, where the check-in agent is more likely to be an airline employee who might actually care about your seating preference.

When you check your luggage (no fee), they slap on a "priority" sticker that sometimes (who knows how often, really?) gets your bags off the plane more quickly on landing. Some airlines automatically invite you to their business "lounge." Even if it's only a place to sit, a cup of coffee, and some packaged crackers, it's better than waiting in the rush-hour chaos of the airport, with the drone of security warnings, fast-food fragrances, and incessant "Airport Network" broadcasts emanating from gateside monitors at 50 US airports.

Once on board, there's plenty of room, a flight attendant hands you high-tech noise-cancelling headphones to watch the personal pop-up LCD screen. A drink in a glass, then a choice of meal (rarely anything to savor, but still actual food) and a decent wine. After dinner, there's a reasonable chance of getting some sleep, on a real pillow with a clean blanket, stretched out on your convertible seat, before they wake you an hour prior to landing with a microwaved croissant and coffee (even if it's two a.m. on your internal clock). On arrival, you join the special "fast track" lane at Heathrow to clear Her Majesty's Customs and EU immigration. If all goes well, you're in decent shape to handle a morning business meeting in the City or even a half a day of sightseeing before you crash at teatime. In the back, using a laptop is an acrobatic exercise and the main job of the flight attendants seems to be monitoring the inmates for buckle-up compliance, with occasional cries of "seat

belts!"—usually just when you are about to snatch a few seconds of miserable upright sleep.

It's not just the greater personal space, or even the relative lack
of hassle. Business Class connoisseurs will tell you that it's really all
about the Seat—your airborne "home," sometimes for hours on end. A
decade ago, Business Class seats were just seats. They reclined several
inches, but if you really wanted to sleep, you needed a couple of stiff
martinis and an unusually elastic spine. In 2000, though, British Airways launched the Seat War as a weapon in its battle with arch-rival
Virgin Atlantic for the lucrative transatlantic Business Class traveler.
Where Virgin's stylish new "Upper Class" offered "guests" in-flight
neck massages, designer cocktails, and lots of entertainment options,
traditionally staid BA (self-described as "the World's Favourite Airline")
promised Business passengers "beds" that "lie flat"—really, a seat that
folds fully back with a leg-rest that simultaneously extends to create a
flat surface. (Think of a La-Z-Boy that reclines to horizontal.) Packed
with yards of high-tech electronics, the new seats massaged, adjusted
lumbar pressure, provided high-tech entertainment, and with all the
bells and whistles cost the airline almost as much as the average 4-year
tuition at a public university—some $50,000 to $75,000.

Today, the lie-flat seat is just the price of admission in the race to
woo long-haul business fliers. Now the battle has advanced to a question
of geometric exactitude: Just how flat is "flat"? British Airways' earlier
versions of "lie-flat" seats were actually "angled-flat"—flat, but also
slightly slanted, such that passengers complained they "slid down" the
seat when sleeping. Airlines could fit more angled seats into the cabin,
though, as one passenger's legs tucked under the reclined seatback of
the passenger in front, taking up less space between rows. But the "full-
flat" seat soon became the Holy Grail. A trivial distinction? Maybe to
the guy crammed in coach who'd just like to cross his legs, but not to the
Wall Street exec who's paying $5,000 each way in Business for a decent
shot at three or four hours of sleep before starting another workday. So

important has the Seat become to the top of the business travel market that United, American, and Delta are spending hundreds of millions of dollars to outfit their fleets with honest-to-God "full flat" seats.

Business Class is the airlines' profit sweet spot, where the revenues they earn from higher fares far outweigh the extra costs they pay. If the airline can fill the front cabin of its Boeing 737 with either 30 Economy seats or 16 Business Class seats, it makes better business sense for it to choose the Business seats—as long as it can collect twice as much money for each of them on average. The fact is that the airline can often collect much *more* than double; domestic Business Class fares can be three to five times as much as coach, even though many Business Class fliers don't actually pay "full" retail fares, what with corporate discounts and upgrades. So the airline comes out ahead by focusing on the front cabin. The economics of *international* Business Class are even clearer. At least on some unusually business-heavy routes like between New York and London, the relatively few "premium" passengers can generate nearly three-quarters of what the flight takes in. In May 2012, American's chief commercial officer revealed that 25 percent of the airline's customers produce 70 percent of revenues.

Movin' On Up

People don't pay five or ten times more for Business Class just for crea-ture comforts. They also crave something less tangible, something as ancient as the wolf pack: status and recognition. One of the big perks of Business Class has nothing to do with better food or wider seats—it's that the flight attendant addresses you by name when she or he takes your meal order. That's right, your very own name, read right off the torn sheet of computer-generated flight manifest! In the grimly impersonal, rigorously standardized experience of modern mass air travel, any hint of personal recognition or status is a rare, valued—and eminently salable—commodity. Can you blame Cathay Pacific flight attendants for trying to monetize the value of a smile when, as part of labor negotiations for a 5 percent pay hike in December, 2012, they threatened not to serve booze and food—and to stop smiling at passengers?

This is hardly lost on the global airlines that cater to comfort-seeking, world-beating business travelers, either. Why else would high-end travelers willingly pay a premium of thousands of dollars to fly on a relatively small airline based in a tiny equatorial country the size of New York City—Singapore Airlines? Sure, they get a gourmet meal, an excellent wine, and a comfy sleep, but more important, they also get the fiction that, even at 35,000 feet, they remain in control of their Type-A lives. They get to *choose* when to eat—they can even order online before the flight. They get to choose between *two* world-class Champagnes—not because standard-issue vintage Dom Pérignon is anything but faultless, but because there must be a choice. On some flights, there's a choice of nine types of dinner rolls. And Singapore flight attendants are schooled in the art of wine—not because the airline couldn't easily print a list describing the half dozen wines on board, but because choosing the wine is an event that affirms the passenger's autonomy.

Singapore's not alone. Closer to home, genius airline marketing goads business fliers to pursue "status" almost for its own sake. Flying a lot becomes personally transformative. To be "elite" you needn't be rich or smart or beautiful, or graduate from Harvard or Amherst or race yachts on Nantucket Sound or have ancestors on the *Mayflower*. The biggest US airlines are each thought to have upward of a million "elites" of some stripe, and frequent-flier expert Randy Petersen, founder of the popular InsideFlyer.com and FlyerTalk.com websites, estimates there are 4.2 million "elites" worldwide (out of some 320 million frequent-flyer members), according to a *New York Times* report. Heck, you're sort of elite just by paying the Business Class fare. To be *really* special, though, you also need to be "loyal" to the airline. The basic measure of true fealty remains how many miles you've flown on the airline, though that's changing as airlines start to focus on how much money you "contribute" to the carrier, not just how much territory you've crossed in low-fare, low-profit "mileage runs" taken for the sole purpose of accumulating miles.

Loyalty also begets special titles—you're "preferred" or "gold" or "diamond" or, better yet, a Mao-like "Chairman's Preferred." You can even "earn" an impressive list of compound titles, say "Executive Premier" or "Executive Platinum" or "Diamond Medallion." The *truly* "elite"—those itinerant souls whose if-it's-Tuesday-it-must-be-Akron jobs keep them in the air nearly constantly—are even "invited" to join "exclusive" secret airline societies, so secret their name is rarely spoken. A kind of mysterious airborne fraternal order where your discreet membership card—"Global Services" or "Concierge Key"—gets you a "special" phone number and a good chance for free upgrades. Airlines don't say, but estimates are that the top elite status levels are bestowed on only about 1 percent of each airline's top "revenue contributors." These are the folks who spend a cool quarter million or so buying tickets for themselves or their businesses and so rate what American's sales exec calls "high-touch end-to-end" service—which sounds uncomfortably more like TSA's "enhanced" screening.

Fly a million miles on American and you're "Lifetime Gold"; another million and you're "Lifetime Platinum." And any poor wretch who flies four *million* miles on United—equivalent to circling the entire globe 160 times!—gets to be super-"elite" for life, or whatever remains of it. Beyond the perks and honorific titles, there's the recognition. Elites on some carriers are specially "invited" by the harried gate agent to "walk across the red carpet" to the jetway—so *everyone* can see who ranks. Then there's the chance to climb aboard the plane first ("preferred" boarding) along with the infants and "those needing special assistance."

According to Peterson, there are more than 400,000 "mileage millionaires," but a man named Tom Stuker has actually flown more than *ten* million miles on United. To celebrate his accomplishment in 2012, the 56-year-old auto-sales consultant was awarded a "Titanium Mileage

Plus Membership Card," had his name painted on a jumbo jet, and was
feted at a party with the airline's CEO. What he seems to enjoy particularly, though, is the special recognition from telephone reservations
agents. "They know me," the ultra-elite Mr. Stuker told *Time* magazine
in 2009. "I got my own 1-800-KISS MY ASS hotline."

If it all seems a little much, status is deadly serious to the airlines
and to their loyal flying "elites." Airlines fight to maintain the "integrity" of their elite check-in lines, battling "line pollution" by ordinary
passengers. Elite road warriors—grown men and women, for goodness
sake—can be heard to denigrate the "gate lice," a term occasionally used
for less elite travelers who crowd the boarding gate, sometimes trying
to cadge a free upgrade or sneak aboard before their allotted priority
in order to snag overhead bin space. Maybe it's some deep human need
for social stratification, but the sense of entitlement, even superiority,
is palpable. Even before it starts, super-elites get their phone calls to
one major airline answered within 10 seconds, reports consumer travel
writer Christopher Elliott; the rest of us are lucky to endure only two
minutes of "Your call is important to us."

It's all reinforced throughout the journey. Merely boarding the plane
involves lots of parsing of status and priority—distinguishing the sera-
phim from the cherubim, an elaborate ritual that can extend the time
to load a 150-seat domestic jet to nearly 40 minutes. That's nearly half
again as long as the 30 minutes it typically took in the 1980s (though
planes were much less full then) and nearly double the time it took less-
hierarchical Southwest to fill up in its glory days. Once aboard, your
relative "eliteness" dictates other things—for example, what you eat.
Some airlines follow a strict priority for taking meal orders in the front
of the plane; woe betide the busy flight attendant who offers the last filet
mignon (the airplane version anyway) to a Premium Executive before
she asks a Global Services member. Never mind the greater legroom
and wider seat—it's all about status and "personal" recognition. You're
a person, not just a fare!

America's Second Currency

Not many fliers can afford actually to pay to escape Economy Class. Some fly Business because their companies can afford it. Most of the folks up front, as we've seen, are in the big seats because they regularly and reliably produce revenue for the airline. To keep these precious frequent customers from the clutches of lower-fare competitors or luxury foreign carriers, for that matter, airlines reward them with a powerful incentive—free escape from coach misery with the almighty "upgrade."

Marketing innovator American Airlines launched the first mileage-based frequent-flier program in May 1981, as a way to keep passengers "loyal" in the face of new competition unleashed by US airline deregulation three years earlier. What could be simpler in concept? If you buy 12 cookies, they toss another one in the bag. To identify worthy "members" of its new frequent-flier "club," American simply searched its then-rudimentary computer reservation system for recurring telephone numbers. To that list of its 130,000 most frequent fliers, it added 60,000 members of its Admirals Club airport lounges. Grasping the potential, United and TWA followed suit in a matter of days.

Thirty years later, collecting—or, rather, "earning"—miles has become almost a national obsession. And not just for road warriors and airfare geeks. American's original membership of less than a quarter million grew to more than 69 million by the end of 2011, according to the *Dallas News*. By then, there were half as many US frequent-flier members as there were adults living in the United States—and, according to InsideFlyer.com, some 10 to 15 *trillion* frequent-flier "miles" outstanding and unredeemed (all of them angling for free flights to Hawaii at Christmas). Uncounted websites and chat rooms and online "communities" obsess about "miles"—how to get them, how to sell them, how to use them to beat the airlines. By 2012, an estimated 320 million humans across the globe were hoarding "miles." *BusinessWeek* in 1999 dubbed them America's "second currency."

And why not? Who doesn't love to get a "reward"? For millions of occasional air travelers—regular folks with regular salaries who drive the kids' carpool or go downtown to work each day—frequent-flier programs offer the best, maybe the *only,* way they're going to see the grandeur of the Alps or the Great Wall without shelling out thousands they don't have. On the large US airlines, some 7 to 9 percent of passengers use award tickets in a given year. Airlines, in turn, get an incredibly effective marketing hook that keeps "their" core customers from straying to competitors, a hook that drives serious revenue.

It sounds like a fair bargain, except that, over the last decade, the "exchange" has gotten increasingly one-sided. As carriers started cutting back on the number of seats they fly, both "free" and paid, they've also flooded the market with more and more miles. More miles chasing fewer seats make it ever more difficult to redeem award seats or upgrades, and there's no Treasury Department or Federal Reserve to oversee the devaluation of *this* currency. Frequent-flier programs are practically unregulated, and airlines have used their free hand—deciding unilaterally how much a mile is worth (how many you need for each award or status level), how many "free" seats to make available, and what extra fees to charge to redeem those seats.

The only serious check is the very remote possibility that an airline's most reliable consumers will stop griping on frequent-flier online chat rooms and jump ship to Southwest, or maybe Greyhound or NetJets. To make sure that doesn't happen, though, airlines rarely mess with the perks for their very, *very* top customers—those top-level elites who fly the equivalent of at least twice around the globe every year. As for the rest of the Silvers and Golds, though, they're largely captive. With only three or four US airlines offering global networks, and half the major US hubs dominated by a single airline, where exactly are they going to go?

What's the disincentive, after all, for carriers to keep raising the number of miles needed for a free trip or an upgrade? That 60,000 miles you saved for the anniversary trip to Paris? Sorry—that'll now be

75,000 miles. Mileage expert Tim Winship estimates that the value of a frequent-flier mile has dropped from the old "rule-of-thumb" 2 cents to closer to 1.2 cents. Or a slightly more subtle approach taken by some airlines: create a new "preferred" mileage "tier." Maybe you can still cruise the Seine for 60,000 miles, but only in the middle of damp and snowy February, when the kids are in school and planes are half empty and nobody else wants to go to France. Or you can just declare unilaterally that miles "expire" after an arbitrary period of account inactivity. Continuing "mileage creep" has already put popular travel rewards out of reach for many would-be vacationers. Try taking your spouse on a peak summer jaunt to Europe in Business Class. You'll need about 500,000 frequent-flier miles in your account—what you earn by circumnavigating planet Earth *20 times*.

Airlines don't even have to play with the award-seat mileage requirements, though. To reduce their costs on loyalty programs, they can just make fewer award seats available. One airline promises to keep "a select number of seats" for frequent fliers, but who's "selecting" that "number"? With paying passengers filling so many flights, it's no wonder award seats seem ever harder to snag. The last DOT Inspector General report on the subject in 2006 found the number of seats in fact dropped 11 percent between 2000 and 2005. Are airlines really about to happily give away lots of free seats they're confident of selling for cold, hard cash?

Even if the absolute number of award seats remains the same, miles are worth less when everybody's got them. Over the last decade, collecting miles has had less and less to do with actually flying. Swiping your airline co-branded Visa card gets you miles for your morning coffee, your mortgage, even your funeral. Banks, credit card firms, hotels, rental-car companies, and retailers buy miles by the millions from the airlines for cash, to give them away to their own customers as incentives. American in 2010 actually sold almost twice as many miles to other companies, including Citibank, than it awarded directly to its own passengers, according to a 2011 study by IdeaWorks. Citibank gives them to its credit card holders to get them to swipe the plastic. Of course, airlines don't want to upset their frequent actual *fliers*, the folks who stick with the darn airlines month after month in hopes of snagging a free trip to Hawaii, by flooding the market with miles, but the temptation has to be huge. United made an estimated $3 billion selling miles to third parties in 2010 and, according to IdeaWorks, the carrier's subsidiary for its Mileage Plus program was the only profitable piece of its globe-spanning empire when the company declared bankruptcy in 2002. So the good news is that it gets ever easier to accrue miles, but don't count on using them to see the sunrise over Mauna Kea for free; the rest of humanity has plenty of miles too.

The whole mileage game is very good business for the industry. Airlines value a "mile" as a liability on their financial books at only a small fraction of a cent, and estimate that about 15 to 20 percent of those miles will never be redeemed. According to InsideFlyer.com, a favorite website of the mileage-obsessed, American's AAdvantage program, for instance, effectively "owes" participants the equivalent of 5.9 million round-trip Business Class flights to Europe in frequent-flier miles they haven't redeemed.

On the other side of the ledger, mileage programs turn the airlines' "distressed merchandise"—seats that may otherwise go empty—into rich sources of ancillary fees and other revenues. "Free" tickets—a term airlines now avoid—aren't really free anymore. Reward tickets come with lots of their own gotchas. You still pay "surcharges" and à la carte fees (for instance, for checked bags and seat assignments), but there are also "redemption" fees, co-pays, sometimes special "booking fees" merely to reserve an award seat. At least one carrier charges a $25 "award redemption processing fee" that jumps to $50 if you're flying to Hawaii (a top award destination) where processing must be uniquely expensive.

Beyond generating revenue, though, frequent-flier programs are potent competitive weapons for global airlines. Road warriors chasing status, upgrades, and escape from the hoi polloi are bound by their carrier's golden mileage handcuffs—almost no matter how much they hate its service or fares. In the real world, not many United Premier and Delta Gold Medallions will "waste" 2,269 miles—another step on the journey to Premier *Gold* and *Platinum* Medallion—by flying cross-country on JetBlue or Virgin America. James T. Kane, a business consultant on customer loyalty, put it succinctly: "I'm not loyal. I'm just a hostage."

In the end, the whole frequent-flier mileage obsession can seem a little ridiculous. Respected business executives fly at ungodly hours, make strange connections and same-day "mileage run" flights to random destinations, even pay higher fares just to score enough miles on "their" airline to retain or advance their "status." Some spend hours on frequent-flier websites and online communities dedicated to the obsessive accretion of miles, just for the joy of beating the system. There are endless discussions of surefire strategies for exploiting airline reservation systems or outsmarting the upgrade process, as well as Talmudic debates on such arcana as how to wangle a "status" upgrade on a code-share flight when holding a discounted Business ticket. Get a life! Here's how one rueful business traveler blogged about his quest in March 2008, in a *USA Today* online comment:

> I just got the congratulatory notice that my elite membership had been renewed for another year. My wife read it to me while I was at the airport, on the same day it was my son's 5th birthday. I have come to realize the price you pay to be a Platinum, Diamond, or Blue Chip member is to watch your kids grow up and your marriage deteriorate from an airport lounge in some distant town. When I first started to travel I would envy those as I walked down the aisle of first class on my way back to economy. . . . But I did not know the price you have to pay.

You have to ask: Is this frequent-flier obsession totally irrational? Is it all a sucker's game? Is it just plain silly?

Yes, yes, and yes. And I have another embarrassing confession to make.

Two years ago, I actually paid my hub airline $799 in hard-earned cash for the privilege of "fast-tracking" my elevation to low-level elite status. In effect, I bought my way up, purchasing the 10,000 miles needed to attain "Premiere"-ship. Why would I do that?

Because I wanted a little relief from the air-travel grind. A shorter airport check-in line manned by a knowledgeable airline employee. No extra fee for a checked bag. Access to the "premium" security inspection line, where, in a rush, I was less likely to be trapped behind a multigenerational family of tourists. Not having to push for overhead space for my carry-on. An exit-row or aisle seat with a few more inches of room. The possibility, however remote, of an upgrade to Business Class that would buy me a "free" drink, a smile from the flight attendant, and a touch of humanity. Small comforts, but still a modicum of escape.

The Dream of First

If Business Class is designed to make flying a non-event, a transit from which you emerge relatively unscathed, First Class (the international version, not the domestic service that some US carriers *call* First Class) is in a way just the opposite. It's flying as an experience to be savored, more about enjoyment and luxury than mere comfort or efficiency. This is the realm that few fliers attain but all aspire to, the place you glance at covetously, your view blocked by the purser as you turn right at the aircraft door on the way to *your* seat.

For most folks, it's really not worth vaulting the fare chasm. At the end of 2012, the 12-hour flight from San Francisco to Beijing that cost $5,000 in Business was more than *double* that in First. Transatlantic fares are similarly skewed. A weekday Chicago-to-Paris flight, about $1,500 in coach, ran $6,800 in Business and a whopping $17,500—that's $2,000 per airborne hour—in First.

What does the extra $10,000 buy you? Maybe a great wine and as good a dinner as can be prepared in a convection oven at 35,000 feet. Enough movies and music to last a week instead of a weekend. And likely a very nice preflight lounge—though how much can you sit and eat while waiting to take off? For decades, the greatest distinction between First and Business was, again, the Seat. The First Class seat was typically a big, plush affair, with tons of stretch-out room, a deep back recline, and ample, electronically controlled footrests. Clearly better than in Business. But when airlines began installing "lie-flat" seats not just for the aristocracy in First but also for the mere merchant class in Business, even the wealthiest fliers had to ask if it was really worth the immense price leap. To justify that difference now, First had to be far more than a marginal improvement; it had to be over the top.

But how much wonderfulness can you cram—legally, at least—into 12 hours in an aluminum tube? What else but, as Singapore Airlines hypes it, "Beyond First Class"? A kind of battle of excess ensued. For the select few flying on carriers like Emirates and Cathay and Singapore, the new "Beyond First Class" meant this:

> Sleep: full lie-flat beds that convert at the touch of a button, real pillows and Egyptian-cotton sheets and duvets; personal Givenchy robes and pajamas; combinable privacy "suites" where couples can enjoy their very own stand-alone double bed—coyly advertised with rose petals strewn on top (Singapore Airlines cautions occupants to "observe standards that don't cause offence to other customers and crew," but who's kidding who?).

> Serious privacy: private mini-pods spaced far apart with electric sliding doors, and complete segregation from the Economy Class hoi polloi—from boarding via a separate jetway to being escorted upon arrival through special exits and immigration lines to a private arrival lounge.

> A vast array of entertainment choices: full-size personal television

screens with scores of in-flight video choices, first-run movies, and nearly a thousand musical selections.

> Extravagant dining—whenever you choose—including generous servings of caviar (over $1,000-a-pound retail Caspian Ossetra), lobster, and even fresh sushi prepared by an onboard chef. (Korean Airlines' organic farm on Jeju Island grows its own beef, chicken, and vegetables for First Class palates.)

> Endless top-quality Champagne and vintage "Grand Cru" Burgundies and fine spirits, plus exclusive cocktail lounges where onboard bartenders mix exotic drinks.

> A bathroom freshened by cut flowers kept sparkling throughout the flight for you and maybe six or seven other passengers, not the four or five dozen per head in Economy. (Carriers like Air Canada, Lufthansa, and British Airways feature windows in some lavs, but not to be outdone, Oman Air's First-only lavatory on its new A330 reportedly features a bidet.) The "ultimate" bathroom perk, so far offered only by Emirates and only on its A380s, is the in-flight hot shower and steam in two "spa" rooms whose comfortably heated floors are continually kept spotless by dedicated bath/shower attendants. (Consider the opportunity cost of hauling the extra half ton of water across the globe in lieu of a half dozen paying passengers.)

> Constant personal attention from a specially trained flight attendant, one for as few as every four to six "guests."

Is all this wretched excess really good business? Delta and Continental, outgunned and outclassed in the ultraluxury department, dropped First entirely in favor of a larger Business Class in the late 1990s. United and American blanched at the cost of running a First Class sufficiently over-the-top to compete, and they've commandeered some First Class real estate to expand Business Class. Yet they couldn't entirely eliminate First if they hoped to battle for super-high-end transoceanic passengers with the likes of Singapore, an airline that spends $16 million annually just on vintage wines and is historically the world's second largest buyer of Dom Pérignon Champagne.

Theoretically, at least, the extra operating expense is more than off-set by the ultra-high First Class fares airlines command for ultra-luxe service. Consider a British Airways 747 flying from New York to London in mid-March 2013. The advance-purchase round-trip coach fare was about $800, while fully-refundable First Class was an eye-popping $19,500. If—and it's a *very* big "if"—even 5 of the 14 cushy sleeping pods up front were actually paid for in full, the front cabin would generate more than $100,000 for the airline—roughly the same as the entire 177-seat coach section at normal 80 percent loads (about $113,000). In other words, the handful of super-spenders in First could be worth to the carrier—again, theoretically—almost as much as the entire mass of "regular" passengers.

In reality, only a small cohort actually pays the full First Class fare, no matter how luxurious the ride. Airlines tend to treat that precise pro-portion as top-secret, and it varies widely by flight, route, and carrier, but industry veterans estimate that full-fare passengers fill as little as 5 to 10 percent of most First Class cabins. (Even *paying* First Class pas-sengers don't all pay retail, considering corporate discounts and other deals for high-volume purchasers.) The rest of those up front are more likely to be upgraded "elites" risen from Business Class, frequent fliers who've hoarded "miles" for the trip of a lifetime, and a sizable cadre of "non-revenue" passengers—including lucky (and presentably dressed) airline employees who fly free based on seniority when, rarely, there are otherwise empty seats. All that said, Delta disclosed in 2011 that it sold 14 percent of its seats in *domestic* First Class (really a hybrid Business Class named "Business Elite"), and some well-timed business-heavy international flights like New York–London can reportedly rack up double that percentage of honest-to-God paid-up First Class fliers.

Airlines don't like to talk about freebies and upgrades to First, of course, and say they strive mightily to maintain the "integrity of the

First Class product." Who wants to be the only sucker in the front cabin who's coughing up real cash for the big seat and glass of bubbly? A very few carriers even keep First Class semi-sacrosanct by making it almost impossible to gain access without paying the fare. Singapore Airlines, for example, reputedly releases only one or two First Class seats for upgrade on any given flight, and then only if the supplicant has demonstrated *extreme* past loyalty to the airline. A "full" First Class mileage upgrade round-trip between New York and Tokyo at peak times in 2012 required, in addition to the hefty Business Class fare, one *million* frequent-flier miles. That's just over two round-trips to the moon.

For many global airlines, the business rationale for maintaining a world-beating First Class is ultimately about more than generating revenue from a relative few ultra-high fares. Just Google "Emirates showers" to appreciate the massive free publicity a couple of glorified (OK, glorious) onboard lavatories can generate. It's also about image and publicity. A great First Class enhances the airline's overall reputation—if First Class is so great, coach can't be that bad—just as the hugely expensive Concorde burnished the image of its owners Air France and British Airways. In the end, First Class is largely about aspiration. It creates a dream of air travel, a goal for the poor soul stuck back in Row 41 for nine hours, or the sales guy flying monthly from O'Hare to Omaha and diligently tracking his "status" and "miles."

Membership Has Its Privileges

There's only so much you can do in the air to separate the merely big spenders in Business from the true price-is-no-object First Class flier, but there's a lot you can do on the ground to create the aura of exclusive luxury. Like much else in the industry, the airline "club" or "lounge" is a world of stratified privilege and privacy—for a fee. Especially since 9/11 turned the airport into a high-stress zone, the airport club has been a key part of the total air-travel experience.

Airline clubs originally were, literally, clubs. When American opened its first "Admirals Club" in 1939 at New York's LaGuardia, entry was by invitation only; the airline's top executives chose the invitees. With mass travel and the jet age, airline "clubs" became freestanding enterprises—open to anyone for a fee, daily or annual. Though often crowded and hardly posh, they still offered escape from the noise and bustle and grime of the terminal, a relatively tidy bathroom, a free biscuit and coffee or modest glass of wine, and a place to plug in the laptop. But far from luxurious, as one blogger-flier described his airline's "bus terminal" lounge at ultrabusy O'Hare:

> It used to be a membership Club, but is now available to persons buying day passes, signing up for credit cards, paying with points . . . in fact, virtually anyone with a pulse and money can now enter, which means it's overcrowded. Showers [don't] work, the attendant said [the airline] doesn't maintain them. The lounge attendants are rude and unhelpful. Cheap drinks are on the house, but not an open bar. Anything of quality must be paid for. A pretzel is [the airline's] definition of food. Absolutely abysmal.

The "real" First Class lounge—not for the mere road warrior—is often in another universe. You need an airport map to find it—and *that* only comes with an International First Class ticket or extreme eliteness. Hidden away from the crowds, up the elevator, around the corner, down the hallway, there's actual food, cushy armchairs, a clean shower and private dressing room, even a touch of design elegance. Cognoscenti have favorites. Virgin Atlantic's Heathrow outpost—the "Clubhouse of all Clubhouses" it gushes—offers shoulder massages, a Martini Loft, and a "poolside lounge." United's First Class club at San Francisco—a preferred gateway for wealthy travelers to Asia—resembles a luxury hotel lobby, complete with Chinese wall hangings, a constantly refreshed international buffet, and suited attendants who speak in hushed tones.

Lounge lizards also speak fondly of Thai Airways' Bangkok club, Qantas' lounge in Sydney and British Airways' modestly self-described "sanctuary away from the outside world" and "the epitome of elegance" at Heathrow.

In the ongoing competitive battle for the world's ultra-premium fliers, though, Lufthansa has taken the club concept to the next level—with not just a premium club, but an entire, stand-alone First Class–only *terminal* at its Frankfurt hub. Don't even try to get in with a Business Class ticket, much less a First Class ticket on another, lesser, airline, even if it's one of Lufthansa's "alliance" partners. That lets me out, but a senior West Coast airport executive I know who visited the establishment not long ago testified that it is all, well . . . first class.

You pull your limo right up to the door, next to another passenger's half-million-dollar McLaren roadster, and the valet will happily take care of it. Your elegantly suited "personal assistant" waits at the entry to take your coat and escort you through your private security screening, taking care not to crease your suit jacket. Up the elevator to the chic, minimalist lobby done in rich earth tones and filled with white orchids. You're whisked to an elegant lounge area, where you can relax with a crystal glass of bubbly and a few imported olives as they take your ticket and handle all those bothersome check-in formalities. (Your passport and documents are returned as you board the plane, after a private immigration check.)

While waiting, your private spa room is available for a massage shower, a facial or, should you prefer, a milk bath (a deal at €60), complete with premium toiletries and a fluffy bathrobe. Then it's time to unwind at an elegantly sleek cocktail bar with a liberal pour of single malt or 85 other whiskeys. Should you wish to dine, a top-flight restaurant (gratis) awaits across the terrazzo slate floor. After dinner, check the scores of international periodicals in the library, watch a new movie on a private DVD player, or enjoy the cigar lounge—presumably stocked with mellow Havanas and some old brandy.

Prefer a preflight nap? There are private sleeping rooms with full beds and private baths and, don't worry, your personal assistant will make sure to wake you for the flight—but not too soon. He or she is in direct contact with your plane to make sure that *it* waits for *you*. Only then are you escorted down the airside elevator to the waiting new Mercedes or Porsche, your luggage already stowed, that whisks you to the door of the First Class cabin. All in all, it sure beats shuffling through the twelve-deep check-in line at Newark on a rush hour Thursday afternoon.

It's tough to top Lufthansa's palace, but luxury airlines continue to try. Singapore's ultra-super-duper First Class lounge is called—what else?—"The Private Room." It's so exclusive that when it first opened, reportedly even a First Class ticket wouldn't get you in. To be "invited" you also had to have paid full fare for that ticket. After the 2008 economic downturn, the airline relaxed the rules a mite, but until then, pretenders to true First Class status, through upgrades or frequent-flier awards, were said to be discretely directed elsewhere.

Today's International First Class travel is all about privacy and seamlessness. A world of isolation where, from the time you reach the airport until you arrive at your destination, you need never even glimpse the rest of the passengers, much less rub shoulders with them, except for the select few—rarely more than a dozen—in First. Of the 526 seats on Lufthansa's superjumbo A380, only *eight* are in First. It's a rarefied universe where the goal is, really, to emulate the experience of a private jet (but with the long-haul range and technical reliability of a major airline). As one Wall Street analyst observed in *Newsweek*, "real" First Class fliers today could "probably afford to take their own Gulfstream." If "super-first class is edging close to the cost of hiring a private aircraft," the analyst mused, "why would you bother" with the airlines?

Why, indeed?

Real Players

No matter how cushy your First Class crib or how luscious your after-dinner chocolate truffles, you're still in the commercial aviation system. The only complete escape is to stop "flying commercial" altogether—and take a private jet. The infamous "master of the universe," fictional financier and villain Gordon Gekko put it this way in his immortal rant to an aspiring acolyte in the 1987 movie *Wall Street*:

> Wake up, will ya, pal? If you're not inside, you're outside, OK? And I'm not talking a $400,000-a-year working Wall Street stiff flying First Class and being "comfortable." I'm talking about liquid. Rich enough to fly in your own jet, rich enough not to waste time. Fifty, a hundred million dollars, buddy. A player . . .

Not only do you not "waste time," but flying outside the commercial airline system you escape:

> Lines at the airport terminal: Typically, there's no terminal as such at all. Your driver pulls up to the front door of the airport's "fixed base operator," or "FBO" (a firm like Jet Aviation or Signature Flight Support or Million Air that services private aircraft), and you walk right into the executive lounge, where someone takes your luggage, offers you a drink, and tells your waiting pilot you've arrived. (Big FBOs have nice *pilot* waiting lounges.) On landing, your plane taxis right up to the door; your car waits at the curb to whisk you to your business meeting or the hotel they've reserved for you. No muss, no fuss.

> Security drama: So far, there's no TSA screening at all of individual passengers unless in the very rare case the pilot requests it. No magnetometers, no wands, no groping, and no lines. When TSA had the audacity to try to collect background information on private-jet

passengers, operators successfully rebuffed this "invasion of privacy" of their elite fliers. As the CEO of a leading corporate jet-maker once observed mildly, albeit in a different context, "[aircraft] owners are influential people."

> Boarding delays: The plane waits for you. Just give the FBO receptionist your plane's tail number (the identifying numbers on the back of the plane, starting with the letter "N," in the United States, called the "N-number") and he notifies the pilot that you've arrived. Don't worry about airline schedules. Generally, you can change your FAA-required instrument flight plan 30 minutes before departure.

> Airline food: What you want to eat or drink is delivered fresh to your aircraft door by a local charter-catering firm. Some focus on the high-end palate, but even the omnipresent "deli platter," fruit plate, and defrosted shrimp cocktail still easily beats a $6 snack pack.

> Publicity: It's a matter of public knowledge where your commercial flight is traveling. Its altitude, speed, direction, and arrival time are all available in real time to anyone with an Internet connection. Not so for private planes. Only the FAA knows for sure your flight details. Your whereabouts can in most cases be hidden from the public and prying news media—amazingly useful if you're a top executive visiting a potential corporate takeover target, a football coach courting a hot prospect, or, better yet, an unloved head of state fleeing with the national treasury. During the 2011 "Arab Spring" uprisings, demand for private charters in the Gulf Region soared so fast that one-hour flights on an 18-seater were reportedly going for as much as $18,000.

> Destination restrictions: Commercial airlines fly to fewer than 500 or so of the nation's 5,000-plus public airports. Private planes access the rest—rural areas and small cities, not to mention remote airstrips.

All in all, air travel off the grid is liberating. You drive to the plane, get on board, and go. No tiresome process, no mass herding, no mystery. And it's the only way to go when time is really tight—corporate jets cruise at about to normal airliner speeds—or when complex itineraries are changing fast.

But don't let anyone tell you that flying private is just about business efficiency. There's an undeniable emotional charge of being above it all (literally and figuratively) in a private jet. You're a "player"—as Mr. Gekko would say. It's everyone's dream. Why else would Playboy's Hugh Hefner, the ultimate dream marketer, buy an old DC-9 (last sold to AeroMexico and stripped for parts) and call it "Big Bunny"? Why else was Donald Trump's recently replaced vintage Boeing 727, fuselage emblazoned eponymously (reportedly in 23-karat gold leaf, no less), so often parked in full view of a busy runway at New York's close-in LaGuardia Airport? Why do Google's founders have their own *fleet* of jet aircraft?

I've been fortunate, while in government, to experience flying off the commercial grid—on Learjets piloted by my boss the FAA administrator, on the agency's premier plane, registration "N-1," a 1989 Gulfstream IV painted light blue and white, and emblazoned with UNITED STATES OF AMERICA on the side; even once, wide-eyed, on President Clinton's *Air Force One*. After traveling on N-1 for a two-week, multi-stop journey through Asia to negotiate liberalized aviation agreements, it was tough to return to my normal perch in commercial Economy. Not because the government jet was super-plush—it wasn't; our onboard catering consisted mainly of bring-on-board corn chips and bottled salsa—but because the plane was always there and ready when we needed to move: no boarding line, no seat assignment, no announcements. True freedom to move about the globe.

No wonder the masters of the universe love it—though there's sometimes a downside: facing the jealous outrage. Everyone detests those who fly on private jets. OK, that's more than a bit overstated, but there's a modern cultural reality: In the eyes of many, corporate-jet flying is antisocial, elitist, even somehow a little corrupt. Flying private can rile folks up almost viscerally.

The CEOs of the Big Three automakers learned that the hard way when they came to Washington, DC, to beg Congress for a $25 billion taxpayer bailout in the midst of the 2008 recession. They could easily have flown commercial—on almost-hourly flights to convenient Reagan National Airport. Instead, each auto bigwig took his own deluxe corporate jet for the 90-minute flight. The round-trip cost? About $20,000 (each) compared to the $837 First Class fare. Congress was decidedly unimpressed: "I mean, couldn't you all have downgraded to First Class or jet pooled or something to get here?" jabbed Congressman Gary Ackerman of the House Financial Services Committee. "It could have at least sent a message that you do get it. . . . It's almost like seeing a guy show up at the soup kitchen in high hat and tuxedo." A disgusted Congress stalled the massive bailout package, demanding that the automakers' jets be sold.

The lesson wasn't lost on other corporate high-fliers. Within a year, Citigroup and Time Warner, for instance, were selling down their considerable corporate fleets. And the price of high-end corporate jets— having soared after 9/11 as businesses sought executive transportation with less "hassle"—tumbled. The year before the automakers' PR disaster, more than 1,000 US corporate jets were sold, buyers were waiting years for the newest models, and owners were "flipping" used jets like McMansions before the 2008 recession. Just two years later, prices had dropped more than 30 percent, some as much as 50 percent. Owning a private jet, bemoaned one aviation executive in *Executive Travel* magazine in 2011, became "akin to maintaining a mistress on the side."

Of course, you don't have to buy a private jet to fly on one. At the low end of the high-end business are air taxis—essentially mini-charters where you can buy a single seat "on demand." There are more than 2,000 air-charter operators in the United States alone, and brokers will be happy to find you just the ride you need to meet your flight-distance range, seat, configuration, and schedule requirements—figure $10,000 to $15,000 an hour all-inclusive to charter a large Boeing 737 airliner.

It's the only way to go for presidential aspirants trying to hit half a dozen cities per day with media in tow, or a pro basketball team whose elite athletes are entitled by contract to tons of extra legroom.

Or, if you really want to own something, but not a *whole* jet, how about just a little piece of one? Billionaire financier Warren Buffett's NetJets popularized the jet "fractional ownership" idea, starting in 1986; now that business model accounts for about 15 percent of all US business aviation flying. NetJets buys business jets by the dozen—in 2011 alone, it acquired 120 Bombardier jets, total cost $6.7 billion—then sells them in pieces as small as one-sixteenth. Your share of the price plus a monthly fee affords access to "your" jet, or one just like it, on as little as four hours' notice for about 50 hours of flying a year. You still pay a fixed hourly charge, but it's less than the rate to charter a plane *and* you can sell your share of the aircraft—think timeshare condo. Prices change, and they don't like to talk prices anyway (If you have to ask . . .), but the cost for one-eighth of a mid-sized jet (equivalent to 100 hours of flying) in 2012 was close to $1 million—plus maintenance and operating costs. For the less-frequent flier, NetJets offers Marquis "debit cards" (others have similar products) that let you buy as little as 25 hours a year flying time on a spiffy seven-passenger light corporate jet—prices start at about $125,000, fuel extra.

In recent years the market for "entry-level jets" or "personal" jets has started to recover. The Brazilian Embraer Phenom 100, for example, priced around $3.5 million, normally carries just four passengers. Sometimes compared to flying in an extra-large SUV with a tiny toilet—if you can call it that—its maximum cabin headroom is less than five feet. Among its customers: the Pakistan Air Force, which reportedly purchased three or four for—believe it or not—flying VIPs. An even cheaper alternative, the Eclipse, was sold in large numbers to an air-taxi firm founded in 2002 named—what else?—Jetson Systems.

The prices of private jets climb rapidly with greater seating capacity, speed, range, and luxury. In the mid-size market, there's the iconic

Learjet, originally introduced nearly 50 years ago and "designed for the upwardly mobile" in the words of manufacturer Bombardier. Toward the upper end of the corporate jet market, the "Cadillac" of private jets may be the ultra-long-range $50 million Gulfstream 550, a plane meant to ease those tedious New York–Tokyo commutes for up to 18 passengers. Aside from its high-end entertainment system and optional beds, there's a broadband multilink system—"an office in the sky"—that lets passengers e-mail and surf the net at data speeds up to 3.5 MB per second, even at 40,000 feet over Siberia. At the top of the luxury heap—list prices start over $60 million—is the Boeing Business Jet (Airbus has its own version), known simply as the Bizjet. It's essentially a VIP version of Boeing's ubiquitous 737, a plane that carries more than 150 passengers in commercial service, but just two dozen or so in private luxury. A third of the BBJs sold to private owners since the launch in 1996 are heading to the Middle East, according to CNNgo.com. What could be handier for an extended family (or the Family)?

Jet-purchasing decisions aren't just about utility, of course. Add a healthy dose of testosterone. With $80 million burning a hole in your pocket, you want the next greatest thing. Why spend $50 million on a Gulfstream V when there's a Gulfstream VI just around the corner for only another $20 million or so? For near $65 million, the Gulfstream 650 promised to be faster and more technologically advanced than anything else on the market, the fastest non-military jet in the world. Even four or five years before scheduled production, demand was so huge that Gulfstream had to devise a special process for would-be purchasers. Just to get on the waiting list entailed a $500,000 deposit, and orders would be taken in the order the deposit money arrived at J.P. Morgan's Midwest branch—starting at exactly 12:01 a.m. on April 15, 2008. Smart buyers opened local accounts at the bank branch in hopes of making an instant electronic-funds transfer precisely when the window opened. Roughly 500 deposits arrived in the first 24 hours, enough to fill the manufacturing schedule for years. The plane Morgan Stanley analysts dubbed the "crown jewel of business jets" begins service in early 2013.

The only way to top a plane that promises to fly near the speed of sound is to fly faster than it. Enter the Aerion, a supersonic 12-seat business jet expected to be built in the next several years and to sell for a mere $80 million. Although it's still a concept, Aerion says there's been plenty of interest in a plane that will let you have two breakfast meetings the same day, on either side of the Atlantic; it has 50 letters of intent to buy from potential purchasers, each accompanied by a $250,000 deposit. One of the first orders was signed at the 2007 Dubai Air Show. Sheikh Humaid bin Rashid al-Nuaimi, the 80-year-old emir of Ajman, one of the UAE's seven emirates, must be in a hurry.

Beyond the Aerion, there's only the private A380 being outfitted for Saudi prince Al-waleed bin Talal, Citigroup's largest individual shareholder. Hyped as "The Flying Palace" by Airbus, the $488 million behemoth, certified by the FAA to carry up to 853 people in the commercial version, will house an onboard garage (for the Rolls). A cylindrical elevator will rise from the owner's private entrance to the five king-bedded master suites, each complete with computer-generated prayer mats that always face Mecca, plus a couple dozen First Class sleeper seats, presumably for the help. On one of the jet's three floors is a concert hall complete with baby grand that seats ten, which is not far from the marble steam room, the "wellness" room with "scented breezes," and the boardroom with holographic screens of world financial markets. All something to contemplate as we battle for the armrest back in 42B.

Three Unimaginable Things That Changed Everything

Next time you're shuffling shoeless through security toward the scanner imaging machine, or groping for a credit card to buy a $3 package of chips, don't blame it all on the mean and greedy airlines. Save some blame for three things that nobody in his right mind could have imagined happening to commercial aviation before September 2001.

September 11 itself—more precisely, its security-consumed aftermath—infused the whole journey with a new kind of dread and disquietude. Then came the late-decade surge in the price of jet fuel—a shock that triggered a near panic of cost-cutting and efficiency-seeking that cemented commercial aviation's "business, *all* business" future. Meanwhile, the decade after 9/11 saw the remarkable revival and ascension of the low-cost airlines, whose simpler "no-frills" business model influenced and terrified their old-school competitors.

Not that change—even turbulent change—was something new to commercial aviation, but the US airline industry and its customers had never experienced anything like the tectonic shocks the decade had generated. These three things changed everything, for good and ill, leaving behind a new normal likely to last for years to come.

1. From Daddy Moments to Groin Checks

Before 9/11, flying was different—in ways everyone remembers through a different lens. For me, it was the "Daddy moments." When my kids were young, I was working in the Clinton administration's Department of Transportation, trying to open global aviation markets so that US airlines could compete more freely around the world. Some weeks, this quest for "Open Skies" had me spending literally more time in the air than on the ground. Finally returning to Dulles, I'd normally just grab a cab home, except on those rare and wonderful occasions when, if pre-school was over and it was not yet bedtime, my ever-loving wife would drag the brood out to the airport to welcome me back. As I trudged up the jetway into the brightness of the busy terminal, I'd hear the excited squeal: "Daddy!" Then the leap into outstretched arms, followed—after the 30-second interval that protocol demanded—by "what did you bring me?" A column by travel writer Harriet Baskas jogged my memory of those jetway greetings. It was a little thing, but it made arriving a true homecoming. Sadly, it's one of the casualties of post-9/11 security; now only ticketed passengers are allowed past the screening area.

September 11 is said to have "changed everything," but nothing so profoundly as everyday air travel. From the "enhanced" screenings and baggies for toothpaste, from unlaced shoes, unbelted waists, and locked cockpits to the new gauntlet we're forced to run from airport door to air-plane seat, the whole texture of the experience suddenly morphed into something alien. After 9/11, we didn't so much fly as we were "flown" as a kind of fragile, unwilling, self-loading cargo. It's no mystery why air travel dropped nearly a third in the immediate aftermath of the attacks.

The decade after 9/11 was our "Security Decade." Flying was not just a hassle; it became downright scary. Boarding a plane was a risk-defying act. Orange Alerts, black-clad police strolling past the Cinnabon coun-ter cradling automatic weapons, nervous flight attendants, security "experts" who never tired of telling us how anxious the bad guys were to bring down planes full of helpless passengers, how it was "not a matter of if, but when." We were targets and suspects at the same time. Look-ing back, for air travelers, there were really three overlapping phases to our Security Decade. Call them Panic, Overkill, and finally, Adaptation.

Panic and First Response

With only slight overstatement, aviation security before 9/11 has been called, in expert Bruce Schneier's phrase, "Security Theater." Since the 1970s, it was handled by private contractors hired by the airlines, with an assist from local airport law enforcement. It was all under the aegis of the FAA, but the big security-screening contracts went to the lowest bidders—the ones who paid near minimum wage and didn't always look too hard at screeners' prior employment, or even their criminal records. FAA rules didn't even *require* criminal record checks for all screeners unless applicants had "specific deficiencies" in their employment histories like long, unexplained gaps. Even convictions for violent felonies—even air piracy (hijacking) and armed robbery—didn't necessarily disqualify applicants if the crimes were more than 10 years old.

What did they expect? At some of the nation's largest airports, as GAO reported to Congress nine days after the 9/11 attacks, screeners sometimes made less money than they would flipping burgers at the airport fast-food joint at the other end of the terminals they were supposed to be guarding. And the turnover rate was astronomical. At a half dozen major airport hubs in 1999, the average screener lasted less than a year, sometimes only a few months. At big airports like Atlanta and St. Louis, annual turnover rates approached 400 percent.

The reliability of the screening reflected the level of professionalism. The FAA measured it directly by testing how often officers missed a standard "threat object"—initially, think dummy guns or grenades in uncluttered carry-on bags—as it passed through. In 1987, some 20 percent of threats got through undetected—and that may well be the best it's ever been since. When more realistic test objects like simulated improvised explosive devices were later used, reliability proved to be even worse—so much so that the GAO stopped publishing or discussing test results on the grounds that they were "sensitive security information," as claimed in a 2001 GAO report. (GAO had acknowledged "room for substantial improvement in airport screening.") Detection failure rates for screening in 2004 and 2005 were reported to be as high as 70 percent at some airports, though TSA said these later tests were designed to be much tougher, so as to ferret out points of screening vulnerability.

Meanwhile, airports themselves were "porous." Testers from DOT's Inspector General's office in 1998 and 1999 succeeded 68 percent of the time in sneaking into secure areas of eight major airports, even managing to climb into the cockpits of parked jets more than 100 times. Just two weeks after the 9/11 attacks, when Congress understandably demanded to know what had gone wrong, GAO's response was a classic of understatement: "Limited action . . . has too often characterized the response to aviation security concerns" and "more needs to be done."

What followed was a massive game of security catch-up played at lightning speed, at least by government standards. Created in just two months, the Transportation Security Administration—in its own words, the "largest civilian undertaking in the history of the US government"— was approved in the Senate by a vote of 100 to 0. Within a year, the new federal security force, initially numbering 45,000 people, took over at nearly 450 commercial airports and started screening every checked bag. Ten years later, the TSA employed roughly 60,000, with an annual budget of more than $8 billion.

The government also rushed to crank up a languishing effort to spot and stop would-be terrorists before they got off the ground. That meant keeping lists—no-fly lists, watch lists, "selectee" lists. The list of *real* bad guys, the "no-fly" list kept by the FBI, had only 16 names on it on September 10, 2001. Within 60 days, responsibility for that list had shifted to the FAA, and it had grown to 400 names, then to 1,000-plus names by the end of 2002. A decade later, the number of "no-fliers" had reportedly ballooned to 21,000 (though only about 500 Americans). More impressive still was the much larger "Terrorist Watch List" managed by the FBI's Terrorist Screening Center. By summer 2011, this list of some 400,000 names bedeviled thousands of air travelers with common names—like the late US senator Edward H. Kennedy who shared a nick-name (Ted) with an IRA bad guy and about 7,000 other American men to whom "T. Kennedy" could apply.

The passage of time after the World Trade Center attacks did surprisingly little to diminish the aviation security hyperdrive, mainly because new "real world" events kept reigniting travel fears. Just 60 days after the attacks, American Flight 587 crashed into the Queens section of New York City, killing 260. Though ruled an accident, many simply refused to believe it wasn't terrorism. In December 2001, a scowling "shoe bomber" named Richard Reid tried to blow up American Flight 63 en route from Paris to Miami with a combination of plastic explosives (PETN and TATP) stuffed into his shoe, an event that to this day keeps us shuffling unshod across airport floors. Later that frightening spring of 2002, authorities arrested a Chicago gang member on his way back from the Middle East for allegedly planning a "dirty bomb" radiological attack. The next autumn, terrorists fired two shoulder-held surface-to-air missiles at an Israeli charter jet in Mombasa, Kenya.

Each new threat kept air travelers on edge and ratcheted up the security scramble. In August 2006, authorities in London charged two dozen people with a failed plot to detonate liquid explosives on transatlantic flights; restrictions on liquids packed in carry-on bags quickly ensued. On Christmas Day 2009, a Nigerian with PETN stuffed into his underwear tried to blow up a Northwest flight from Amsterdam to Detroit and was subdued by passengers and flight attendants—ergo, "enhanced" pat-downs. Less than a year later, authorities intercepted two plastic explosive bombs packed in printer cartridges sent from Yemen on cargo planes bound for the United States; calls to screen 100 percent of inbound merchandise on cargo flights followed.

Experts competed for the scariest—albeit by nature unprovable—predictions of doom. "Only a matter of time" became the mantra. Would-be travelers called it a "hassle"—as in, "I'd prefer to drive all night to my business meeting to avoid the hassle"—but it was mostly just macho-speak for being scared. And who wouldn't be? In the airport, taped announcements droned endless warnings that "unaccompanied bags" would be vaporized. The screening line was a place of special tension, drama, and sometimes confusion, with lots of guys with large weapons standing around. Remove your coat and disgorge your pockets and possessions and hurry up, please. Every week, frazzled travelers left more than 12,000 laptop computers at airports, mostly at screening, according to a 2008 study by Dell, not to mention $409,000 worth of loose change that rushing travelers left behind in plastic screening bins in 2010 alone.

Onboard, we were supposed to "be alert," prepared for a cockpit death struggle, all soldiers in the "Global War on Terror." Flight attendants "assessed" passengers as they came aboard, looking not just for "suspects" to keep an eye on, but also for a few big, strong potential allies, just in case. As it turned out, ordinary passengers were the most effective antiterrorist airborne defense—responsible for stopping not only the "shoe bomber," but also for crashing hijacked United Flight 93 in Pennsylvania before it could reach its probable Washington, DC, target. Self-preservation is a powerful motivator.

Overkill

As the last "successful" attack on aviation receded in time, security annoyance began to eclipse security fear. Did they really need to confiscate all those nail scissors and penknives and cigarette lighters? The TSA announced its annual screening "haul" in 2006: the agency screened 708 million travelers at checkpoints and well over a half billion pieces of checked luggage and opened 16 percent (86 million) of those checked bags. The officers found close to 14 million "prohibited items" at the checkpoints—about 85 percent of them were lighters and another 12 percent were knives of unspecified size. The number of nail clippers was not disclosed.

It all started to seem just a little ridiculous. YouTube offered a near-daily diet of "reality screening" episodes. Cupcakes were prohibited no-fly substances, but only if they had a lot of icing. Too much icing looked like a potentially explosive liquid gel. Snow globes were OK only if you could stuff them into your quart-sized baggie for liquids. Airline pilots heading for the cockpit of their fully loaded jumbo jets had to surrender their penknives. Then there was the TSA "freeze drill," where screeners practiced shutting down a breached airport checkpoint, a process that apparently involved lots of yelling "Code Bravo! Freeze!" As the *New York Times'* Joe Sharkey reported, everyone within earshot, even passengers already *past* security, actually "froze" as though playing a game of Simon Says.

And it was all very expensive, too. In the eleven years following 9/11, missile-loaded F-16 fighter jets based at Andrews Air Force Base—the 113th Wing of the DC Air National Guard known as "The Capital Guardians"—scrambled nearly 2,000 times, almost daily on average, to intercept an errant aircraft straying over the capital's "air defense identification zone." And as complaints mounted about long screening waits, TSA hired more screeners. All that service isn't free. Then there was the travel-suppressing economic impact of it all. Some 64 percent of fliers told a 2010 Consensus Research Group survey they would fly more often if security were less intrusive and time-consuming. According to the US Travel Association, the same survey found that screening hassles deterred fliers from making two to three trips per year.

Was there an end to it? More precisely, could we ever really hope to win the game of cat-and-mouse with terrorists? Few thought so. One descriptive term was "security whack-a-mole." Here's Bruce Schneier's succinct "short history of airport security," from a *New York Times* op-ed:

> We screen for guns and bombs, so the terrorists use box cutters. We confiscate box cutters and corkscrews, so they put explosives in their sneakers. We screen footwear, so they try to use liquids. We confiscate liquids, so they put PETN bombs in their underwear. We

roll out full-body scanners, even though they wouldn't have caught the Underwear Bomber, so they put a bomb in a printer cartridge. We ban printer cartridges over 16 ounces—the level of magical thinking here is amazing—and they're going to do something else.

Americans were willing to accept the inconvenience trade-offs, up to a point. But layered-on security procedures—a new layer for each new threat—tested our tolerance. For many, that line was crossed by "enhanced" screening—what happened if you declined the invitation to be scanned or if the scan showed an "anomaly" that needed a further look—an exercise sometimes known as "the groin check." Thanks to the Christmas "Underwear Bomber," just in time for Thanksgiving 2010, we were introduced to "Advanced Imaging Technology." That meant full-body scans that displayed to a remotely located screener *everything* underneath your clothes. If that included an "anomaly" (think: nipple rings) or you'd rather not be scanned, you got the "enhanced" physical search—please, not a grope, just a friendly "pat-down."

Though fewer than 3 percent of travelers got the pat-down in late 2010, according to TSA's official blog, complaints about the new screening spiked 40 percent during the first half of 2011, and came loudly from all quarters. The scanners were dosing us with harmful radiation; the images of naked bodies seen by TSA were too explicit (new software was installed on one type of scanner to "degrade" the image to a sexless generic line drawing, though the more explicit "backscatter" scanners had to be pulled in 2013); the pat-down alternative was tantamount to assault! Passengers still had options but, as several bloggers put it, they amounted to "naked scan or grope?" Plans for a "National Opt-Out Day" went viral. A major pilots' union, American Airlines' Allied Pilots Association, advised members to "politely decline" the body imagers. DON'T TOUCH MY JUNK T-shirts became the rage.

With the personal honor of upstanding citizens at stake, politicians naturally chimed in. When Kentucky senator Rand Paul was detained at a Nashville TSA checkpoint for refusing a pat-down, his father, congressman and Republican presidential aspirant Ron Paul, decried "a police state ... growing out of control," where TSA "gropes and grabs our children, our seniors, and our loved ones." In May 2011, the Texas House voted 138–0 to make it a misdemeanor for a TSA screener to "touch ..." anyone "in a manner that would be offensive to a reasonable person"—until federal authorities explained that Texas could find itself a no-fly zone if TSA screeners were prevented from doing their jobs.

Even with all the media hype and political hoopla, though, everyday fliers themselves seemed to take the new security in stride. Maybe they figured that underwear bombs are hard to find without looking for them in underwear, or that hassles were to be expected in air travel anyway, or that there was simply not much point in complaining. Opinion polls were mixed, but the limit of passenger tolerance seemed to fall somewhere between machine scans (acceptable) and the full grope (not so much). A CBS News poll a week before Thanksgiving 2010 found 81 percent of travelers approving the full-body scans; 64 percent approved them a week later in an ABC/*Washington Post* poll. Attitudes were different, though, when it came to "enhanced" pat-downs. Half the passengers in the ABC poll said they went too far. The head of the TSA summarized passengers' attitude this way in a *New York Times* report: "When somebody gets on a plane, they want to know that everybody else—O.K., maybe not themselves, but everyone else—has been thoroughly screened."

Ten years after 9/11, an uneasy equilibrium seemed to be emerging between the fear of falling victim to terrorism and the annoyance at intrusive security. By the summer of 2012, a Gallup poll found that a majority of Americans (54 percent) thought the TSA was doing a good or excellent job handling airport screening, and 85 percent thought it was at least somewhat effective in preventing aviation terrorism. Call it grudging acquiescence for now, but what happens when we confront what one screening expert calls the "nightmare scenario"—explosives implanted *inside* the body of somebody willing to die to bring down a plane? A Saudi suicide bomber tried it in August 2009 in an attempt to kill the Kingdom's counterterrorism chief. Complaints about TSA folks rummaging through our hand luggage start to seem almost quaint.

Is the security rigmarole working? It *has* kept lots of stuff that shouldn't be in airplane cabins from getting there. Every day on average, the TSA says it finds four firearms in carry-on bags at airport screening checkpoints. Some have live rounds in the chamber. "There are people who are not focused on the security protocols," the TSA administrator recently deadpanned in congressional testimony.

Adaptation

Nobody would have believed 20 years ago what we now readily accept as the price of catching a plane. It's not all that different from standard intake procedures at county jails: check identity, match government-issued ID to intake form, pat down for weapons or contraband, remove shoes, belt, jewelry, and extra clothing layers, and stand in multiple lines until directed to stand somewhere else. True, there are some differences—you don't have to get fingerprinted or have a mug shot to board a flight; on the other hand, jail intake might just be a little calmer—without banging bins, shouted directions, and endlessly looped security warnings.

A decade after 9/11, though, we've largely adapted. Along the way we've shed some of the loonier security measures launched in the immediate wake of the 2001 attacks. Color-coded alerts—which remained forever "orange" since the summer of 2006—have given way to a less melodramatic advisory system that highlights only specific and imminent threats. Bans on curbside bag check-in—how exactly does that stop terrorists?—are gone. And when was the last time anyone asked "who packed your bags" or if they've been "out of your possession"?—a quaint throwback to the days when terrorists politely requested unwitting strangers to please take a ticking alarm clock home to Mom. National

Guardsmen brandishing automatic weapons in crowded airport lobbies have moved on to more pressing duties.

Overall, passenger security complaints to the TSA dropped to their lowest-ever levels in November 2011 according to Bloomberg News. Even in the wake of "enhanced" pat-downs, they were down 59 percent from their peak in May 2004. TSA says it gets complaints from only .001 percent of passengers—though that's still a non-trivial 6,000 to 7,000 complaints a year, close to 20 every day. "Wait times" to get security-screened are at least more predictable, even as passengers avoiding new checked-bag fees dumped 59 million more carry-on bags onto the screening belts in 2010 than the year before. "Peak" rush hour wait times at the busiest airports can still exceed a half hour, but the TSA says 99 percent of passengers make it through in less than 20 minutes. A good measure of our adaptation to post-9/11 security: far fewer half-full plastic bottles of contraband water tossed into pre-security trash bins.

In large airports, the locus of security activity and, thus, security stress, has become increasingly invisible. Aside from personal carry-on bag screening, the bigger security job has moved belowground. That's where the monster luggage X-ray machines that used to dominate airport check-in lobbies can screen 500 to 600 bags every hour and where TSA folks peering at screens in dimly lit rooms try to make the right call every single time about what's going on your flight. We've all adapted, but in a quiet room in the bowels of San Francisco International, where the security folks do their job, there's still a huge banner lining one wall, with only four words: NOT ON OUR WATCH.

RATCHETING DOWN THE HASSLE FACTOR

By the end of the post-9/11 decade, optimists could sense a subtle shift in the security zeitgeist. If the idea after the attacks was to scare the bejeezus out of us, to keep us "alert" and on edge, the ground seemed to be shifting under the weight of widespread security fatigue and a growing acceptance of the reality that security can never be absolute. All bets were off, of course, if terrorists managed another hellacious attack, but stung by public upset over groin checks and YouTube videos of eight-year-olds getting the rubber-glove treatment, officials started looking for ways to ratchet down—not up—the tension and inconvenience. Very frequent travelers willing to disclose personal data could apply for "pre-check," a program designed to speed screening of "known" travelers. Babies got to keep their booties on, young kids and older folks 75 and up rarely got frisked, and airline pilots were spared the full monty.

Even the once-heretical notion that not all passengers pose the same potential threat or merit the same intensity of screening became a legitimate topic. The core idea was straightforward: Screening would improve if TSA could pick out and focus on those folks who needed extra watching, and ease up on toddlers and grandmas and others who were searched "just to be fair." But how to identify those slightly more suspicious characters who deserve a closer look? A majority of Americans in some polls—54 percent in a Zogby poll released in February 2011—think ethnic, even religious, profiling is OK when it comes to aviation security. But that debate—whether security profiling is ethical, Constitutional, or even effective—has a long way to go.

Are there better ways? Israeli security has made an art form of identifying potential bad guys by another method called "behavioral evaluation." Passengers don't even get close to the bag-screening line at Tel Aviv's Ben Gurion International until they're interviewed by trained security experts who watch for not-quite-kosher verbal responses or subtle behavioral signals. This low-tech alternative to the game of technology catch-up seems still to work after many years: Israeli flag carrier El Al hasn't faced a successful hijacking in four decades. In 1986, El Al agents found 3.3 pounds of explosives a Jordanian man had hidden in the hand luggage of his pregnant young Irish fiancée, who thought she was flying from London to Israel to meet the family of her husband-to-be. The story—her traveling alone, him carefully packing her heavy bag—just didn't seem quite right. The TSA is working on a similar approach, so if an unusually friendly TSA officer starts a casual conversation next time you're waiting to check in, act natural; he or she just may be a "Behavior Detection Officer."

2. Fill 'Er Up—50,000 Gallons, Please

Except for September 11 itself, nothing changed the business, and everyday experience, of air travel so much as the massive surges in the cost of jet fuel in the decade that followed. By the time the price per gallon hit $4 around the Fourth of July 2008—near five times its price on September 11—it was clear that the only airline survivors would be those hardheaded enough to focus ruthlessly on efficiency and the bottom line. The hard lesson was learned and relearned as successive waves of soaring prices hit again in early 2011 and early 2012.

Air travel uses oceans of fuel—jets alone burn enough every year to gas up every automobile on the face of the Earth. Commercial jetliners—more than 25,000 are estimated to be flying worldwide—are basically flying gas tanks. Instead of measuring miles per gallon, they're clocking *gallons per mile*. The Hong Kong–bound 747 jumbo jet throttling up for a 12-hour journey at the end of San Francisco's longest runway, 28-Right, is loaded literally to the wingtips. For nearly an hour, high-pressure fuel pumps have been shooting up to 1,000 gallons every minute—a rate that would fill the family SUV in a few seconds—into the plane's center fuel tank below the fuselage, then into the vast hollow spaces of each wing.

As the massive engines spool up to maximum thrust, the 400 tons of aluminum loaded with 385 passengers rolls, grudgingly at first, down the two-mile tarmac that juts into the blue-gray waters of San Francisco Bay. The plane struggles aloft and slowly turns west over the Pacific, as nearly 1,000 gallons course through its engines in the first three to five minutes. (Just taxiing the huge plane on four engines burns roughly 20 gallons every minute.) Some 3,000 gallons are gone by the time it gets to its initial cruise altitude, a testament to the task of hurling the behemoth five miles high at four-fifths the speed of sound. By touchdown late the next day at Hong Kong International, the tanks have little fuel left. That single flight—one of thousands every day—consumes close to 50,000 gallons of jet fuel.

THE ROLLER-COASTER RIDE

To appreciate the transformative effect on airlines of the repeated fuel-price surges, consider that this indispensable liquid—"go juice" in military pilot slang—is the costliest ingredient in the business *and* that its price is beyond the industry's control. Airlines can press unions for wage concessions, play Boeing against Airbus for aircraft discounts, stiff creditors in bankruptcy court and lobby for favors from regulators, but they can't change the price at the pump. Every time that price rises a single penny per gallon, US airline fuel bills rise $175 million a year. On Wall Street, airline stocks and fuel prices move in almost mirror image.

The amazing thing is that hardly anybody in the airline industry paid serious attention to fuel prices for decades. Until the mid-2000s, fuel was a "given." It cost what it cost; better to worry about labor, which used to be the number one airline cost. Fuel was a reliably stable, highly predictable entry in airline financial ledgers—about 52 cents a gallon in June 1986, 49 cents in 1990, 49 cents in 1994, and 44 cents in 1999. Adjusted for inflation, the price of fuel in 2003 was *still* lower than it was in the mid-1980s.

In economics and finance, there's an iconic power in big round numbers. Dow 15,000. Unemployment at 10 percent. Jet fuel at $1 a gallon. When the latter boundary was crossed in 2004, the airlines' trade association warned that the industry's profitability was in jeopardy, but it was only the start. Prices accelerated past $1.66 a gallon in 2005, then near $2 in 2006, and worry grew to alarm. Wall Street's top airline analysts warned that no major US airlines could remain profitable at these wild prices. They were right. Hit by the back-to-back crises of 9/11 and fuel prices, five of the seven largest US airlines had gone bankrupt by 2006.

Still, prices were destined to go much higher, and faster. On the first trading day of 2008, crude oil hit another milestone—$100 per barrel for the first time in history—and kept heading skyward. By late spring, an already-frantic industry was spooked even further by an ominous Wall Street prediction. Influential investment banking firm Goldman Sachs predicted a crude-oil "super-spike" up to $200 per barrel. Wild volatility added to the distress. The price of a barrel had risen just $2 a barrel over the entire *decade* of the 1990s, but it shot up nearly $17 a barrel on two successive days in June 2008 when an Israeli parliamentarian predicted military confrontation with Iran. That two-day price jump approached what had been the entire cost of a barrel on the world market at the beginning of 2002.

The ultimate peak in jet fuel's price—near $4 per gallon—came the week after Independence Day 2008 as crude oil (a less-refined commodity) briefly topped $147 a barrel. The lifeblood of commercial aviation— now almost 40 percent of the total cost of running an airline—had more than doubled in just three years. It was as if gas for the family car had hit $8 a gallon.

The financial effect was dire. Nearly 40 percent of every ticket sold in 2008 went just to pay for fuel, up from just 15 percent in 2000. In just over a year in 2008, fuel costs sucked an extra $12 billion from US airlines—twice the amount of all the profits they had earned the year before. By the summer of 2008, airline-industry share prices (measured by the Amex Airline Index) had dropped to one-tenth their level on the day before the September 11 attacks; more than a dozen US passenger and cargo airlines filed for bankruptcy that year alone.

Then came the breathtaking collapse. Oil prices plummeted in late 2008 into 2009 even faster than they had soared. Less than four months after their peak, they had fallen by half. By the end of 2008, the price of crude oil on the New York Mercantile Exchange stood at less than a third of its summer peak. Had it all been just a bad dream? For a while, it seemed so. In 2009, while crude-oil prices hovered in a modest range of $50 to $70 a barrel, US airlines began to recoup the staggering losses of the year before. For the dozen large passenger airlines tracked by MIT's Airline Data Project, combined operating losses of nearly $22 billion in 2008 improved to near breakeven in 2009. Not all that much to cheer about, but some relief.

The fuel-price specter returned in early 2011, and again in early and late 2012, as crude oil again crossed the $100-per-barrel barrier, heading upward largely in response to geopolitics and natural disasters. And even when the fuel roller coaster stabilized, it did so at levels that would have been *extreme* a decade earlier. The curse of fuel was here to stay, a threatening cloud looming over the new world of air travel.

SURVIVAL AND RESPONSE

The airline industry in 2008 was frantic to stem the tide of red ink, and the first and most obvious solution was just to use less of the now-exorbitant commodity. The effects on everyday travel were both trivial and profound.

Fly Less

The quickest way to burn less fuel was simply to fly less. As fuel prices approached their summer 2008 peak, the large carriers started to slash the number of seats they would fly after that summer season and into 2009—some of them cut drastically, by double-digit percentages. Especially hard hit were smaller cities, some served by relatively inefficient 50-seat regional jets made suddenly unprofitable by soaring fuel. More than 50 small markets lost air service at some point in 2008; some fell off the route maps entirely.

Slim down

Reducing fuel cost also meant cutting fuel-sucking airborne weight. In the mid-2000s, there was still plenty to cut. The old, heavy seatback telephones went first, then the "real" glassware. (US Airways tried light-weight plastic but had to bring back the glass Champagne flutes when First Class international passengers protested.) Removing the heavy galleys themselves was a no-brainer on domestic planes. It was the death knell for hot meals, but it shed tons of actual weight—the metal ovens and trash compactors, not to mention the older-style food and drink carts that weighed almost 50 pounds empty, up to 200 pounds loaded. Eliminating galleys also made room for another row or two of revenue-generating seats.

US Airways dumped its entire in-flight entertainment system on domestic flights and saved 500 pounds of videotape and DVD machines and associated wiring. And no more free (and weighty) magazines— not even those ubiquitous dog-eared copies of *Golf Digest* that always seemed the last to go. Want to read? There's always the airline's "in-flight shopping mall" catalog tucked neatly in the seatback, printed on ultra-lightweight paper stock.

Some weight could be cut with nobody noticing. Leaving the air-plane fuselage bare of paint could save some 300 pounds in the weight of a Boeing 737. Cleaning the jet engines overnight more frequently with high-pressure hoses reduced aerodynamic drag caused by tiny dirt specks. Lighter, skinnier passenger seats saved weight too. So did drink carts that weighed 12 pounds less (American bought 19,000 of them), lighter-weight cabin carpeting, even 25 percent lighter seat belts on Allegiant's MD-80 planes. Desperate to cut any source of avoidable weight, Japan Airlines even reduced the size of the spoons and forks it carried, saving 2 grams (0.07 ounces) each. Even with a few thousand utensils on a transpacific Boeing 747 flight, that totals less than 20 pounds. And so-called "electronic flight bags"—laptops and sometimes iPads—could serve as lightweight digital substitutes for the 38 pounds of paper flight manuals and navigation charts that each pilot had to haul into the cockpit.

Lavatories got special attention. Gone were the heavy electric-razor outlets built into the walls. Who shaves in there anyway? For that matter, who needs all that water? Finding lavatory tanks still wet on landing, Northwest cut the amount of water loaded aboard. Japan's ANA even asked passengers to visit the bathroom before boarding, portraying it as a "green" initiative that also cut weight. Even the very top of the premium passenger food chain sacrificed. When Emirates discovered that some of its ultra–First Class fliers were passing up the five-minute onboard showers the airline offered on its Airbus 380s, it reduced the ton of extra water carried aboard. Cutting all of this weight improved fuel burn, but only marginally. Huge jets are massive objects. Consider that the maximum takeoff weight of a Boeing 747-400 jumbo jet is some 400 *tons*—about eight times the weight of all its 400 passengers and their luggage.

Carry Less—Up to a Point

The heaviest thing carried aloft was the fuel itself, near seven pounds a gallon. When a 747 jumbo jet takes off, close to 40 percent of its entire weight is the fuel it carries. To burn less fuel, airlines needed to carry less fuel. Hauling enough extra fuel to keep the plane flying for just 15 minutes more at the end of a long flight (depending on altitude, speed, wind and lots of other factors)—can add more fuel-burning weight than carrying two dozen paying passengers, enough to turn some profitable flights into money-losers. So keeping fuel loads down seemed like an obvious imperative to airline budgeters, though not always to the conservative-minded pilots who bear the ultimate responsibility for the safety of the flight.

Under FAA rules and eons of tradition, the "pilot in command" has the final discretion to load as much fuel as he or she deems appropriate, though the airline flight planners and dispatchers make the initial call. And as an old pilots' saying goes: "The only time you have too much fuel is when you're on fire." Pilots concerned about weather delays or unusual headwinds or potential course diversions can and do order more fuel than the FAA requires or dispatchers recommend. Rules require enough fuel to reach not only the planned destination but also a predetermined alternate airport, plus an extra safety "cushion" of 45 minutes' flying time. That's one reason commercial jets almost never run out of gas.

So airlines rarely squawked when their pilots loaded an extra few hundred gallons—until prices hit the roof. The issue came to a head at busy Newark International in late 2007 when air traffic controllers noticed an extraordinary jump in arriving flights declaring "minimum fuel" or fuel emergencies—up from 44 in 2005 to 151 in 2007. Called to investigate, DOT's Inspector General found that one-sixth of all incidents involved a single Continental flight—from Barcelona to New York against prevailing Atlantic winds on a narrow-body Boeing 757. The Inspector General found no rule violations and no safety threat, but he did uncover a couple of questionable bulletins from the airline to its pilots. According to the IG's briefing to New Jersey senator Frank Lautenberg at the time, the memos exhorted pilots to be aware of the "opportunity to improve reducing unwarranted crew-initiated addition of fuel" and warned that "adding fuel indiscriminately without critical thinking ultimately reduces profit sharing and possibly pension funding." Would pilots worried about their pensions think twice before ordering those extra gallons?

Accusations flew. The week fuel prices hit their all-time peak, pilots at US Airways penned a full-page "open letter" to "our valued customers" in *USA Today,* the road warriors' bible. In it, they accused the airline of a "program of intimidation to pressure your captain to reduce fuel loads," which the airline heatedly denied. Just the week before, American had written to *its* flight dispatchers—ground-based FAA-certified staff responsible for managing each flight—that "carrying unnecessary fuel adversely affects American's financial success" and that it would "review every dispatcher's performance." The controversy over excess fuel abated along with fuel prices in 2009, but it returned in 2011, coincidentally as prices resurged. Due mainly to unusually strong west-to-east headwinds in early winter 2011, dozens of the same transatlantic flights to Newark on the same types of Boeing 757s—pushing to the limits of their 3,900-nautical-mile range—found themselves again short on fuel. In December 2011 alone, they were forced to land 43 times (out of 1,100 flights) to refuel in spots like Gander, Newfoundland, and Bangor, Maine.

Airlines tried almost anything to save a little fuel, even flying planes differently. Southwest expected to save $42 million in fuel costs in 2008 just by flying a few miles an hour slower. Arriving planes taxied to the gate on only a single engine, shut down the engines as soon as the chocks that hold the tires were placed around the nose gear, and immediately switched to the airport's electrical "ground power" for cabin ventilation and lighting. (Southwest tries to hook up within 90 seconds of parking the plane.) Support grew for improved air traffic control technology that would let planes fly more direct routes without the fuel-wasting zigs and zags and stair steps now required to keep planes a safe distance apart.

No Panaceas

By 2011, the US airlines had become more fuel efficient, burning 11 percent less fuel than in 2000, while carrying almost 16 percent more "ton-miles" of passengers and cargo, according to industry figures. Less direct cures for the fuel-cost blues didn't always pan out, though. A favorite, for a while, was a financial ploy known as "hedging," common in buying and selling commodities, from gold to pork bellies. If you're an airline decision-maker, you basically bet on what the price of fuel will be on some future date, paying to "lock in" today's price for your future fuel needs. If world oil prices go up, you win, and pay less at the pump than your un-hedged competitors. But if prices drop below the price you locked in, you're screwed. That's exactly what happened during the roller-coaster ride of fuel prices from 2008 to 2010.

The undisputed world champ of fuel hedging was Southwest. Consistently guessing right that pump prices would rise in the decade before they peaked in mid-2008, the airline made about $4 billion on fuel hedging and so stayed profitable even as rivals foundered. Jealous traditional airlines eventually jumped in to place their own hedging bets and lock in fuel prices—in some cases, unfortunately, just as those prices were about to turn sharply south. Caught by the breathtaking price collapse that followed, hedging latecomers were hit hard. United, for example, racked up more than half a billion dollars in hedging-related accounting losses in the third quarter of 2008 alone. Even Southwest itself eventually lost its price bet, suffering its first quarterly loss in 17 years. Chastened, most major airlines in 2012 hedged a modest 20 to 40 percent of fuel costs.

A cheaper alternative to petroleum-based jet fuel has also eluded the industry. One problem is that jet engines are very picky. Any safe replacement for the real thing has to pass some extreme performance tests:

> It can't auto-ignite, even at broiling temperatures near 400 degrees Fahrenheit when sitting in the wing tanks on Persian Gulf tarmacs in midsummer, but must still be explosive enough when ignited to power super-high-thrust jet engines without fail.
> It can't freeze (and so risk blocking fuel lines) cruising high over the Arctic in the dead of a winter night when temperatures hit 65 below.
> It must be capable of being produced in vast quantities, without turning forests or croplands into deserts, and usable in existing aircraft.

All a tall order, not likely to be filled easily or soon. Believers hope algae (think: pond scum) could supply one-third of all jet fuel by 2030, and all you need to grow it are pools of brackish water, not farmland. But so far at least, today's experimental algae is expected to yield only about 1,000 gallons of fuel per acre. (Advocates envision twice to 10 times that production efficiency eventually.) In a Boeing engineer's estimate reported by author James Fallows in *China Airborne*, supplying world airline needs would require algae fields the size of Belgium. As for other biomass fuels, Cathay Pacific predicts they could halve the price of today's fuel—but only in 20 years or so. The ultimate hedge against soaring fuel prices? Buy your own refinery like Delta did in 2012. For $150 million, the airline bought an aging Pennsylvania facility from ConocoPhillips in hopes it will reduce the carrier's annual fuel expense related to refining costs by $300 million, supplying 80 percent of the carrier's domestic jet fuel needs.

/ / /

The consternation over fuel in 2008 gave birth to the big-dollar surcharge but, in doing so, it also had a broader, profound effect on the airline business model. The "success" of fuel surcharges, and the willingness of air travelers to acquiesce to them, helped usher in the wondrous new world of ancillary fees, a river of new revenues limited only by the creative minds in the executive suites. There was a delicious irony: the fearsome explosion of world fuel prices had, in a sense, saved the industry from itself by forcing a tough new focus on profitability and the bottom line. The fuel hysteria also left in its wake a whole new frame of reference for the business of commercial aviation. Whatever vestige remained of the "customer service" ethos of the early Jet Age was supplanted by a hard-nosed business calculus: Don't fly a plane you can't fill. Cut flights and charge more for scarcity. (Don't worry about competitors stealing your market share—they're cutting too.) Peanuts for dinner will do in Economy. There was still plenty of marketing hype about customer service, maybe more than ever, and flying was as safe as ever. But "sit back and relax" had become "you get what you pay for."

3. Riding the Flying Bus

Nobody quite knew what to make of them at first—or even what to call them—when they emerged as unloved stepchildren of airline deregulation 30 years ago. But low-cost carriers/discounters/no-frills/upstarts/ value airlines not only survived; to the chagrin of their traditional airline rivals, some ultimately flourished. By example, they dragged the whole airline business kicking and screaming into the new century and profoundly changed the way we fly. The CEO of Southwest, the quintessential "upstart" carrier, summed it up this way in a December 2011 memo to employees the week after American Airlines, the quintessential traditional "legacy" airline, filed for bankruptcy: "The sloth-like industry you remember competing against is now officially dead and buried. We fought them and we won."

With lower costs, simpler fares, one-class service, fewer fees, and even fewer amenities (in their original "pure" form), the low-cost carriers seemed to lots of ordinary fliers somehow a little less soulless, manipulative, and money-hungry than the traditional carriers they challenged. Consumers complain about them to DOT less than a third as often as they complain about the large network airlines on average, and Southwest fliers complain least of all. Polls too confirm that US fliers hate them less than the large network airlines. In March 2012, J.D. Power and Associates' annual survey of 800 US companies in 20 industries ranked only three airlines among the top 50 "Customer Service Champions"—Southwest, JetBlue, and Virgin America.

Before 9/11, who could have imagined, for instance, that Southwest— once a four-jet outfit conceived apocryphally on the back of a cocktail napkin in a San Antonio bar—would become America's largest, richest domestic airline, with 40 profitable years in succession, a competitive threat so powerful it struck fear in the hearts of every mega-carrier and would discipline airfares across the land? Or that these rag-tag discounters would today carry one-third of all US fliers, compete on almost three-quarters of the country's city-to-city routes, *and* make money year after year. Before they could become a game-changing force in an industry grown cozy under years of regulation, though, they had to survive the wrath of the established older rivals whose lunch they were trying to eat.

AN EXISTENTIAL THREAT

Fear is a powerful motivator, and traditional airlines feared what the low-cost newcomers seemed to do best: keep fares down. Exploiting lower costs and greater efficiencies, and cherry-picking only the more lucrative (and overpriced) bigger-city markets, they could offer fares their legacy rivals just could not profitably sustain. For network airline execs, the appearance of Southwest at the doorstep of your comfortable high-fare hub was a cause for dread. Competition was about to drop the fares you could charge, and so, too, your revenues.

Aviation economists even had a name for it: the "Southwest Effect." When Southwest started flying from Baltimore in 1993, fares dropped 73 percent and traffic soared. When the airline invaded the high-priced Philadelphia market in 2004, average fares cratered there, too. And where Southwest *stopped* competing, fares could skyrocket. On the 259-mile route from Philadelphia to Pittsburgh, the cheapest advance-purchase round-trip fare jumped *sixfold*, from $118 to $698, plus taxes, when Southwest left the market at the start of 2012, according to *USA Today*. Similarly, when JetBlue left the Pittsburgh–New York route in early 2013, some competitors quickly offered alternatives—at more than five times the price. Put it this way: if a serious low-cost carrier chose to compete for "your" price-conscious customers, you really had only three options: slash your own fares to keep those customers, try to drive the new carrier away, or leave the market with your tail between your legs. All three happened.

From the perspective of the Old Guard pre-deregulation airlines—Delta, American, United, and US Airways, plus long-gone TWA, Pan Am, and Eastern—there were *already* "enough" airlines to fly travelers where they needed to go at government-approved fares. "Cutthroat" competition, after all, could benefit only consumers.

Traditional airlines took whatever steps were legal—and maybe then some—to keep the new guys from gaining a toehold, and they were successful. If a new carrier tried to compete by starting a couple of daily flights on your established route, you added four more flights of your own to "bracket" the new service, slashed your own fares—temporarily, of course—and loaded on extra "loyalty" or "mileage" awards that the start-ups couldn't offer. You might even try to punish the newcomer by throwing a few cheaply priced flights of your own on some other route where the upstart was actually making money. And plenty of would-be airline entrepreneurs tried to play without adequate start-up funds or even a realistic business plan, naïve about the battle they could expect to face from longtime incumbent carriers. By the mid-1990s, close to 100 airlines spawned by deregulation had gone out of business.

The killer blow, in fact, had little to do with aggressive tactics by the traditional airlines. It was, in a word, ValuJet. Starting with a single used DC-9 in 1993, this hot new outfit was seen as a model of the breed. That same year, DOT had giddily declared the growth of Southwest, the most successful of the new genre, to be "the principal driving force behind dramatic fundamental changes" in the airline industry. In its first year of operation, ValuJet Airlines lowered fares in the high-priced Atlanta market, turned a profit, and added 15 planes, then ordered 50 more the next year. Regulators applauded the new competition. Success seemed inevitable until ValuJet's Flight 592 corkscrewed into the Florida Everglades in May 1996. Though the NTSB ultimately determined the crash wasn't entirely ValuJet's fault (a contractor had improperly packed on board five boxes of flammable oxygen generators), it didn't really matter whose fault it was. Would-be customers of *any* "no-frills" airline now asked the sale-killing question: "But are they safe?"

Left for near-dead after ValuJet, the surviving airlines eventually staged a resurgence. It was a testament to the power of their low-cost business model, but also to hard lessons learned about the rigors of airline competition, and support from competition-promoting regulators charged with allocating limited available rights to access the most popular, congested airports. And this time around, the new "little guys" weren't always so little; they began with enough money to survive the by-then appreciated firepower of incumbent competitors. JetBlue didn't even think about entering the fierce New York market in 2000 until after it had amassed a war chest of $130 million; Virgin America tapped its association with Virgin Atlantic Airways and its media-genius chairman, Richard Branson, to raise $177 million in start-up capital before its 2007 launch.

The newbies had gotten smarter, too. Rather than confront their deep-pocketed network rivals at their hub fortresses, the upstarts flew the same lucrative big-city routes, but often used secondary airports—Long Beach instead of LAX, Oakland instead of SFO, Islip instead of JFK or LaGuardia, Baltimore instead of Reagan National, and Midway instead of O'Hare. And they invested to maintain their critical cost advantage, acquiring new planes that would be cheaper to fly and to maintain. The "but are they safe?" question all but disappeared.

Low-cost carriers still pressure fares, but not quite like they used to. Traditional airlines too can now offer low, low, base fares and make up some of the revenue hit with expensive premium-class tickets and hefty ancillary fees. Even powerful discounter Southwest has lost some of its fare-disciplining mojo as it tries to cover its own rising costs, and so more often "goes along" with industrywide fare hikes. When fuel prices spiked in the middle of 2008, Southwest raised its fares an average of 8.4 percent, almost exactly the same as the legacy airlines, and fare levels at some of its airport strongholds have since climbed faster

than the national average. The more lasting impact of the low-cost airlines, though, lies in the triumph of an innovative business model based
on high productivity, dedication to simplicity, and carefully nurtured,
distinctive "culture."

MORE BANG

Low-cost carriers don't pay less than the big airlines for their fuel or
labor or airplanes, but they get more for each dollar they spend. More
performance, more flights, and ultimately more passenger revenue
from the same operating expense. Until 2008, it added up to a nearly
25 percent cost advantage. That gap has since narrowed by half in the
United States, though, according to a 2011 study by consulting firm Oliver Wyman, as fuel (everybody pays about the same pump price) grows
as a proportion of every airline's operating costs.

   Even with lower overall labor expenses, though, low-cost carriers
(though not all of them) actually pay their employees *better* than traditional airlines. In 2011, Southwest's pilots' and copilots' average total
compensation of $237,000 (including benefits) outstripped the average
of the other large US passenger airlines by almost one-third. On the
other hand, those pilots also had many years' experience and reportedly worked longer—almost an extra hour every day, though it varies
from month to month. Non-pilot airline employees also make more at
the typical low-cost carrier, though that gap is considerably narrower,
according to MIT data. By paying more but also getting more work for
that higher pay, low-cost airlines lower their *true* cost of operating—of
flying each airplane seat a mile.

   It's much the same when it comes to making fuel more productive.
Everybody pays the same price for the combustible liquid, but low-cost
carriers generally cram more paying seats into the fuel-filled planes they
fly, partly by eliminating First Class. Delta's 737-700 carries 124 passengers, while the exact same plane flown by Southwest holds 137 paying

seats. Spirit jams 174 "pre-reclined" Economy seats into its Airbus 320, while United carries 138 or 144 in *its* A320, depending on model.

There's an even starker contrast when you compare where the two types of airlines "live." United's ultramodern operations center, soon to be joined by its global corporate headquarters, occupies a dozen floors in the tallest building in the United States, Chicago's magnificent Willis Tower, formerly known as the Sears Tower. American, as revealed in its bankruptcy filings, housed its top international executive in Europe in a stately five-bedroom town house in one of London's poshest neighborhoods—a lovely pied-à-terre worth upward of $20 million. Meanwhile, until 2012, JetBlue crammed almost everybody into several floors of a nondescript office building on Queens Boulevard, boasting a mid-rise view of the borough. It since moved to a century-old former auto assembly building in Long Island City, New York—still a subway ride from midtown Manhattan.

There are a lot of smaller things—call them "process inventions"—that boost the low-cost carrier productivity edge. The textbook example is the Southwest "turn"—the rapid-fire choreography that airlines have mastered to get an arriving jet—unloading, cleaning, servicing, refueling, reloading—quickly back in the air. The faster, the better; planes earn nothing sitting on the ground, as they say. It takes a lot of teamwork, motivation, and drilled-in coordination. Think NASCAR pit crew. Just watch the ballet when an incoming plane rounds the taxiway heading to its gate. Airline ground crew are on their feet, cradling refueling hoses, poised to crawl into cargo holds, plug in electric connections, and position the waiting baggage carts while fueling and waste trucks stand at the ready yards away.

The upshot is that Southwest can turn its Boeing 737 jets in roughly 30 minutes, sometimes as little as 25 minutes. (The airline's average turn time has slowed a little since it began serving more congested airports like New York's.) It learned how by necessity; as a fledgling carrier in the 1970s, it sold one of its four jets and had to "turn" the remaining three in as little as 10 minutes to meet its schedule. Traditional airlines turn the same domestic planes in 40 minutes on a good day, often closer to an hour depending on the airport, time of day, weather, and lots of other variables. So what's ten minutes? Boeing says that saving ten minutes of on-the-ground time translates into 8 percent more time flying—and earning fares. Plus, it means Southwest can get more use out of the airport boarding gates it pays to lease from airports—at some busy airports, it can move as many as 10 flights per day through each gate it leases.

KEEPING IT SIMPLE, STUPID

At the heart of low-cost carriers' success is a devotion to simplicity. Start with their aircraft fleets. United, for instance, flies more than a half dozen basic types of planes (excluding variants), while Southwest flies just one, the popular 737 (its merger with AirTran temporarily added a second, the smaller Boeing 717), and JetBlue uses two. Ideally, aircraft fleet uniformity means that every certified mechanic and technician can fix and clean and service most every plane. The hydraulics and fasteners and sophisticated avionics are the same, one plane to the next. So you need only one set of parts, one set of maintenance manuals, one warehouse system, one training program, one way of doing things—and all of your pilots are qualified and approved ("type-rated") to fly all of your planes. Network airlines with long-haul and international service can't do the same. They need very different aircraft to make it across the Pacific or over the Poles from the ones they use for the Atlanta–Dallas run. It's one reason low-cost carriers in the United States don't venture too far overseas (exceptions are Central America and the Caribbean)— they just don't want the operational complication.

Simplicity also means flying to fewer places—the bigger the market, the better. Shuttling full planes back and forth between big cities works just fine; low-cost airlines serve very few of the country's smaller airports. Of the 500 smallest ("non-hub" airports), only five had low-cost airline service in 2005, according to the GAO. Why worry about the intricacies of collecting Beijing-bound passengers in ones and twos from Lansing and Oshkosh and Greensboro, shoving them through big, expensive hubs, and sending them out again to Asia? Choreographing tight domestic hub connections, racing across tarmacs to make "hot" bag transfers between connecting flights, and scheduling rafts of gates, lounges, and crew facilities at city-sized hubs is costly, labor-intensive, and bound to tick off passengers who get caught in the inevitable screwups.

It's not that low-cost carriers were uniquely creative business strategists. More that they could get away with kinds of "reinvention" their established rivals weren't ready for and, more important, didn't think their *customers* could tolerate. Take the elimination of onboard meals. Since United opened the first airline flight kitchens in 1936, there was *always* food on airplanes. Even if we mocked it, hated it, or ignored it, a meal was a fundamental part of the flying experience, a gesture of "taking care." In the soft light of memory, some of it wasn't all that bad, but more important was the anticipation, the diversion and, ask any kid, the thrilling otherworldliness of eating—who cared what it was?—above the clouds!

For the airlines, though, meals were an unwelcome expense—$5 to $6 per passenger in 2008, about 2 percent of operating expenses—and an operational and logistics headache. Even though most airlines left the cooking, chilling, prepping, storing, and hauling to a handful of "in-flight catering" contractors, there's was still the waste, hygiene issues, and tracking who gets Vegan, who gets Halal, and who gets Kosher. Hauling heavy galley ovens burns fuel. Heavily loaded food carts bash knees, block aisles, and strain employee backs. Galleys themselves displace paying seats; and crews have to heat, serve, and clean up. Onboard meals were just something else to worry about when trying to get the flight out on time.

The large carriers quietly ended meals on short flights immediately after 9/11, but dropping coach meals *entirely* on nearly *all* domestic flights? Wouldn't passengers balk, maybe even switch to another carrier that still fed them? The proudly meal-less low-cost carriers provided "cover" for the whole industry to end coach meals once and for all. Southwest had never offered meal service—and bragged about it. Almost defiantly, it tossed bags of peanuts at its budget-minded passengers—a statement, even a subliminal compliment, to the frugality of its (still-hungry) customers. Hipper JetBlue offered signature "Terra Blue" potato chips in lieu of meals. If the millions who made Southwest the most profitable US carrier and JetBlue the country's sixth largest airline in its first decade could live without free meals, so could fliers on American and Delta and United. Effectively killing the last free meals on domestic flights in 2010, Continental claimed the move reflected "today's market and customer preference"—not to mention that it would save the airline some $35 million annually.

Traditional carriers couldn't afford to emulate some kinds of low-cost airline simplification, though, like eliminating the elaborate stratification of service according to each flier's "status" or fare. Distributing "perks" in proportion to what each passenger "contributes" to airline revenue, in the industry lexicon, remains a key revenue tool for the big airlines.

What better example than the network airlines' ritualistic process of getting everybody onto the plane? As we've seen, each caste—starting with Platinum Gold Premier Chairman or whatever, working down to the Untouchables who are entirely without "status"—must be recognized in strict rank order by the harried gate agent. Compare Southwest's "cattle call," as it was known in its pure form until late 2007. It was simplicity itself: passengers lined up at the jetway door, got on, and grabbed any open seat.

HUMANIZING THE CULTURE

Most difficult to replicate, though, was an intangible ingredient in the low-cost airline success story—call it culture, spirit, or personality.

It's an ingredient that makes no-frills, tight-pitch, cram-aboard flying palatable—even preferable—for many ordinary passengers. When peanuts for dinner was still a joke instead of an expectation, the low-cost carriers' less-robotic, up-front culture sent a message: "We won't insult your intelligence by pretending coach air travel is a pleasant adventure, but we're in this together, so let's make it as decent as we can while we get you where you're going." At least it avoided the bland insincerity of "sit back and relax." Less blowing smoke, fewer false expectations, no overpromising or broken bargains.

The ethos varied by carrier. Southwest perfected the easygoing "we-don't-take-ourselves-too-seriously-and-you-shouldn't-either" persona. JetBlue and Virgin America projected a cooler, urban vibe—where crew wore monochromatic uniforms, mood lighting tinted the cabin ceiling, and a menu of "Signature Cocktails" complemented the buy-on-board tapas. At the other end of the spectrum, there was the ultra-cheap, "just-get-me-there" spirit of Spirit and its successful counterparts in Europe, Ryanair and Easyjet, favored by holidaymakers and weekend soccer hooligans alike. JetBlue explicitly professed itself "dedicated to bringing humanity back to air travel." Whatever, at least it seemed sincere.

Not that the Old Guard didn't try to create an appealing new "culture," but when they did, it felt more like fiftysomethings trying to act cool with their kids' friends. Some tried to graft an "irreverent" vibe onto newly formed "airline-within-an-airline" subsidiaries that would offer stripped-down service in return for cheaper fares in big markets, in competition with the low-cost carriers. Who can forget short-lived experiments like "Ted" from 2003 to 2005—"part of UniTED" (get it?)—or Delta's "Song," with its Apple Martinis, singing flight attendants (for the safety instructions), and tightly packed Boeing 757s painted an unlovely lime green?

The low-cost-carrier cultures weren't always all that organic or spontaneous, either. Southwest, for instance, established a "culture committee" in the 1990s to promote "the Southwest Way." To find employees with the right attitude, its hiring became so selective—only 1 percent of résumé applicants got a job—that, by 2009, according to the *New York Times*' Jad Mouawad, it was easier statistically to get into an Ivy League college than to get a job at Southwest slinging bags. Savvy management understood that an imbued culture gave workers a sense of ownership and responsibility—for the enterprise and for keeping customers happy. Culture Committee theme for 2010: "Count on Me to Own It!"

COMING TOGETHER

As the dust cleared a decade past September 11, traditional carriers had become more like the "backpacker airlines" they had once disdained. When US Airways merged with America West in 2005, it paid the ultimate compliment, choosing "LCC" (for "low-cost carrier") as its new Wall Street ticker symbol. If you can't beat 'em, join 'em. The once-yawning "cost gap" between the two kinds of airlines began to narrow. Low-cost-carrier labor and fuel costs rose, while traditional carriers used bankruptcy to escape all manner of expense; as their finances improved, they acquired more fuel-efficient planes that would further narrow the competitive cost advantage. As business travelers and frequent fliers came to see the Southwests and JetBlues as decent alternatives for domestic flying, the fare premiums passengers once paid to fly on "real" airlines began to disappear.

For the ordinary air traveler in back, it made ever less difference whether you were flying on Southwest or American, Virgin or United. *Nobody* provided free meals or much free anything, and please pass your trash. All flights were crowded, all offered much the same tight seat pitch and just-get-me-there ambience. Experts talked about the "hybridization" of the airline industry, but for the non-elites, the airline we flew mattered less and less. Now we're pretty much *all* aboard the flying bus.

10

Forecast

CLOUDY WITH SOME SIGNS OF CLEARING

Attend enough aviation industry gatherings and eventually you're bound to hear some self-important after-dinner speaker invoke Heraclitus, the Greek philosopher who observed, about 2,500 years ago, that "change is the only constant." Especially over the last decade, it's been an apt cliché for an airline business that seems always in crisis. Today, though, the truism is ever *less* true. Thirty-five years after the trauma of airline deregulation and more than a decade past September 11, the turbulence and uncertainty that seemed woven into the fabric of commercial aviation appear to be giving way to a new status quo—more stable and likely more enduring than most aviation folks could have imagined.

In this emerging aero-business environment, airlines turn a profit as often as not. Maybe it's not enough to make investors happy—but it keeps companies in the black. Only recently, though, have owners and investors even begun to earn the kind of returns that, if sustained over a full multiyear business cycle, would cover their "cost of capital"—what investors normally expect from their investments. (All US airlines combined are still worth less in market capitalization than Starbucks.) Passengers pay more, one way or another, whether in fares or fees or surcharges or wasted time. Financial uncertainty remains, but at least the key variables are clear: the price of jet fuel, the strength of the economy (which translates into the demand to fly), the control of capacity, and, as always in today's airline world, the avoidance of some unimagi-nable out-of-the-blue catastrophe.

A telling bit of evidence about the industry's new durability from *Airline Weekly:* When fuel prices soared to $100 a barrel in 2008, US airlines lost $4 billion. When prices climbed nearly as high ($95 per barrel) in 2011, they *made* $2.5 billion. And they kept eking out profits through 2012, even after fuel again peaked above $100. As the industry association's chief economist explained in August 2012, "What used to be a threat to [airlines'] existence [$100 per barrel oil] is now a threat to earnings." The CEO of US Airways put it another way at an aviation conference in Dallas: "I think we're finally on the brink of stability." In other words, something fundamental about the industry is changing, and—fingers crossed in the executive suites—it's likely to continue. What, exactly, happened? Essentially three things.

First, the industry shrank. Consolidation hasn't reached the point where we just dial up "Airline" when we want to fly somewhere, but we're approaching the logical end point that competition regulators once feared, a world of "3 + 3 + 3": three huge network airlines, three nationwide low-cost carriers—each with more than 3 percent of the market (plus a few niche players)—and three global airline alliances. It's been a long time coming—scores of new airlines have appeared and disappeared just since deregulation—but the last five years have wit-nessed a denouement as Delta swallowed Northwest, United merged with Continental, US Airways joined America West, and Southwest bought AirTran.

The final shoe drops if, as widely predicted, American's 2012 bank-ruptcy leads to another merger, this time with US Airways. If the pro-posed $11 bilion merger to create the world's largest airline happens, says an April 2012 analysis by J.P.Morgan, the Big Three airlines plus Southwest would control "close to 90 percent of domestic capacity," compared to the roughly 50 percent they controlled in 2005. *That's* a world that Wall Street has long yearned for—a much cozier market-place for the fare-focused survivors. For investors, says J.P.Morgan airline analyst Jamie Baker, it would "represent the optimal industry structure, and should allow for consistent return generation going forward. . . ."

"Optimal" for airline owners, perhaps, but advice to consumers: at least over the long haul, hang on to your wallets.

Second, the airlines found ingenious new ways to extract more cash from fliers without raising basic airfares. "Unbundling" the product (once quaintly known as a "flight") into lots of little chargeable services may not have added all that much to basic fares—about $22 to a $316 near-average round-trip in 2011, according to Airlines for America—but that's still the same as a 7 percent fare hike. And that doesn't include other uncounted "extras" that DOT doesn't yet require airlines to report specifically, like buy-on-board meals, Wi-Fi and in-flight enter-tainment, blankets, certain assigned seats, telephone reservations, early boarding privileges—the whole shebang.

Without these ancillary fees, airline profits would remain almost as elusive and uncertain as ever. Whine all you want about fees, fellow fli-ers, as we've seen before, there's just too much money at stake to expect them to end. They compose roughly 10 percent of all revenue for some of the largest traditional airlines, up to a whopping one-third for carri-ers like Spirit. Ancillary fees are here to stay and so, for that matter, are crowded planes.

Third, the decade since 9/11 saw a profound, if subtle, shift in the way airlines thought about the business. Forget the sentiment and the cowboy mentality of the risk-taking flyboys who started it all. As ever-quotable airline consulting guru Michael Boyd put it, "The crazy people are gone and now we're going to have a reasonable airline indus-try that will make some money." Soaring fuel prices? Dump the galleys, cut flights, and burn less, and do it quick. Rising labor costs? Lay off a quarter of the industry workforce—about 150,000 full-time jobs at the major airlines—and automate. Aircraft-maintenance expense rising as planes age? Park those gas-guzzlers in the desert. By 2012, mainline US fleets were 17 percent smaller than in 2000 as older, larger jets were replaced by newer, smaller, and more fuel-efficient planes. Passenger service? It depends what you mean by "service"—you get what you pay for. Computer algorithms dictate who gets the upgrade, no matter how much you smile at the gate attendant. And if you want the whole can of Coke, you have to ask.

These changes were foundational, philosophical, and signaled a whole new way of doing business for commercial aviation. Not that we're somehow approaching the "end of history," to borrow noted political scientist Francis Fukuyama's phrase. The industry is still evolving, including internationally. Compare lists of the world's ten largest airlines measured by paid passenger-miles in 2000 and in 2010, as compiled by the Centre for Aviation analytic and consulting organization. Only six carriers make both "top ten" lists; two of the 2010 top ten—Emirates and China Southern—didn't even make the top 25 just a decade earlier. Or look at it this way: only about half of the world's 25 biggest airlines (measured by total passengers) in 2010 made that category ten years earlier. Add to that the unique and constant vulnerability of the airline business. For all of its newfound stability, the entire industry remains one body-implanted bomb or major new Mideast war away from renewed financial grief.

What does this more stable and businesslike industry bode for everyday air travelers? Even if it's far from utopian, it doesn't have to be dystopian, either. After all, it's an industry that's already proven itself capable of surviving catastrophic terrorism, plagues, and widespread bankruptcy. With stronger finances, relatively stable fuel prices, and steady demand for flying, couldn't it also deliver the "miracle" of human flight to everyday air travelers with a little more humaneness, civility, and comfort. There are reasons to be optimistic.

1. THE KIOSK

Harried travelers have grown to love the airport self-check-in "kiosk," a promising herald of our automated flying future. Take it from a guy who once resisted even supermarket self-checkout lines: When you're hustling to catch a flight, the kiosk is a godsend. It doesn't just eliminate long line waits—how do I inevitably pick the understaffed check-in line behind the nice couple planning their fiftieth-anniversary around-the-world trip?—it's empowering. You lose the human touch, but when you have to move fast, the "new" automation—at least when it works—can make flying a whole lot less grueling and stressful.

It's no longer just about cutting labor costs, or shifting them to passengers forced to pay in wasted time holding on endless telephone trees. Today's information technology supports a whole new level of automation, one that still saves airlines cash but also lets halfway-savvy passengers help themselves online and at the airport. Add to kiosks plenty of other new technologies like travel software applications for tracking flights in real time, airport guides that electronically walk you through the terminal bedlam to your gate or to the closest watering hole, apps that monitor security-line wait times, and radio-frequency bag tags that track the precise location of your luggage as it moves along the journey, not to mention digital check-in and boarding and the wonder of Wi-Fi at 37,000 feet. Call it DIY air travel, except for the actual flying.

The self-service journey has happened fast—maybe too fast for some. As noted, costly-to-handle paper tickets disappeared in less than a decade, for example, but not every flier—my elderly aunt included—joyfully embraces the brave new world of downloading and flashing barcodes on smart phone screens at boarding gate scanners. And there can be false economies. A pet peeve: Is it really faster to make busy TSA name-checkers squint at your electronic boarding pass on your iPhone screen (the pass still needs to be scanned, verified, and compared to your ID) than to simply print out the bloody thing at the kiosk in the airport lobby and hand it to the officer along with your driver's license?

And despite its huge promise, automated self-service doesn't always work, period. Just ask Virgin America, one of the world's most tech-friendly airlines, based in San Francisco, up the highway from Silicon Valley where hardly anybody "calls" an airline. When its web-based reservations system crashed in 2011, Virgin's tech-savvy clientele reportedly waited up to an hour on the *telephone* to make or change reservations or to check in. With high expectations for technology, don't expect much patience from the young and tech-reliant, either; remember the guy in New Orleans arrested for a violent assault on a balky Continental Airlines check-in kiosk.

2. THE DREAMLINER

Even with the initial safety angst over Boeing's new 787 superplane, a new generation of airplanes using innovative technologies—put aside the 787's battery problems—promises passengers a better flying experience soon. Beaten down by hard times after 9/11, traditional US airlines initially stopped buying new airplanes. Just stopped. By late in the decade, their fleets were aging—according to Airfleets.net, about 12 to 16 years old on average compared to about nine years at Air France and KLM, 10 to 11 years at Cathay Pacific, Japan Airlines, or Qantas, and six to seven years at Emirates and Singapore. By 2013, Delta was still flying more than a dozen DC-9 jets inherited from Northwest that averaged close to 35 years old.

Deferring aircraft replacement saved money in the short term, but aging fleets bore their own cost consequences, like higher fuel and maintenance expense. When United bought 50 new-generation long-haul jets in December 2009 to replace older 747s and 767s, for example, it projected 40 percent savings in lifetime maintenance costs per seat-mile for each retired plane, and fuel-cost reductions of some 33 percent. So when industry finances began to improve, replacing aircraft—en masse in some cases—climbed corporate agendas. In July 2011, months before it went bankrupt, American announced the biggest airplane order in history—460 new jets, plus options for another slew of about the same number—and other carriers went shopping too.

New passenger-friendly airplanes promise to meet the imperatives of lower operating costs, but the leaps of technology on which they rely are just that—true leaps of both engineering and manufacturing processes that, as the Boeing 787 saga attests, can be much tougher to execute than anyone expects. Hyped as the "Dreamliner," no less, the plane took a decade to build, arrived three years late at the end of 2011, and suffered what may be the worst US market debut of any airship since the *Hindenburg*. After a full-on, pop-the-evacuation-slides emergency landing in Japan, regulators had to ground the whole fleet to investigate what the NTSB called "very serious safety concerns" related to battery overheating. (The planes' powerful lithium-ion batteries help provide the copious electricity—the plane generates enough to power some 500 homes—that lets fuel-saving components substitute for heavier, traditional mechanical systems.)

Once eventually back in the air, the Dreamliner won't be any less crowded, offer more legroom, or make pricey snack packs more satisfying, but two unseen improvements should enhance physical comfort: a lower "virtual" altitude and higher cabin humidity. Both are made possible by the plane's innovative construction—it uses carbon-fiber composite sections, not the typical sheets of airplane aluminum that are vulnerable to metal fatigue. (Airbus's "new-generation" long-range A350, due in service as soon as late next year, takes the same approach to airframe materials.) Passengers should feel more like they're sitting in a Denver high-rise than in a desert-mountain pass. Cabin humidity will also be higher than the Saharan levels of most planes—15 to 16 percent humidity is promised—and a new gas filtration system removes, ahem, odors and "gaseous contaminants."

At least as noticeable as the physical improvement will be the psychic comforts of the interior of the new planes, the feng shui. For a decade, teams of psychologists worked with Boeing's "director of passenger satisfaction" on the challenge: how to improve the flying experience while still letting their airline customers squeeze in as many bodies and burn as little fuel as possible. The physical dimensions of an airplane cabin can't change that much, so designers tried to change passengers' *perception* of their spatial environment—to leave them a little less stressed, more relaxed, and even less bored. Boeing's aim to "reconnect passengers to flying" is an unabashed throwback to an earlier day when the air journey still held a little wonder.

Start with the 787 windows—they're about 65 percent larger than on "standard" jets, another feature made possible by the strength of the plane's carbon-composite construction, and they're positioned higher, at the passengers' eye level. Forget staring at the mindless sitcom rerun on the seatback screen; welcome to the sky and earth and clouds. And electronic virtual window shades darken the windows through five levels with the touch of a button by activating an electro-chromatic film, without entirely blocking out the view. Inside the cabin, light levels and ceiling colors can be adjusted across an almost infinite spectrum, say to mimic the blue sky, or a dawn or sunset on long-haul flights across time zones. At the plane's main entry door, a spacious foyer is intended to emphasize the welcoming transition from the cramped, dark jetway, a psychological transit from the "compression" of the boarding line to— dare we say it?—the "magic" of flight.

Airlines think passengers will eat it up, ordering 850 planes before even the first test flight. So don't be surprised to see—eventually at least—a Dreamliner surcharge.

3. NEXTGEN

It's an awkward moniker, but this monster federal program promises to drag air traffic control out of the post–World War II era, reducing delays, improving safety, and even shortening flights by letting planes fly closer together and on more direct routes. NextGen is really an umbrella for a bunch of new tools and technologies meant to change the way air traffic is managed. The basic idea is to transfer much of the job from controllers in darkened rooms watching radar screens to a satellite-based system using GPS that gives pilots in the cockpit more control and responsibility for safe and efficient routing. The package includes lots of other improvements—new digital communications and data networking, precision weather forecasting, and new airport systems.

Truth be told, not many folks fully understand all the pieces of this huge air traffic rework, how they're supposed to fit together, precisely what it will cost, or who exactly will pay for what. Cost estimates approach $40 billion, with taxpayers picking up most of the tab and airlines the rest. But suffice it to say that NextGen is, as the *Washington Post* put it, the "most expensive and complicated transportation project since the launch of the interstate highway system."

Putting aside the surfeit of NextGen hype, though, the problem it aims to fix is very real: an obsolete US air traffic control system that is operating at, and sometimes beyond, its limits. Controllers tracking the 7,000 or so aircraft over the United States at any given time on any given day still use radar, a rudimentary technology for locating things that is light-years behind even the $199 GPS navigation system plugged into your car's dashboard outlet.

Before your eyes glaze over, understand that NextGen—particularly its GPS component—should make a concrete difference for fliers, speeding travel time and cutting delays. While delays have already dropped significantly since the forgettable summer of 2000, that's at least partly due to fewer airline flights and padded flight schedules. The reprieve won't last forever, though; even as airlines keep a tight reign on capacity, economic growth spurs profitable demand and air traffic continues its long, slow rebound. The FAA optimisticaly predicts that in a decade or so, a *billion* passengers will crowd US airspace, 37 percent more in 2024 than flew in 2011. So if you thought delays *used* to be bad . . .

Here's how NextGen promises to help: Consider a raft of planes converging on a fog-bound hub at rush hour. Air traffic controllers' top safety priority is just to "maintain separation" between them—or, as normal humans might say, to keep them from crashing into each other and plummeting to earth in horrifying fireballs. If things get overloaded and controllers start wondering where DL 432 went or why UA 92 is heading to the wrong runway, they have to slow everything down, imposing a ground delay or airspace-flow program that meters flight activity. Sometimes, the FAA has to just blow the whistle—putting a "ground stop" on all flights to the overloaded airports or regions until things get less crazy. More commonly, planes are directed to zigzag between virtual "waypoints" in the sky at precisely staggered altitudes—think of a sailboat tacking upwind—so that traffic controllers can be sure they know where every airplane is headed in the three-dimensional chess game known as the National Airspace System.

Hopscotching and zigzagging between waypoints burns extra fuel, emits greenhouse gases, delays flights, and sometimes triggers a cascade of further downstream delays. And it invariably lengthens the actual distance you have to fly to get to your destination—you notice it most on what should be short hops in congested metro regions. An extreme example cited by the airlines in 2007 Senate testimony: flights between Boston and Washington in the congested Northeast corridor that had to be routed via western New York and central Pennsylvania, lengthening the intercity journey by 35 percent. And that's when radar and other control technologies are working reliably. Radar sometimes breaks down, reflects "ghost" images, or tracks flocks of birds. Remote mountaintop radar antennas can be tough to maintain. NextGen technologies should eventually let airlines abandon the old jagged waypoint-to-waypoint "highways in the sky" in favor of near-direct routings.

At the heart of the NextGen fix is a piece of techno-magic known as—it's a mouthful—automatic dependent surveillance-broadcast (everybody says "ADS-B"). What that does, in essence, is let air traffic controllers see precisely and almost instantly where your plane is—by using satellite-based GPS surveillance. Radar can't do that. One reason is that long-range radar dishes take about 12 seconds to rotate, 5 or 6 seconds for radar near airports, so controllers can see only where your plane *used* to be 12 seconds ago—that's a mile away when you're flying at 300 miles per hour. ADS-B should update your plane's position at least every single second, and GPS will show more precisely how fast you're moving and where you're headed.

And get this: Pilots in their cockpits will see it all too—their own console screens showing the same picture of the airspace and other planes around them that air traffic controllers sitting on the ground see on *their* screens. It's all designed to make it easier for planes to see and avoid one another—so they can get where they're going directly, and so more of them can fit safely into congested airspace without the time-consuming "safety cushion" of extra separation and airborne maneuvering that today's less-precise system requires. By 2020, the FAA expects the improvements to cut delays 38 percent and at the same time save 1.4 billion gallons of fuel. At least, that's the theory.

Even though the need for it is close at hand, NextGen truly does mean *next generation*, and much of the core hardware won't be in place for nearly a decade. Meanwhile, the FAA has, to put it politely, a blemished history of implementing big-bang new technologies, especially those involving complex new software. It comes as little surprise, therefore, that two government watchdogs, the GAO and DOT's Inspector General, have warned of costly delays in the program. In April 2012, DOT's Inspector General concluded rather drily that "it is uncertain when the [NextGen] programs will start delivering benefits . . ."; in September, it was "come the promised land, when NextGen is in place." In 2012 the GAO found that more than a third of the program's 30 key contracts were already over budget, with half of them behind schedule. The FAA still speaks hopefully about a "goal" of getting the whole whizz-bang program up and running by 2025—they call this vision "Destination 2025." But consider the fact that, as late as the mid-1990s, the FAA was the world's largest consumer of old-style vacuum tubes.

4. T-2 AND THE YOGA ROOM

Airports aren't always happy places. People arrive stressed. They're leaving something or someone; they're about to embark on something new; they're rushing to make a flight, a meeting, a deadline; they're being scanned and maybe frisked—and they know why. Venues of anguished leave-takings and joyous reunions, they're also gateways to the new normal of air travel, often the first corridors of travel angst. In response, airports have historically aspired to be, from a functional standpoint, largely invisible. The mission of these highly ordered systems was to move passengers through the pipeline to their planes like clockwork, without drama.

At the same time, though, mega-airports were monuments to modernity—witness LAX's retro-futuristic "Theme" building or the Saarinen terminals at JFK and Dulles. From Southeast Asia to the Persian Gulf, airports have become "statements," testaments to having arrived on the world stage. The new Beijing International Terminal 3 is not only the world's largest airport but, by some measure, the world's largest building of *any kind,* an edifice twice the square footage of the Pentagon. Air travelers traversing such vast marble icons seem diminutive, almost afterthoughts.

Today that vision of the monumental "aerodrome" is starting to be eclipsed, at least in the United States, by a new idea of the airport's role in the air-travel journey. Leading airports are trying to pick up the slack in the passenger experience, reintroducing a little humanity, civility, and even fun. They're motivated partly by money—happier, relaxed passengers spend more, park more, and fly more—and partly by civic pride and a sense of responsibility to their communities. Attracting a new international flight can bring huge benefits to the local economy—Denver projected $142 million a year for a new daily Boeing 747 flight to Asia. And most are creatures of municipal government; their bosses answer to local elected politicos and their constituents, after all.

Add a simple fact of aviation life after September 11: airports are where travelers often spend the bulk of their journey, more time than in the air—it's known as "dwell time." There's plenty of it to spare at the world's mega-hubs. A Dallas-Fort Worth airport survey of 1,600 travelers at the end of 2008 found that departing passengers spent about 95 minutes between the time they cleared security until they boarded their plane; nearly a quarter of them spent more than two hours waiting. For travelers connecting to other flights at the hub, the wait was 134 minutes on average. At ultrabusy London Heathrow, one study found an average total dwell time of 161 minutes—*nearly three hours*. Long dwell times aren't only at huge hubs, though. Even the nice, new airport in Bismarck, North Dakota, with less than a dozen daily airline flights and fewer than 600 passengers a day on average in 2011, cautions fliers to arrive at least 90 minutes early.

But who's complaining about the end of sprints to the boarding gate? For airlines, the extra time ensures that even once-a-year "Christmas fliers" get to the gate on time, that bags have time to get tagged accurately, and presumably that check-in desks can be more tightly staffed. For airports, dwell time means cash. Air travelers have money, they're bored, and they're captive after the security screening—almost perfect consumers. Their $88,000 median income in 2010 far exceeded the national median income of just under $50,000. And, according to an Arbitron survey in 2007, more than two-thirds of air travelers hit the demographic sweet spot—between 25 and 54 years old, with nearly 60 percent having at least a college degree.

To access passenger wallets, retailers pay airports serious rents and a piece of the revenue action. Even before 9/11, a little See's Candies cart in a terminal lobby at SFO grossed well over a million dollars a year. Clothing retailer Brooks Brothers caught on early to the airport-as-shopping-mall; its motto: "Bad Weather Is Good for Business," according to a *New York Times* story. Good, too, for the airport—it typically takes well over 10 percent of the non-food retail gross, and double that percentage from rental-car companies. Airport retail is getting even more lucrative. By 2011, fliers at large airports were shelling out an estimated $10 on average on airport purchases, not including duty-free goods. The demise of free food onboard must have made gold mines out of some airport eateries. How can you lose selling water at $3 a quart? Since 9/11 swelled "dwell time," airport revenues from retail stores and food and beverage concessions have by some estimates jumped over 40 percent (from 2002 to 2009), according to one research study. And that's not including airport parking and ground transportation—where the biggest chunk of passenger purchase revenue comes from.

Whether by design or default, leading US airports are becoming more than forgettable pass-throughs from the curb to the plane, or vice versa. Who else is taking care of the traveler? Since so much of the nation's travel is concentrated in relatively few large airports—the 16 largest handle half of all US passengers and the top 25, known as "Category X" airports, serve more than two-thirds of them—a dozen or two truly passenger-friendly hubs could make a real difference in the whole country's air travel experience.

That said, fliers aren't likely soon to see airports, no matter how attractive, as stand-alone destinations—despite the fondest hopes of some airport entrepreneurs. More than a few high-end restaurateurs have lost their shirts trying to attract upscale diners to white-tablecloth "destination" restaurants stuck in airport terminals. (An after-dinner stroll through baggage claim, anyone?) But more and more, leading airports are becoming "real" *places* that, at the very least, take the edge off the air-travel experience.

Check out, for example, San Francisco International's Terminal 2

("T-2"), opened in 2011 as the 14-gate home of American and Virgin America.

To get to T-2, you still have to transit standard TSA security screening, but then everything changes. You emerge into a serene "recomposure zone"—heavily sound-insulated and terrazzo-floored, eerily quiet, with soaring ceilings drawing natural light from large skylights and clerestories. Soft lighting emphasizes the gently billowing, cloudlike fabric installation created by a New York artist. Stylishly upholstered platforms are positioned to let fliers re-dress and re-shoe and re-gather belongings after the usual screening indignities. Calming background sounds—not Muzak, not droning security "alerts," more like a little sophisticated soft jazz—emanate from hidden speakers, the volume and even the tempo programmed to fit the time of day and activity level of the terminal.

Having "recomposed," you stroll down a "street" of retailers and restaurants. Every passenger passes every concession, and antsy fliers can keep an eye on their boarding gate from every eatery. (According to the terminal's acclaimed architect, Gensler, "passengers want to stay within 250 feet of their gate.") The food is serious, healthy, and local— "sustainable" in the vernacular. Some of the Bay Area's celebrated foodie outlets offer to pack you a gourmet onboard lunch that would shame any First Class microwaved product—maybe a roasted porchetta sandwich or a half slab of dry-rubbed ribs or a rotisserie chicken, and the wine bar is pouring crisp vintage Taittinger Champagne, though a little pricey at $19 a glass. To attract these premium food purveyors, the airport takes a lighter-than-normal cut of revenues—far less than the hefty portion big airports typically extract, for instance, from on-airport rental car companies (one reason airport car renters see that airport "concession recovery" surcharge on their credit card receipts). At T-2, relaxed fliers do spend more, a lot more. As of early 2012, they spent about 22 percent more on retail and food and beverage combined than they did at the airport's other domestic terminals. By the end of 2011, the average flier at SFO spent more per capita than passengers at any other international airport in the United States, except JFK.

Think of places like T-2 as partial antidotes to the cold new world of mass air travel—like airline clubs and lounges for the elite traveler. If today's flying demands that travelers budget extra time, places like T-2 respond with free Wi-Fi (it's not cheap to provide), hundreds of gateside electric outlets, and workstations and elevated work counters right at the gate for last minute lap-topping.

And of course the New Age airport terminal is "green." A monument to environmental sensitivity and sustainability, T-2 is the nation's first LEED Gold-certified airport terminal. A special ventilation system filters the indoor air using 20 percent less energy; a direct connection to the region's BART subway system cuts car trips; and the building uses reclaimed water for toilets. There's high-efficiency lighting and sustainable-material terrazzo floors made of recycled glass. And perish those Earth-killing plastic bottles of designer water sold in other terminals; T-2 glorifies the humble water fountain. At SFO, "hydration stations" located past security offer, the sign says, "delicious water delivered direct from the Sierra Nevada Mountains." Oh, and for stress, there's the airport's new "yoga room." Seriously. It opens at four thirty a.m.

SFO is hardly alone in trying to transform the nowhere/everywhere twilight zone of airport "travelspace" into a real, even authentically local, experience. Enjoy Amsterdam at Schipol Airport—there's a branch of the world-renowned Rijksmuseum, not to mention the Schipol Love Club, an establishment that advertises "hostesses . . . for business or pleasure" just "a stone's throw" from the airport. Or get a Finnish sauna or "stone bath" steam treatment at Helsinki Airport. At Munich, sample the local beer at a Bavarian beer garden—it's made in the airport's own on-site brewery. Or tour Phoenix Sky Harbor's 500-piece art collection that includes work assembled from local galleries and museums. Las Vegas International is famous for its thousand-plus slot machines located throughout the terminals, some near baggage-claim carousels—why waste time when you're waiting for luggage? Not to mention the indoor putting green at Palm Beach International, an IMAX theater in Hong Kong, a "five-star" in-terminal hotel in Dubai, and even a rooftop swimming pool and Jacuzzi at Singapore's Changi Airport.

And for the truly hassled, airports have faith. At least three-dozen of the larger US airports have chapels, now mostly interfaith. Boston's Our Lady of the Airways, opened in 1951, may have been the first, but JFK now has four chapels side by side—Catholic, Protestant, Muslim, and what is reportedly the only Jewish airport synagogue in the Western Hemisphere. At SFO, the floor of the "meditation room" incorporates a Compass Rose to help devout Muslims find Mecca.

All oases in the psychological desert of modern air travel.

5. "TRANSPARENCY" AND THE GOTCHAS

Life for everyday fliers stands to get at least a little less complicated as federal regulators keep the heat on airlines to level better with their customers about the real cost of flying. Consumerists bemoan a lack of "transparency," but even fliers who understand and appreciate the overall value of flying can't stand the "gotchas."

Let's be realistic. Airlines on their own aren't necessarily going to champion the utmost "transparency" in all their dealings with consumers. Can they really be expected to? Telling potential ticket purchasers the whole truth and nothing but the truth about what they will ultimately have to shell out to get where they're going—taxes, fees, and surcharges included—is bound to cut into sales, especially when fliers seeking the very cheapest fare online will take their business wherever they can save a few dollars. Why muddy—or clarify (depending on your perspective)—the sales pitch with premature, unpleasant warnings about added fees and surcharges, and caveats about cancellation or checked bags?

That leaves DOT's designated consumer "protectors" to use their unique legal authority over "unfair or deceptive" airline practices, and they're starting to. By 2012, DOT had issued nearly a dozen new consumer-protection rules and begun to beef up a historically over-stretched, outgunned staff responsible for enforcing them. Despite some anguished industry hyperbole about how the feds were bent on reversing 35 years of deregulation, DOT's recent push for consumer "transparency" hardly seems radical. Seeing that air travelers get the clearest possible information, in a timely fashion, about what they'll have to pay (in part so they can better comparison-shop) is mighty hard to see as creeping Socialism. The Federal Trade Commission did much the same in December 2012 when it warned hotel chains about potentially deceptive "drip pricing" tactics—where unavoidable "resort fees" or "convenience fees" aren't disclosed in a timely manner to hotel guests checking advertised room prices. Nobody's telling airlines to dispense free snacks or provide more legroom or to charge less, after all.

In fact, it's not in DOT's bureaucratic DNA to get too aggressive about dictating the way the airline industry markets and advertises its product, whether that's due to a commendable reluctance to tell airlines how to run their hellishly complex businesses or just an exaggerated fear of political and industry blowback. Today's get-tougher approach to consumer transparency is a predictable reponse to the last decade's evolution of the airline-passenger commercial equilibrium. Everyday consumers simply need more help in the challenging world of ancillary fees, surcharges, and ever-fewer competitors wielding super-sophisticated technology to reach into their wallets. Bound to champion the *public* interest in aviation, DOT could only try to help consumers navigate the new terrain.

Not everyone agrees. Even a seemingly commonsense new rule—that airlines must make clear to passengers *upfront* the full amount they will actually have to pay to fly, including taxes and mandatory fees—drew heavy industry flak. So did other DOT rules requiring airlines to warn more clearly of bag fees and carry-on allowances and, a particular irritant for some, to give customers 24 hours to comparison-shop without penalty.

To many airlines, these rules didn't seem like common sense at all. Several quickly sued, as noted, and anti-tax legislators were enlisted to try to roll back the full-fare rule in Congress on the theory that regulators were trying to "hide" the tax burden (what Spirit referred to as "the Government's Cut") from a presumed-to-be outraged public. In fact, the rule does not bar separately displaying taxes as long as the total fare, including those taxes, is clear and more prominent.

There was a fusillade of additional arguments, too. Some asked why airlines should have to be more open upfront about total prices than other businesses—like the beloved telephone companies—are in billing their customers. Then there was a claim—later rejected by a federal appeals court in July 2012—that requiring the "total fare" disclosure would abridge airlines' "free speech" rights to show how high taxes on air travelers had become. Industry-supportive economists weighed in too, arguing that the new fare disclosure rule would somehow "burden" US air carriers to the tune of more than one *billion* dollars a year and cost 12,000 industry jobs by raising prices and depressing demand. The litigant airlines appealed to the Supreme Court to protect their commercial free expression, but some thought their real beef was less lofty— that ticket-buyers might get sticker shock if they knew earlier in their purchase process the "real" total cost of their journey.

Debate over the new transparency rules goes on, but they're largely coming into effect. That said, regulating more "transparency" may not be the optimal solution; ultimately, it could prove unnecessary and inflexible in an industry where intense competition has delivered extraordinary consumer value. And airlines fairly ask how much "extra" price disclosure burden they should be required to shoulder compared to other consumer retail businesses. But for now, for ordinary consumers trying to navigate the increasing complexity of fares, fees, and myriad new charges, reasonable rules may be the only realistic way to help them get a fair shot.

6. RANDOM ACTS

It's not that airline folks are cruel or uncaring. Some of the nicest people you'd ever want to meet work for America's airlines—and that's not a wisecrack, it's true. But with nearly two million fliers and more than 25,000 US commercial flights every day, they're trying to hold the line in a high-pressure super-securitized mass travel system that depends on standardization, routine, and efficiency. There's just not much time or space for empathy, sympathy, and individual kindness.

OK, but does it all have to be quite so dehumanized, a place where the tragedy of a Carol Gotbaum is nobody's fault? Not always. There are moments of humanity in airline travel, random acts of kindness—the gate agent who manages to find an open seat for a "lap infant" without a ticket, a First Class flier whom someone saw trading his seat with a soldier returning home from Afghanistan, a flight attendant who finds a few seconds to chat with an elderly gentleman traveling alone. Or the air traffic controllers who in April 2012 briefly shut down the country's twentieth busiest airport, LaGuardia, to save a stray puppy who had escaped from her Delta Airlines transport crate and wandered onto the tarmac. Some airlines are starting to get it too. Virgin America, for instance, lowered the height of the check-in counters at its hub to reduce the sense of barrier to its "guests," while airport agents for an Asian carrier step out from behind their podiums to welcome passengers and take their tickets. And, credit where credit is due, US airlines overall are improving their government-measured performance for on-time arrivals, mishandled bags, and cancellations.

Is there hope for a more humane kind of flying experience? Hard to say, but at least there's the story, first reported by consumer travel writer Christopher Elliot, of Mark Dickinson, a traveler who was living a nightmare in January 2011. His two-year-old grandson lay near death in Colorado and he was desperate to catch the next Southwest flight from Los Angeles to say good-bye. Stuck in a snaking security screening line, though, Dickinson couldn't convince officials to let him jump the queue, so he waited, and waited, as his flight's departure time passed. Finally through security, he ran in his socks to the boarding gate, praying the flight had been delayed. It *had* been—held for 12 minutes by the plane's captain, who had learned of Dickinson's plight from the passenger's wife's urgent call begging the airline to hold the plane. Standing at the boarding gate waiting for this one last passenger, the pilot said simply: "They can't go anywhere without me and I wasn't going anywhere without you."

The act of kindness quickly made headlines around the globe—from London's *Daily Mirror* to Sydney's *Australian*. A great story, but therein lies the problem: an act of simple humanity in commercial air travel was big, big news.

ACKNOWLEDGMENTS

The world of commercial air travel is a strange terrain marked by rivers of statistics, mountains of expert (and not-so-expert) analysis, swamps of impenetrable acronyms, and myriad technical complexities, all of it at times obscured by a fog of marketing and public relations smoke. Everything's debatable—or at least constantly debated. Everybody's got more than an opinion about air travel—they *know* wherein the truth lies. After all, everybody flies.

To explore this vast and murky landscape and illuminate it for the everyday air traveler, you need good guides, even if you've spent twenty years trekking through it, as I have. Knowing about airline economics or regulatory aero-politics doesn't mean you know anything about piloting a Boeing 777 or making "hot" bag transfers at busy connecting hubs or closing virtual fare buckets or calculating fuel burn or searching suitcases for hidden explosives. For all that and more, I've been fortunate in writing this book to have had good guides—more than can be (or wish to be) named here individually.

Senior airline pilots took the time to sit with me for extensive interviews; a former director of pricing for a large network carrier schooled me in the intricacies of airfares and ticket buckets; the director of a city-sized airport hub invited me to shadow him for a day; leading industry and independent economists, as well as lobbyists and aviation lawyers, shared their perspectives, insights, and data; and federal aviation officials and regulators, present and former, helped me focus the consumer issues. Along the way, I've watched bags being screened in the "Bomb Room" (it's not called that anymore), checked out the pilots' private quarters behind the A380 flight deck, discussed corporate culture with airline officers, timed "the turn" of a rush-hour flight, and even interviewed one flight attendant on horseback (but that's another story). Individuals at US airlines and their high-powered trade association provided facts and tried to set me straight.

I'm indebted to the many folks in various corners of the commercial aviation world who took the time to patiently answer my nagging email questions and personal inquiries, and especially grateful to my longtime consulting business partner Pat Murphy, who's forgotten more about the airline business than most in that business are likely ever to learn. I'm also grateful to the array of extraordinary journalists and enlightening bloggers (plus informative web sites and online forums) whose insightful work this book also draws on, as the extensive bibliography reflects. Two veteran journalists, Marilyn Adams and Dan Reed, especially helped advise and edit and keep me honest.

Beyond the support of aviation experts, my sincere thanks go to my editor, Brendan Curry of W. W. Norton, who skillfully kept it all on track with grace, patience, and a fine editor's pen. Many thanks also to my talented literary agent, Rafe Sagalyn, who stuck with me to make this book happen, as well as to his creative colleague Shannon O'Neill and to my longtime associate Linda Miller, who for years has tried in vain to keep me organized. Others owed thanks include William Swelbar of MIT, journalist Laura Parker, copy editor Rachelle Mandik, and editorial assistant Will Glovinsky.

Most important, this book would not have been realized without the support, love, and patience of my wife, Lisa. Beside her unfailing encouragement, her skill as both an elegant wordsmith and a discerning editor vastly improved this work. Finally, thanks are due to my amazing kids: Charlotte, my intergenerational sounding board, and Adam, for whom air travel has always been something very special.

BIBLIOGRAPHY

An Explanatory Note

The world of commercial aviation is saturated with information. Daily, weekly, monthly, and annual statistics on safety, fuel prices, financial, legal, even medical issues mix with a copious stream of analyses, reports, legal filings, and press releases from everyone with an interest in aviation—not just airlines, but regulators, consumers, labor, airports, manufacturers, security experts, politicians, and many, many more. Everyone who's ever flown has *something* to say about it.

The following chapter-by-chapter bibliography includes not just the extensive, sometimes-arcane mix of information and analysis on which this book draws, but also a selection of thoughtful and illuminating material in popular media readily accessible to the curious reader. Even taken together, though, all of the writings included here form only part of the basis for this book.

Both in this endeavor and in my two decades in aviation, first at the FAA and DOT, then as a Washington aviation consultant, I've interviewed, consulted, conversed, and corresponded with dozens of experts and industry leaders and critics. They range from senior pilots to airport directors, economists and lobbyists, airline and union officials, government regulators and political appointees, and more. Though these individuals are not listed—understandably in such an ultrasensitive business, some explicitly preferred not to be named—their information and their perspectives all contributed to this book.

Chapter 1: The Disconnect: How We Fly Now

BOOKS AND ARTICLES

Belobaba, Peter. *The Global Airline Industry.* Edited by Amedeo Odoni and Cynthia Barnhart. West Sussex: John Wiley & Sons Ltd., 2009.

Brannigan, Martha, Susan Carey, and Scott McCartney. "Business Travelers Rebel, Fly Cheaper." *Wall Street Journal,* August 28, 2011.

Compart, Andrew. "US Regionals Cannot Grow to Success." *Aviation Week,* May 16, 2011.

Dempsey, Paul Stephen. "The Financial Performance of the Airline Industry Post-deregulation." *Houston Law Review* 45, no. 2 (2008): 421–85.

Elliott, Christopher. "Now Arriving: The Golden Age of Air Travel." msnbc.msn.com, January 4, 2011.

Higgins, Michelle. "Class Conflict." *New York Times,* November 25, 2007.

Karp, Aaron. "Solid Profitability." atwonline.com, March 3, 2006.

Lukas, Paul. "On Wings of Commerce the Wright Brothers Were First." *Fortune,* March 22, 2004.

Retrowow. "Air Travel in the 60s." retrowow.co.uk, n.d.

Robson, John. "Airline Deregulation: Twenty Years of Success and Counting." *Regulation* (Spring 1998): 17–22.

INDUSTRY, GOVERNMENT, AND OTHER MATERIALS

Airlines for America. "Toward Global Competitiveness, Economic Empowerment and Sustained Profitability." Report, January 25, 2012.

———. "US Airline Bankruptcies and Service Cessations." Report, n.d.

Arbitron, Inc. "The Arbitron Airport Advertising Study: Exploring an Undiscovered Upscale Medium." July 2004.

Belobaba, Peter. "The Airline Industry Since 9/11: Overview of Recovery and Challenges Ahead." Presentation for MIT Global Airline Industry Program, Washington, DC, March 26, 2002.

Bowen, Erin E., Brent D. Bowen, and Dean E. Headley. "Frequent Flier Perceptions & Air Travel Satisfaction." airlinequalityrating.com, April 2, 2012.

CAPA. "A Decade of Change for the Global Airline Industry: A New and Altered Reality in the Rankings." centreforaviation.com, July 18, 2011.

_____. "Aviation's Lost Decade? 9/11 and Beyond." centreforaviation.com, September 9, 2011.

_____. "United Ends 2011 as World's Largest Airline as Emirates Encroaches on the Number Three Spot." centerforaviation.com, December 9, 2011.

Dempsey, Paul Stephen. "The Cyclical Crisis in Commercial Aviation." Report, 2011.

Hazel, Bob, Aaron Taylor, and Andrew Watterson. "Airline Economic Analysis." Oliver Wyman. Paper prepared for Raymond James Global Airline Conference, New York, NY, February 3, 2011.

US Government Accountability Office. "Airline Industry Contraction Due to Volatile Fuel Prices and Falling Demand Affects Airports, Passengers and Federal Government Revenues." (GAO-09-393), April 2009.

Chapter 2: The Hassle Factor

BOOKS AND ARTICLES

Airfarewatchdog.com. "Why You Should Buy a Four-Wheeled Suitcase." February 17, 2012.

Associated Press. "DOT Seeks More Transparency from New Ancillary Fees Reporting Rule." aviationweek.com, July 15, 2011.

Ball, Aimee Lee. "Sexy in the Sky: A History of the Stewardess." msnbc.msn.com, January 24, 2011.

Bardach, A. L. "Why Flying Now Can Kill." *Washington Post,* October 14, 2007.

Baskas, Harriet. "Shut Up and Fly! Debate Over Cell Phones on Flights Continues." msnbc .msn.com, January 13, 2011.

Bomkamp, Samantha. "Overstuffed Carry-on Bags Getting More Scrutiny." Associated Press, December 15, 2011.

Celizic, Mark. "Thrown Off Plane for Outfit Deemed Too Skimpy." msnbc.msn.com, September 11, 2007.

Consumer Reports. "Carriers Continue to Squeeze with Fees." June 2011.

Defazio, Peter. "Allowing Cellphones In-Flight Would Make Air Travel Even Worse." usnews.com, August 24, 2009.

Eberwein, Elise. "US Airways Responds." *Washington Post,* October 18, 2007.

The Economist. "Take this Flight and Shove It." August 11, 2010.

_____. "Sometimes You Just Can't Take It Anymore." November 22, 2011.

_____. "Money Bags." July 10, 2012.

Eligon, John. "Gotbaum's Death Is Ruled an Accident; Alcohol and Prescription Drugs Found." *New York Times,* November 9, 2007.

Elliott, Christopher. "Passengers Say They Miss Luggage-Inclusive Fares the Most." elliott .org/blog, December 12, 2010.

Fallows, James. "Thankfulness Is Great, But What Is the NYT Thinking?" theatlantic.com, November 22, 2007.

Flightaware.com. "Delays—There's More Than Meets the Eye!" n.d.

Flint, Perry. "Baggage Asphyxia." *Air Transport World,* March 2007.

Friedman, Richard. "Just Think of the Hassles as Character Building." *New York Times,* September 17, 2007.

Halsey III, Ashley. "Airplane Annoyance Leads to Brouhaha in the Skies Over D.C." *Washington Post,* May 31, 2011.

Hawley, Chris. "Report: Flight Delays in NYC Region Bad as Ever." Associated Press, November 4, 2010.

Hester, Elliott Neal. "Flying in the Age of Air Rage." salon.com. September 7, 1999.

———. "Welcome to the Mile-High Club." salon.com, September 21, 1999.

Hewitt, Ed. "Surviving the Middle Seat." independenttraveler.com, n.d.

Hill, Kashmir. "Cathay Pacific Cockpit Sex Photos Ground New Ad Campaign, but Web Team Doesn't Get the Memo." forbes.com, August 17, 2011.

Hobica, George. "Confessions of an Airline Baggage 'Thrower': Why You Should Buy a Four-Wheel Suitcase." huffingtonpost.com, December 16, 2011.

Hunter, Marnie. "Airlines Post Record Lows for Bumping, Mishandled Bags." cnn.com, February 14, 2012.

Hurst, Nathan. "Tight Planes: Fliers Aren't Happy, But Full Planes Key to Airlines' Survival." *Detroit News,* December 23, 2008.

Karp, Aaron. "Baggage Blues." *Air Transport World,* March 2007.

Koenig, David. "Airlines: You Can't Wear That." Associated Press, August 26, 2012.

Konigsberg, Eric. "Life of Comfort and Pain Ends in an Airport Cell." *New York Times,* October 6, 2007.

Jarvis, Jeff. "Customer Omega for the Airlines." buzzmachine.com, April 11, 2008.

Jones, Charisse. "For Some, Hassles Dim the Appeal of Air Travel." January 12, 2010.

Limone, Jerry. "Company Designs Stand-Up Seat, Says Airlines Are Interested." travel weekly.com. September 9, 2010.

Lippman, Daniel. "FAA Center Works to Keep Your Flight On Time, or Close." McClatchy Newspapers, August 23, 2011.

Lovitt, Rob. "New Developments in Do-It-Yourself Travel." msnbc.msn.com, December 9, 2010.

Martin, Hugo. "U.S. Airlines in No Rush to Allow In-Flight Cellphone Use." *Los Angeles Times,* October 3, 2012.

Mayerowitz, Scott. "Now Arriving in Alabama: Your Lost Luggage." Associated Press, April 14, 2011.

McCartney, Scott. "Flying Foul: Passengers Behaving Badly." *Wall Street Journal,* May 6, 2008.

———. "What It Costs An Airline to Fly Your Luggage." *Wall Street Journal,* November 25, 2008.

_____. "Why a Six-Hour Flight Now Takes Seven." *Wall Street Journal,* February 4, 2010.

_____. "Better Odds of Getting Your Bags." *Wall Street Journal,* December 2, 2010.

_____. "The One Airport to Avoid Is . . ." *Wall Street Journal,* August 4, 2011.

_____. "Cracking Down on Crime in the Skies." *Wall Street Journal,* February 23, 2012.

Mouawad, Jad. "Most Annoying Airline Delays Might Just Be in the Boarding." *New York Times,* October 31, 2011.

_____. "N.Y. Airports Account for Half of All Flight Delays." *New York Times,* January 27, 2012.

Mulvihill, Keith. "4 Most Common Reasons Airlines Lose Luggage." budgettravel.com, July 27, 2011.

Mutzabaugh, Ben. "Police: Unruly Flier Enraged by Neighbor's Reading Light." *USA Today,* July 30, 2012.

Negroni, Christine. "Less Baggage, Big Savings to Airlines." *New York Times,* April 6, 2010.

Newman, Maria. "Man Found Not Guilty of Attack on Airline Worker." *New York Times,* April 4, 2001.

New York Daily News. "Airline Allows Cell Phone Calls on Planes 35,000 Feet in the Sky." May 15, 2012.

Nomani, Asra Q. "A New Problem for the Airlines: Sexual Misconduct at 37,000 Feet." *Wall Street Journal,* June 10, 1998.

Okada, Bryon. "Unseen Protectors: Screeners Under Airport Provide Human Element in Automated System." *Star-Telegram* (Fort Worth), June 25, 2006.

Patterson, Thom. "Airline Squeeze: It's Not You, 'It's the Seat.'" cnn.com, June 1, 2012.

Pawlowski, A. "Air Rage: Is Reclining Your Seat a Right?" cnn.com, December 9, 2010.

Reed, Dan. "Airlines May Never Fly Right on Customer Service, Experts Warn." *USA Today,* October 17, 2007.

Robinson, Bryan, "Flight Attendants Say Air Rage Ignored." abcnews.go.com, July 6, 2001.

Schlangenstein, Mary, and Mary Jane Credeur. "U.S. Reviews JetBlue Strandings That Prompted Tears, Shouts." bloomberg.com, October 31, 2011.

Schrader, Ann. "Frontier Airlines to Discontinue Complimentary Chocolate Cookies After April." *Denver Post,* April 2, 2012.

Scottberg, Erin. "Anatomy of Lost Luggage: How to Track Your Bags (and Save 'Em)." *Popular Mechanics,* October 1, 2009.

Sharkey, Joe. "Foreign Airlines Ahead of U.S. on Cellphone Use." *New York Times,* September 29, 2009.

_____. "Airlines Weighing Fee for Oversize Carry-On." *New York Times,* June 4, 2012.

Stellin, Susan. "A Boarding Pass on Your Screen." *New York Times,* November 2, 2011.

Stoller, Gary. "Airline Passengers' Complaints on Upswing." *USA Today,* January 14, 2009.

Strunsky, Steve. "Half of Nation's Airport Delays Traced to Problems in This Region." blog.nj.com, September 13, 2012.

Summers, K.C. "More on the Carol Gotbaum Case." *Washington Post,* November 1, 2007.

Wall Street Journal. "Slow Motion: The Top 100 Ranked Flights in the U.S. in Terms of Delays." August 4, 2011.

Wassener, Bettina. "Cathay Pacific Delays International Ad Campaign Amid Photo Scandal." *New York Times,* August 15, 2011.

Wilber, Del Quentin. "Like Clockwork: Hour of Delay, Hour of Flight." *Washington Post,* November 13, 2006.

Zimmerman, Neetzan. "Cell Phones on a Plane. Virgin Atlantic to Allow Cell Phone Calls During Flights." gawker.com, May 16, 2012.

Zumbrun, Joshua. "How Airports Profit from Your Wait." forbes.com, June 13, 2008.

INDUSTRY, GOVERNMENT, AND OTHER MATERIALS

Air Transport Association. "When America Flies, It Works: 2010 Economic Report."

———. "The Economic Climb-Out for U.S. Airlines: Global Competitiveness and Long-Term Viability." September 21, 2011.

Bowen, Brent, and Dean E. Headley. "Airline Quality Rating, 2012." airlinequalityrating. com. April 2012.

Bricker, Jonathan B. "Development and Evaluation of the Air Travel Stress Scale." *Journal of Counseling Psychology* 52, no. 4 (2005): 615–28.

CAPA. "Babbitt Attacks Over-Scheduling, Parker Fights Back. Everyone Whines, Nothing Changes." centreforaviation.com, May 20, 2010.

Dahlberg, Angela. "Air Rage—A Human Factor Issue; Managing for Prevention." Dahlberg & Associates, n.d.

Flint, Perry. "Baggage Asphyxia." *Air Transport World,* March 2007.

Guy, Ann Brody. "Flight Delays Cost $32.9 Billion, Passengers Foot Half the Bill." Institute of Transportation Studies, October 18, 2010.

J.D. Power and Associates. "2008 North America Airlines Satisfaction Study." June 17, 2008.

———. "2012 North American Airlines Satisfaction Study." June 13, 2012.

Marketwire. "Travel Survey Shows People Would Rather Go to the Dentist Than Sit in the Middle Seat on an Airplane." Press statement, July 1, 2009.

National Transportation Safety Board. Accident Report for Piper PA-34-200T on December 23, 1991. (MIA92FA051). Issued May 5, 1993.

NEXTOR. "Total Delay Impact Study: A Comprehensive Assessment of the Costs and Impacts of Flight Delay in the United States." October 2010.

SITA. "SITA Reports Large Drop in Mishandled Baggage as Airlines Save $460 Million." Press statement, March 25, 2010.

———. "Baggage Report 2011."

———. "Baggage Report 2012."

Tomer, Adie, and Robert Puentes. "Expect Delays: An Analysis of Air Travel Trends in the United States." Brookings Institution, October 2009.

Travel Industry Association. "Landmark Survey Reveals Deep Frustration Among Air Travelers—42 Million Trips Avoided, $26.5 Billion Blow to Economy." Press statement, May 29, 2008.

Travelocity. "2009 Rudeness Poll North America." August 19, 2009.

US Congress/Joint Economic Committee. "Your Flight Has Been Delayed Again: Flight Delays Cost Passengers, Airlines, and the US Economy Billions." May 2008.

US Department of Transportation. "Enhancing Airline Passenger Protections, Notice of Proposed Rulemaking." (DOT-OST-2007-0022), November 17, 2008.

US Department of Transportation/Aviation Consumer Protection Division. "Air Travel Consumer Report." August 2012.

US Department of Transportation/Federal Aviation Administration. "Fact Sheet—Update: New York–New Jersey–Philadelphia Metropolitan Area Airspace Redesign Implementation." October 20, 2011.

———. Chart of FAA enforcement of "unruly passenger violations," 1995–2010.

———. "Study of the Use of Cell Phones on Passenger Aircraft." (DOT/FAA/AR-12/30), July 2012.

US Department of Transportation/Research and Innovative Technology Administration. "Understanding the Reporting of Causes of Flight Delays and Cancellations," n.d.

———. "Opinions on Cell Phone Use on Airplanes, Congestion, and Telecommuting— From the 2006 and 2007 Omnibus Household Survey." Special report, July 2008.

———. "US Air Travel On-Time Performance." 2012.

US General Accounting Office. "Long-Term Capacity Planning Needed Despite Recent Reduction in Flight Delays." (GAO-02-185), December 14, 2001.

US Government Accountability Office. "DOT and FAA Actions Will Likely Have a Limited Effect on Reducing Delays During Summer 2008 Travel Season." (GAO-08-934T), July 15, 2008.

———. "Setting On-Time Performance Targets at Congested Airport Could Help Focus FAA's Actions." (GAO-10-542), May 26, 2010.

———. "More Data and Analysis Needed to Understand Effects of Flight Delays." (GAO-11-733), September 7, 2011.

———. "Delayed Baggage Trends and Options for Compensating Passengers." (GAO-12-804R), June 14, 2012.

US House of Representatives/Committee on Transportation and Infrastructure/Subcommittee on Aviation. "Testimony of Patrick Forrey, president, National Air Traffic Controllers Association." September 26, 2007.

University of Washington. "Number of Passengers Experiencing Air Travel Stress Jumps to 81 Percent." Press statement, March 21, 2002.

US Senate/Committee on Commerce, Science and Transportation/Subcommittee on

Aviation. "Statement of Robert A. Sturgell, FAA Acting Administrator." September 17, 2007.

US Travel Association. "Traveler Perspectives on Aviation Security 10 Years After the Creation of TSA." Survey, November 16, 2011.

Chapter 3: The Margin

BOOKS AND ARTICLES

Agarwal, Vibhuti. "New Guidelines Say Co-Pilots Need to Speak Up." *Wall Street Journal.* August 11, 2010.

Ahlers, Michael. "US Airways, United Face FAA Fines for Safety Violations." cnn.com, October 14, 2009.

AirSafe.com. "Top 10 Airline Safety Questions." airsafe.com, December 13, 2011.

———. "Average Fleet Age for Selected Airlines." airsafe.com, April 19, 2012.

———. "Fatal Plane Crash Rates for Selected Airliner Models." airsafe.com, June 3, 2012.

Associated Press. "Schumer: Pilot Safety Regulations Being Weakened." February 13, 2011.

———. "FAA Gives Controllers an Extra Hour to Rest Between Shifts, But Rejects On-the-Job Napping." April 18, 2011.

———. "FAA Never Acted on Plan to Aid Fatigued Air Traffic Controllers, Airline Pilots and Mechanics." April 23, 2011.

Aviation Daily. "FAA Proposes $9.2 Million Civil Penalties Against US Airways, United." aviationweek.com, October 15, 2009.

———. "ATA Blasts Pilot Fatigue Proposals As Costly, Duplicative and Unscientific." aviationweek.com, November 18, 2010.

———. "Airlines Rely on Third-Party MROs to Rein in Costs." aviationweek.com, February 23, 2011.

———. "FAA Implements 'Interim Plan' to Prevent Absent Controller Incidents." aviationweek.com, March 28, 2011.

———. "DOT Chief Ends Single-Staffed Towers After Another Sleeping Incident." aviationweek.com, April 14, 2011.

———. "FAA Tightens Scheduling Rules to Address Controller Fatigue." aviationweek .com, April 19, 2011.

———. "Pilot, Controller Professionalism Targeted on NTSB Wish List." aviationweek .com, June 27, 2011.

Aviation Knowledge. "English as the Official Aviation Language." aviationknowledge.wiki dot.com, n.d.

Aviation Today. "Legging It. The FAA's Last Word on Extended Range Safety Issues." January 15, 2007.

Baron, Robert. "Guest Editorial: Barriers to Effective Communications: Implications for the Cockpit." airlinesafety.com, n.d.

Barron, James. "FAA Proposes Rules to Prevent Pilot Fatigue." *New York Times,* September 10, 2010.

Belson, Ken, and Christine Negroni. "Smaller Planes Are Taking on a Bigger Share of the Skies." *New York Times,* February 15, 2009.

Borenstein, Seth. "Experts: Airliner Crashes More Survivable Recently." *USA Today,* January 16, 2009.

Borrell, Brendan. "What Is a Bird Strike? How Can We Keep Planes Safe from Them in the Future?" scientificamerican.com, January 15, 2009.

BusinessWeek. "Danger in the Repair Shop." businessweek.com, July 30, 2007.

Carey, Susan. "Delta Flies New Route to Profits: Older Jets." *Wall Street Journal,* November 15, 2012.

Carey, Susan, and Andy Pasztor. "AMR Faces $162 Million in Penalties." *Wall Street Journal,* August 6, 2012.

CBS News. "Jet Engine Failures Rare, Usually Not Fatal." cbsnews.com, November 4, 2010.

Chernoff, Allan. "FAA Moving to Prevent Aging Aircraft Dangers." cnn.com, November 12, 2010.

Chiles, Patrick. "ETOPS Redefined. A New Name and Sweeping New Rules for 'Extended Operations.'" *AeroSafety World,* March 2007.

Clark, Pilita. "The Final Approach." *Financial Times,* February 7, 2011.

CNN. "FAA Knew Controllers Nap, Ignored Fatigue Issue." cnn.com, April 26, 2011.

_____. "FAA Proposes $1.45 Million Fine Against Northwest Airlines." cnn.com, March 23, 2010.

Couch, Aaron. "Should Snoozing Controller at Reagan Airport Have Had Backup?" *Christian Science Monitor,* March 25, 2011.

Cox, John. "Ask the Captain: Responding to an In-Flight Crisis." *USA Today,* November 29, 2010.

Croft, John. "Engine Certification: Meet the Flockers." Flightglobal.com, March 14, 2011.

The Daily Beast. "Airline Safety: From First to Worst." thedailybeast.com, May 21, 2010.

_____. "America's Most Dangerous Airlines." thedailybeast.com, May 24, 2010.

Englund, Will. "Russian Aviation Meets Global Safety Standards." *Baltimore Sun,* October 15, 1994.

Fernandez, Colin. "Want the Safest Seat on a Plane? Sit on the Aisle Near an Exit." dailymail.co.uk, June 27, 2008.

Foley, Meraiah, and Nicola Clark. "Officials Detail Peril of Qantas Jet Saved by Crew." *New York Times,* December 3, 2010.

Freed, Joshua. "It's Never Been Safer to Fly; Deaths at Record Low." Associated Press, December 31, 2011.

Freeman, Sholnn. "Federal Air Safety Initiatives Run into Opposition." *Washington Post,* October 1, 2009.

Gallup Politics. "Americans' Fear of Terrorism in US Is Near Low Point." gallup.com, September 2, 2011.

Gates, Dominic. "At Boeing, Pushback on 787 Grounding." *Seattle Times*, January 20, 2013.

Great Circle Mapper. "FAQ: What Is ETOPS?" gcmap.com, n.d.

Halsey III, Ashley. "Mistakes Rise for Washington Region's Air Traffic Controllers." *Washington Post*, August 30, 2010.

———. "Tower at Reagan National Goes Silent as Planes Attempt to Land." *Washington Post*, March 23, 2011.

———. "FAA Chief Orders New Air Traffic Control Procedures." *Washington Post*, March 26, 2011.

———. "At National Airport, Aborted Landings Are Not Uncommon." *Washington Post*, March 29, 2011.

———. "Report: FAA Should Improve Control of Birds, Wildlife Near Airports." *Washington Post*, September 2, 2012.

Hauser, Christine. "Boeing Urges Tests on 737s After More Cracks Surface." *New York Times*, April 4, 2011.

James, Frank. "American Air Inspection Failures Draw $24.2 Mln FAA Fine." npr.org, August 26, 2010.

Jaunted. "World's Most Dangerous Airports." jaunted.com, n.d.

Jansen, Bart. "Danger of Turbulence Remains Safety Threat to Air Travel." *USA Today*, September 11, 2012.

Joseph, Claudia. "Attention First-Class Passengers, This Is Your Captain Speaking . . . Crash Test Proves That It Is Much Safer to Sit in the Back of the Plane." dailymail .co.uk, September 15, 2012.

Karp, Aaron. "FAA: US Commercial Aircraft Fleet Shrank in 2011." atwonline.com, March 13, 2012.

Koenig, David. "Aviation Technology Advances, FAA Tries to Keep Up." Associated Press, January 20, 2013.

Levin, Alan. "Bills Seek Ban of Pilots' Use of Electronic Devices in Cockpit." *USA Today*, November 19, 2009.

———. "Airbus, Boeing Models Draw Scrutiny After Accidents." *USA Today*, November 15, 2010.

———. "Air India Pilot's 'Sleep Inertia' Caused Crash." *USA Today*, November 18, 2010.

———. "Aircraft Collisions with Birds Increase." *USA Today*, March 11, 2011.

———. "Recent Air Controller Incidents No Sign of Crisis, Experts Say." *USA Today*, April 22, 2011.

Lowy, Joan. "Gov't Watchdog Pans FAA Safety Reporting Program." Associated Press, May 19, 2009.

———. "FAA Says Airlines Are No Longer Its 'Customers.'" Associated Press, September 17, 2009.

_____. "Safety Board Pins NY Crash Cause on Pilot Errors." Associated Press, February 2, 2010.

_____. "Air Traffic Control Error Numbers Double." Associated Press, February 11, 2011.

_____. "FAA Proposes to Strengthen Airline Pilot Training After Pilot Error Caused Air Crash." Associated Press, May 11, 2011.

Lynch, Kerry. "ADs Under the Microscope." *AviationWeek's Overhaul & Maintenance Magazine,* June 2008.

Maksel, Rebecca. "What Determines an Airplane's Lifespan?" airspacemag.com, March 1, 2008.

Matlack, Carol. "Younger Fleets Boost Non-US Airlines." businessweek.com, June 2, 2008.

McCartney, Scott. "The Difficulty in Improving Airline Safety Now." *Wall Street Journal,* September 2, 2010.

McGee, Bill. "Airbags on Airplanes: Your Seatbelt May Hide a Lifesaving Surprise." *USA Today,* March 31, 2010.

McGee, William J. "Forcing the FAA to Fly Blind." *New York Times,* April 9, 2011.

Muggeridge, Tessa. "Shhhh! Your Pilot Is Napping." msnbc.msn.com, September 27, 2010.

Niles, Russ. " 'First World' Airlines Fatality-Free." avweb.com, January 23, 2011.

Noah, Timothy. "The PATCO Echo." Slate.com, March 30, 2011.

Noland, David. "Safest Seat on a Plane: PM Investigates How to Survive a Crash." popular mechanics.com, July 18, 2007.

Norris, Guy. "Boeing 787 Test Priority Shifts to ETOPS." *Aviation Week,* January 28, 2011.

Negroni, Christine. "Interfering with Flight?" *New York Times,* January 17, 2011.

New York Times. "Do Pilots Get Enough Sleep?" Editorial, October 23, 2009.

Ostrower, Jon, Andy Pasztor, and Yoree Koh. "Fire Fears Spur FAA to Ground Dreamliner." *Wall Street Journal*, January 17, 2013.

Pasztor, Andy. "U.S. to Impose Tougher Rules for Pilot Rest on Long Routes." *Wall Street Journal,* November 14, 2008.

_____. "Latest Air-Safety Idea: Naps in the Cockpit. Airlines, Unions Urge FAA to Allow Pilots to Sleep Midflight to Alleviate Fatigue; a Tough Sell." *Wall Street Journal,* October 9, 2009.

_____. "Airbus Takes on Test-Flight Hazards." *Wall Street Journal,* November 18, 2009.

_____. "Watchdog Faults FAA for Lax Oversight of Southwest." *Wall Street Journal,* March 19, 2010.

_____. Air Controllers Press for Break-Time Naps." *Wall Street Journal,* April 23, 2011.

_____. "Would Pilot 'Panic Button' Save the Day or Tie Hands?" *Wall Street Journal,* July 23, 2011.

Pasztor, Andy, and Susan Carey. "Commuter Airlines: Questions of Safety." *Wall Street Journal,* December 1, 2009.

Pasztor, Andy, and Christopher Conkey. "Safety Pushes Stall at Embattled FAA." *Wall Street Journal,* June 26, 2008.

Patterson, Thom. "Air Traffic Overhaul Hinges on 'Human Factor.'" cnn.com, March 9, 2011.

Paur, Jason. "Boeing 787 Passes Incredible Wing Flex Test." wired.com, March 29, 2010.

Pawlowski, A. "What It's Like to Be an Air Traffic Controller." cnn.com, April 15, 2011.

PlaneCrashInfo. "Last Words . . . Cockpit Voice Recordings, Transcripts, Air Traffic Control Tapes." planecrashinfo.com, n.d.

———. "Airline Accident Rates." planecrashinfo.com, n.d.

Polek, Gregory. "Boeing's New ETOPS Offering Brings Asia Closer to the Rest of the World." ainonline.com, February 14, 2012.

Professional Pilots Rumor Network. "What's the Hardest Airport to Land At?" Comments Thread, pprune.org, April–December 2002.

Ranson, Lori. "MRO USA: FAA Dissolves Carrier Customer Service Mentality." flightglobal .com, April 19, 2010.

Reed, Ted. "AMR's In-House Maintenance Commitment Set to Decline." thestreet.com, May 14, 2012.

Reuters. "Dangers of Flying Vary Around the Globe." September 5, 2010.

———. "Airline Fatality Rate Improves, Some Exceptions." February 8, 2011.

———. "Airlines Say Pilot Fatigue Rule Would Cost Jobs." September 15, 2011.

Scott, Alwyn, and Mari Saito. "Insight—Boeing 787 Battery Woes Put FAA Approval under Scrutiny," Reuters, January 22, 2013.

Shami, Hamooda. "America's Safest Airlines: When You Look at the Numbers, Commercial Air Travel in the United States Today Is About As Safe As It Gets." usnews.com, January 26, 2011.

Sherwood, Ben. "The Great Plane Crash Myth." thedailybeast.com, January 17, 2009.

Simon, Jordan. "FAA Doling Out Record Fines." news.travel.aol.com, August 27, 2010.

SKYbrary. "Aircraft Certification for Bird Strike Risk." Reference for Aviation Safety Knowledge. Skybrary.aero.

Smith, Geri, and Justin Bachman. "The Offshoring of Airplane Care." businessweek.com, April 10, 2008.

Smith, Patrick. "Aging Planes and Safety Records." salon.com, April 26, 2010.

Stark, Lisa. "FAA Holds Regional Airline Safety Summit." abcnews.go.com, June 15, 2009.

Stoller, Gary. "Planes with Maintenance Problems Have Flown Anyway." *USA Today,* February 1, 2010.

———. "FAA Fines Show Extent of Airline Problems." *USA Today,* February 1, 2010.

Tatge, Mark, and Emily Schmall. "America's Most Dangerous Airports." forbes.com, February 23, 2007.

Trottman, Melanie, and Andy Pasztor. "Airlines Fight Cost of Safety Measure." *Wall Street Journal,* March 15, 2010.

View from the Tower Blog. "Wake Turbulence: Part 2—Controller Requirements." fromthecontroltower.blogspot.com, January 4, 2010.

Wald, Matthew L. "Report on Pilots Who Overshot Airport." *New York Times,* December 16, 2009.

Webster, Ben. "In a Plane Crash Safest Seats Are in Aisle." timesonline.co.uk, June 26, 2008.

———. "Polish Pilots' Poor English Almost Led to Crash." timesonline.co.uk, June 12, 2008.

Wilber, Del Quentin. "Airline Safety Alarms Unheeded." *Washington Post,* April 4, 2008.

Woods, Richard, and Matthew Campbell. "Air France 447: The Computer Crash." times online.co.uk, June 7, 2009.

Zwerdling, Daniel. "To Cut Costs, Airlines Send Repairs Abroad." npr.org, October 19, 2009.

INDUSTRY, GOVERNMENT, AND OTHER MATERIALS

Barnett, Arnold. "Cross-National Differences in Aviation Safety Records." *Transportation Science* 44, no. 3 (August 2010): 322–32.

Bachtel, Brad. "ETOPS, Extended Operations, and En Route Alternate Airports." Boeing Commercial Airplanes. Presentation to FAA/AAAE Basic Airport Safety & Operations Specialists School, October 22, 2003.

Baron, Robert. "The Cockpit, the Cabin and Social Psychology." The Aviation Consulting Group, n.d.

Boeing Commercial Airplanes. "Statistical Summary of Commercial Jet Airplane Accidents Worldwide Operations 1959–2009." July 2010.

Centre for Asia Pacific Aviation. "Complacency Is the Biggest Risk to Airline Safety Record in the U.S." centreforaviation.com, May 24, 2010.

Congressional Research Service. "U.S. Airline Industry: Issues and Role of Congress." (RL34467), July 29, 2008.

European Aviation Safety Agency. "Annual Safety Review 2011." easa.europa.eu, n.d.

Holden, Richard J. "People or Systems? To Blame Is Human. The Fix Is to Engineer." (Appendix). *Professional Safety,* December 2009.

International Air Transport Association. "Aircraft Accident Rate Is Lowest in History—Still Room for Improvement, Regional Concerns Remain." Press statement, iata.org, February 23, 2011.

———. "Unlocking Africa's Aviation Potential." Release no. 35, iata.org., September 3, 2012.

Midkiff, Alan H., R. John Hansman, and Tom G. Reynolds. "Air Carrier Flight Operations." MIT International Center for Air Transportation (ICAT-2004-3), July 2004.

National Sleep Foundation. "Poll Explores Transportation Workers' Sleep." Press statement, March 3, 2012.

National Transportation Safety Board. "Survivability of Accidents Involving Part 121 U.S.

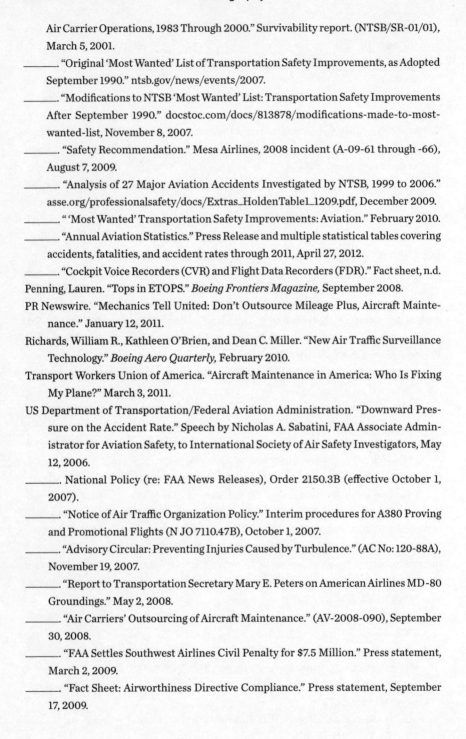

Air Carrier Operations, 1983 Through 2000." Survivability report. (NTSB/SR-01/01), March 5, 2001.

_____. "Original 'Most Wanted' List of Transportation Safety Improvements, as Adopted September 1990." ntsb.gov/news/events/2007.

_____. "Modifications to NTSB 'Most Wanted' List: Transportation Safety Improvements After September 1990." docstoc.com/docs/813878/modifications-made-to-most-wanted-list, November 8, 2007.

_____. "Safety Recommendation." Mesa Airlines, 2008 incident (A-09-61 through -66), August 7, 2009.

_____. "Analysis of 27 Major Aviation Accidents Investigated by NTSB, 1999 to 2006." asse.org/professionalsafety/docs/Extras_HoldenTable1_1209.pdf, December 2009.

_____. " 'Most Wanted' Transportation Safety Improvements: Aviation." February 2010.

_____. "Annual Aviation Statistics." Press Release and multiple statistical tables covering accidents, fatalities, and accident rates through 2011, April 27, 2012.

_____. "Cockpit Voice Recorders (CVR) and Flight Data Recorders (FDR)." Fact sheet, n.d.

Penning, Lauren. "Tops in ETOPS." *Boeing Frontiers Magazine,* September 2008.

PR Newswire. "Mechanics Tell United: Don't Outsource Mileage Plus, Aircraft Maintenance." January 12, 2011.

Richards, William R., Kathleen O'Brien, and Dean C. Miller. "New Air Traffic Surveillance Technology." *Boeing Aero Quarterly,* February 2010.

Transport Workers Union of America. "Aircraft Maintenance in America: Who Is Fixing My Plane?" March 3, 2011.

US Department of Transportation/Federal Aviation Administration. "Downward Pressure on the Accident Rate." Speech by Nicholas A. Sabatini, FAA Associate Administrator for Aviation Safety, to International Society of Air Safety Investigators, May 12, 2006.

_____. National Policy (re: FAA News Releases), Order 2150.3B (effective October 1, 2007).

_____. "Notice of Air Traffic Organization Policy." Interim procedures for A380 Proving and Promotional Flights (N JO 7110.47B), October 1, 2007.

_____. "Advisory Circular: Preventing Injuries Caused by Turbulence." (AC No: 120-88A), November 19, 2007.

_____. "Report to Transportation Secretary Mary E. Peters on American Airlines MD-80 Groundings." May 2, 2008.

_____. "Air Carriers' Outsourcing of Aircraft Maintenance." (AV-2008-090), September 30, 2008.

_____. "FAA Settles Southwest Airlines Civil Penalty for $7.5 Million." Press statement, March 2, 2009.

_____. "Fact Sheet: Airworthiness Directive Compliance." Press statement, September 17, 2009.

———. "Traffic Flow Management in the National Airspace System." October 2009.

———. "Statement of Peggy Gilligan, Associate Administrator for Aviation Safety." Before the Senate Committee on Commerce, Science and Transportation/Subcommittee on Aviation, December 1, 2009.———. "Fact Sheet—Pilot Flight Time, Rest, and Fatigue." Press statement, January 27, 2010.

———. "Slowing Down Is a Mistake." Speech (as prepared for delivery) by FAA Administrator J. Randolph Babbitt, to the FAA Annual Forecast Conference, Washington, DC, March 9, 2010.

———. "FAA Proposes Civil Penalty Against American Airlines." Press statement, August 26, 2010.

———. "Serious Runway Incursions Cut in Half for Second Straight Year." Press statement, October 8, 2010.

———. "Keynote Address by Peggy Gilligan, Associate Administrator for Aviation Safety to Aeronautical Repair Station Association Symposium." April 1, 2011.

———. "Fact Sheet—Pilot Fatigue Rule Comparison." Press statement, December 21, 2011.

———. "Establishing and Implementing Limits of Validity to Prevent Widespread Fatigue Damage." (AC No: 120-104), January 10, 2011.

US Department of Transportation/Office of the Inspector General. "Aviation Safety: FAA Oversight of Foreign Repair Stations." Statement of Calvin L. Scovel III, Inspector General, US Department of Transportation Before the House of Representatives/Committee on Transportation and Infrastructure/Subcommittee on Aviation, June 20, 2007.

———. "FAA's Oversight of American Airlines' Maintenance Programs." (AV-2010-42), February 16, 2010.

———. "Enhanced Oversight of Staffing and Training at FAA's Critical Faculties Is Needed to Maintain Continuity of Operations." (AV-2012-039), January 12, 2012.

———. "The State of Aviation Safety and FAA's Oversight of the National Airspace System." Statement of Jeffrey B. Guzzetti, Assistant Inspector General, US Department of Transportation, April 25, 2012.

———. "FAA Has Not Effectively Implemented Its Wildlife Hazard Mitigation Program." (AV-2012-170), August 22, 2012.

US Government Accountability Office. "FAA's Safety Efforts Generally Strong but Face Challenges." (GAO-06-1091T), September 20, 2006.

———. "Enhanced Oversight and Improved Availability of Risk-Based Data Could Further Improve Safety." (GAO-12-24), October 5, 2011.

———. "FAA Is Taking Steps to Improve Data, but Challenges for Managing Safety Risks Remain." (GAO-12-660T), April 25, 2012.

Chapter 4: The Pointy End

BOOKS AND ARTICLES

Airline Nightmare. "What Do Pilots Actually Do During Cruise Flight, on a Long Flight in the Cockpit?" Parts 3A and B. airlinenightmare.com, March 18 and 19, 2010.

The Australian. "Half of Pilots Admit to Sleeping Mid-Flight." February 10, 2011.

AvWeb. "Letter of the Week: Airbuses Fly 'Like a Video Game.'" avweb.com, June 6, 2011.

Borough, Jimmy. "Southwest Airlines Pilot's Rant—Transcript, Here's What He Said." sure-start.com, June 22, 2011.

Calio, Nicholas. "Airlines Will Shrink, Jobs Will Go If FAA Implements Pilot Rule." thehill .com/blogs, September 22, 2011.

Clark, Nicola, and Marcus Mabry. "You Think You're a Frequent Flier." *New York Times,* March 17, 2012.

CNN. "Southwest Disciplines Pilot for Rant During Flight." cnn.com, June 22, 2011.

Frank, Thomas. "More Than 10% of Pilots Allowed to Fly Armed." *USA Today,* April 1, 2003.

Halbfinger, David, Matthew Wald, and Christopher Drew. "Pilots' Lives Defy Glamorous Stereotype." *New York Times,* May 17, 2009.

Halpin, Tony. "Passengers Stop Flight After 'Drunk' Pilot Sparks Panic." timesonline.co.uk, February 3, 2009.

Higgins, Michelle. "Flying the Unfriendly Skies." *New York Times,* September 14, 2008.

Hobica, George. "Confessions of a Regional Jet Pilot." foxnews.com, February 1, 2012.

Jones, Charisse. "Demand for Airline Pilots Set to Soar." *USA Today,* June 21, 2011.

Levin, Alan. "Pilots Alcohol Limits Debated." *USA Today,* September 16, 2010.

———. "NTSB: Sleep Aids Should Be OK in Fighting Pilot Fatigue." *USA Today,* March 15, 2011.

Mathieu, Stevie. "Video in the Cockpit: Privacy vs. Safety." msnbc.msn.com, September 28, 2010.

Maxon, Terry. "American Airlines Pilots Are an Aging Bunch." dallasnews.com, May 6, 2011.

McCartney, Scott. "Pilot Pay: Want to Know How Much Your Captain Earns?" blogs.wsj. com, June 16, 2009.

Pasztor, Andy, and Daniel Michaels. "Black Boxes Point to Pilot Error." blogs.wsj.com, May 24, 2011.

Reuters. "JetBlue Pilot Who Disrupted Flight Declared Insane." July 4, 2012.

Scheck, William. "Lawrence Sperry: Autopilot Inventor and Aviation Innovator." *Aviation History,* November 2004 (available online at historynet.com).

Smith, Patrick. "Behind the Underwear Bomber." salon.com, May 10, 2012.

———. "Boredom and Fatigue at 35,000 Feet." salon.com, October 29, 2009.

Sydney Morning Herald. "Engine Explosion Qantas A380 Returns to Australia." April 23, 2012.

Times Herald-Record. "As Pilots Age, Airlines Hire Fewer From Military." recordonline. com, January 17, 2009.

Wien, Kent. "Cockpit Chronicles: Is It Time for Pilots to Ditch the Hat?" gadling.com, March 22, 2011.

_____. "Cockpit Chronicles: Nearly a Near Midair Collision." gadling.com, November 12, 2010.

INDUSTRY, GOVERNMENT, AND OTHER MATERIALS

Air Line Pilots Association. "Air Line Pilot Readership Poll." Conducted by the Wilson Center, alpa.org, May 2001.

Bureau d' Enquêtes et d'Analyses. "Accident to the Airbus A330-203 Flight AF on 1st of June, 2009." May 2011.

ExpectMore.gov. "Detailed Information on the Transportation Security Administration: Flight Crew Training Assessment." georgewbush-whitehouse.archives.gov.

Flight Attendants Training Online. "Cruise Level Procedures for Flight Attendants." flight attendantcabincrewtraining.com.

Morrell, Paul A. "We Are Airline Pilots." alpa.org, June 5, 2004.

National Transportation Safety Board. Final accident report, EgyptAir Flight 990. (NTSB/AAB-02/01), March 13, 2002.

_____. Final accident report, Air Midwest Flight 5481. (NTSB/AAR-04/01), February 26, 2004.

Pilot Career Info. "Common Questions & Answers for Aspiring Aviators." pilotcareer.info, n.d.

Proulx, Jim. "Behind Door No. 2: Boeing Meets Tough Deadline for Enhanced-Security Flight Deck Doors." *Boeing Frontiers,* May 2003.

Saenz, Rogelio, and Louwanda Evans. "The Changing Demography of U.S. Flight Attendants." Population Reference Bureau, prb.org, June 3, 2009.

US Department of Transportation. "In-flight Medical Incapacitation and Impairment of U.S. Airline Pilots: 1993 to 1998." (DOT/FAA/AM-04/16), October 2004.

_____. "Comparison of Minimum Fuel, Emergency Fuel, and Reserve Fuel." InFO for Operators (InFO 08004), February 7, 2008.

US Department of Transportation/Federal Aviation Administration. "Random Drug and Alcohol Testing Percentage Ranges of Covered Aviation Employees for the Period of January 1, 2011, Through December 31, 2011." (75 Federal Register 76069), December 7, 2010.

_____. "Cockpit Distractions." (InFO), April 26, 2010.

_____. *Federal Air Surgeon's Medical Bulletin* 41, no. 3, Fall 2003.

Chapter 5: Fares, Fees, and Other Games

BOOKS AND ARTICLES

Aho, Karen. "The Secrets Behind Crazy Air-Travel Prices." moneycentral.msn.com, April 22, 2009.

Airline Weekly. "Ancillary Revenue: It's Not Non-Core Anymore." Special report, quarterly supplement, airlineweekly.com, February 2010.

———. "Taming the Wilds: U.S. Airlines Get Caught in a Q1 Storm, but Come Out Largely Unscathed." airlineweekly.com, September 1, 2012.

Ashley, Mark. "Reality Check: Fare Fearmongering?" upgradetravelbetter.com, April 14, 2009.

Associated Press. "Higher Oil Means More Airline Fees. Extra, Heavy Bags Will Cost You. How About a Cushier Seat?" March 31, 2011.

Bachman, Justin. "Forget Gas Prices—Air Fares Are Getting More Painful." Bloomberg.com, April 2, 2012.

Bennett, Andrea. "Deciphering Airline Fare Codes." airfarewatchdog.com, October 21, 2008.

Bloomberg Businessweek. "Point of View: Airline Deregulation, Revisited." bloomberg.com, January 20, 2011.

Bloomberg News. "USAirways to Add Sales of Pillows, Blankets." November 1, 2008.

Bly, Laura. "Fare Errors on the Web: Savvy Fliers Run with 'Em." *USA Today,* May 5, 2005.

Boehmer, Jay. "DOT Adds Teeth to Fuel Surcharge Rules." businesstravelnews.com, March 15, 2012.

Bonné, Jon. "Making Sense of the Airline Business." msnbc.msn.com, January 23, 2003.

———. "Inside the Mysteries of Airline Fares." msnbc.msn.com, May 8, 2003.

Borenstein, Severin. "Why U.S. Airlines Need to Adapt to a Slow-Growth Future." bloomberg.com, June 3, 2012.

Brancatelli, Joe. "All-Business-Class All the Time." *USA Today,* October 27, 2006.

———. "Nothing Fair About Airfares." portfolio.com, June 9, 2010.

Bryant, Adam. "Some Airlines Break Ranks Over Fees Paid Travel Agents." *New York Times,* March 29, 1995.

Chen, Stephanie. "Starting Today, No More Free Water on US Air." blogs.wsj.com, August 1, 2008.

Clark, Nicola. "Sticker Shock for Travelers as Airfares Climb." *New York Times,* November 8, 2010.

Cohen, Amon. "CWT: Airline Fuel Surcharge Hikes Easily Outpacing Oil Price Increases." businesstravelnews.com, July 26, 2012.

Connelly, Eileen AJ. "Fee-Weary Customers Breaking from Big Banks." Associated Press, October 23, 2011.

Crankyflier. "What's the Deal with Bereavement Fares?" crankyflier.com, July 14, 2010.

Demerjian, Dave. "Behind the Fiendish Complexities of Airfare Pricing." wired.com, July 10, 2007.

Dickler, Jessica. "Airline Fees: The $500 Surprise." cnn.com, May 2, 2011.

Elliott, Christopher. "Should Airlines Honor Fares That Are Obvious Mistakes?" frommers .com, February 4, 2010.

Esterl, Mike. "Delta Makes Fliers Bid to Get Bumped." *Wall Street Journal,* January 14, 2011.

―――. "Airlines Revamp Sites to Sell More Than Seats." *Wall Street Journal,* January 25, 2011.

Fallows, James. "Why Your Plane Is Always Full." theatlantic.com, July 15, 2010.

Flint, Perry. "Editorial: The Final Round." *Air Transport World,* May 2008.

FlyerTalk. "Thread Listing All Known UA Revenue and Award Booking Codes and a Summary of Each One." flyertalk.com, September 24, 2002.

Fox News. "7,500 Online Shoppers Unknowingly Sold Their Souls." foxnews.com, April 15, 2010.

Grant, Alison. "The Best Time to Buy an Airline Ticket Is at 3 PM on a Tuesday." *Plain Dealer,* December 26, 2010.

Harrison, Michael. "BA Customers Face Air Fuel Surcharge as Oil Prices Rise." independent .co.uk, May 12, 2004.

Halsey, Ashley III. "As Airlines Raise Fees Instead of Fares, Taxpayers Pick up Tab." *Washington Post,* October 21, 2012.

Hawkins, Robert J. "Flying to LA From Lindbergh? Hang on to Your Seat." *San Diego Union-Tribune,* January 12, 2011.

Higgins, Michelle. "When to Buy That Plane Ticket." *New York Times,* April 11, 2012.

Hume, Tim. "Too Good to Be True: New York to Hong Kong for $43." cnn.com, July 23, 2012.

Hobica, George. "Confessions of a Fat-fingered Airline Pricing Analyst." airfarewatchdog .com, March 5, 2009.

―――. "How to Find Cheap Airfares in Any Season." airfarewatchdog.com, December 8, 2011.

Jones, Charisse. "Airfares Up for Summer Travel, Likely to Keep Climbing." *USA Today,* April 26, 2012.

―――. "Is Spirit the Nation's True Low-Cost Airline?" *USA Today,* October 18, 2012.

Knowledge@Wharton. "The Domino Effect: Will Airlines Follow One Another in the Consolidation Game?" knowledge.wharton.upenn.edu, February 20, 2008.

Koenig, David. "U.S. Airlines Make Money Again by Flying Less." Associated Press, January 25, 2011.

―――. "DOT Says It Will Fine American over Vouchers." Associated Press, February 28, 2011.

Kralev, Nicholas. "Airlines Refuse to Honor Mistake Fares." *Washington Times,* January 11, 2010.

Kropff, Allison. "Jerry Meekins Denied Airline Refund After Diagnosed with Terminal Cancer; Spirit CEO Ben Baldanza Says It's Company Policy." wtsp.com, April 27, 2012.

Lovitt, Rob. "Spirit Raises Baggage Fees Again—Pay Early or Pay a Lot!" msnbc.msn.com, May 4, 2012.

Marks, Gene. "Pricing Lessons from the Airline Industry." businessweek.com, April 26, 2010.

Marotte, Bertrand. "High Taxes Driving Tourists Away: IATA." theglobeandmail.com, August 23, 2012.

Martin, Hugo. "Airlines' Fuel Surcharges Far Outpacing Fuel Prices." *Los Angeles Times,* July 23, 2012.

Martin, Timothy W., and Jennifer Levitz. "Oil Falls, but Surcharges Stay Aloft." *Wall Street Journal,* August 11, 2011.

McCartney, Scott. "Bag of High-Tech Tricks Helps to Keep Airlines Financially Afloat." *Wall Street Journal,* January 20, 2000.

———. "What It Costs An Airline to Fly Your Luggage." *Wall Street Journal,* November 25, 2008.

———. "You Paid What for That Flight?" *Wall Street Journal,* August 26, 2010.

———. "Now, Even the Cheap Seats on Airplanes Come with a Fee." *Wall Street Journal,* November 3, 2011.

Michaels, Daniel. "Extra Airline Fees a Growth Market." *Wall Street Journal,* May 31, 2011.

Mouawad, Jad, and Michelle Higgins. "Airlines Look to Limit Bumping." *New York Times,* April 5, 2010.

———. "After Bargains of Recession, Air Fares Soar." *New York Times,* September 4, 2010.

Negroni, Christine. "More Fees, More Carry-Ons." *New York Times,* March 28, 2011.

NV Flyer. "ATPCO Not Liable to Alitalia for Fare Coding Mistake." nvflyer.wordpress.com, September 9, 2008.

Pearlstein, Steven. "Executives Raid the Tip Jar to Feed Their Piggy Banks." *Washington Post,* April 9, 2008.

Perkins, Ed. "The Truth About Airline Fuel Surcharges." *USA Today,* May 11, 2011.

Perone, Joseph R. "Airlines Have No Plans to Roll Back Fuel Surcharges." *Seattle Times,* October 26, 2008.

Recio, Maria. "Want an Aisle Seat? Not for $2,000, Ralph Nader Tells American Airlines." miamiherald.com, February 9, 2012.

Reed, Dan. "Fliers Go for Cheap Fares, with Al La Carte Fees for Bags, Food." *USA Today,* November 12, 2008.

Schlangenstein, Mary. "Fliers Pay More Peak-Day Surcharges as U.S. Travel Demand Rises." bloomberg.com, August 17, 2010.

Seaney, Rick. "Understanding Airline Ticket Prices: Why Your Seatmate's Airfare Cost More (Or Less) Than Yours." Farecompare.com, May 17, 2010.

———. "Airfare Expert: How Taxes and Fees Make 'Cheap' Europe Flights Expensive." *USA Today,* January 25, 2012.

Sharkey, Joe. "A Bonanza for Airlines as Taxes End." *New York Times,* July 25, 2011.

———. "With Fees Here to Stay, Trying to Crack the Code." *New York Times,* September 12, 2011.

Silver, Nate. "Which Airports Have the Most Unfair Fares?" *New York Times,* April 6, 2011.

Smith, Oliver. "Fuel Surcharges Rise Twice as Fast as Oil Prices." telegraph.co.uk, July 24, 2012.

Sokolow, Jese. "British Airways Launches 'Know Me' Customer Recognition Program." *Frequent Business Traveler,* October 29, 2012.

Starmer-Smith, Charles. "Surcharges All But Paying Airlines' Fuel Bills," telegraph.co.uk, October 17, 2008.

Stellin, Susan. "Taxes and Fees Grow for Air Travelers." *New York Times,* March 1, 2010.

———. "Where 'Free' Costs a Lot." *New York Times,* May 30, 2011.

Stoller, Gary. "All-business-class Airlines Take Off Despite Past Failures." *USA Today,* May 28, 2008.

———. "Airline Fees Reach $400 Mark, USA Today Survey Finds." *USA Today,* September 20, 2011.

———. "Airlines See Revenue Increase from Fees." *USA Today,* September 20, 2011.

Yeo, Ghim-Lay. "Interview: Spirit Airlines Chief Executive Ben Baldanza." flightglobal .com, April 26, 2012.

INDUSTRY, GOVERNMENT, AND OTHER MATERIALS

Airlines for America. "U.S. Airlines: An Economic Update." airlines.org, March 2012.

Airline Tariff Publishing Company. "Life Cycle of the Fare." Report, atpco.net, n.d.

ARC. "ARC Reports Lowest-Priced Air Tickets Are Purchased Six Weeks Before Flight." Press statement, arccorp.com, January 17, 2012.

Calio, Nicholas E. "Remarks to the International Aviation Club." Air Transport Association, September 27, 2011.

CAPA. "Why Google Doesn't Need to Sell Air Fares. It's All About Data. Facebook Will Be Next." centreforaviation.com, July 2, 2010.

———. "US Airlines' Ancillary Revenues Continue to Grow, But at a Slower Pace for Legacy Carriers." centreforaviation.com, November 15, 2011.

Cordle, Vaughn. "Mergers—the Best Solution for Network Airlines." airlineforecasts.com, June 1, 2010.

Hazel, Bob, Aaron Taylor, and Andrew Watterson. "Airline Economic Analysis." Oliver
    Wyman. Paper prepared for Raymond James Global Airline Conference, New York,
    NY, February 3, 2011.

Hazel, Bob, Tom Stalnaker, and Aaron Taylor. "Airline Economic Analysis." Oliver Wyman,
    February 2012.

IdeaWorks. "Airline Revenue from Optional Services & Frequent Flier Programs Grows
    $20 Billion Since 2007." Report. ideaworkscompany.com, August 29, 2012.

———. "Ancillary Revenue Training Camp." ideaworkscompany.com, September 12, 2012.

Mathematical Association of America. "The Crazy Math of Airline Ticket Pricing." maa
    .org, September 2002.

Pan Am. "All Year Transatlantic Fares." timetableimages.com, n.d.

PRNewswire. "American Airlines Introduces 'Your Choice' Services to Give Customers
    More Options, Greater Control Over Travel Experience." Press statement, aa.com,
    June 15, 2010.

Ryanair. "Ryanair to Introduce EU261 Compensation Levy of [€]2." Press statement,
    Ryanair.com, March 30, 2011.

Spirit Airlines. "Statement from Ben Baldanza, CEO of Spirit Airlines." spirit.com, May
    4, 2012.

US Department of Transportation. "BTS Releases 4th-Quarter 2011 Air Fare Data." Report
    (BTS 21-12), April 30, 2012.

US Department of Transportation/Federal Aviation Administration. "Aircraft Weight and
    Balance Control." (AC 120-27D), August 11, 2004.

US Department of Transportation/Office of the Inspector General. "New York Flight
    Delays Have Three Main Causes, but More Work Is Needed to Understand Their
    Nationwide Effect." (AV-2011-007), October 28, 2010.

US Department of Transportation/Research and Innovative Technology Administration.
    "Annual US Domestic Average Itinerary Fare in Current and Constant Dollars." bts
    .gov, n.d.

US Government Accountability Office. "Impact of Changes in the Airline Ticket Distribu-
    tion Industry." (GAO-03-749), July 14, 2003.

———. "Consumers Could Benefit from Better Information About Airline-Imposed Fees
    and Refundability of Government-Imposed Taxes and Fees." (GAO-10-785), July
    2010.

US Senate/Department of Homeland Security Appropriations Bill, 2012. (Senate Report
    112-074), September 11, 2011.

Chapter 6: Sickening

BOOKS AND ARTICLES

Air Safety Week. "Special Report: Cabin Safety: Bodily Fluids a Fact of Life for In-Flight Heart Emergencies." March 13, 2000.

Associated Press. "Dealing with Death at 30,000 Feet." February 28, 2008.

———. "Swine Flu's Spread Tracked Through Air Travel." msnbc.msn.com, June 29, 2009.

Alcock, Charles. "Cabin Humidity Emerges as Service Differentiator for High-Yield Passengers." ainonline.com, September 24, 2010.

Aleccia, JoNel. "Cats on a Plane? Allergy Sufferers Can't Escape." msnbc.msn.com, November 19, 2010.

Aviation Daily. "Germ Exposure Highest During Boarding, Deplaning." aviationweek.com, May 5, 2008.

Bear, David. "Sky-High Stress: Are New Rigors of Air Travel Taking a Medical Toll?" post-gazette.com, September 7, 2008.

Brown, Sally. "Eyes Wide Open." *Business Traveller,* May 25, 2011.

Butler, Carolyn. "Air Travel Isn't Sure to Make You Sick, but You Can Take Some Precautions." *Washington Post,* January 3, 2011.

Clark, Andrew. "Airline's New Fleet Includes a Cupboard for Corpses." guardian.com.co.uk, May 10, 2004.

Clark, Duncan. "Business Class Fliers Leave Far Larger Carbon Footprint." guardian.co.uk, February 17, 2010.

Cohen, Elizabeth. "Five Ways to Avoid Germs While Traveling." cnn.com, November 7, 2008.

Crewdson, John. "How Many People Die on Airplanes?" *Chicago Tribune,* June 30, 1996.

Dakss, Brian. "Beware Airplane Water." cbsnews.com, March 7, 2005.

Davis, Robert, and Anthony DeBarros. "In the Air, Health Emergencies Rise Quietly." *USA Today,* March 12, 2008.

Donnelly, Sally B. "Travel: MedAire Is Everywhere." *Time,* September 6, 2004.

The Economist. "Breathing More Easily." September 17, 2009.

Fallows, James. "The Future of Flight." travelandleisure.com, December 2003.

FlightGlobal. "In Focus: Manufacturers Aim for More Comfortable Cabin Climate." flightglobal.com, March 19, 2012.

Gendreau, Mark. "Swine Flu and Your Health on a Plane." cnn.com. April 30, 2009.

Gold, Jim. "Boeing Suit Settlement Stirs Jetliner Air Safety Debate." msnbc.msn.com, October 6, 2011.

Gross, Samantha. "When Passengers Die on Planes, Everyday Flights Turn Macabre." *Seattle Times,* February 28, 2008.

Hafner, Katie. "When Doctors Are Called to the Rescue in Midflight." *New York Times,* May 23, 2011.

Heavey, Susan, and John Crawley. "Update 1—U.S. Warns Airline over Paint Chips in Water Tank." Reuters, May 20, 2008.

Higgins, Michelle. "Need a Doctor in the Air? Fly with One." *New York Times,* March 16, 2008.

———. "How Not to Get Sick from a Flight." *New York Times,* March 2, 2011.

Hocking, M. B. "Passenger Aircraft Cabin Air Quality: Trends, Effects, Societal Costs, Proposals." *Chemosphere* 41, no. 4 (August 2000): 603–15.

Independent. "Cathay Pacific Launches Campaign to Stop Toilet Blocking." December 2, 2009.

Johnson, Julie. "United, Others Get Serious About Clean Planes." chicagotribune.com, January 29, 2009.

Keates, Nancy, and Jane Costello. "How Safe Is Airline Water? Bring Your Own Bottle!" *Wall Street Journal,* November 1, 2002.

KGO-TV San Francisco. "Tests Show Contaminated Water on Airplanes." abclocal.go.com, February 14, 2008.

———. "Airlines We Don't Have Test Results For." abclocal.go.com, February 27, 2008.

Marcinkowski, Victoria. "Coffee, Tea, or Bacteria?" *Science World,* January 24, 2003.

Marquette University. "Marquette University Study Shows Radiation from Airport Scanners Extends into Organs; Still Lower than Health Standards." marquette.edu, June 11, 2012.

Maynard, Micheline. "A Respiratory Illness: Airlines; Carriers Respond as Disease Raises Concerns over Air Circulation in Passenger Cabins." *New York Times,* April 4, 2003.

McCartney, Scott. "Why Air Quality on Planes Can Seem Stagnant." *Wall Street Journal,* July 16, 2009.

Michels, Jennifer. "Biden, FAA, DOT Weigh In on Swine Flu." aviationweek.com, May 2, 2009.

Nair, Drishya. "North Carolina Couple Sues Airline for $100,000 for Cockroaches on Flight." ibtimes.com, November 13, 2007.

New York Times. "Lawyer Infected with Tuberculosis Apologizes to Airline Passengers." June 1, 2007.

Norton, Amy. "Is There Such a Thing as 'Airplane Headache'?" Reuters, June 7, 2012.

Padilla, Adriana. "Airline Meals Prepared in Unsanitary Conditions, FDA Finds." petergreenberg.com, June 30, 2010.

Parker-Pope, Tara. "What's Really in That Seat-Back-Pocket." *New York Times,* May 9, 2008.

Peterson, Barbara S. "Airplane Air Is No Riskier Than Other Closed Spaces, Study Says." *New York Times,* October 4, 2010.

Reichman, Judith. "Germs on a Plane: Can You Get Sick Flying?" msnbc.msn.com, October 9, 2006.

Rosenkrans, Wayne. "Beating the Odds." Flight Safety Foundation. *Aerosafety World,* May 2010.

Ruppel, Glenn, Jim Avila, and Mark Greenblatt. "Mice, Roaches Seen by FDA Inspecting Airline Food." ABC News, November 16, 2012.

Smith, Lizzie. "Pilot Forced to Make Early Landing After All Ten Toilets Break." dailymail .co.uk, November 25, 2009.

Sood, Suemedha. "Travelwise: Death on a Plane." bbc.com, January 6, 2012.

Spengler, John D., et al. "In-Flight/Onboard Monitoring: ACER's Component for ASHRAE 1262, Part 2." National Air Transportation Center of Excellence for Research in the Intermodal Transport Environment, Final Report, April 2012.

Stoller, Gary. "Inspectors Find Safety Flaws Where Airline Food Is Prepared." *USA Today,* June 27, 2010.

———. "FDA Report Reveals Airline Food Could Pose Health Threat." *USA Today,* June 28, 2010.

Stellin, Susan. "Practical Traveler; Assessing Air Quality Aloft." *New York Times,* May 18, 2003.

Thomas, Geoffrey. "A Toxic Debate on Cabin Air." atwonline.com, January 1, 2010.

Tito (username). "Aircraft Cleaning." Airliners.net online discussion forum, January 3, 2007.

Vass, Beck. "Airlines Use Plastic Cutlery Up to 10 Times." nzherald.co.nz, May 19, 2010.

Wall Street Journal. "Thinking of Drinking Airplane Water? Read This." blogs.wsj.com, August 28, 2008.

Wright, Douglas. "6 Places Germs Breed in a Plane." msnbc.msn.com, January 20, 2011.

Yancey, Kitty Bean. "The Germiest Parts of Plane Travel and How to Avoid Getting Sick." *USA Today,* February 22, 2011.

Young, Alison. "People Shouldn't Fly When They're Sick, but They Do." *Atlanta Journal-Constitution,* December 21, 2008.

———. "Reports of Sick Travelers Climb." *USA Today,* July 27, 2010.

INDUSTRY, GOVERNMENT, AND OTHER MATERIALS

Association of Flight Attendants, AFL-CIO. "Aircraft Air Quality: What's Wrong with It and What Needs to Be Done." Report submitted to US House Committee on Transportation and Infrastructure, Subcommittee on Aviation, June 4, 2003.

Boeing Commercial Airplanes. "Cabin Air Systems." boeing.com/commercial/cabinair, n.d.

Cocks, Robert, and Michele Liew. "Commercial Aviation In-Flight Emergencies and the Physician." *Emergency Medicine Australasia* 19, no. 3 (June 2007): 286.

DeHart, R. L. "Health Issues of Air Travel." *Annual Review of Public Health,* October 23, 2002.

DeJohn, C. A., Véronneau, S. J., Wolbrink, A. M., et al. "The Evaluation of In-Flight Medical Care Aboard Selected U.S. Air Carriers: 1996 to 1997." Federal Aviation Administration, Office of Aviation Medicine. Technical report, (DOT/FAA/AM-0013), May 2000.

Delaune, E. F. III, R. H. Lucas, and P. Illig. "In-Flight Medical Events and Aircraft Diversions: One Airline's Experience." *Aviation, Space and Environmental Medicine* 74, no. 1 (January 2003): 62–68.

Finneran, Michael. "Thousand-Fold Rise in Polar Flights Hike Radiation Risk." NASA .gov, February 18, 2011.

Gallagher, Nancy M., et al. "Air Travel—2010 Yellow Book." Centers for Disease Control and Prevention, July 2009.

Gendreau, Mark A., and Charles DeJohn. "Responding to Medical Events During Commercial Airline Flights." *New England Journal of Medicine* 346, no. 14 (April 4, 2002): 1067–073.

Harvey, Gordon, et al. "Air Travel by Passengers with Mental Disorder." *The Psychiatrist* 28 (2004): 295–97.

Health Physics Society. "Radiation Exposure During Commercial Airline Flights." Summary of multiple articles, hps.org, n.d.

HealthWatch/Commercial Aviation. "Stats Reveal Most Common In-Flight Medical Emergencies." medaire.com, March/April 2001.

Hocking, M. B. "Indoor Air Quality: Recommendations Relevant to Aircraft Passenger Cabins." *American Industrial Hygiene Association Journal* 59, no. 7 (July 1998): 446–54.

———. "Passenger Aircraft Cabin Air Quality: Trends, Effects, Societal Costs, Proposals." *Chemosphere* 41, no. 4 (August 2000): 603–15.

Hocking, Martin B., and Harold D. Foster. "Common Cold Transmissions in Commercial Aircraft: Industry and Passenger Implications." *Journal of Environmental Health Research* 1, no. 3 (2004).

Hunt, Elwood H., and David R. Space. "The Airplane Cabin Environment: Issues Pertaining to Flight Attendant Comfort." donaldson.com, n.d.

Hung, Kevin K. C., et al. "Predictors of Flight Diversions and Deaths for In-Flight Medical Emergencies in Commercial Aviation." *Archives of Internal Medicine* 170, no. 15 (August 2010): 1401-402.

Kharas, Ruby J. "Air Line Hygiene in Civil Aviation: Jet Airways' Perspective." *Indian Journal of Aerospace Medicine* 46, no. 2 (2002): 39–43.

Liao, Mark. "Handling In-Flight Medical Emergencies." *Journal of Emergency Medical Services*, jems.com, June 3, 2010.

Lindgren, Torsten, Kjell Andersson, and Dan Norbäck. "Perception of Cockpit Environment Among Pilots on Commercial Aircraft." *Aviation, Space and Environmental Medicine* 77, no. 8 (August, 2006): 832–37.

Mangili, Alexandra, and Mark A. Gendreau. "Transmission of Infectious Diseases During Commercial Air Travel." *The Lancet* 365 (March 2005): 989–96.

Mendis, Shanthi, Derek Yach, and Ala Alwan. "Air Travel and Venous Thromboembolism." *Bulletin of the World Health Organization* 80, no. 5 (2002): 403–06.

Medline. "Abstracts for Management of Inflight (CQ) Medical Emergencies on Commercial Airlines." (Abstracts 3, 4, 5, 8, 9), 1989–2003 (updated 2012). (uptodate.com/contents/management-of-inflight-medical-emergencies-on-commercial-airlines)

Merck Manual. "Air Travel: Medical Aspects of Travel." merckmanuals.com, February 2009.

National Research Council. "The Airliner Cabin Environment and the Health of Passengers and Crew." December 6, 2001.

PRNewswire. "Thomson-Reuters-NPR Health Poll Finds Nearly One in Four Americans Would Refuse a Full Body Scan at Airport Security." December 23, 2011.

Ruskin, Keith J., et al. "Management of In-Flight Medical Emergencies." *Anesthesiology* 108, no. 4 (April 2008): 749–55.

Sand, Michael, Bechara Falk-Georges, Daniel Sand, et al. "Surgical and Medical Emergencies on Board European Aircraft: A Retrospective Study on 10,189 Cases." National Center for Biotechnology Information. ncbi.nlm.nih.gov, January 20, 2009.

Scurr, J. H., et al. "Frequency and Prevention of Symptomless Deep-Vein Thrombosis in Long-Haul Flights: a Randomised Trial." National Center for Biotechnology Information. ncbi.nlm.nih.gov, May 12, 2001.

Stockholm Environment Institute/Carbon Offset Research and Education (CORE). "Average Seat Room Based on Seat Class." co2offsetresearch.org, 2010.

Transguard Group. "Spotless Record in the World of Hygiene." Press release, Zaywa.com Business News, September 4, 2008.

US Department of Health and Human Services/Centers for Disease Control and Prevention. "Cockpit Card Notifying Public Health About Ill Passengers or Crew on Flights Arriving in the United States." February 2007.

US Department of Health and Human Services/Food and Drug Administration/Inspections, Compliance, Enforcement and Criminal Investigations. "LSG SkyChefs: Warning Letter and Notice of Provisional Status." (DEN-10-04 WL), December 10, 2009.

US Department of Transportation/Federal Aviation Administration. "Radiation Exposure of Air Carrier Crewmembers." (FAA AC 120-52), March 5, 1990.

———. "Inflight Medical Care: An Update." (DOT/FAA/AM-97/2), February 1997.

———. "Code of Federal Regulations: FAR Part 121 Sec. A121.1, effective May 12, 2004."

———. "Chicago O'Hare FSDO—Blue Water & Blue Ice." Updated November 12, 2010.

US Environmental Protection Agency. "Fact Sheet: Aircraft Drinking Water Rule." (EPA 816-F-08-011), March 2008.

———. "Economic and Supporting Analyses for the Final Aircraft Drinking Water Rule. (EPA 816-R-09-007), October 2009.

———. "Aircraft Drinking Water Rule." October 19, 2009.

US General Accounting Office. "More Research Needed on the Effects of Air Quality on Airliner Cabin Occupants." (GAO-04-54), January 16, 2004.

US House of Representatives/Committee on Transportation and Infrastructure/Subcommittee on Aviation. "Statement of Dr. Anne Schuchat, Acting Director, National Center for Infectious Diseases, Center for Disease Control and Prevention." April 6, 2005.

Walkinshaw, Douglas S. "Germs, Flying and the Truth." *ASHRAE Journal* 52, no. 4 (April 2010): 71–74.

World Health Organization. "Cosmic Radiation and Air Travel." who.org, November 2005.

Zitter, Jessica Nutik, et al. "Aircraft Cabin Air Recirculation and Symptoms of the Common Cold." *Journal of the American Medical Association* 288, no. 4 (July 2002): 483–86.

Chapter 7: No-Brainer

BOOKS AND ARTICLES

Abrams, Jim. "House Moves to Protect Air Passengers." Associated Press, September 20, 2007.

Adams, Marilyn. "The DOT's Growing Mountain of Airline Service Complaints." *USA Today,* November 16, 2007.

Associated Press. "House Passes Aviation Bill, Targets Safety Rules." *USA Today,* April 1, 2011.

———. "Tarmac Nightmare Shows Delays Are Still a Problem." October 31, 2011.

Aviation Daily. "Washington Lobbyists Cashing In on Regulatory, Financial Uncertainties." aviationweek.com, April 22, 2011.

Bachman, Justin. "Airline Passengers' Rights Delayed." businessweek.com, March 26, 2008.

———. "Continental Boss Raises the Flight Cancellation Bogeyman." businessweek.com, March 9, 2010.

Bailey, Jeff. "JetBlue's CEO Is 'Mortified' After Fliers Are Stranded." *New York Times,* February 19, 2007.

———. "An Air Travel Activist Is Born." *New York Times,* September 20, 2007.

———. "No Limit for Waits on Runways." *New York Times,* September 26, 2007.

Bence, Dan. "Airline Passenger Rights Activist Kate Hanni Accuses Delta of Hacking Her Email." petergreenberg.com, October 14, 2009.

Breyer, US Supreme Court Justice Stephen. "Airline Deregulation, Revisited." businessweek.com, January 20, 2011.

Carey, Susan. "Seven Hours of Sitting and Waiting Leaves Northwest Passengers Near Breaking Point." *Wall Street Journal,* April 28, 1999.

Cohn, Amy, and Peter Belobaba. "Still Stuck on the Tarmac." forbes.com, August 13, 2009.

Compart, Andrew. "U.S. Airlines Blast Proposal for More Detailed Reporting of Fees." *Aviation Week,* September 16, 2011.

Consumer Travel Alliance. "DOT Rulemaking on Final Stretch—Here's Our Take on Expanded Tarmac Delay Rules." consumertravelalliance.org, July 30, 2010.

Cooper, Aaron. "Spirit Airlines Adding 'Unintended Consequences Fee.'" cnn.com, February 1, 2012.

Eggen, Dan. "Airline Lobbying Group to Hire Nicholas Calio, a Former Bush Aide, as CEO." *Washington Post,* November 29, 2010.

Elliot, Christopher. "Can Airlines Police Themselves?" elliott.org, February 21, 2007.

———. "JetBlue's Apology." elliott.org, February 21, 2007.

———. "Transportation Department Steps Up Efforts in Aviation Consumer Protection." elliott.org, January 17, 2010.

———. "The Navigator: Tarmac-Delay Rule Gives Air Travelers More Respect." *Washington Post,* September 21, 2010.

———. "New Airfare Pricing Rule Challenges in Congress." *Seattle Times,* February 7, 2012.

Goodwyn, Wade. "Aging Controllers, Lax Rules Trouble FAA." npr.org, January 12, 2009.

Graham, Mark R. "Salaries Reach New High for Top Association CEOs." ceoupdate.com, November 30, 2012.

Hughes, John. "Pilot-Rest Rules May Be 15 Times More Costly Than Projected, Airlines Say." bloomberg.com, November 16, 2010.

Independent Traveler. "The Airline Passenger's Bill of Rights." independenttraveler.com, February 21, 2007.

Jenkins, Darryl. "DOT's War Against the Airline Industry." aviationweek.com, January 24, 2012.

Lovitt, Rob. "Airlines Cancel Flights Before Snow Flies." msnbc.msn.com, February 10, 2011.

Lowy, Joan. "Gov't Asking Why Airline Passengers Were Stranded." Associated Press, August 12, 2009.

———. "Ex-CEO Backs Limit on Leaving Passengers on Tarmac." Associated Press, September 22, 2009.

———. "Changes Coming to Prevent Tarmac Delays." Associated Press, November 30, 2011.

Marr, Kendra, and Del Quentin Wilber. "Airlines Reject Guidelines on Delays; Time-Limits Plan Criticized in House." *Washington Post,* September 27, 2007.

Mayerowitz, Scott. "Obama Administration Gets Tough on Airlines." abcnews.go.com, May 6, 2010.

McCartney, Scott. "While Fliers Fume, Fewer Fines for Airlines." *Wall Street Journal,* January 13, 2009.

———. "How Snow (and Libyan Soldiers) Led to Airport Logjams." *Wall Street Journal,* November 10, 2011.

Mitchell, Josh, and Susan Carey. "Airlines Face Big Fines for Delays." *Wall Street Journal,* December 22, 2009.

Morgan, David. "Northwest Settles in Detroit Blizzard Lawsuit." abcnews.go.com, January 9, 2001.

The New Yorker. "Talk of the Town: Dining Up." July 22, 1961.

New York Times. "The Tarmac's Madding Crowds." Editorial, November 21, 2008.

The NV Flyer. "Airline Passenger 'Bill of Rights' Legislation Resurrected." nvflyer.word press.com, April 26, 2009.

Pasztor, Andy. "Southwest's Cozy Ties Triggered FAA Tumult." *Wall Street Journal,* April 3, 2008.

Reed, Dan. "Airlines Grapple with Increased Regulatory Focus." *USA Today,* September 23, 2010.

Sharkey, Joe. "Continental: Faced with Fines for Tarmac Strandings, We Will Cancel Flights." joesharkeyat.blogspot.com, March 10, 2010.

———. "Tough Rule Eliminates Most Tarmac Strandings." *New York Times,* May 4, 2011.

Siegel, Robert. "Delta CEO Pushes for National Airline Policy That Lets 'Free Market Work.'" npr.org, June 6, 2012.

Sniffen, Michael J. "Limits Sought for Waiting Time on Planes." Associated Press, September 25, 2007.

Stellin, Susan. "U.S. Orders Airlines to State Fees More Clearly." *New York Times,* April 20, 2011.

Stieghorst, Tom. "Flight Delay Issue Heats Up." *Sun-Sentinel,* September 27, 2007.

Stoller, Gary. "Fliers Trapped on Tarmac Push for Rules on Release." *USA Today,* July 28, 2009.

———. "New Government Committee Supposed to Stick Up for Fliers." *USA Today*, May 7, 2012.

Stoller, Gary, and Dan Reed. "Passengers Stranded on a Plane Really Are Stuck." *USA Today,* August 12, 2009.

Wald, Matthew L. "Airlines Pay for Stranding Passengers." *New York Times,* November 25, 2009.

Wald, Matthew L., and Micheline Maynard. "Behind Air Chaos, an FAA Pendulum Swing." *New York Times,* April 13, 2008.

Washington Post. "A Flying Shame; The Federal Aviation Administration and The Airlines Forget Who The Customer Really Is." Editorial, April 13, 2008.

Weinstein, Andrew. "Crossing the Finish Line on Hidden Airline Fees." aviationweek.com, May 2, 2011.

Wilber, Del Quentin. "Airlines, FAA Under Fire on the Hill." *Washington Post,* April 2, 2008.

Yamanouchi, Kelly. "Delta Objects to New Passenger Rules." *Atlanta Journal-Constitution,* September 29, 2010.

INDUSTRY, GOVERNMENT, AND OTHER MATERIALS

Airlines for America. "Customers First 12-Point Customer Service Commitment." airlines. org, November 24, 2011.

———. "A4A Responds to Chairman Issa and Chairman Jordan Regarding Regulations That Have Harmed Job Growth in the Aviation Industry." Letter, airlines.org, June 2, 2012.

———. "The Case for a U.S. National Airline Policy." airlines.org, March 2012.

Air Transport Association. "Statement on DOT Passenger Protections Rules." Press statement, April 20, 2011.

———. "Airline Customer Service Commitment." June 17, 1999.

American Airlines. "Conditions of Carriage." aa.com, n.d.

Calio, Nicholas. "Remarks to the Aero Club of Washington." Air Transport Association, October 18, 2011.

CAPA. "Study Indicates Tarmac Rule Still Doing Damage." centreforaviation.com, November 22, 2010.

Center for Responsive Politics. "Lobbying Airlines Industry Profile 2011." opensecrets .org, n.d.

Continental Airlines. "Customer First." continental.com, n.d.

Delta Air Lines. "Delta Air Lines Endorses DOT Inspector General's Recommendations on Airline Service." Press statement, October 25, 2007.

Jenkins, Darryl, and Joshua Marks. "Impact of Three-Hour Tarmac Delay Rules and Fines on Passenger Travel Time and Welfare." The Airline Zone and Marks Aviation, July 20, 2010.

JetBlue. "Customer Bill of Rights and Tarmac Contingency Plan." jetblue.com, n.d.

LaHood, Ray. "Letters to the Editors: Stranded on the Tarmac." *New York Times,* May 6, 2011.

May, James C., "Airline Delays and Consumer Issues." September 26, 2007.

PBS. *Commanding Heights. The Battle for the World Economy.* Directed by William Cran. Written by William Cran and Daniel Yergin. Episode 1. PBS Studios, 2002.

Siddiqi, Asif. "The Federal Aviation Administration and Its Predecessor Agencies." US Centennial of Flight Commission, n.d.

US Court of Appeals. *Air Transport Association v. Cuomo,* 520 F.3d 218 (2d Cir. 2008).

US Department of Transportation. "New DOT Fact Sheet to Help Travelers Cope with Flight Delays." (DOT 218-00), November 2, 2000.

———. "Welcome to the Fast Lane: Outrage on Tarmac Delays—You Want to Know, DOT Wants to Know." Official blog of the Secretary of Transportation, August 11, 2009.

———. "Memorandum to Docket Re Meeting of General Counsel with Representatives of the Air Transport Association." (DOT-OST-2007-0022), September 22, 2009.

———. "Final Regulatory Impact Analysis of Rulemaking on Enhanced Airline Passenger Protections." Final Regulatory Evaluation, December 17, 2009.

_____. Consent Order, "American Eagle Airlines, Inc. Violation of 14 CFR Part 259 and 49 U.S.C. §41712." (OST-2011-0003), November 14, 2011.

_____. "New Airline Passenger Protections Take Effect This Week." Press statement, (DOT 08-12), January 23, 2012.

_____. "January 2012 Passenger Airline Employment Rose 2.1 Percent from January 2011." (BTS 16-12), March 28, 2012.

US Department of Transportation/Aviation Consumer Protection Division. "Consumer Protection of Air Travelers in the USA." Slide presentation, August 19, 2008.

_____. "Fly-Rights; A Consumer Guide to Air Travel." n.d.

US Department of Transportation/Federal Aviation Administration. "A Brief History of the FAA." faa.gov/about/history/brief_history.

_____. "Update to FAA Historical Chronology: Civil Aviation and the Federal Government, 1926–1996." faa.gov/about/media/1997-2011chronology.pdf (updated through December 2011).

_____. "FAA Proposes $330,000 Civil Penalty Against American Eagle Airlines." Press statement, December 22, 2010.

_____. "FAA Issues Final Rule on Pilot Fatigue." Press statement, December 21, 2011.

_____. "FAA Proposes $13.57 Million Civil Penalty Against Boeing Company." Press statement, July 13, 2012.

US Department of Transportation/Office of the Inspector General. "Airline Customer Service Commitment." Statement of Kenneth Mead, June 28, 2000.

_____. "Follow-Up Review: Performance of U.S. Airlines in Implementing Selected Provisions of the Airline Customer Service Commitment." (AV-2007-012), November 21, 2006.

_____. "Actions Needed to Minimize Long, On-Board Flight Delays." (AV-2007-077), September 25, 2007.

_____. "Statement of Calvin L. Scovel III, Inspector General of U.S. Department of Transportation." April 20, 2007.

US Department of Transportation/Office of the Secretary. "Enhancing Airline Passenger Protections, Advance Notice of Proposed Rulemaking." (72 Fed. Reg. 65233), November 20, 2007.

_____. "Enhancing Airline Passenger Protections, Final Rule." (74 Fed. Reg. 68983), December 30, 2009.

US Governmental Accountability Office. "Further Reform Is Needed to Address Longstanding Problems." (GAO-02-821), July 9, 2001.

_____. "Consumers Could Benefit from Better Information About Airline-Imposed Fees and Refundability of Government-Imposed Taxes and Fees." (GAO-10-785), July 14, 2010.

_____. "More Data and Analysis Needed to Understand Effects of Flight Delays." (GAO-11-733), September 7, 2011.

US House of Representatives. "Bill Text of H.R. 3528.IH from 101st Congress (1989–1990)."

US House of Representatives/Committee on Transportation and Infrastructure/Subcommittee on Aviation. "Airline Passenger Rights, H.R. 780, and H.R. 908." Hearing transcript, March 18, 1999.

US Senate. "Letter from US Sens. Barbara Boxer and Olympia Snowe to Secretary of Transportation Mary Peters." January 22, 2008.

———. "Bill Text of S. 213.IS from 111th Congress (2009–2010)."

Chapter 8: Escape

BOOKS AND ARTICLES

Ahles, Andrea. "American Airlines Touts Its Performance During Bankruptcy." *Star-Telegram* (Fort Worth), May 12, 2012.

Alexander, Bryan. "Up in the Air Fantasies: What Does 10 Million Miles Get You?" *Time*, December 22, 2009.

Associated Press. "Cathay Pacific Cabin Crew Threatens No Smiles, No Booze in Pay Dispute with Hong Kong Airline." December 13, 2012.

Aviation Daily. "Five Good Questions With United SVP-Airport Ops Scott Dolan." aviationweek.com, April 9, 2008.

Blomquist, Cord. "What Are Frequent Flyer Programs Really Worth?" marginalrevolution.com, November 5, 2005.

Bloomberg Business Week. "Arriving on a Jet Plane." businessweek.com, May 20, 2006.

Boehmer, Jay. "AA Ramps Up Personalization in Selling and Tailoring Services." travelweekly.com, May 24, 2012.

Booth, Darren. "OMG! Elite United Passengers Will Be Boarding with the Masses." CNBC, January 11, 2013.

Brancatelli, Joe. "Think You're Special Because You Have Platinum Status?" portfolio.com, November 4, 2008.

———. "A Classy Move: Delta and Continental Add Premium Seats." portfolio.com, March 9, 2011.

Brett, Victoria. "Celebrity Chefs Preparing First-Class Airline Food." Associated Press, April 25, 2008.

Charette, Robert N. "The Psychology of Comfortable Air Travel." IEEE Spectrum, September 2008.

Cirillo, Greg. "Gulfstream G650. Rollout (Part One): Defining a Market for the Best." *World Aircraft Sales Magazine.* avbuyer.com, August 2008.

———. "Gulfstream G650 Rollout (Part Two): The G650 Program Takes Shape." *World Aircraft Sales Magazine.* avbuyer.com, September 1, 2008.

Elliott, Christopher. "The Navigator: Frequent-Flier Programs' Rules Spur Boom in 'Mileage Consultants.' " *Washington Post,* February 22, 2010.

———. "5 Fascinating Facts about the New United Airlines." elliott.org, August 4, 2012.

Fabrikant, Geraldine. "Market for Corporate Jets Goes Into Free-Fall." *New York Times,* December 24, 2008.

Frank, Robert. "Living Large While Being Green." wsj.com, August 24, 2007.

Garrett, Jerry. "Ten Million Frequent Flier Miles: Actual Miles or Myth?" jerrygarrett .wordpress.com, January 1, 2010.

Glab, Jim. "Using Private Jets for Business Making a Quiet Comeback." executivetravel magazine.com, May–June, 2011.

Grabell, Michael, and Sebastian Jones. "Review: Federal Program Used to Hide Flights from Public." *USA Today,* April 10, 2010.

Grant, Kelli B. "How to Save on 'Free' Airline Tickets." smartmoney.com, May 25, 2012.

Grose, Thomas. "Why the Snowpocalypse Is a Paradise for Private Jets." *Time,* January 27, 2011.

Grossman, David. "Packed Planes, Older Fliers Spur Long Lavatory Lines." *USA Today,* May 9, 2011.

Gulf News. "Oman Air Unveils Aircraft Lavatory Dubbed 'Poshest in the Business.' " gulf news.com, October 7, 2009.

Harvard Business Review. "The Shrinking Space Between Airline Seats." November 24, 2010.

InsideFlyer. "10-K Award Statistics." insideflyer.com, n.d.

Jones, Charisse. "Airlines Up Chase for Corporate Traveler with New Come-ons." *USA Today,* June 19, 2012.

Kesmodel, David. "Private Jets Tempt Rich in New Ways." *Wall Street Journal,* April 3, 2012.

Kuang, Cliff. "A Peek Inside a Saudi Prince's $485 Million Flying Palace." *Fast Company,* June 5, 2009.

Levere, Jane L. "Airlines Focus Rewards on Those Who Pay More." *New York Times,* October 17, 2011.

———. "The Executive Lounge as a Distinctive Marketing Lure." *New York Times,* February 20, 2012.

Levine, Shira. "How Singapore Airlines Keeps Its Brand Strong in An Age Where Everybody Hates Flying." businessinsider.com, February 4, 2012.

Lichtblau, Eric. "Industry Set for Fight to Keep Corporate Tax Breaks." *New York Times,* July 7, 2011.

Lynch, Kerry, and George Larson. "Investigators Seek Clues in G650 Crash." *Aviation Week,* April 12, 2011.

MacNeille, Suzanne. "No Extra Points for This Quiz." *New York Times,* June 8, 2012.

Mayerowitz, Scott. "Does Airline Food Always Have to Suck?" abcnews.com, March 1, 2010.

McCartney, Scott. "The Star Treatment: Flying Like Jennifer Aniston." *Wall Street Journal,* April 1, 2008.

―――. "Which Airlines Are Generous With Frequent-Flier Award Seats and Which Aren't." *Wall Street Journal,* May 13, 2010.

McGinn, Daniel. "Making Airline Travel Feel Less Like Torture." newsweek.com, March 15, 2008.

McKinley, Jesse. "Whatever Happened to First Class?" *New York Times,* February 10, 2012.

McMillan, Graeme. "British Airways Flight Attendants to Be Outfitted with iPads." *Time Techland,* September 2, 2011.

McMillin, Molly. "TSA Rules Could Hurt Business Jets." *Wichita Eagle,* January 8, 2009.

Meyer, George. "The Privileged Few." *The New Yorker,* May 25, 2009.

Millbank, Dana. "Auto Execs Fly Corporate Jets to D.C., Tin Cups in Hand." *Washington Post,* November 20, 2008.

Mouawad, Jad. "Taking First-Class Coddling Above and Beyond." *New York Times,* November 20, 2011.

―――. "Beyond Mile-High Grub: Can Airline Food Be Tasty?" *New York Times,* March 10, 2012.

Mutzabaugh, Ben. "5,962 Flights: United Frequent-flier Tops 10 Million Miles." *USA Today,* July 12, 2011.

Negroni, Christine. "For Many Carriers, Business Class Is the Premium Choice." *New York Times,* May 4, 2011.

―――. "Air Security Could Involve Private Jets." *New York Times,* January 5, 2009.

Nicas, Jack. "The Long, Slow Death of the First Class Seat." *Wall Street Journal,* July 19, 2012.

Noel, Josh. "Be Savvy About Seating." *Chicago Tribune,* May 3, 2011.

Pew, Glenn. "NTSB Prelim On G650 Crash." avweb.com, April 7, 2011.

Phillips, Matt. "Barbarians at the Gate? Elite Fliers Bemoan 'Gate Lice.'" blogs.wsj.com, October 20, 2008.

Reuters. "Private Jets Boom As Unrest Sweeps Mideast." March 31, 2011.

―――. "Etihad Raises Hens, Bees to Beat Competition." June 21, 2012.

Sharkey, Joe. "Travel Bug: A Million Miles vs. a Few More Smiles." *New York Times,* January 13, 2008.

―――. "On the Road: You Still Fly Commercial? That's So Down Market." *New York Times,* June 17, 2008.

Stellin, Susan. "Airlines' New Cash Cow: Frequent Flier Programs." *New York Times,* April 1, 2008.

Stoller, Gary. "All-Business-Class Airlines Take Off Despite Past Failures." *USA Today,* May 29, 2008.

Teague, Lettie. "Are the Wines in First Class Truly First-Rate?" *Wall Street Journal,* September 4, 2010.

Thurber, Matt. "Restoring Business Aviation's Image." bjtonline.com, June 1, 2010.

Van Riper, Tom. "How to Travel Like the Pros." *Forbes,* May 16, 2008.

Wall Street Oasis. "Hey Pal, Are You a Wannabe Working Stiff, Or are You a Player?" wallstreetoasis.com, October 16, 2010.

Walton, John. "The Lie-Flat Lie: Business Class Lie-Flat Seats Vs Fully Flat Beds." *Australian Business Traveller.* ausbt.com, April 12, 2012.

Watson, Blair. "Your Private Air Travel Options Are Growing." msnbc.msn.com, April 16, 2008.

Winship, Tim. "Elite Status: The Ultimate Frequent Flier Perk." *USA Today,* March 13, 2008.

Yamanouchi, Kelly. "Delta Pitching Discount First Class Upgrades." *Atlanta Journal-Constitution,* May 24, 2011.

Zoglin, Richard, and Christine Lim. "Frequent Flyer Seats: Sorry, All Full." *Time,* June 10, 2010.

INDUSTRY, GOVERNMENT, AND OTHER MATERIALS

CAPA. "What's Driving the World's Busiest Airports?" centreforaviation.com, March 31, 2011.

Consumer Reports. "Best and Worst Airlines." June 2011.

Collins, Chuck, Sarah Anderson, and Dedrick Muhammad. "High Flyers: How Private Jet Travel Is Straining the System." Institute for Policy Studies, June 2008.

FrequentFlier. "History of Loyalty Programs." frequentflier.com, n.d.

IdeaWorks. "Value Airlines Offer Best Seat Award Availability, British and United Improve Most Among Majors." Report, ideaworkscompany.com, May 17, 2012.

Petersen, Randy. "History of Frequent Flyer Programs." frequentflyerservices.com, May 2001.

Sorensen, Jay. "Loyalty by the Billions: IdeaWorks Analyzes How Frequent Flier Programs Pour Cash Into Airline Coffers." Loyalty Marketing Report Series, 2011.

The Travel Insider. "Who Flies First Class Anymore?" thetravelinsider.info, October 6, 2006.

United Airlines. "Million Miles and Beyond Rewards." united.com, n.d.

Chapter 9: Three Unimaginable Things That Changed Everything

BOOKS AND ARTICLES

ABC News. "TSA Fact Sheet: Amid Checkpoint Confusion, Some Real Numbers from the Airport." abcnews.go.com, November 22, 2010.

Adams, Marilyn, Barbara De Lollis, and Barbara Hansen. "Fliers in for Pain as Airlines Pack It In." *USA Today,* June 4, 2008.

Airline Weekly. "The Ryan King." April 9, 2012.

Anders, George. "Why Rivals Don't Copy Southwest's Hedging." *Wall Street Journal,* May 28, 2008.

Associated Press. "US Airways Pilots: We're Pressured to Cut Fuel." July 17, 2008.

Aviation Daily. "Half of LCCs Have Evolved into 'Hybrids,' New Study Says." aviationweek .com, May 8, 2008.

_____. "Study Finds 12,000 Laptops Lost or Stolen Each Week." aviationweek.com, July 9, 2008.

_____. "Pratt & Whitney Growing EcoPower Engine Wash Business." Market briefing, aviationweek.com, January 21, 2011.

Baskas, Harriet. "Free Meals on Planes Fly into the Sunset." msnbc.msn.com, October 12, 2010.

_____. "How the Airport Experience Has Changed Since 9/11." *USA Today,* September 7, 2011.

Bloomberg News. "Fuel Expense Is Forecast to Erase 62% of Profit for Airlines." *New York Times,* March 20, 2012.

Blumenfeld, Laura. "The Flight Watchmen." *Washington Post Magazine,* June 22, 2008.

Borman, Laurie. "A Day in the Life of an Airline Meal." news.travel.aol.com, July 22, 2010.

Carey, Susan, and Andy Pasztor. "Nonstop Flights Stop for Fuel." *Wall Street Journal,* January 11, 2012.

Cauchi, Marietta. "In Midst of Crisis, Advantage to Budget Carriers." *Wall Street Journal,* June 18, 2012.

Church, Aaron M. U. "Capital Defenders." airforce-magazine.com, December 2012.

Consumer Reports. "Air Security: Why You're Not As Safe As You Think." consumerreports .org, February, 2008.

Davis, Aaron. "Scrambling at the Siren's Call." *Washington Post,* August 10, 2008.

Dickler, Jessica. "Post 9/11 Travel: What Airport Security Costs Us." cnn.com, September 8, 2011.

The Economist. "What's the TSA's Current Failure Rate?" economist.com. January 2, 2011.

Frank, Thomas. "Airports Seek Millions to Screen Few." *USA Today,* March 5, 2008.

_____. "Anxiety-detecting Machines Could Spot Terrorists." *USA Today,* September 18, 2008.

_____. "TSA's 'Behavior Detection' Leads to Few Arrests." *USA Today,* November 18, 2008.

_____. "Poll: 70% Applaud Air-Security Effort." *USA Today,* December 8, 2008.

Freed, Joshua. "Airlines Cut Small Jets as Fuel Prices Soar." Associated Press, November 25, 2011.

Goldberg, Jeffrey. "Why Cavity Bombs Would Make the TSA Irrelevant." theatlantic.com, November 21, 2010.

Grabell, Michael. "Crimes by Air Marshals Raise Questions About Hiring." *USA Today,* November 12, 2008.

Green, Heather. "Security Wait Times for All Major U.S. Airports." farecompare.com, August 5, 2011.

Greenemeier, Larry. "Screening Test: Are al Qaeda's Airline Bombing Attempts Becoming More Sophisticated?" scientificamerican.com, May 9, 2012.

Halsey III, Ashley. "New Guidance System for Skies Could Face Delays." *Washington Post,* July 3, 2011.

Jansen, Bart. "More People Being Caught with Guns at Airports." *USA Today,* January 8, 2012.

Johnson, Keith, and Siobhan Gorman. "Bomb Implants Emerge as Airline Terror Threat." *Wall Street Journal,* July 7, 2011.

Jones, Jeffrey. "In U.S. Air Travelers Take Body Scans in Stride." gallup.com, January 11, 2010.

Jones, Rhys, and Chris Wickham. "Exclusive: American Airlines' $30 Million London Town House." Reuters, December 14, 2011.

Karp, Aaron. "US Majors Had Profitable 2011 Despite $2 Billion AMR Loss." atwonline .com, February 21, 2012.

King, Ledyard. "About $400,000 in Coins Forgotten at TSA Checkpoints in 2010." *USA Today,* January 11, 2012.

Lowy, Joan. "Pilots Complain Airline Restricts Fuel to Cut Cost." Associated Press, in *USA Today*, August 8, 2008.

MacVicar, Sheila. "Al Qaeda Bombers Learn from Drug Smugglers." cbsnews.com, September 28, 2009.

Mapes, Diane. "Private Piercings Raising Public Alarm: TSA Advises Removing Nipple Rings and Other Personal Jewelry Before Flying." msnbc.msn.com, May 15, 2008.

Martin, Hugo. "10 Years After 9/11, the Airline Industry Is Looking Up." *Los Angeles Times,* September 10, 2011.

_____. "Amid Criticism, TSA Finds Weapons in Walker and Stuffed Animals." *Los Angeles Times,* May 13, 2012.

Matlack, Carol. "Younger Fleets Boost Non-U.S. Airlines." businessweek.com, June 2, 2008.

Mayerowitz, Scott. "Virgin America CEO Looks to Make Flying Fun Again." sfgate.com, November 25, 2011.

Maynard, Micheline. "To Save Fuel, Airlines Find No Speck Too Small." *New York Times,* June 11, 2008.

McCartney, Scott. "Unusual Route: Discount Airlines Woo Business Set." *Wall Street Journal,* February 19, 2008.

———. "The Gap Between Airlines Is Shrinking." *Wall Street Journal,* February 17, 2011.

Miller, David. "22 Things We Miss About Travel Before 9/11." matadornetwork.com, September 12, 2011.

Millman, Gregory J. "Delta Refines a Fallacy." *Wall Street Journal,* May 15, 2012.

Mola, Roger. "Then & Now: A Weighty Matter." *Air & Space Magazine,* February 2009.

Mouawad, Jad. "Pushing 40, Southwest Is Still Playing the Rebel." *New York Times,* November 20, 2010.

———. "The Challenge of Starting an Airline." *New York Times,* May 25, 2012.

NBC News. "Gun Parts, Ammo Found Hidden Inside Stuffed Animals at Rhode Island Airport." msnbc.msn.com, May 9, 2012.

Negroni, Christine. "Air Security Could Involve Private Jets." *New York Times,* January 6, 2009.

———. "Questioning Safety of Heavy Passengers on Planes." *New York Times,* May 7, 2012.

New York Times. "We'll Have to Check, Sir." Editorial, May 15, 2008.

Pae, Peter. "Low-Cost Airfares Flying Under Radar." chicagotribune.com, May 19, 2008.

Prada, Paulo. "Low-Fare Airlines Discount Growth Plans." *Wall Street Journal,* June 19, 2008.

Reed, Dan. "High-Priced Fuel Scares Airlines." *USA Today,* March 24, 2008.

———. "Southwest Airlines Adds Cities, Courts Business Travelers." *USA Today,* December 26, 2008.

———. "Chicken Parts As Jet Fuel? Pond Scum? It's Possible." *USA Today,* January 27, 2009.

———. "Low-Cost Airlines Grab 30% of Travel Market vs. Full-Price Rivals." *USA Today,* November 9, 2009.

Reed, Dan, and Barbara Hansen. "Some of USA's Busiest Airports to Lose 10% of Domestic Flights." *USA Today,* June 30, 2008.

Reuters. "Texas Passes Airport 'Anti-Groping' Bill." June 28, 2011.

Saad, Lydia. " 'Grin and Bear It' Is Motto for Most Air Travelers." Gallup News Service, September 6, 2006.

Schillinglaw, James. "Travel Leaders Survey Finds Higher Satisfaction with Airport Security." travelpulse.com, June 11, 2012.

Schlangenstein, Mary. "Southwest Fights 'Cost Enemy' After AMR Bankruptcy Filing." bloomberg.com, December 6, 2011.

Schneier, Bruce. "A Waste of Money and Time." *New York Times,* November 23, 2010.

———. "Stop the Panic on Air Security." cnn.com, January 7, 2011.

Searles, Robert. "Maintaining for Fuel Efficiency." Aviationweek.com, October 26, 2006.

Segal, David. "Don't Come Crying to This Airline." *New York Times,* March 29, 2009.

Sharkey, Joe. "The Terrorist Watch List, Jumbled in Translation." *New York Times,* September 2, 2008.

———. "Screening Protests Grow as Holiday Crunch Looms." *New York Times,* November 15, 2010.

———. "Playing Simon Says at Airport Security." *New York Times,* March 28, 2011.

Smith, Patrick. "Ten Years After 9/11, Airport Security Still Not Getting It." salon.com, April 19, 2011.

Stoller, Gary. "Spirit Airlines Is Cheap and CEO Ben Baldanza's Proud of It." *USA Today,* June 22, 2009.

———. "Taking a Trip Can Be a 'Degrading' Experience for Fliers." *USA Today,* January 26, 2012.

Sullivan, Eileen. "Fed's Secret No-Fly List More Than Doubles in a Year." Associated Press, February 2, 2012.

INDUSTRY, GOVERNMENT, AND OTHER MATERIALS

"American Airlines Letter to Dispatchers (re 'Fuel Discussions')," alliedpilots.org, July 7, 2008. (alliedpilots.org/public/fuel_discussions_dispatch_letter081308.pdf)

Bennett, Randy, Patrick Murphy, and Jack Schmidt. "A Competitive Analysis of an Industry in Transition." Gerchick-Murphy Associates, LLC., Report, July 2007.

Boeing Commercial Airplanes. "767 Fun Facts." n.d. (boeing.com/commercial/767family/pf/pf_facts.html)

CAPA. "There Will Be Blood: Oil Prices Beyond Imagination." centreforaviation.com, May 22, 2008.

———. "Unstoppable and Irreversible: LCCs Spread Around the World: Regional Round-Up." centreforaviation.com, December 2, 2009.

———. "Ryanair Raises Full Year Result Outlook as Profits Increase and Yields Improve." centreforaviation.com, November 2, 2010.

———. "Security, Cancellations to Cost U.S. Airlines: View from America Pt. I." centreforaviation.com, December 20, 2010.

———. "Virgin America Closes 3Q Facing Stiff Headwinds for 2012, but Still Breaking Even." centreforaviation.com, December 28, 2011.

Heimlich, John. "Coping with Sky-High Jet Fuel Prices." Air Transport Association, April 21, 2008.

———. "The Price of Jet Fuel and Its Impact on U.S. Airlines." Air Transport Association, 2011.

J.D. Power and Associates. "Customer Satisfaction with Airlines Increases for a Second Consecutive Year." Press statement, June 8, 2011.

Johnson, Eric, and Joseph M. Hall. "Enhancing Service at Southwest Airlines." Dartmouth College/Tuck School of Business, 2009.

Mirza, Mansoor. "Economic Impact of Airplane Turn-Times." *The Boeing Company Aero Magazine* (fourth quarter), 2008.

MIT Global Airline Industry Program. "Airline Industry Overview." mit.edu, n.d.

Newport, Frank, and Steve Ander. "Americans' Views of TSA More Positive Than Negative." Gallup, Inc., August 8, 2012.

Ponemon Institute/Dell. "Airport Insecurity: The Case of Lost Laptops." U.S. research, June 30, 2008.

PR Newswire. "Thomson Reuters-NPR Health Poll Finds Nearly One in Four Americans Would Refuse a Full Body Scan at Airport Security." prnewswire.com, December 23, 2011.

US Department of Homeland Security/Transportation Security Administration. "Myth Buster: TSA's Watch List Is More Than One Million People Strong." Report, n.d.

———. "Screening Statistics: Facts and Figures for 2006." Report, n.d.

US Department of Transportation/Office of the Inspector General. "Emergency and Minimum Fuel Declarations on Flights Into Newark Liberty International Airport." Congressional briefing, February 12, 2008.

US Department of Transportation/Research and Innovative Technology Administration. "Airline Fuel Cost and Consumption (All Majors—Scheduled)." January 2000–October 2011 (published monthly).

———. "A Decade of Change in Fuel Prices and U.S. Domestic Passenger Aviation Operations." Special Report, March 2012.

———. "Table 2-16b: Prohibited Items Intercepted at Airport Screening Checkpoints." 2010.

US Government Accountability Office. "Terrorist Acts Demonstrate Urgent Need to Improve Security at the Nation's Airports." (GAO-01-1162T), September 20, 2001.

———. "Despite Industry Turmoil, Low Cost Airlines Are Growing and Profitable." (GAO-04-837T), June 3, 2004.

———. "Initial Small Community Air Service Development Projects Have Achieved Mixed Results." (GAO-06-21), November 30, 2005.

———. "Potential Mergers and Acquisitions Driven by Financial and Competitive Pressures." (GAO-08-845), July 31, 2008.

———. "Vulnerabilities in, and Alternatives for, Preboard Screening Security Operations." (GAO-01-1171T), September 25, 2011.

Chapter 10: Forecast: Cloudy with Some Signs of Clearing

BOOK AND ARTICLES

Airline Weekly. "The Crazy People Are Gone." September 24, 2012.

American Aviation Institute. "Consumer Regulation and Taxation of the U.S. Airline Industry." aviationinstitute.org, November 16, 2011.

Avon, Natalie. "Pilot Holds Flight for Man Going to See Dying Grandson." cnn.com, January 14, 2011.

Baskas, Harriet. "Better Than a Key Chain." *USA Today,* September 5, 2006.

Carey, Susan. "Airlines Face September Stall: Worries About Weaker Travel Ahead Have Wall Street Paring Earnings Forecasts." *Wall Street Journal,* August 31, 2012.

Cranky Flier. "What Airlines Spend on Food." crankyflier.com, July 12, 2010.

Elliott, Christopher. "The Travel Industry Shows Its Kinder, Gentler Side." *Washington Post,* December 15, 2011.

Epstein, Edward, and Benjamin Pimentel. "SFO Reaches for the Sky." sfgate.com, August 17, 1997.

Halsey, Ashley III. "NextGen Air Traffic Control System Behind Schedule and Over Budget." *Washington Post,* September 12, 2012.

Hinton, Christopher. "Airlines Uneasy Over Costly Bid to Replace Radar." marketwatch. com, May 19, 2011.

Jones, Charisse. "Fliers More Satisfied with Airlines, New Survey Says." *USA Today,* June 19, 2012.

Krystal, Becky. "On Planes, the Future Is Now. Sort Of." *Washington Post,* August 31, 2012.

LaGanga, Maria, and Dan Weikel. "When It Comes to Amenities, San Francisco Airport Soars Above the Competition." *Los Angeles Times,* July 3, 2011.

Levin, Alan. "NextGen FAA Contracts Are $4.2 Billion over Budget, GAO Says." bloomberg. com, February 16, 2012.

Lowy, Joan. "Court Denies Bid by Spirit, Southwest Airlines to Block Consumer Protection Regulations." Associated Press, July 24, 2012.

McCartney, Scott. "Flying on a Wing and a Prayer." *Wall Street Journal,* March 10, 2011.

Mouawad, Jad. "Service Cuts May Follow Merger of Airlines." *New York Times*, February 14, 2013.

Mutzabaugh, Ben. "Southwest Pilot Holds Flight for Grieving Grandfather." *USA Today,* January 17, 2011.

Nicas, Jack, and Daniel Michaels. "The Self-Service Airport." *Wall Street Journal,* August 27, 2012.

Reuters. "No End Yet to U.S. Jetliner Buying Spree." September 5, 2012.

Sanders, Peter. "Airlines Promise: It Will Get Better." *Wall Street Journal,* May 23, 2011.

Sanderson, Bill. "La Guardia Flights Delayed When Dog Flees Delta Jet and Sprints to Runway." *New York Post,* April 26, 2012.

Smith, Aaron. "Airports Cash in on Flight Delays." cnn.com, July 2, 2008.

Stellin, Susan. "Yes! Download that Airline App." *New York Times,* February 29, 2012.

Sullivan, Mark. "Best (and Worst) Tech Airports." pcworld.com, December 14, 2011.

Yu, Roger. "More Airport Restaurants Open Closer to Gates and Fliers." *USA Today,* January 4, 2011.

INDUSTRY, GOVERNMENT, AND OTHER MATERIALS

Airports Council International/North America. "2010 ACI-NA Airport Concessions Benchmarking Survey." Presented at Phoenix, AZ, November 8, 2010.

——. "ACI-NA Economic Bulletin." July 2012.

Airline Media. "Significant Facts." umbrellamedia.com.

Airlines International. "Cutting Catering Costs." iata.org, February–March 2010.

Air Transport Association. "The Economic Climb-Out for US Airlines: Global Competitiveness and Long-Term Viability." Presented at the ATA Economics meeting, Washington, DC, September 21, 2011.

Borenstein, Severin. "On the Persistent Financial Losses of US Airlines: A Preliminary Exploration." Working Paper 16744. National Bureau of Economic Research, Cambridge, MA, January 2011.

CAPA. "A Decade of Change for the Global Airline Industry: A New and Altered Realty in the Rankings." centreforaviation.com, July 18, 2011.

——. "Aviation's Lost Decade? 9/11 and Beyond. Cause for Optimism in the Wake of 9/11 Changes." centreforaviation.com, September 9, 2011.

HNTB Corp. "Evolving Airport Can Make Travel More Enjoyable." America THINKS Aviation Survey, 2012.

——. "2012 ACI/IPI Parking Survey Results." leighfisher.com, April 2012.

Miller, Richard K. "The 2011–2012 Travel & Tourism Market Research Handbook." May 2011.

PRWeb. "America THINKS: Making Air Travel Fun Again." prweb.com, January 26, 2012.

Transportation Research Board. "Resource Manual for Airport In-Terminal Concessions." ACRP Report 54. trb.org, 2011.

United Airlines. "United Invests in the Future, Places Order for Next-Generation Aircraft." Press release, December 8, 2009.

US Department of Transportation/Federal Aviation Administration. "Next Generation Air Transportation System." Fact sheet, December 18, 2008.

US Department of Transportation/Office of the Inspector General. "Audit. Status of Transformational Programs and Risks to Achieving NextGen Goals." (AV-2012-094), April 23, 2012.

——. "Aviation Industry Performance: A Review of the Aviation Industry, 2008–2011." Controlled correspondence, (2012-029), September 24, 2012.